The Changing Face of Central Banking

Central banks have emerged as the key player in national and international financial policy making. This book explores their evolution since World War II in 20 industrial countries. The study considers the mix of economic, political, and institutional forces that have affected central bank behavior and its relationship with government. The analysis reconciles vastly different views about the role of central banks in the making of economic policies. One finding is that monetary policy is an evolutionary process. The emphasis on clarity of objectives, transparency of the decision-making process, and a clear understanding of the accountability of the central bank cannot be understood in isolation from the previous 50 years of policy making. The changing face of central banking, born out of the turbulence of the first half of the last century, nurtured by evolution and revolution in policies, defines the history of key financial events in the second half of the twentieth century.

Pierre L. Siklos is Professor of Economics at Wilfrid Laurier University, Waterloo, Ontario, Canada, and Associate Director of its Viessmann Centre for the Study of Modern Europe. He is the author of several books, including the leading textbook in Canada on money and banking and another on the Hungarian hyperinflation of 1945–6. Professor Siklos has served as a visiting professor at Oxford University and the University of California, San Diego, and as an Erskine Fellow at the University of Canterbury, Christchurch, New Zealand. He has also published numerous articles in eminent economics journals. In 2000–1 he was Wilfrid Laurier University's University Research Professor.

Studies in Macroeconomic History

SERIES EDITOR: Michael D. Bordo, *Rutgers University*

EDITORS: Forrest Capie, *City University Business School, U.K.*
Barry Eichengreen, *University of California, Berkeley*
Nick Crafts, *London School of Economics*
Angela Redish, *University of British Columbia*

The titles in this series investigate themes of interest to economists and economic historians in the rapidly developing field of macroeconomic history. The four areas covered include the application of monetary and finance theory, international economics, and quantitative methods to historical problems; the historical application of growth and development theory and theories of business fluctuations; the history of domestic and international monetary, financial, and other macroeconomic institutions; and the history of international monetary and financial systems. The series amalgamates the former Cambridge University Press series *Studies in Monetary and Financial History* and *Studies in Quantitative Economic History*.

Other books in the series:

*A History of Banking in
Antebellum America*
Howard Bodenhorn
0-521-66999-5

*The Gold Standard and Related
Regimes*
Michael D. Bordo
0-521-55006-8

Monetary Regimes in Transition
Michael D. Bordo and
Forrest Capie, editors
0-521-41906-9

*Transferring Wealth and Power
from the Old to the New
World*
Michael D. Bordo and
Roberto Cortés-Conde,
editors
0-521-77305-9

Canada and the Gold Standard
Trevor J. O. Dick and
John E. Floyd
0-521-40408-8

Elusive Stability
Barry Eichengreen
0-521-44847-6

Europe's Postwar Recovery
Barry Eichengreen, editor
0-521-48279-8

A Monetary History of Italy
Michele Fratianni and
Franco Spinelli
0-521-44315-6

The Economics of World War II
Mark Harrison, editor
0-521-62046-5

Continued after the index

The Changing Face of Central Banking

Evolutionary Trends Since World War II

PIERRE L. SIKLOS
Wilfrid Laurier University, Canada

PUBLISHED BY THE PRESS SYNDICATE OF THE UNIVERSITY OF CAMBRIDGE
The Pitt Building, Trumpington Street, Cambridge, United Kingdom

CAMBRIDGE UNIVERSITY PRESS
The Edinburgh Building, Cambridge CB2 2RU, UK
40 West 20th Street, New York, NY 10011-4211, USA
477 Williamstown Road, Port Melbourne, VIC 3207, Australia
Ruiz de Alarcón 13, 28014 Madrid, Spain
Dock House, The Waterfront, Cape Town 8001, South Africa

http://www.cambridge.org

First published 2002

Printed in the United Kingdom at the University Press, Cambridge

Typeface Times Ten 10/13 pt.   *System* QuarkXPress [BTS]

A catalog record for this book is available from the British Library.

Library of Congress Cataloging in Publication Data available

ISBN   0 521 78025 X   hardback

To Nancy, the "big" guy and the "little" guy

Contents

Figures

Tables

Preface

Throughout much of my professional career I have investigated economic issues that affect central banks directly or indirectly. My earliest involvement in this area dealt with conditions that lead to a hyperinflation and their termination, an extreme illustration of total subjugation of a central bank to government demands. By the early 1990s I became interested in the relationship between central banks and governments and the monetary policy choices made by these same authorities. Parallel literatures, with important contributions by Canadians, had emerged wherein a central bank either was an optimizing agent that could fine-tune the economy or behaved as a bureaucratic institution determined to maintain its special role via obfuscation and secrecy. At the same time political economists, and political science, claimed that central banks were constantly pressured by the political authorities to change their policies to facilitate reelection prospects or support partisan economic programs. Throughout, these various strands of the literature continued to grow, though some floundered by the late 1980s due to a lack of empirical support or an inability to address the issues that were the concern of the day.

Little did I know that, in 1993, a topic that lay largely dormant in economists' minds (but not in the minds of political scientists) would get its second wind so to speak. The catalyst was, of course, the publication of John Taylor's article on the Fed and its interest rate setting behavior. This led to an explosion of research into the "new" economics of central bank reaction functions. It was also when I undertook (initially with a colleague at Wilfrid Laurier University) a research program to investigate how central banks react to both the economic and political pressures they face. In a very real sense then, this study began in 1993.

Yet, despite the increased scrutiny faced by central banks, there is little emphasis in the literature on the connection between the economic and political pressures on them. Moreover, there is relatively little known about how and why central bank policies have evolved over time, how the institutions themselves have changed, or the proximate causes for these changes. It is with this in mind that the present study mixes economic history with a quantitative analysis of central banks and their policies, roughly since the end of World War II. The aim is to try and isolate how monetary policies have been shaped by economic, political, and institutional forces. As will become clear, bits and pieces of the main arguments in this study can be found elsewhere. I hope, however, that I have not reinvented too much.

I have tried to make the study as accessible as possible. While technical details cannot be avoided entirely, they are kept to a minimum. It will also become apparent from a reading of the text that central banks, as institutions, are best understood as having evolved over time. Hence, the notion of "game playing" between the monetary and fiscal authorities, while a useful tool under specific circumstances, is seen as a profoundly unsatisfactory way of explaining the changing face of central banking since World War II.

There are too many people to thank for their help, directly and indirectly, in the preparation of this study. They are, in any event, acknowledged in the various articles I have written over the years on the topics of greatest concern for this study. Nevertheless, I do wish to add a special thanks to Professor Michael Bordo and his referees for their valuable assistance in ensuring that the coverage of topics would appeal to economists and to a broader audience of individuals interested in central banking issues. I am also grateful to Elsie Grogan for assisting me with the manuscript and making endless corrections to many drafts. I also owe a debt of gratitude to the many officials of central banks who assisted me by providing valuable historical and other information, and for the many discussions I had with various officials over the years. Finally, I am grateful to the Social Science and Humanities Research Council of Canada, the German-American Academic Council Foundation, and Wilfrid Laurier University for financial support. I am particularly grateful to Wilfrid Laurier University for providing me with the time to complete this manuscript as recipient of the 2000–1 University Research Professor award. I was able to indulge in a year of research free of teaching and administrative responsibilities for which I am very thankful. Indeed, I was able to put the finishing touches to the manuscript in

Sydney, Australia, as a visiting professor at the University of Technology, Sydney. The vistas of Sydney provided, I believe, some wonderful inspiration about central banks and central banking. Finally, I appreciate the opportunity to publish this research with Cambridge University Press, and the help of Scott Parris in shepherding the manuscript to completion.

Pierre L. Siklos
Waterloo, Ontario, CANADA
June 2002

1 | The Institutional Make-up and Evolution of Central Bank–Government Relations: An Introduction

INTRODUCTION

As the twenty-first century begins, central banking would appear to be at a crossroads. From lender of last resort, to active participant in stabilizing economic fluctuations, and now as the guardian of price stability, much is expected from the monetary authority. Indeed, where once fiscal policy was considered the main instrument of economic policy, the ascendancy of monetary policy became especially noticeable by the late 1980s in much of the industrialized world with profound implications for the role of the central bank. Yet, as this is written, financial innovations seemingly threaten once again the position of central banks as the dominant force responsible for ensuring financial stability and in influencing economic outcomes.[1]

There is an important sense in which, over the past several decades, central banking has been at the mercy of whim or fashion. "At a time when the price level is rising and employment is relatively full, price stability takes precedence over full employment as a policy objective. At a time when prices are stable and unemployment is rising, on the other hand, employment becomes the prime objective. A better measure of central bank conservatism might be the length of time it takes for him to accept a change in conditions and adjust his thinking accordingly" (Whittlesey 1970: p. 225).

The above quote highlights the fact that the practice of central banking involves a considerable amount of learning and adaptation to a

---

[1] Since the present study is not about the future of central banking I shall, for the most part, avoid the question of whether central banks are indeed even necessary. See, however, Chapter 2, Friedman (1999) and Goodhart (1999).

changing environment, a theme now gaining wider acceptance, both in terms of formal models (as in Sargent 1999) as well as in historical descriptions of central bank policies throughout this century (see Howitt 2000; Siklos 1999a). Yet, an understanding of such developments requires more evidence than has heretofore been brought to bear on the issues.

This study examines, using both qualitative and quantitative evidence, the evolution of central banks and their policies since the end of World War II. The degree to which central banks have tended to be cast as separate, if not at times autonomous, institutions from the rest of government has changed considerably over the past fifty years. This separation has been the cause of considerable tension, particularly when the preferences of elected officials seem to conflict with those who manage monetary policy. Among the questions considered in this study is how seriously one ought to take institutional elements in central bank–government relations as the crucial ingredient in gaining an appreciation for the evolution of the monetary authority's influence vis-à-vis government. The conclusions, as we shall see, are very much in the mold of the proposition that institutions matter and that it is of inherent interest to explore how central banks have evolved the way they have over the past fifty years or so.

Nevertheless, central bank behavior cannot simply be about what banks are legislated to do. No statutory relationship can define either day-to-day central banking operations, nor can it ultimately dictate the influence of the personalities who set the direction of monetary policy. Therefore, politics and the preferences of the central bank may intrude on the institution's evolution and performance. Louis Rasminsky, a former governor of the Bank of Canada, put it best in his Per Jacobsson Lecture (1966: p. 116): "The formal status of the central bank varies a great deal from country to country. In any case this is a field in which the real situation is not likely to be revealed by the terms of the statute. Much depends on history and tradition and a fair amount even on the personalities involved."

Despite the appeal of institutional economics there are some limitations to the approach as will become apparent. We simply do not yet know enough about why certain central banking and monetary policy frameworks work better in some countries than in others. In part for this reason the present study resorts at times to the case method approach to illustrate the significance of institutional or economic factors which are relevant to an understanding of central bank behavior. We have, however, learned a great deal over the decades about key aspects of monetary policy implementation and central bank–government relations that work and these do highlight the central role of the institutional structure in place.

This study is also prompted by the need for more comparative evidence on the activities of central banks and their place in government. While economists have, very recently, embarked on such a task, the available comparative evidence is relatively thin. Moreover, a significant portion of recent research tends to be cast in terms of an approach introduced by economists in the 1990s to characterize the conduct of monetary policy, primarily in the United States. Perhaps more importantly, there has been a gulf between various strands of literature dealing with central banks. Some view central bank operations solely through the lens of statutory and other legal aspects of central bank behavior. Other literature presumes complete freedom of action by the monetary authority to set interest rates and the question then becomes what weight the central bankers place on controlling inflation versus some real objective such as output growth or unemployment. Finally, an altogether separate literature interprets central bank behavior as being significantly affected by political forces.

Discussions of the myriad of pressures on monetary policy in one place is not available and this study hopes to at least make a start at looking at the relative importance and influence of each across countries and over time. Existing theories in each strand of the literature are now fairly well developed and, though some modest points about the relevance of existing theories will be made, the study is mainly about building and sifting through the available evidence about what central banks have done, and why, over the last half century.

INFLATION THEN AND NOW

A few words are in order about the choice of the post-World War II era for analysis. First, as will be seen in the next chapter, the economic environment and mission governing almost all central banks being studied here altered substantially following the decade of the 1940s. It is fair to say that while central banks have always been viewed as lenders of last resort, their role in stabilization policy was far more passive in the pre-World War II era than thereafter. Moreover, cataclysmic events such as wars and revolutions were relatively more prevalent prior to the 1950s. Finally, the behavior of inflation is sufficiently different in the years before World War II which suggests that other forces were at play rather than the ones that are the prime concern of this study. To illustrate, Figure 1.1 plots inflation in Germany and the United Kingdom since the middle of the nineteenth century. In the case of Germany the plot omits the years of hyperinflation, another feature of the pre-1950s history of inflation (also see Siklos 2000a). Two important distinguishing features of the pre-World War II era include the more-or-less regular appearance of periods of deflation, and the relatively greater volatility of inflation. While there are no doubt several proximate causes for these distinctive characteristics in the inflation process, the Gold Standard and the Great Depression clearly come to mind as the main explanations for this outcome. In contrast, as we shall see, the post-World War II era is dominated by persistently positive inflation rates and changes in policy regimes that shall be the focus of the discussion in the remainder of this study. To illustrate, Figure 1.1c shows inflation in New Zealand since 1930. There is a consistent upward trend in inflation until the middle 1980s when major reforms, not just ones affecting the position of the central bank, produced a sharp decline in inflation that has been maintained ever since (see Chapters 2 and 7).

There are additional reasons to treat the years since the 1940s somewhat differently from the monetary policy experience of preceding decades. Consider a simple description of the relationship between the amount of slack in economic activity, referred to as the output gap (see Chapter 2)[2] and inflation. The resulting trade-off, usually referred to as the Phillips curve, can be written in simplified form as

$$\pi_t = \pi_t^e + a\tilde{y}_t + e_t \tag{1.1}$$

where π is the actual inflation rate at time t, π^e are inflation expectations also at time t (though possibly conditioned on information available only up to time $t-1$), $\tilde{y}$ is the output gap and e_t are random "shocks" to inflation. The latter can be thought of as having a zero mean and a constant variance. The coefficient a is positive suggestive of the notion that inflation is lower when there is excess capacity in the economy ($\tilde{y} < 0$) than when the economy produces more than its potential (that is, $\tilde{y} > 0$). Versions of Equation 1.1 are part and parcel of most standard macroeconomic models. There is, of course, continuing controversy over the existence of the Phillips curve trade-off, whether linearity is an appropriate characterization, as well as the extent to which the trade-off is "exploitable" by governments and central banks. We shall return to some

---

[2] The output gap is simply the (percent) spread between actual and some measure of potential aggregate output.

(a) Germany

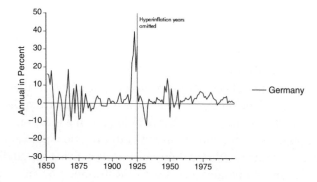

(b) UK

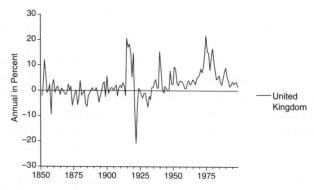

(c) New Zealand

Figure 1.1 Inflation in Germany, the United Kingdom, and New Zealand over the Last Century (*Sources*: Mitchell (1992), updated from sources described in Chapter 2, and at http://www.wlu.ca/~wwwsbe/faculty/psiklos/centralbanks.htm.)

of these questions throughout this study.[3] Nevertheless, what is germane for the moment is the role played by central banks and the policy regime in place. One reason is that, as we shall see, some policies or institutions are better able to anchor expectations than others. This has the effect of minimizing deviations between π_t and π_t^e with implications for the behavior of $\tilde{y}_t$, other things being equal. Indeed, it is apparent from the foregoing discussion that, since policies aimed at influencing inflation and the output gap also lead to more variability in both variables,[4] delivering the best possible monetary policy should aim at minimizing variability in both. Recognition of this idea has led to the formulation of a "new" policy trade-off, namely one between inflation and output variability.[5] Nevertheless, these developments also suggest the necessity of a fairly good understanding of what drives expectations, the ability to model economic relationships that recognize forward looking behavior, as well as identifying economic shocks, among other requirements.

Figure 1.2a makes clear that, in terms of the "new" trade-off, the performance of monetary policy was, for the most part, substantially different after World War II than in earlier decades, at least if we take the U.S. experience as representative. Figure 1.2b makes the same point but via comparisons across policy regimes, again for U.S. data. Hence, we find that inflation and output volatility are considerably smaller during the period of pegged exchange rates, known as the Bretton Woods era, and still better under inflation targeting. The respective roles played by central banks and institutions during these regimes will also figure prominently in the present study.

The remainder of this chapter gives a taste of what is to follow as well as briefly highlighting the need to bring together the separate elements of the literature on central banks.

GOVERNING STRUCTURES

In most industrialized countries, the legislation governing central banks has the same status as that of any other government body. Hence, the structure of government, electoral, and partisan activity, as well as inter-

---

[3] A recent, and highly readable, view of the current state of key aspects of the debate may be found in, for example, Akerlof, Dickens, and Perry (2000).

[4] Recognition of some facets of the debate owes a considerable debt to, for example, Friedman's Nobel Lecture (1977).

[5] Taylor's (1993) work probably originated this line of debate. Also see, however, the 1996 and 1999 Symposia held by the Federal Reserve Bank of Kansas City (most notably Fischer 1996, and Taylor 1996), Svensson (2001), Taylor (2000), and Walsh (2000a) for highly readable accounts of the principles behind the "new" trade-off.

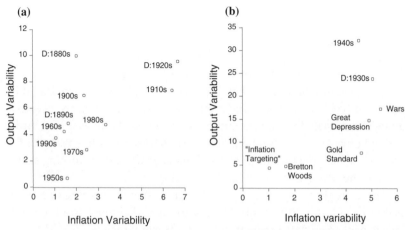

Figure 1.2 Inflation and Output Variability: The U.S. Historical Experience (*Note*: The plots show the variance of real GDP and CPI inflation by decade (part a), and by regime (part b), based on annual data. The Great Slump is the 1928–32 period; wars are 1914–18, 1939–45, and 1950–53; Bretton Woods is 1959–72; the Gold Standard is 1873–1919; "inflation targeting" is 1987–2000. *Sources*: See Figure 1.1.)

national considerations, in large part via the choice of exchange rate regimes, will contribute to explaining central bank performance. In other words, legislation covering the central bank is not typically organic in that it is not protected by some constitutional provision and can, therefore, be amended with relative ease. Hence, a central bank is usually a creature of the central government, to whom it ordinarily pays seigniorage profits, even under a federative structure although the latter can, as we shall also see, have the potential to indirectly influence central bank behavior. In part for this reason the question of appointments and the manner in which central banks govern themselves are potentially important questions though only the former has, until recently, attracted considerable academic interest. While this development is understandable, it will be argued here that such focus on appointments procedures is partly misplaced. First, central bank personalities tend to matter more in times of crises rather than as a rule. Second, central banks, in recognition of changing objectives of governments and society, and due to a growing desire for accountability and openness on the part of public institutions, have formally or informally changed how monetary policy decisions are made and communicated to the public. Issues of governance have thus become paramount, an aspect downplayed in the current literature. Why is governance important? As Williamson (2000:

p. 599) points out ". . . governance is an effort to craft *order*, thereby to mitigate *conflict* and realize *neutral* gains. So conceived, a governance structure obviously reshapes incentives" (italics in original). The foregoing quote clearly suggests that the changing face of central banks since World War II will be marked by such considerations.

Complicating matters is that, if the central bank is not mandated to supervise banks or the financial sector more generally, a separate piece of legislation will govern that authority as well as the degree of coordination between the central bank and the supervisory authority. Table 1.1 provides some general information about central bank governing structures in the countries to be examined in this study.

There are three aspects worth highlighting about governing structures as they exist today. First, central banks are overwhelmingly state-owned. This is not a new development but its roots can largely be traced to the aftermath of the Great Depression and the early post-1940s view that significant government intervention in the economy is warranted. Second, the typical term of office for a central bank governor tends to correspond or exceed the term of office of the political authorities. Nevertheless, terms of office for central bank governors or presidents vary widely, from four years to indefinite terms of office. In this respect, central bank observers have long argued about the desirability of having terms of office long enough to overcome the potential for political or partisan business cycles. Yet, there are also widely held beliefs about the significance of political economy influences on economic activity based on a large body of empirical evidence. The two views come into conflict in part because of difficulties in measuring the impact of political influences on central bank policies because of the role of the term of office in determining the degree of autonomy of the central bank, as well as other factors to be considered throughout this study (see also, Waller and Walsh 1996).

Finally, a more recent development has been the shift away from giving central banks responsibility for supervision of the banking system. Here too the evolution of policies reflects the tension between the need to avoid potential conflicts of interest between the central bank and the banks it supervises versus the need to ensure financial stability. Indeed, it is the growing importance of financial stability as a separate objective of monetary policy that, as we shall see, raises a potentially important drawback with recent reaction, function-based approaches to modeling central bank behavior.

Chapters 2 and 3 use the information in Table 1.1 and explore its implications in greater detail. A final comment is in order. The early

Table 1.1. Principal Ingredients of Governing Structures of Central Banks

Country	Ownership[1]	Profits[5]	Governor/President Term of Office[9]	Banking Supervision?[7]
Australia	State[2] (1948)	Finance Minister	7 years (R)	No (1998)
Austria	Public-Private (1965)	State according to formula	5 years (R)	No (see ECB)
Belgium	State-Others[3] (1948)	State in excess of 3%	5 years (R)	No (see ECB)
Canada	State[4] (1938)	State according to formula	7 years (R)	No (1992)
Denmark	State (1936)	Fixed amount to Finance Minister	Indefinite[6]	No
Finland	State (1933)	State according to formula	7 years[8] (R)	No (see ECB)
France	State (1945)	State according to formula	6 years[8] (R)	Combined
Germany	State[4] (1957)	State according to formula	5–8 years (R)	No (see ECB)
Ireland	State (1942)	Central bank with provisions for distribution	7 years (R)	Yes
Italy	State–Public Co. (1948)	Shareholders	Indefinite	Yes
Japan	State[3] (1942)	State according to formula	5 years (R)	Combined
Netherlands	State (1948)	State	7 years (R)	Yes
New Zealand	State (1936)	State subject to central bank budget	5 years (R)	Yes
Norway	State (1949)	State according to formula	6 years[8] (R)	No (1985)
Portugal	State (1931)	State according to formula	5 years (R)	Yes
Spain	State (1946)	Minister of Finance	6 years[8] (NR)	Yes
Sweden	State (1934)	Parliament with provision for central bank share	6 years[8] (R)	Yes
Switzerland	Public-Private	Shareholders	6 years (R)	No
UK	State (1946)	Treasury	5 years (R)	No (1998)
US	Banks	Shareholders	4 years (R)	Combined
ECB	National Central Banks (1999)	Allocation to member CB according to formula	8 years (NR)	No (1999)

[1] In parenthesis the approximate year central banks were nationalized or became state owned.
[2] Commonwealth owned.
[3] Bearer shares or "nongovernmental persons."
[4] Federal government.
[5] In the case of eleven EMU members (Austria, Belgium (Luxembourg), Finland, France, Germany, Ireland, Italy, Netherlands, Portugal, Spain) distribution information is prior to ECB formulation. Formula refers to allocation for expenses or reserve funds.
[6] Subject to maximum age (for example, seventy-five years).
[7] Refers to supervision of the banking and financial system. Central banks ordinarily retain authority over the payments system. Combined signifies a sharing of responsibility with either the finance ministry or other supervisory agencies. Even in the case where the central bank does not formally supervise the banking system there exist vehicles or arrangements that may directly or indirectly involve central bank actions.
[8] Most recent legislation has clarified term of office. Previously, that is, prior to the Maastricht Treaty, term of office was interpreted as indefinite.
[9] R = renewable; NR = nonrenewable.

Sources: Aufricht (1967), Capie, Fischer, Goodhart, and Schnadt (1994), Eijffinger and de Haan (1996), Goodhart and Shoenmaker (1995), Grilli, Masciandaro, and Tabellini (1991), and various publications from national central banks. See www.wlu.ca/~wwwsbe/faculty/psiklos/centralbanks.htm.

history of central banks, and of central banking, involved the establishment of monopoly note issuing authority and lender of last resort functions. Indeed, as shown in Table 1.2, central banks were institutions created to finance wars, manage the public debt, or consolidate note issuing authority, ostensibly to restore confidence and stability in the monetary system. More cynically, they also served the interests of governments via the seigniorage revenues they generated. By the early decades of the twentieth century, the lender of last resort function took on greater importance. The history of central banking since World War II is principally about the establishment and evolution of autonomy and the manner in which monetary policy is conducted. That is the primary interest of the present study. There are several excellent references to the early development of central banking (for example, Eichengreen 1992a; Goodhart 1988, 1995).

CONFLICTS AND CONFLICT RESOLUTION

The potential for conflict between central banks and governments suggests that disagreements about objectives, policies, or both, can emerge with far-reaching consequences. Again, statutory arrangements, politics, and personalities all play a role in the likelihood of such conflicts surfacing. However, economic activity will undoubtedly be the proximate cause for any conflicts since it is to be expected that, particularly at times when the economy is under stress, the preferences of the central bank and the government may deviate most from each other. Nevertheless, once conflict develops, the other factors mentioned above may prove to be decisive in the outcome. Many authors (for example, Capie, Fischer, Goodhart, and Schnadt 1994; Cukierman 1992; and Eijffinger and de Haan 1996 represent a partial list) have pointed out the importance of conflict between the monetary and political authorities. However, it appears that these authors have treated the role of conflicts, and the procedures invoked to resolve them, as no more important than the many other characteristics that define government–central bank relationships. Details about how one can proxy conflicts and conflict resolution processes are discussed in the next chapter. Historical examples from several countries in our study, most notably Canada, New Zealand, Germany, the United Kingdom, and the United States, suggest that while conflicts are comparatively rare events, they can have a lasting impact on the extent of political pressures applied on central banks.

Table 1.2. The Origins of Central Banks

Year	Country	Name	Motivation
1668	Sweden	Bank of the Estates of the Realm. Forerunner of the Riksbank	Finance war
1694	UK	Bank of England	Finance war
1782	Spain	Forerunner of Bank of Spain	Finance war
1800	France	Banque de France	Manage public debt, generate seignorage
1811	Finland	Bank of Finland	Monetary sovereignty
1814	Netherlands	Nederlandsche Bank	Promote economic growth
1816	Austria	Austrian National Bank	Manage public debt as a result of war finance
1816	Norway	Bank of Norway	Economic crisis in Denmark prompts monetary reform
1818	Denmark	Denmark Nationalbank	Restore stability in aftermath of war finance
1846	Portugal	Banco de Portugal	Restore credibility to previous monetary regime
1850	Belgium	Belgian National Bank	Reform prompted by banking crises
1876	Germany	Reichsbank. Forerunner of Bundesbank	Consolidation of previous note issuing authorities following unification
1882	Japan	Bank of Japan	Part of modernization of Meiji regime
1893	Italy	Banca d'Italia	Consolidation of previous note issuing authorities following unification
1907	Switzerland	Swiss National Bank	Elimination of note issuing competition
1911	Australia	Commonwealth Bank of Australia. Forerunner of Reserve Bank of Australia	Creation of a single note issuing authority
1913	USA	Federal Reserve System	Creation of lender of last resort and other banking related functions
1934	Canada	Bank of Canada	Lender of last resort
1934	New Zealand	Reserve Bank of New Zealand	Lender of last resort
1942	Ireland	Bank of Ireland	Lender of last resort
1999	European Union	European Central Bank	Foster monetary and political union in Europe

Sources: Capie, Fischer, Goodhart, and Schnadt (1994) and individual country central banks. See www.wlu.ca/~wwwsbe/faculty/psiklos/centralbanks.htm.

It is also important to recognize that, even if conflict resolution procedures are clearly laid out, another proximate source of crisis in central bank–government relations is the presence or absence of clear objectives for monetary policy. Therefore, putting into place a well-articulated monetary policy strategy is also of crucial importance. The latter, as we shall see in Chapter 7 especially, is perhaps the single most important development of the 1980s and 1990s in central banking circles.

OBJECTIVES AND RESPONSIBILITIES IN MONETARY POLICY: FROM EXPERIMENTATION AND AUTONOMY TO ACCOUNTABILITY AND DISCLOSURE

In the immediate aftermath of the wave of nationalization or state domination of central banks that took place around the end of World War II, central banks were, for the most part, viewed simply as subservient to governments. What was less clear were the expectations for monetary policy in fulfilling society's wish for steady economic growth and the maintenance of the purchasing power of money. Indeed, monetary policy was deemed capable of carrying out multiple objectives simultaneously and there were few concerns expressed about the limitations of monetary policy. Indeed, there was little indication that policy makers understood that the ending of the Gold Standard necessitated that more careful thought ought to be given to specifying and outlining the proper objectives of monetary policy. This is partly reflected in the following critics of monetary policy going back at least to the 1930s. "For the internal economy of Great Britain, it is equally necessary that British monetary policy should have a *definite objective*. But as far as is publicly known, there is none . . ." (Cassel 1932: p. 12). Another critic would state: "Public opinion must demand in future that the government of the day should have a defined and constructive monetary policy, and have the courage to state it" (Behrens 1932: p. 7). Later events in the history of central banking would prove that governments, and economies more generally, would pay a dear price for ignoring such recommendations.

In an era where there was considerably more emphasis placed on the role of fiscal policy, monetary policy was viewed as passively supplying the ingredients required to guarantee aggregate economic well-being. This was in large part due to the breakdown of the Gold Standard, the failure of international coordination among central banks, as well as the response of governments to the global slump triggered by the Great Depression of the 1930s. Nevertheless, with fiscal activism came inflation.

Moreover, the adoption of quasi-fixed exchange rates in the aftermath of the Bretton Woods Conference meant that domestic monetary policy was subordinated to the monetary policies of the United States and, to a lesser extent, of Germany, at least in the continental European context. This reflected the insistence on the part of monetary policy makers that international policy coordination, despite its rather checkered past, was the "only" solution. "We recognize, of course, that monetary objectives ... can only be fully attained by broad international action" (Bennett 1932).[6] It would take a few decades, and considerable experimentation to recognize that "good" monetary policy begins with a domestic solution but one that would eventually be "exported" internationally.

To be sure, there were other forces affecting the role and responsibilities of some central banks. For example, Germany and Austria, both victims of hyperinflation in the 1920s, sought to enshrine notions of price stability long before they became fashionable elsewhere.

The exchange rate as a nominal anchor of monetary policy also served a useful purpose so long as economic activity was strong and inflation was relatively low (for example, see Bordo 1993). However, when Bretton Woods ended, the different reactions of central banks and governments worldwide to the oil price shocks of the 1970s led to cross-country divergences in monetary policies as countries were, in principle, freer to choose their own inflation rates in a floating exchange rate environment. But along with inflation rates that were drifting higher came more sluggish economic growth and the chorus of discontent about the kind of economic performance delivered by the existing package of monetary and fiscal policies grew louder. This led to considerable experimentation in the area of monetary policy, as governments and central banks sought more flexible means to deliver their economies from economic stagnation and inflation. It is not that central banks somehow became less resistant to the siren calls for inflationary finance on the part of governments who continued to believe such policies would stimulate output. Quite the contrary, for some of the best-known and vocal opponents of inflation headed the major central banks at the time. Instead, as we shall see, the era of experimentation captured the mood of the times as central banks grappled with the search for a reliable anchor for monetary policy. Nevertheless, weaknesses in the institutional structure of many central banks, and perhaps of some central bankers, became increasingly apparent.

---

[6] The quote is from the Canadian prime minister at the time, but is representative of the tone and goal of the Imperial Economic Conference held in Ottawa in 1932.

Whether newer forms of exchange rate pegging, or targets in money supply growth, were adopted did not matter so much as the search for a credible anchor for monetary policy. Increasingly, however, fiscal policies began to make the often murky objectives of monetary policy in most industrial countries incompatible with stable inflation rates or exchange rates. In any event, the era of experimentation did not produce satisfactory economic outcomes.

To be sure, pressure for change was much stronger in some countries than in others, but the late 1980s saw the beginning of a movement in the industrial world to change the direction of monetary policy first and, belatedly, of fiscal policy. Indeed, among those who question various arguments put forward in favor of increasing central bank autonomy – these tend to center around questions of democratic accountability – it is not sufficiently recognized that institutional reforms in the area of monetary policy have generally preceded reforms aimed at improving fiscal balances and government debt.[7] We return to these issues at the end of Chapter 2.

There was a fairly broad consensus among industrialized countries after World War II to place central banks under state ownership and, for a time at least, to anchor domestic monetary policy to the United States (or, to a lesser extent, Germany). By the 1990s there was, similarly, widespread agreement about the need to ensure some form of price stability. However, the institutional mechanisms by which an era of stable prices was to be achieved differed considerably across the industrialized world. In some countries (for example, New Zealand), price stability was chosen as the sole objective of monetary policy. Other countries also chose to focus on price stability (for example, Canada, Australia) but without changing the statutory mandate of the central bank. Still other central banks obtained no formal mechanisms to guarantee price stability but instead chose to rely on past reputation for inflation performance and autonomy (for example, as in the United States). Finally, a few countries simply placed renewed emphasis on the goal of price stability that was already part of their statutory objective (for example, Germany), while others chose to express the goal of price stability as one that ought to be achieved so long as it did not prejudice the overall objectives of government economic policies (for example, the European Central Bank, the United Kingdom). Figures 1.3 and 1.4 and Table 1.3, illustrate some of the complexities regarding the links between central bank's status and

---

[7] But perhaps no reforms aimed at reducing the regulatory burden in the economy.

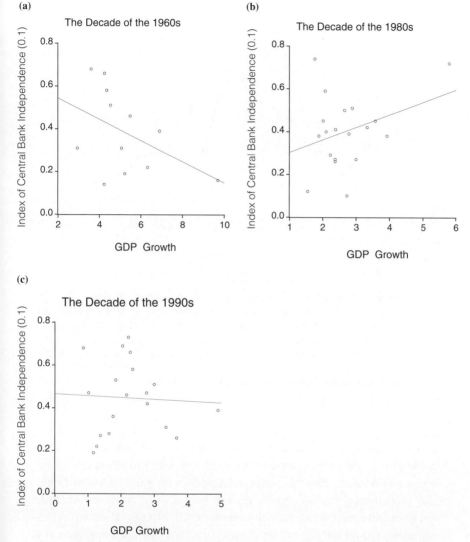

Figure 1.3 Economic Growth and Central Bank Independence, 1960–1999 (*Note*: Index of central bank independence devised by Cukierman (1992) is used for part (a) of the figure. For parts (b) and (c) adjusted and updated indexes were used. GDP growth is average GDP growth rate for the decades in question. See chapter 2 and www.wlu.ca/~wwwsbe/faculty/psiklos/centralbanks.htm for more details.)

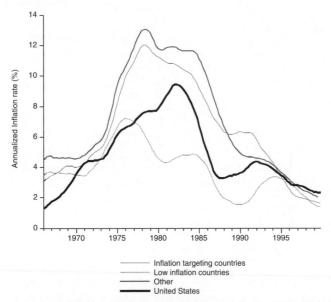

Figure 1.4 Inflation Performance in Selected Country Groups, 1969–1999 (*Note*: Inflation is measured as a twenty-quarter (five-year) moving average of annual inflation based on quarterly data for the CPI. *Inflation targeting* countries are: Australia, Canada, Finland, New Zealand, Sweden, and the United Kingdom. *Low inflation* countries are: Netherlands, Austria, Switzerland, and Germany. *Other countries* are: Norway, France, Belgium, Denmark, Ireland, Italy, Portugal, Spain, and Japan.)

economic performance. Figure 1.3a shows the connection between a statutory measure of central bank independence – details are provided in Chapter 2 – and Gross Domestic Product (GDP) growth in the 1960s. Figures 1.3b and c show the same relationship for the 1980s and 1990s. The 1960s reveal that economic growth was slightly better on average when central banks were less autonomous. Of course, as we shall see, this relationship does not control for the fact that those same economies were operating under the Bretton Woods regime. By the 1980s, the correlation is reversed, and the relationship essentially disappears by the 1990s. Not only do these results contradict some of the earlier evidence (for example, see Alesina and Summers 1993), they also reveal that any connection between real economic activity and the statutory position of a central bank within government is far from being robust. This despite the fact that output growth over the four decades considered is highly persistent. This means that countries with relatively higher growth rates

Table 1.3. Unemployment Rate and Output Gap Performance in Twenty Countries

	Decade							
	Unemployment (%)				Deviation from "Natural" Rate			
Country	1960s	1970s	1980s	1990s	1960s	1970s	1980s	1990s
Australia	1.59	3.95	7.64	8.90	0.17	−0.14	0.14	−0.18
Austria	2.83	1.95	4.28	6.51	−0.31	0.27	−0.41	0.37
Belgium	3.48	6.37	15.66	13.33	−0.23	0.45	−0.30	0.09
Canada	5.03	6.71	9.37	9.58	0.42	−0.61	0.48	−0.29
Denmark	1.08	4.17	8.96	9.44	−0.69	0.36	0.01	−0.24
Finland	2.13	3.61	4.93	12.99	n/a	−0.20	0.50	−0.33
France	0.84	3.89	9.09	11.20	n/a	−0.19	0.19	.0001
Germany	0.96	2.86	7.92	9.05	−0.26	0.35	−0.48	0.39
Ireland	6.14	7.92	15.23	12.68	0.05	0.46	0.27	−0.39
Italy	5.14	6.36	10.24	11.43	−0.61	0.01	0.49	0.12
Japan	1.29	1.69	2.51	3.05	−0.08	0.24	−0.60	0.44
Netherlands	0.86	3.49	10.59	5.45	n/a	−0.49	−0.09	0.25
New Zealand	0.18	0.65	5.12	7.97	n/a	n/a	0.51	−0.40
Norway	1.12	0.95	2.58	4.96	−0.28	0.26	0.77	−0.28
Portugal	n/a	N/a	7.23	5.26	n/a	−0.49	−0.10	0.28
Spain	n/a.	4.20	17.51	19.79	n/a	0.03	−0.05	0.02
Sweden	1.47	2.05	2.48	6.12	n/a	0.17	0.09	−0.16
Switzerland	0.02	0.22	0.58	3.46	n/a	−0.16	0.06	0.10
United Kingdom	1.91	3.42	9.24	7.43	0.27	−0.47	0.10	0.10
United States	4.78	6.21	7.28	5.72	0.03	−0.04	0.02	−0.01

Data are averages of quarterly data over the decade in question. Data for Austria (1964.Q1), Denmark (1968.Q1) and Norway (1961.Q1), Portugal, Netherlands (1977.Q1), New Zealand (1982.Q2) begin in the year, quarter indicated in parenthesis. Data for the output gap for Austria, Belgium, Finland, France, Italy, Norway, Portugal, Spain, Sweden (1998.Q4), Ireland (1998.Q3), United Kingdom, Japan, New Zealand, Switzerland (1999.Q3), Netherlands (1999.Q1) end in the year, quarter shown. Otherwise data begin in 1960.Q1 and end 1999.Q4. Output gap is actual less potential output with latter estimated via an H-P filter with a smoothing parameter of 3200. More information about the data can be found at www.wlu.ca/~wwwsbe/faculty/psiklos/centralbanks.htm.

in the 1960s also tended to outperform others in the 1970s through the 1990s.[8]

In contrast, there appears to be a more robust relationship between unemployment rates and central bank independence with the more autonomous central banks over each decade associated with, on average, lower unemployment rates. As seen in Table 1.3, average unemployment

---

[8] The correlation is weakest between GDP growth in the 1960s and 1990s.

rates have tended to rise in almost every country considered through the 1980s. By the 1990s, however, we begin seeing unemployment rates falling in a few countries. Despite the apparently clear relationship between unemployment and central bank independence, included among the countries with lower average unemployment rates during the 1990s are countries that virtually span the spectrum of autonomy central banks enjoy vis-à-vis their government. Part of the difficulty in interpreting these data is that unemployment rates in the table are not expressed relative to some natural, or nonaccelerating inflation rate. But this cannot be the whole story as there is considerable uncertainty about the evolution of benchmark unemployment rates (for the United States see Symposium 1997).

The evidence based on the output gap, the currently most fashionable expression of real economic influences on central bank behavior, tells a less striking tale. Here too there are a number of data-related difficulties to consider. First, of course, there is the thorny issue of how to estimate such gaps. While this study avoids getting into the controversy, the relevant measurement issues are highlighted. Most countries appear to have experienced boom and bust cycles over the four decades since 1960. However, there is no obvious pattern that emerges by country bloc (for example, Europe versus North America, Anglo-Saxon versus other countries). However, it is interesting to note that virtually all countries that formally targeted inflation through most of the 1990s,[9] including the United States, have managed both lower inflation and relatively better output performance during that same decade. Whether the strategy of inflation targeting deserves the lion's share of the credit remains to be seen, as we shall see, but it does appear to be an ingredient in the outcome.

Finally, Figure 1.4 plots a five-year moving average of inflation for three groups of countries and the United States. Inflation is, after all, the fulcrum of monetary policy. The inflation targeting countries adopted quantitative inflation objectives during the 1990s. A second group of countries, consisting of Germany, Austria, Switzerland, and the Netherlands, have a long-standing policy of requiring the central bank to deliver price stability. The United States, by contrast, has historically provided the U.S. Federal Reserve with de facto autonomy and has built up a reputation of delivering moderate inflation. The remaining group of countries are difficult to describe as a block but they tend to include countries where formal autonomy between the central bank and the gov-

---

[9] Namely, Australia, Canada, Finland, New Zealand, and Sweden.

ernment is not deemed essential, or desirable, or where the central bank has never accumulated a reputation for low or stable inflation. The striking result of the figure is that, for over two decades, namely the 1970s and 1980s, and into the 1990s, inflation rates between these countries diverged substantially. During the 1960s, the Bretton Woods exchange rate standard kept inflation rates fairly close together. Finally, by the mid-1990s, inflation rates showed a remarkable convergence. Disentangling the role of institutions, politics, and policies in the following chapters will, hopefully, add to our understanding of the role each of these factors play in explaining inflation and central bank performance.

Clearly then, delivering good monetary policy via statutory means need not be necessary nor sufficient. Credibility, reputation, and interdependence of economic shocks among industrial countries were also factors in the brew that produced a consensus in favor of adopting price stability objectives. We explore these questions in Chapters 4 through 7. One notable phenomenon of the 1980s and 1990s is the formulation of an explicit goal for inflation, eventually adopted in one form or another in sixteen of the twenty countries examined in this study. Given the attention paid to inflation targets in both academic and policy circles, and their apparent popularity, Chapter 7 places emphasis on their role in the changing face of central banking over the last half century.

Implementing a coherent strategy for monetary policy may still not be enough if the elements of the strategy are not sufficiently well communicated or understood, and if responsibility for the outcomes of monetary policy actions are not clearly delineated. Accordingly, transparency and accountability have become the new watchwords for how good monetary policy outcomes ought to be delivered. But, as is sometimes the case, these questions are often addressed outside the historical context. Could central banks have been more transparent before the 1990s? Is accountability a feature of central bank–government relations that emerged because of recent economic circumstances industrial economies have found themselves in, or did the question show up in previous decades as well? As we shall see, before transparency was possible it was necessary to reach some consensus over what constitutes a successful monetary policy strategy. As for accountability, bringing into sharper focus the limits to monetary policy required experimentation and experience with monetary policy regimes that failed to make these clear to policy makers and the public alike.

Yet, there is a sense in which the literature in this connection exaggerates the appropriate onus that ought to be placed on the central bank to "perform" well as far as society is concerned. The point, it cannot be emphasized enough, is that accountability must, to be effective, come with a clear understanding of the role of the central bank vis-à-vis the government. Similarly, openness is occasionally viewed as desirable only if the central bank is an "open book." However, as will be seen, there are a variety of reasons why this condition is not to be literally sought after. The difficulty stems largely from inadequate definitions and opaque measurement of the useful characteristics of accountability and openness in the current literature.

Nevertheless, even if these drawbacks are overcome, there remains the perception of a "cultural" aspect to the issues. Thus, for example, the continuing debate over the performance of the fledgling European Central Bank (ECB) suggests possibly an Anglo-Saxon versus a continental European divide. There are those who feel that dissent, or the absence of consensus, is detrimental to good conduct in the delivery of monetary policy while others are strongly in favor of openness. Hence, for example, when the ECB resisted interest rate reductions in early 2001, at a time when the U.S. Fed rapidly cut interest rates, there were public complaints about a poor communications strategy and opacity in public pronouncement on the state of thinking at the ECB, especially in the Anglo-Saxon press. By contrast, the European press was somewhat less critical pointing out that the relatively greater transparency of the U.S. Fed actually led to more criticism of its policies and not to a better understanding of the uncertainties in the conduct of monetary policy.[10]

However, a great deal of the difficulty with such questions involves institutional design and the structure of government–central bank relations, as we shall see and, in this connection, the ECB provides examples of both good and bad elements in the design of a successful monetary policy strategy. Indeed, there are also international forces at work that are creating a greater "convergence" of sorts in views about accountability and transparency. For example, the Financial Stability Forum, established in 1999, includes nine of the twenty countries considered in this study.[11] Among the many questions being considered by this group include a set of rules aimed at ensuring inflation control objectives as well as rules to prevent lax budgetary policies. More importantly, the

---

[10] It is, of course, dangerous to generalize on the basis of a small sample of views but see, for example, Barber (2001) and Cohen (2001).

[11] They are the G7, Australia, and the Netherlands. The Forum also includes Hong Kong and Singapore.

Forum hopes to ensure that a set of international standards in the disclosure of economic information be implemented. As we shall see in Chapter 6, the International Monetary Fund (IMF) has already begun to play an active role in this process. These developments hardly represent the stuff of a continuing "cultural" divide in perceptions about how transparent monetary policy should be. In any event, the results of this study suggest that better accountability and more openness are both desirable, if well executed, and can overcome an Anglo-Saxon continental European divide.

There is also, however, an additional explanation about why the meaning of transparency might differ across countries. It is customary, in both Anglo-Saxon and in continental Europe, for governments to at least notionally speak with one voice. It is conceivable then that some central banks, in an attempt to protect their autonomy, feel that a similar dose of solidarity, even in the presence of disagreement or of dissent within the institution, is called for. Here, the emphasis is on less transparency as a bulwark against political pressure on monetary policy. This could be one interpretation of, say, the Bundesbank's behavior (also see Chapter 2 and Deutsche Bundesbank 1998a). In contrast, central bank transparency is seen as a device both to inform markets about uncertainties in the conduct of monetary policy, and, by implication, to demonstrate competence thereby earning or retaining credibility. This might be considered one aspect of the Anglo-Saxon view of transparency.

It should be emphasized, however, that notions of transparency are fairly recent, and that central bank secrecy was the norm in earlier decades in both Anglo-Saxon countries and elsewhere. Hence, it is possible that so-called "cultural" factors reflect political and institutional considerations instead of purely philosophical differences about how best to communicate monetary policy decisions.

THE CENTRAL BANK AND THE STATE

As creatures of the state, central banks used to believe that, in return for a measure of autonomy, communication about any disagreements with government should be done in private. Indeed, most central banks, either formally or informally, have an arrangement whereby there is regular consultation with the government, usually through the minister of finance. Moreover, many central bankers felt it necessary to go out of their way to, as one former deputy governor of the Bank of England put it, avoid public disagreements ". . . consistent with the avoidance of unnecessary publicity" (as quoted in Bopp 1944: p. 261). In fact, tradition also dictated that central bankers comment only on matters of direct relevance to monetary policy and to studiously avoid fiscal or exchange rate issues. But there are at least two important exceptions to this rule with perhaps significant implications for how monetary policy increasingly came to be implemented by central banks in most industrial countries. In both the United States and Germany there has long been a tradition of commenting on fiscal policy. In the United States this tradition probably began with the introduction of the Full Employment Act of 1946 that, it can be argued, provided the first legislated set of objectives for the U.S. Fed. The chair of the Board of Governors of the U.S. Fed at the time, Marriner Eccles, commented on specific fiscal measures and the practice continues to this day with Alan Greenspan, the current chair, who also comments on fiscal and tax measures. However, even if one accepts that the Act first outlined objectives of sorts for the Fed to meet, there were no provisions as such to clearly define how monetary and fiscal policy would be coordinated. Further clarification would await the Humphrey-Hawkins bill of 1978[12] that mandated regular reporting to Congress on the conduct of monetary policy. Hence, via largely informal means, the U.S. experience recognized, more so than in almost every other industrial country, that fiscal and monetary policy should be coordinated. In the case of Germany, the recognition of joint responsibility is formally recognized as the Bundesbank was expected ". . . to support the general economic policy . . ." of government (Deutsche Bundesbank Act, section 12) but was also mandated to provide advice to the federal government on ". . . monetary policy matters of major importance . . ." (Deutsche Bundesbank Act, section 13). As noted earlier, while such approaches also raise the possibility of conflict between the central bank and government they do at least underline the important point that central banks can only be autonomous *within* government and that monetary and fiscal issues cannot be entirely divorced from each other.

By the 1980s, the appearance of more autonomous central banks and the need for greater accountability and openness also meant that central banks could no longer avoid publicity. Indeed, as a result of these developments, public communication by central bank officials became increasingly important. Although it is unclear from the data the extent to which the intensity of public communication has increased over the past few

---

[12] The Act has since expired but it is highly likely that the Fed will continue providing monetary policy forecasts, in particular, to the Congress.

decades (see Chapters 3 and 7), the evidence does point to more focused discussions of issues that relate to the principal objectives and responsibilities of the central bank, namely inflation control, and to providing views about the economic outlook from the central bank's perspective. Therefore, whereas central banks used to speak softly they now speak more loudly, and mechanisms that clarify and ensure the joint responsibilities of fiscal and monetary arms of government are now more firmly in place than ever. For this reason Parkin (2000) and Fischer (2000), for example, describe current goals for inflation as "constrained discretion."

THE DOMAIN OF CENTRAL BANKING

Certain features of what central banks do have become widely accepted or at least controversies surrounding them have been muted over the years. Thus, central banks are still, by and large, lenders of last resort and supervise and regulate the payments system. There has been somewhat more controversy, as noted earlier, over whether central banks ought to supervise the banking system, with some empirical evidence suggesting that central banks that are not directly responsible for banking supervision are relatively more autonomous and deliver better inflation performance.

Interestingly enough, however, there has been less discussion about the appropriateness of permitting central banks to become involved in the choice of the exchange rate regime. Clearly, as is now well known, the connection between the exchange rate regime on the one hand, and central bank autonomy and freedom of action in setting policy instruments on the other, is well known but much of the literature, though not all, has tended to relegate these questions to the background. It is, therefore, appropriate to ask whether the choice of exchange rate regimes should be the sole purview of government, as opposed to, say, a joint responsibility of both government and the central bank. History offers no definitive answers. Nevertheless, it would be an exaggeration to state that politicians will typically exhibit the wrong sentiments regarding such choices. A case in point is Britain's return to the Gold Standard in 1925. "Nearly all the *bien-pensant* sources of advice were unanimous that it was in Britain's interest and duty to return to the Gold Standard ..." (Jenkins 2001: p. 398; an important dissenter was Keynes). The ideology of the Gold Standard had blinded many supposedly in the know. Yet, Churchill, himself no expert, appears to have harbored considerable doubts about the return to gold. Indeed, Jenkins (op. cit.: p. 399) writes that the responses to a minute the then chancellor of the exchequer circulated among experts, including Montague Norman, governor of the Bank of England, ". . . were splendid examples of substituting superior wisdom for rational argument. . . . Churchill's doubts took a lot of subduing." It is interesting to note, in light of the significant amount of space in this study devoted to the principle of disclosure in monetary policy, that the dispute about whether and at what parity to return to the Gold Standard, took place in utter secrecy. Contrast this with the very public objections to the prospect of a single currency expressed by the Bundesbank on the eve of the irrevocable fixing of exchange rates in what came to be called the euro area. Yet, political imperatives won the day and the euro was successfully introduced in 2002 following a two-year stint as a "virtual" currency. A major difference between the two episodes is that there was considerably more openness about the process toward monetary union. No doubt luck also played a role, thanks to the helpful state of the business cycle at the end of the 1990s, and the absence of major economic shocks such as World War I and the deflation of the early 1920s. These events only serve to reinforce the importance of political factors as direct or indirect influences with implications for the conduct of monetary policy.

As a consequence, the meaning of central bank autonomy and the freedom to set policy instruments may be vastly different under fixed versus floating regimes. Indeed, Chapters 4 and 5 will argue that central bank autonomy, as it is commonly understood, is compatible only with floating exchange rates for two reasons. One is an argument with a long history in the literature, namely the property that floating exchange rates have in insulating the domestic economy from foreign disturbances. A second reason is that floating exchange rates provide the clearest policy signal that responsibility for domestic monetary policy performance in terms of inflation is placed squarely on the shoulders of the central bank in the first place, and in domestic hands more generally. In other words, floating exchange rates contribute to the accountability and openness characteristics that have become so important for reasons alluded to earlier.

SUMMARY

Understanding the evolution of central banks and monetary policy over the last half century requires that careful attention be paid to the forces shaping institutional change from within and without. Institutional factors, therefore, play a central role in the present study. The personalities at the head of central banks are often thought to play a role but there are good reasons to place far less emphasis on this possibility than on the conflicts between the monetary authority and the governments to whom they are accountable. Events that have affected both governments and central banks have resulted in greater openness and more accountability. These developments profoundly affect how and what central banks do today.

This chapter broadly reviews the questions that are the focus of the study and the position of central banks in industrialized countries. While several common features are identified, differences across the twenty countries examined are at least as interesting if only because they also highlight what we still do not know about how institutions influence central banks and economic activity more generally. Attempting to disentangle the respective roles of policies, institutions, and personalities over the past half century of economic history is the primary task of this study.

2 | Legislation Alone Does Not a Central Bank Make: Political Structure, Governance, and Reputation in Monetary Policy

INTRODUCTION

One of the aims of this book is to blend purely economic analyses of central bank behavior since the end of World War II with what has been learned in related literatures in the political economy and public choice areas. In so doing some familiar ground is covered. However, the various strands of the literature referred to above have taken divergent paths, particularly over the last decade. While this outcome is perhaps understandable, given the complexity of the issues under discussion, it is also one that is profoundly unsatisfactory. In discussions about central bank independence in recent years many observers have lost sight of the fact that monetary policy is ultimately a joint responsibility of the government and the central bank, no matter how much autonomy is permitted by statute. As a result, there may be a connection between a particular political structure, autonomy, and the performance of a central bank.

More surprisingly, there has been relatively less discussion about the process by which decisions are made by central banks. Instead, economics has been preoccupied with the relative importance of inflation versus other potential objectives the monetary authority may pursue and their connection with interest rate developments especially. Consequently, governance issues have yet to make their mark in our understanding of central bank behavior, a significant lacuna already noted in Chapter 1.

An important feature of later chapters of this book is the resort to macroeconomic and institutional data from a cross section of countries. An overview of the data and its limitations is, therefore, in order and some space is devoted in this chapter to important features in the data.

26

It should come as no surprise to observers of central banks that, however important is the statutory relationship between a government and a central bank, actual performance and perceptions of such performance are critical to a proper assessment of the effectiveness of central bank policies. It is, in this sense, that "legislation alone does not a central bank make," as suggested by the title of this chapter. This is not to say that statutory considerations are irrelevant. Quite the contrary. For while the legal relationship between a central bank and the government is important, its role is far from being as mechanical as some have suggested. For example, one of the glaring deficiencies about legislation governing central banks in several countries is that it is either silent or deficient in dealing with the issue of procedures to resolve conflicts that can and do arise between governments and the monetary authority. This question is, therefore, worthy of some attention. The chapter ends by briefly asking if a separate monetary authority from other branches of government is even desirable or whether the separation is a fiction that the modern state can do without.

POLITICAL STRUCTURE AND CENTRAL BANK AUTONOMY

Table 2.1 provides some general information relating to the political environment governing the central banks covered in this study. The first column represents a classification of forms of government based on Lijphart (1999: p. 145).[1] Of the twenty countries examined, four are of the plurality-majority (PM) type, that is, where members of the legislature are elected by a majority or a plurality of the voters, as in, for example, the United States. This is also referred to as a "winner-take-all" system of government. By far the most common form of political structure, however, is the proportional representation (PR) model in which both majority and minority parties are represented. Consequently, as shown in Column 4, PR electoral systems generally involve more political parties than in PM systems of government. As a result, this form of government is more consensus driven. It is conceivable that consensus politics could lead to more inflation relative to a majoritarian system, especially if the latter is dominated by inflation "hawks." However, the connection is not an obvious one since the majoritarian party may also change and lead to a more "dovish" view of inflation. It is, instead,

---

[1] The classification used here is slightly less fine than the one outlined in Lijphart (1999). This appears adequate for the purposes of understanding central bank behavior.

Table 2.1. Characteristics of Political Structure

Country	(1) Type[1]	(2) Political Structure[2]	(3) No. Elections	(4) No. Parties[3]	(5) No. Partisan Changes[4]	(6) Changes in CB Legislation[5]	(7) Average Inflation[6]	(8) Degree of Federalism[7]	(9) Date CB Formed
Australia	PM	Bicameral-federation (prop. repr.)	16	6	3(R); 2(L)	0	5.56	5	1911
Austria	PR	Bicameral-federation (mix)	11	6	4(R); 1(L)	1 (90s)	4.10	4.5	1816
Belgium	PR	Bicameral (mix direct, prop. repr.)	12	12+	1(R); 3(L)	1 (90s)	4.08	3.1	1850
Canada	PM	Bicameral-federation (mix, single member majoritarian, appt.)	12	5	1(R); 3(L)	1 (60s)	4.63	5	1934
Denmark	PR	Unicameral (prop. repr.)	15	12	3(R); 4(L)	0	5.73	2	1818
Finland	PR	Unicameral (prop. repr.)	11	11	1(R); 1(L)	1 (90s)	6.14	2	1811
France	PM	Bicameral (mix, prop. repr., majoritarian)	10	22	3(R); 2(L)	1 (90s)	5.27	1.20	1800
Germany	PR	Bicameral-federation (prop. repr.)	11	7	2(R); 3(L)	1 (90s)	3.01	5	(1876) 1957
Ireland	PR	Bicameral (mix direct, prop. repr.)	11	8	3(R); 3(L)	1 (90s)	6.79	1	1942
Italy*	PR	Bicameral (mix, prop. repr., appt.)	10	15	2(R); 3(L)	1 (90s)	7.86	1.3	1893
Japan*	SPR	Bicameral (mix, prop. repr., direct election)	12	7+	0	1 (90s)	3.98	2	1882
Netherlands	PR	Bicameral (mix indirect, prop. repr.)	11	4+	3(R); 5(L)	1 (90s)	3.98	3	1814
New Zealand*	PM/PR	Unicameral (mix, prop. repr., indirect)	14	9+	2(R); 3(L)	1 (80s)	6.80	1	1934
Norway	PR	Unicameral (prop. repr.)	10	9	5(R); 4(L)	1 (80s)	5.48	2	1816

Portugal	PR	Unicameral (direct)	12	6	2(R); 3(L)	1 (90s)	10.92	1	1846
Spain	PR	Bicameral (mix, prop. repr., indirect)	9	7+	1(R); 1(L)	1 (90s)	8.57	3	1829[8]
Sweden	PR	Unicameral (prop. repr.)	13	9	2(R); 2(L)	1 (80s)	5.65	2	1668
Switzerland	PR	Bicameral-federation (prop. repr.)	10	8+	0	0	3.39	5	1907
United Kingdom	PM	Bicameral (mix appt., single member majoritarian)	10	10	2(R); 3(L)	1 (90s)	6.49	1	1694
United States	PM	Bicameral, direct	11	2	2(R); 3(L)	1 (70s)	4.36	5	1913

[1] PM = plurality majority, PR = proportional representation electoral systems.

[2] prop. repr. signifies proportional representation; appt. means some members appointed to seat in a legislature; majoritarian means that each member must win a plurality of votes to be elected to legislature; indirect signifies that some members elected from lists according to overall size of the popular vote.

[3] + means that smaller parties excluded.

[4] See Chapter 4 for details of the construction and interpretation of partisan changes.

[5] Refers to major amendments or replacement of existing act governing central bank operations. Number of changes since World War II only are recorded.

[6] Rate of change in consumer prices, annual, over the period 1960–99.

[7] The higher the value the greater the degree of federalism.

[8] Forerunner was actually created in 1782.

* Method of electing representatives was changed in 1983 in New Zealand, 1996 Japan, and 1994 Italy. However, only in the case of New Zealand is general classification affected.

Sources: Columns 2, 4, 5, and 6 from sources listed in Table 2.2 and Chapter 4; Columns 1 and 3 from CIA Factbook http://www.odci.gov/cia/publications/factbook/index.html, International Monetary Fund www.imf.org, Goodman (1991), Lijphart (1999), and Pringle (1995).

possible that PM systems of government produce more volatile inflation as shifts in majorities over time lead to sharp changes in the relative importance attached to inflation or output objectives. In part for this reason there does not appear to be a simple connection between the form of government and the degree of central bank autonomy or overall inflation performance.[2]

It is also conceivable that the legislative process may have a bearing on the amount of statutory autonomy awarded to a central bank. The vast majority of governing systems consist of bicameral legislatures. Therefore, the hurdles in changing the legislation governing the central bank, or the influence on its policies, may be greater than in a unicameral system. Once again, however, it is difficult to make a connection with either central bank independence or inflation performance. One reason for the absence of a significant correlation is due to the variety of bicameral structures. In some countries, such as Canada, the second chamber is appointed and the majority party in power in the main legislature can, in principle, override or decide the outcome of voting. In other countries, such as the United States, there are clear divisions of power as between the two chambers and, in some cases, different majority voting requirements depending on the legislation in question. Finally, allegiances to the majority party line may differ across countries and issues. It is not obvious that the number of chambers per se will lead to a direct connection with the status of the central bank in government.

Potentially more promising avenues of influence over both the importance of central bank statutes and the actual policies they follow is via the electoral route. Elections (Column 3) and partisan changes in government (Column 5) put pressure on the government to improve economic conditions in order to favor reelection prospects. Similarly, if partisan factors concerning the relative weight placed on inflation versus output outcomes are identifiable then this may also represent a channel through which central bank policies are influenced. This consideration is all the more important as neither the number of elections nor the number of partisan changes is reflected in the number of changes made to the statutes of central banks (Column 6). Indeed, the vast majority of

---

[2] Johnson and Siklos (1994) consider how the type of government and the length of time a government is in power affect interest rate determination in the 1960–90 period for a group of OECD countries. Data are hard to come by and classification of governments is difficult but, in about half the countries considered, the type of government and the length of time it held office were significant factors affecting interest rate movements.

statutory changes were made during the 1980s and, especially, the 1990s, when it appears that a consensus of sorts about the desirability of low inflation seems to have spread across the industrial world (see Siklos 1999b).

Another potentially promising characteristic of political structure is the degree of decentralization in government decision making. This is reflected in an index of federalism (Column 8). Previous studies (for example, Banaian, Laney, and Willett 1986; Lijphart 1999: pp. 240–1) have suggested a positive relationship between decentralized federal structures (for example, as in the United States or Germany) and central bank autonomy. The more decentralized the structure of government, the less likely it is that the federal Parliament will use the opportunity to influence central bank policies. Alternatively, it is perhaps more difficult to modify the statutory relationship between the central bank and the government in more decentralized federations owing to the costs and complexities of passage of any legislation that can potentially infringe on several jurisdictions at once. Nevertheless, what can be a virtue in terms of the status of a central bank can also be a vice especially if, due to the degree of decentralization, the original statutes of the central bank are viewed as flawed and necessary changes are difficult to implement. Failed proposals to modify the objectives of the Bank of Canada, along the lines consistent with its current inflation control targets (Manley Report 1992),[3] as well as unsuccessful proposals to change the mandate of the U.S. Federal Reserve (Joint Economic Committee 1991) immediately come to mind.

Finally, it is also possible that the length of time a central bank has been the sole monetary authority (see Column 9) may also be a factor in explaining the current status of the central bank. Indeed, there is some evidence (for example, see Elgie and Thompson 1998) that the degree of statutory autonomy has changed rather substantially, but infrequently, over the last century or more, at least in the case of the United Kingdom and France. However, upon closer look, we shall see that changes were largely driven by the type of exchange rate regime in place, and, secondarily, by how much it was in the interests of the state to retain effective control over the central bank.

---

[3] In the Canadian case it could also be argued that the decision not to modify the Bank of Canada Act was a reflection of the philosophy "if it ain't broke, don't fix it." See Laidler (1991) and Siklos (1997a).

THE ROLE OF GOVERNANCE AND CONTRACTS FOR CENTRAL BANKERS

There are two predominant themes in the literature on organizational aspects of central banking. First, central banks are typically perceived as being the agents of the government and are mandated, subject to differing levels of autonomy, to carry out the task of conducting monetary policy operations for the government. The latter acts as the principal in the state-central bank relationship. Until fairly recently, however, little thought was given to the "contract" between the principal and the agent. The literature tended to assume for a considerable period of time that the head of the central bank (hereafter also referred to as the CEO) fundamentally determined its policies and the degree of effective autonomy enjoyed vis-à-vis the government. That so much influence was invested in the CEO of the central bank is evidenced not only by the attention paid to the lives of individual central bankers but is also manifested in the primacy given long ago by Friedman (1962), and many others (for example, Sicilia and Cruikshank 2000), to the role of personalities over policies in central bank performance. Formal expressions of the role of the CEO in determining monetary policy outcomes had to wait until, first, it was demonstrated that, left to their own devices, governments were more apt to impart an inflationary bias in macroeconomic outcomes due to the appeal of exploiting the short-run Phillips curve. The so-called time inconsistency problem (Calvo 1978; Kydland and Prescott 1977) could then be solved via the appointment of a "conservative" central banker who places a relatively greater weight on low inflation outcomes than does the government.[4] Rogoff (1985) was the first to show the implications of such an outcome. A principal-agent problem arises because, whereas governments own their central banks, the relationship centers almost exclusively on the CEO's position vis-à-vis the govern-

---

[4] Recent literature has asked whether the time-inconsistency problem is a significant feature of the inflationary experience in developed countries. But time inconsistency does not produce a particular inflation rate; instead, it arises so long as politicians can generate an inflation rate that is higher than the public expects. Moreover, time inconsistency has no implications for the level of inflation and the length of the electoral cycle (although it may affect the volatility or the direction of change in inflation). Finally, democratic countries should produce lower, not higher, inflation rates because their governments are responsible for an electorate that prefers inflation lower than politicians do (see, for example, Shiller 1997), whereas undemocratic governments clearly are not accountable to an electorate.

ment of the day. As we shall see as follows, this view is somewhat flawed for both institutional and historical reasons.

Granted, relations between a government and its central bank usually offer considerable scope for focusing on the personality of the CEO. First, he or she is often the principal spokesperson for the central bank. Second, regular discussions between a government representative (usually the finance minister) and the central bank's CEO represent an important (and, for the most part nonpublic) tool of communication between the monetary and fiscal authorities. Later developments in central banking history, to be examined in Chapters 4 and 6, refined the question of appointments to the head of a central bank and its impact on inflation and output stabilization. Indeed, with so much at stake in the selection of a CEO, it was natural to take the next step and ask whether social welfare could be improved by formally contracting with the central banker. As a result, there has been keen interest in the properties of the explicit relationship – the "contract" – between the central bank's CEO and the government or, to put the point another way, in finding the "optimal" degree of authority to be delegated to the central banker in charge of monetary policy (Lohmann 1992; Persson and Tabellini 1990; 1993; Svensson 1995; Walsh 1995a).[5] Yet here is the agency problem again: Unless incentives are in place, the effective authority of the central bank's CEO is likely to be considerably more extensive than may be desirable for a government whose ultimate authority rests with elected representatives. Therefore, other than when the mandate and responsibilities are clear, a central bank's CEO may end up being *too* independent.[6] That is why many (for example, Debelle and Fischer 1994) have argued that the central bank's CEO be given an explicit inflation target and be held strictly accountable by way of a contract that specifies the consequences for failure to deliver the quantified objective.

Although current fashion dictates that the CEO be dismissed for missing a target (see, for example, Persson and Tabellini 1993; Walsh 1995b), the New Zealand example suggests that such a solution is fraught with problems and that other considerations may be more decisive in a world of inflation targeting. First, no contract can cover all contingencies, nor does the theory impose such a requirement. In other words, the

---

[5] There is, by now, a fairly voluminous literature on the topic and only some of the key references appear here. A recent comprehensive summary is found in Walsh (2000a).

[6] Russia provides a recent example. There, central bank CEOs have demonstrated their considerable independence by sending the economy into hyperinflation in 1991–2, an extreme manifestation of the failure to properly define the authority of the central bank.

optimality of the contract for the central bank can hold only in a very narrow sense.[7] Moreover, as McCallum (1995; 1996) points out, the existence of a contract simply transfers the enforcement problem to the government and so does not resolve the time-inconsistency problem.

Finally, a survey of central bank structures reveals that de facto, if not de jure, central bank decisions are made by committees (see Chapter 6). "This institutional detail may – and probably does – have important behavioral consequences" (Blinder 1999: p. 16). Indeed, a growing literature, in an area not adequately consulted by those who study central banks, argues that boards represent a vital mechanism to solve agency problems referred to previously that arise in any large organization (for example, see *inter alia*, Fratianni, von Hagen, and Waller 1997; von Hagen and Suppal 1994; Waller 1992; 2000). Nevertheless, as we shall see (in Chapter 3), boards at central banks are not always a product of the legislation. Consequently, governance questions are important for addressing credibility and transparency questions developed in greater detail in Chapter 6. Governance issues are also relevant since, until the recent New Zealand experience, little thought was given to the role of committees and, perhaps more importantly, to how the arm's length relationship between the government and the central bank is structured and defined. In part because many central banks were, at the outset, private institutions, they were set up with a board of directors to ensure that the interests of the shareholders were represented. Following the Great Depression, and certainly by the end of World War II, many central banks became state owned,[8] and the role of boards in monetary policy outcomes was generally subsumed to the direct interests of the state. Yet, the literature dealing with governance issues (for example, Hermalin and Weisbach 1998; 2000; John and Senbir 1998; Shleifer and Vishny 1997), suggests that the effectiveness of the CEO is directly influenced by the board's independence. In the private sector, shareholders, debt holders,

---

[7] Charles Goodhart's suggestion that New Zealand tie the salary of its governor to inflation performance was rejected because of the possibility that his salary might rise if the central bank was successful (personal conversation). One can imagine the scenario that ran through the decision-makers' minds. Suppose that the public expects higher inflation next year than this year and that, as a result of central bank policies, this expectation proves overly pessimistic. When unemployment rises as a result, newspaper headlines will read "Inflation reduced. Hundreds of thousands more unemployed: Central bank governor gets raise."

[8] By the mid 1990s, in thirteen of the twenty countries considered in Table 2.1, the central government owned 100% of the shares of the central bank; in others it owns a majority interest.

and society all have interests in the performance of the firm, roughly in that order. In post-World War II central banking, however, the shareholder is the state for the most part but, as the time-consistency literature suggests, the interests of the two need not coincide. Consequently, appointment procedures and powers of the board responsible for the oversight of the central bank are critical elements in dealing with conflicts between the government and the central bank's management. Similarly, the structure of day-to-day decision making by a committee of senior officials, their appointment, and their de jure responsibilities are also critical to the reputation of the central bank. It is only recently that the literature has begun to pay attention to this question (for example, see Sibert 1999; Siklos 2000b).[9]

Indeed, as we shall see, most decision-making boards at central banks are made up of insiders, namely senior officials at central banks. While these officials are well informed about monetary policy questions it is unclear how independent they are from the CEO. This may be a thorny issue when the CEO is *primus inter pares* ("first among equals") in the institution. On the other hand, unlike the case of many private firms, senior officials want to be seen by the public as making good monetary policy decisions. Such behavior can protect the central bank from undue government interference.

In contrast, few central banks (see Chapter 6) permit "outsiders," namely experts on monetary policy with no direct affiliation with the central bank, to sit on the decision-making board. Outsiders' preferences may be better aligned with those of the public but are perhaps less well informed about monetary conditions than the insiders.

It is conceivable that, just as pressures to reform governance in the private sector have mounted in recent years, demands for changes in how monetary policy decisions are made will grow.[10] We return to the issue in Chapter 6.

---

[9] Complicating matters is that there are often two organs of decision making within a central bank. One board is responsible for general oversight or ratifies the appointment of the CEO. A separate board is often responsible for the conduct of monetary policy. While both types of boards are of considerable interest for the purposes of this study, much of the focus about governance issues will be around the policy-making body in a central bank. Berman and McNamara (1999), for example, argue for public oversight of central banks.

[10] A related question, for example, is how to signal differences between insiders' versus outsiders' preferences to improve the efficiency with which decisions are made. One solution is to publish the votes of monetary policy committee meetings.

The Role of Fiscal Policy

From time to time, governments and commentators tend to ignore or to underemphasize the relationship between fiscal policy and monetary policy. It is easy to lose sight of the fact that, at times, the timing and impact of monetary policy decisions are partially a function of perceptions about the conduct of fiscal policy, if not of actual fiscal policy. Even if the connection between budget deficits, interest rates, and inflation is, empirically at least, a tenuous one (see, *inter alia*, Barro 1990; Burdekin and Wohar 1990; Johnson 1994; Siklos 1988), there are good reasons to believe that monetary policy credibility and success depend in part on perceptions and the actual performance of fiscal policy.

As the date approached for implementation of the Treaty on European Monetary Union (EMU; otherwise known as the Maastricht Treaty), a debate emerged about why the Treaty concentrates so heavily on the monetary aspects of economic union but gives less thought to fiscal transfers and fiscal policy in general. Some evidence (for example, Eichengreen and von Hagen 1997) suggests that what is really important in a monetary union is which level of government controls the tax base. In the European case, the fact that EMU member countries control the tax base makes it more difficult for the supranational European Union (EU) to bail out a member that incurs excessive debts via deficit spending. The issues seem to belong primarily in the politico-economic sphere (Alesina and Perotti 1996). Matters came to a head and nearly derailed EMU a few months before it was to come into force. EMU did, of course, proceed but not before a Stability Pact was negotiated that placed constraints on the size of member countries' deficits and left open the possibility of financial sanctions under limited circumstances of excessively loose fiscal policies (Eichengreen and Wyplosz 1998). There is at least the presumption, not supported by many empirical studies, that the lack of fiscal discipline in one region of EMU will push up eurowide inflation and interest rates. A further consideration is the worry that an accumulation of excessive debt by an EMU member would require a coordinated bail out. As this is written, concerns over lax fiscal policies have reared their ugly heads again and, much as there is doubt over the significance of statutory central bank independence, there are also concerns about the enforceability and, therefore, the credibility of fiscal pacts that are, of necessity, incomplete contracts.

In general, the less dependent subcentral governments are on the central government for financing expenditures, the smaller is their incentive to engage in excessive spending. Hence, to the extent that fiscal policy plays a strong role in determining the costs of inflation and disinflation over time, designing budgetary rules and institutions to ensure good fiscal policy as well as good monetary policy would appear to be critical.

Some preliminary evidence (for example, Ball 1994; Debelle 1996) appears to suggest that inflation-targeting policies have made the costs of disinflation excessively high. Even if one remains skeptical about the methodology used to reach such conclusions (for example, Mayes and Chapple 1995), there is growing realization that fiscal rules do matter (Alesina and Ardagna 1998; Poterba 1994). Hence, if the disinflation costs found for one country are relatively high compared with another, and these can be traced to fiscal policy (among other factors), fiscal reform measures are surely relevant.

A Brief Detour to the Antipodes

Reforms putting government finances on a sounder basis in New Zealand culminated with the 1994 passage of the Fiscal Responsibility Act (Reserve Bank of New Zealand 1993; 1996a). Unlike the United States' Balanced Budget Act of 1985 (also known as the Gramm-Rudman-Hollings Act), which stipulated deficit targets but was vague about how to achieve them and did nothing to prevent the federal government's avoiding the legislated goals via loopholes in the U.S. budgeting system ("off-budget items"), the New Zealand legislation places greater restrictions on the budget constraint. First, public accounts must follow generally accepted accounting rules, as required of any private institution. Second, the minister of finance must publish the government's long-term objectives for fiscal policy and its fiscal intentions for at least two years ahead. Third, the government must announce *before* each general election an update and projection of the anticipated fiscal policy stance for the next three years (the length of the country's election cycle). A positive implication of this requirement is the resulting pressure on opposition parties to also announce before an election their views on fiscal policy should they form the government.

An escape clause from the balanced-budget norm exists, but the government is required to explain to Parliament the reasons and the length of time required to return to a balanced budget. Failure to meet the act's objectives does not trigger penalties, such as the resignation of the minister of finance or the calling of an election. Nevertheless, one ought to consider that the New Zealand government, unlike a central bank, is directly accountable to the citizenry at regular intervals via elections, so such provisions are perhaps unnecessary. Finally, in its regular Monetary Policy Statement, the Reserve Bank of New Zealand states its key assumptions about the anticipated future fiscal policy stance, thereby adding to the perceived harmony between fiscal and monetary policies.

An important source of the New Zealand government's ability to attain what appears to be a highly desirable set of policy rules stems in some measure from its status as a unitary state. Matters are, of course, more difficult in a federal structure, such as in Canada, Australia, Germany, and the United States, to name just a few examples.

Although fiscal processes across the world are perhaps more diverse than central bank structures, and research concerning fiscal institutions is so far at a fairly early stage, it seems safe to say that no central bank mandate, however precise or lofty, can survive poor fiscal policy. Hence, the ultimate credibility of the monetary authority is inextricably tied to that of the fiscal authority.[11]

COMMON FEATURES IN MONETARY AND FISCAL POLICIES AND INDICATORS OF CENTRAL BANK PERFORMANCE

This section has two objectives. First, it broadly describes certain key features of the data. Any multicountry study must face serious hurdles in constructing a usable data set. The same economic variables can actually be constructed rather differently across countries and sources. Another difficulty is finding comparable time series that consistently measure the economic concept of interest for a sufficiently long span of time. Below, some of the choices, calculations, or interpolations that had to be made to carry out the econometric analyses conducted throughout this study are outlined. The web site that accompanies this study (http://www.wlu.ca/~wwwsbe/faculty/psiklos/centralbanks.htm) provides additional details. A wide variety of sources were used and, in several instances, more than one version of the same series was constructed so that comparisons could be made across sources.

A second objective is to provide a glimpse of some of the common features in the data as they pertain to the conduct of monetary policy

---

[11] See, however, OECD (1995) and Poterba (1994) for further discussion on the issues. The material in this subsection draws from Siklos (1997a) which goes into greater detail about the New Zealand experience.

more generally and central bank performance in particular. The description that follows is not meant to be detailed or exhaustive. A more intensive analysis of the data awaits the reader in Chapter 4. The objective here is to point out potential sources of differences in monetary policy and economic performance across the twenty countries in the study as well as highlight common features in the data. Any model will have to reproduce, within acceptable bounds, both the common features and key idiosyncrasies in the experiences of the central banks being considered.

Inflation and Inflation Persistence

The fulcrum of monetary policy actions is, of course, inflation. Figure 2.1 plots selected inflation rates for a group of countries that represent a wide range of inflationary experiences since 1960.[12] One immediately notices at least four broad episodes in the inflationary experience, common not just to the five countries considered in Figure 2.1 but essentially true of all twenty countries included in this study. The period until the early 1970s is characterized by low inflation as is the period since the early 1990s. However, a key distinction between the two eras is that, in all the countries shown in the figure save the United States, the 1990s marks an era of formal inflation targeting (see Chapter 7). In addition, pegged exchange rates dominated the earlier era while most of the countries adopted floating exchange rates by the 1990s.

The 1970s, broadly speaking, reflects the impact of the first oil price shock (1973–4) in all countries resulting in double-digit inflation. However, through the early 1980s, there is considerable diversity in the inflationary experience. Although all the countries considered begin to disinflate by the mid-1980s, there are several reversals in the inflationary fortunes in these and other countries not shown in the figure. It is conceivable that the impact of historically high inflation rates in several countries, combined with weak economic performance (see the following), contributed to institutional changes leading to more autonomy for some central banks, possibly combined with inflation control targets in others.

[12] The data can be found at http://www.wlu.ca\~wwwsbe\faculty\psiklos\centralbanks.htm. The five countries depicted here also run the gamut of highly autonomous central banks (for example, the United States) to central banks with, at least until recently, a low reputation for autonomy (for example, New Zealand). A moving average is used only to emphasize the long-run features in the data.

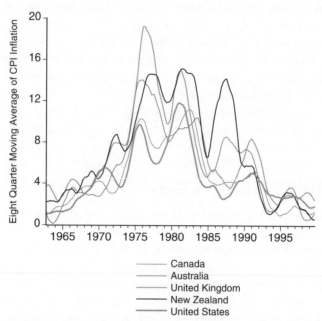

Figure 2.1 Selected Moving Average of Inflation Rates in Consumer Prices

A more formal way of exploring the factors that can explain the evolution of inflation across countries and over time is to think of the inflation process as being driven by a combination of the reputation and credibility of policy makers. Reputation may be viewed as a "stock," that is, it represents the accumulated impact of past successes and failures at delivering good monetary policies with the latter summarized entirely by inflation. Credibility, in turn, represents the public's assessment of current monetary policy. Now, assume that inflation can be adequately described by a first order autoregressive model that is written

$$\pi_t = \alpha_0 + \alpha_1 \pi_{t-1} + \varepsilon_t \tag{2.1}$$

where π is the inflation rate and α_1 measures the degree of inflation persistence. If central banks deliver inflation with a great deal of persistence, that is, α_1 is high, then the accumulated record of the past will weigh far more heavily in determining inflation performance than a change in monetary policy regimes or some other institutional factor. By contrast, if inflation persistence falls without a change in policy goals, because inflation expectations are better anchored, then this can largely be attributed to the reputation of the central bank. Therefore, a change in inflation persistence accompanied by a change in policy goals, may be attributed to the credibility of the central bank at delivering presumably a better inflation outcome under a new framework.[13]

It is, of course, difficult to neatly separate reputation from credibility since the latter does, over time, contribute to the former. Nevertheless, the distinction in terms of Equation 2.1 can help us understand why institutional change may be necessary to deliver good monetary policy in some countries but not others.

There remains the question of how to characterize or date the timing of events leading to a change in inflation persistence. One approach (for example, see Siklos 1999b) is to use the date when a policy was changed de jure. In other words, we can simply assume that a policy change occurs when the legal authorities say it has occurred. However, it is becoming increasingly apparent that this need not be the case. The impact of policy announcements on expectations can occur with a lag. There is also the possibility that policy makers make an announcement of a change in policy direction only after they believe it has a good chance of success or has been effectively in place for some time. In the case of monetary and fiscal policies there are also lags because joint decisions require discussion, and possibly parliamentary approval, prior to enactment, again depending on the reputation and credibility of the institutions in question. The upshot then is that the timing of changes in inflation persistence need not be known a priori. Consequently, an expression such as Equation 2.1 needs to be augmented with additional explanatory variables. If the timing of events that can produce a change in inflation persistence is known then we can write

$$\pi_t = \alpha_0^* + \alpha_1^* \pi_{t-1} + \alpha_2 I_t \pi_{t-1} + \varepsilon_t^* \tag{2.2}$$

where I_t is an indicator that is equal to 1 in the case of a known event, and 0 otherwise. Notice that if the event significantly affects inflation persistence (that is, $I_t = 1$, and the estimated coefficient is statistically significant) then the latter becomes $\alpha_1^* + \alpha_2$ where α_2 can, of course, be

---

[13] In Chapter 7, a more precise definition of what constitutes "good" monetary policy is provided. The treatment of reputation as a stock and credibility as a flow was used in Siklos (1997a) and Burdekin and Siklos (1998; 1999) to explore the connection between exchange rate regimes and inflation performance. Subsequently, I found that Cukierman and Meltzer (1986a; 1986b) also made a similar distinction, not in terms of an AR(1) model of inflation, but to address the question of conditions under which a central bank might want to exploit its reputation.

positive or negative. Alternatively, if the timing of a policy change is not known then one can estimate

$$\pi_t = \alpha_0^+ + \alpha_1^+ \pi_{t-1} + \alpha_2^+ [DU_t] + \alpha_3^+ [DB_t] + \varepsilon_t^+ \tag{2.3}$$

where DU_t and DB_t are dummy variables to capture, respectively, the impact on inflation when a break occurs and the impact of the break on inflation persistence. Therefore, Equation 2.3 suggests that a change in policy or some other shocks that significantly affect inflation persistence can have an immediate impact (referred to, therefore, as an additive effect). Alternatively, the same shock may possibly have a more gradual effect on the series as when there is a change in persistence throughout the postshock period.[14] The dummies are also specified in such a fashion as to, in principle, permit a break to occur at any time in the sample (see Burdekin and Siklos 1999, and references therein, for greater details). Other than the fact that we must specify the statistical criteria used to decide where the most significant breaks occur we must also ask how many such breaks are to be contemplated.[15]

Table 2.2 provides the key results of the estimation of Equations 2.1 to 2.3. The discussion so far clearly suggests that the end of Bretton Woods, the adoption of inflation targets, and the granting of greater autonomy to central banks in the 1990s are prime candidates for events that potentially impact inflation persistence.

The first three columns of Table 2.2 give unconditional estimates of inflation persistence based on Equation 2.1, that is, conditional on events presumed to be known. Columns 4 and 5 provide the dates and inflation persistence measure conditional on not knowing, a priori, when a break takes place. There are at least two noteworthy features in the results. First, whether one believes we can date events with certainty has a significant impact on inflation persistence. Indeed, while inflation persistence has declined in the 1990s in virtually every country considered, the

---

[14] Hence, in the case of DU_t the dummy is set to 1 in the quarter following the break alone and is zero otherwise. The dummy DB is set to 1 in the quarter following the break until the end of the sample and is zero otherwise. Note that this description assumes only a single "break" in the time series. Below the possibility of multiple breaks is also considered. Again, see Burdekin and Siklos (1998; 1999), Bai and Perron (1998), and references therein, for more details. One limitation of the current exercise is that, in effect, the focus is on endogenously determined structural breaks in the intercept and slope parameters of Equation 2.1. The issue of how shifts in α_0 might influence estimates of α_1 is not addressed.

[15] Footnotes to the table provide the necessary information. Technical issues, however, are outside the scope of this study.

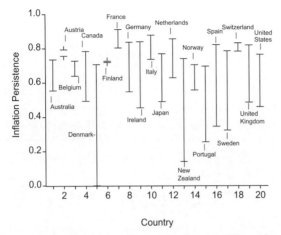

Figure 2.2 Changing Inflation Persistence (*Note*: The top (bottom) gives inflation persistence conditional on the first (second) break detected in the data according to Equation 2.3. Austria and Finland are the only two countries showing greater inflation persistence after the second break. *Source*: Table 2.2, Column (4).)

change is brought out most clearly when the data are allowed to select the timing of the break. Figure 2.2 illustrates graphically how inflation persistence has fallen, dramatically in some cases, since the timing of the first break which occurs anywhere from the early 1970s to the early 1980s. The second break in persistence occurs in the late 1980s and early 1990s, that is, when central banks became more autonomous either de facto or de jure, or, in some cases, when they adopted inflation targets. Second, letting the data select the break produces a series of break points that not only differ considerably from de jure type classifications (shown in Column 5 of Table 2.2) but suggests that monetary policy varied rather substantially from country to country. Therefore, monolithic explanations of the impact of exchange rate regimes or oil price shocks do not fit the inflation record of even a majority of the countries sampled. In particular, only nine of the twenty countries reveal a break in inflation persistence around the time of the end of Bretton Woods and the data often times predict the break before that used in de jure classifications. Similarly, among the inflation targeting countries in the sample, the breaks are estimated to take place after the "official" introduction of the inflation control regime in four of the seven inflation targeting countries considered. Finally, it is interesting to note that the central banks commonly viewed as being the most autonomous, namely those of Germany,

Table 2.2. Measures of Inflation Persistence and Structural Breaks in Persistence*

	Inflation Persistence			Following Endogenous Breaks		(5) Dating Endogenous Breaks[3]		(6) Dating Exogenous Breaks	
	Full[8]	PBW[1]	1990s	1st	2nd	1st	2nd	1st	2nd
Australia	.974	.970	.876	.736	.555	1972:3	1990:3	1974:1	1993:1
Austria	.934	.936	.963	.756	.793	1971:3	1983:4	1973:1	
Belgium	.967	.978	.867	.727	.640	1973:2	1985:1	1973:1	
Canada	.978	.977	.871	.783	.493	1982:1	1991:3	1970:2	1991:1
Denmark[7]	.921	.954	.557	.707	0[2]	1981:4	1992:2	1973:1	
Finland	.971	.984	.887	.719	.726	1973:1	1994:2	1974:1	1993:1
France	.987	.976	.937	.910	.803	1972:4	1984:3	1974:1	
Germany	.949	.933	.847	.837	.548	1981:3	1991:1	1973:1	1990:2[5]
Ireland	.966	.959	.768	.839	.454	1972:3	1985:3	1974:4	
Italy	.978	.984	.974	.877	.737	1973:3	1985:1	1973:1	
Japan	.956	.947	.895	.769	.489	1978:3	1988:4	1973:1	
Netherlands	.946	.977	.769	.855	.629	1981:4	1992:3	1971:2	
New Zealand	.967	.973	.862	.741	.140	1978:4	1990:3	1973:3	1990:1
Norway	.939	.975	.810	.704	.557	1979:2	1993:1	1973:1	
Portugal	.960	.967	.960	.695	.255	1976:2	1985:1	1973:1	

Spain	.958	.984	.947	.821	.345	1972:4	1989:1	1973:1	1995:1
Sweden	.949	.959	.938	.785	.323	1979:1	1989:3	1971:2	1993:1
Switzerland	.952	.955	.967	.831	.782	1974:2	1989:2	1971:2	
UK	.967	.972	.932	.818	.484	1973:2	1988:1	1972:2	1992:4
US	.975	.976	.910	.764	.459	1983:4	1990:3	1972:2	1979:4[6]
Sample	1961:2–1999:4	1999:4	1990:1–1999:4						

1 Sample begins after first set of dates listed in Column 6.
2 Not statistically different from zero.
3 Estimated sequentially via Equation 2.3, first for full sample, next for subsample beginning one year after timing of first break.
4 Based on dates listed in Chapter 4. These were originally specified in Johnson and Siklos (1996) and Siklos (1999b).
5 German economic and monetary union.
6 Change in Fed operating procedure.
7 Data end in 1993:3.
8 Data ends in 1999:4 except for EMU countries where data ends in 1998:4. The countries are: Austria, Belgium, Finland, France, Germany, Ireland, Italy, Netherlands, Portugal, and Spain.
* The technique used to estimate the break points endogenously is explained in Burdekin and Siklos (1999). At most two breaks were permitted in the sample and these were estimated sequentially. Hence, one break was estimated for the full sample and a second one for the subsample beginning one year after the first estimated break only. The break point was estimated according to minimizing the t-statistic for the measure of inflation persistence in (2.3) where a t-statistic is calculated for a break point that can take place in any quarter.

Switzerland, and the United States, all experienced substantial drops in inflation persistence without the benefit of major statutory changes in central bank legislation.[16]

We can further exploit the data to ask whether institutional factors, such as greater central bank autonomy, the adoption of inflation targets, or the political structure of a country, can explain differences in persistence across countries. Therefore, rather than examine the time series properties of inflation for the individual countries in our sample, we now examine whether estimates of the degree of inflation persistence can be explained by institutional factors related to the monetary policy framework and political structures in place. One way of addressing this question is to adopt a cross-section time series analysis of the determinants of estimates of inflation persistence. In other words, we can estimate

$$\alpha_{1i}^{+} = \alpha_0 + \alpha_1 CBI_i + a_2 IT_i + a_3 FED_i + u_t \tag{2.4}$$

where the estimate of inflation persistence in country i, generated from Equation 2.3[17] is determined by CBI_i, an index of central bank independence (discussed later in the chapter), IT_i, an indicator of whether a country adopted inflation targets, while FED is the degree of federalism, as shown in Table 2.1. The estimation is restricted to the 1990s in part based on the evidence generated so far, and also because many of the institutional sources of change in persistence show little variation relative to earlier decades. Table 2.3 reveals that the degree of federalism and greater central bank autonomy can in fact explain some of the cross-country influences on inflation persistence. More autonomous central banks are indeed better able to anchor inflation expectations. In contrast, governments with a more federalist structure deliver more persistent inflation thereby making it more difficult for the central bank to rely on its reputation for delivering good inflation performance. Finally, there appear to be no significant differences in inflation persistence between inflation and noninflation targeting countries, a reflection of the international convergence in inflation noted in Figure 2.1. Hence, it is likely

---

[16] Therefore, as noted earlier, one advantage of letting the data decide the timing of the break is that it may lead to evidence suggesting that, a priori, less explicit or obvious manifestations of institutional change can also influence inflation performance. Far from relegating institutional factors to the background this approach forces one to ask which event can explain the outcome of the test. Otherwise there is always the danger that the location of a break is spurious.

[17] That is, we use estimates of α_{1i}^{+} following the second break estimated in Column 5 of Table 2.2 for reasons explained below.

Table 2.3. Determinants of Inflation Persistence

Dependent Variable: Coefficient of Inflation Persistence[1]

Independent Variables	Coefficient (Standard Error)
Constant	.69 (.13)*
Central Bank Independence[2]	−.64 (.23)*
Inflation Targeting[3]	−.09 (.08)
Degree of Federalism[4]	.06 (.03)*
adj. R^2	.32
F (prob)	3.96 (.03)⁺

[1] From Column 4, Table 2.2, second date of break.
[2] From Table 2.5.
[3] Australia, Canada, Finland, New Zealand, Spain, Sweden, United Kingdom.
[4] See Table 2.1.
* Significant at the 1% (+5%) level of significance.

that inflation targeting is a device used to ensure the credibility of monetary policy, and thence lower inflation persistence, but need not, by itself, improve inflation performance relative to noninflation targeting countries.

Credibility of Policy Regimes

While changes in persistence can tell us something about a central bank's reputation, and breaks in the presumed relationship are informative about how important events can affect its credibility, estimates of the latter are indirect. A more direct test of credibility perhaps – others will be presented later in connection with central banks attempts to increase accountability and transparency – is to ask how important are announced inflation targets in influencing inflation expectations versus the past history of inflation. Table 2.4 considers the case for seven countries with numerical inflation objectives. It is clear that explicit policy objectives in most cases serve to significantly anchor inflation expectations. Three of the seven inflation targeting countries publish explicit inflation forecasts though only two are usable in the analysis presented in Table 2.4.[18] It is also noteworthy that the simple specification explains

---

[18] The United Kingdom produces a "fan" chart (see Britton and Whitley 1996) which shows the probability distribution of future inflation rates at constant interest rates.

Table 2.4. Credibility Effects of Inflation Targeting

	Coefficients[1]		Summary Statistics	
Country[2]	Lagged Inflation	Current Inflation Target	$\bar{R}^2$	D.W.
Australia (93:1)	.39 (.12)*	.32 (.11)*	.78	1.58
Canada (91:1)	.78 (.05)*	.26 (.05)*	.89	2.04
Finland (93:2)[3]	.72 (.12)*	.17 (.11)[4]	.90	1.83
New Zealand (90:1)				
RBNZ[5]	.16 (.06)*	.18 (.07)*	.70	1.43
ZIER[6]	.82 (.06)*	.17 (.09)*	.86	2.15
Spain (95:1)	.42 (.05)*	.80 (.06)*	.99	2.16
Sweden (93:1)[7]	.76 (.07)*	.43 (.08)*	.79	1.23
United Kingdom (92:4)	.53 (.10)*	.53 (.10)*	.52	1.68

[1] Coefficients are from a regression of the current year forecast for inflation on last year's actual inflation rate, and the current target (date of introduction in parenthesis). The latter is defined as the midpoint of the target band where appropriate. In the case of Finland and the RBNZ forecast for New Zealand, a lag in the inflation forecast was added to correct for serial correlation in the original specification. A lag in the output forecast was also added in the case of Finland and Spain.

[2] Private sector forecasts, except for Finland and the RBNZ forecasts for New Zealand.

[3] Forecasts from the Bank of Finland.

[4] Significant at the .14 level of significance.

[5] Reserve Bank of New Zealand (RBNZ) forecast.

[6] New Zealand Institute of Economic Research (NZIER) forecast.

[7] The critical value for the finding of positive serial correlation based on the Durbin-Watson test is 1.26 but other specifications did not correct the problem or lead to substantially different results.

* Indicates statistically significant at the 1% level of significance.

a considerable portion of the behavior in inflation expectations. However, the specifications for Australia, Finland, and Spain suffered from positive serial correlation in the original specification requiring the addition of a lag in the inflation forecast and/or a measure of the forecast of real GDP growth to correct the problem. Since Canada, New Zealand, Sweden, and the United Kingdom have not only operated under inflation control objectives the longest but have, arguably (see Chapter 7), gone the furthest to ensure that the public anchor its expectations to the announced targets, Table 2.4 illustrates how institutional factors can create credibility and contribute to enhancing reputation via the "breaking" of inflation persistence.[19]

[19] Another factor that may affect the results in Table 2.4 is whether the forecasts for inflation are generated by the private sector or are produced by the central bank. In the case

A number of caveats need to be addressed that underlie the difficulty of measuring the credibility of policies via statistical means. For example, in the case of Canada and New Zealand, the first few years of their inflation targeting regimes involved declining inflation control objectives. One could argue that these were specified with a view to maximize the chances of success. However, in both countries, inflation fell faster than expected in part, as noted earlier, due to international considerations. In other countries, such as Sweden, the United Kingdom, Finland, and Australia, the inflation targets either began as bands and were reduced to point targets, or vice versa, or were point targets from the beginning.

The tests carried out in Table 2.2 are repeated in Table 2.5 using forecasts of inflation from a variety of sources. Building upon the results reported in Table 2.4, we ask whether one finds significant changes in forecasters' beliefs, in the form of estimated breaks in forecasts of inflation, about the future course of inflation. One manifestation of credibility would be if the process driving inflationary expectations is subject to a significant revision in light of a change in policy regimes. However, unlike the results presented in Table 2.4, we permit the data to inform us about the timing of such breaks.

The results need to be interpreted with some caution because of certain features of the data. As with the other data used in this study additional details are relegated to the web site. The primary source of data is from *The Economist* magazine's Poll of Forecasters. Each month the magazine reports forecasts for Consumer Price Index (CPI) inflation as reported by large financial institutions.[20] One advantage of the data is that such forecasts are likely to be taken seriously by central banks in setting policy. A disadvantage is that the data are only available since 1990. Therefore, estimates of breaks are limited to the 1990s and are likely to be imprecisely estimated. Supplementing the data are Organization for Economic Cooperation and Development (OECD) forecasts for the GDP deflator since the 1960s. While the deflator is not the variable of interest, in light of the earlier discussion, the length of the time series permits the estimation of several breaks and more precise estimates of inflation persistence over time. Nevertheless, the OECD forecasts are reported only twice yearly. Hence, the data were converted

---

of Finland and New Zealand, central bank forecasts were used with the remaining forecasts generated by the private sector. Only in the case of New Zealand was it possible to produce results using both sets of forecasts.

[20] Real GDP forecasts and current account balance forecasts are also provided.

Table 2.5. Measure of Persistence and Structural Breaks in Inflation Forecasts*

Country	Source of Forecast	Persistence				Dating Breaks in Persistence			
		1st	2nd	3rd	4th	1st	2nd	3rd	4th
Australia	Econ[2]	.73				1994.3			
Belgium	Econ	.62				1997.3			
Canada	Econ	.82				1994.3			
Denmark	OECD[3]	.89	.86	.68		1972.2	1982:2	1996:2	
	Econ	.48				1998.1			
Finland	BOF[4]	.89				1995.4			
France	Econ	.93				1997.3			
Germany	OECD	.93	.83	.48		1972.4	1986:3	1996:3	
	Econ	.78				1982.2			
Italy	OECD	.93	.84	.40		1968.2	1990:4	1996:2	
	Econ	.64				1994.4			
Japan	OECD	.92	.86	.58	.51	1972.2	1983:4	1989:2	1994:2
	Econ	.41				1996.3			
Netherlands	OECD	.88	.84	.81	.20	1975.4	1980:2	1987:4	1994:4
	Econ	.78				1996.1			
New Zealand	NZIER[5]	.61				1992.4			
	RBNZ[6]	.72				1998.3			
Spain	Econ	.82				1998.1			

Sweden	Econ	.81			1991.3		
Switzerland	Econ	.09[1]			1993.3		
United Kingdom	Econ	.72			1996.4		
	OECD	.90	.78	.32	1973.3	1987:4	1993:3
United States	Econ	.15[1]			1994.3		
	OECD	.91	.81	.21[1]	1981.1	1987:4	1992:4
	Greenbook[7]	.33	.33		1982.3	1989:3	

[1] Coefficient is not statistically significant at even the 10% level.
[2] Economist Poll of Forecasters.
[3] Organization of Economic Cooperation and Development.
[4] Bank of Finland.
[5] New Zealand Institute of Economic Research.
[6] Reserve Bank of New Zealand.
[7] Forecasts generated by the Federal Reserve Board of Governors Research and Statistics Division. Placed between green covers and thus referred to as "greenbook" forecasts.
* See Table 2.2 for an explanation of the technique. Estimates are based on Equation 2.3. Sample for Econ is usually 1990:4–1999:4, except for Denmark (1993:1–1999:4), Finland (1993:2–1999:4); for New Zealand RBNZ sample is 1992:1–1999:4, and for U.S. Greenbook sample is 1965:4–1993:4. For OECD sample is 1960:4–1999:4. The original data are monthly and were converted to the quarterly frequency by averaging the monthly forecasts. Forecast data were not available for all countries in the study.

to the quarterly frequency.[21] Finally, in the case of Finland, New Zealand, and the United States, central bank forecasts are also available at the quarterly frequency though here too there are data limitations.[22] Other forecasts are also available but the chosen ones are possibly more consistent across countries.[23] We return to the question of the role of central bank forecasts in Chapter 6.

Generally, it is found that persistence in forecasts of inflation mirror those of actual inflation, though the former tend to be somewhat higher. Nevertheless, just as inflation persistence has fallen so has persistence in inflation forecasts, at least as measured by the available long-run OECD forecasts for the G7 countries. Moreover, forecast persistence does not appear to be significantly higher or lower in the two G7 countries which adopted explicit inflation targets in the 1990s, namely Canada and the United Kingdom.

Of perhaps greater interest in the present context is the timing of structural changes in the process driving inflation forecasts. It would be useful to know the structure of the models used to generate the various forecasts as well as the loss function implicit in generating such forecasts.[24] In the absence of such information, however, we can only presume that any estimated structural break in inflation forecasts is related to the environment (that is, the policy regime) in place. Restricting attention to forecasts published in the 1990s in *The Economist*, the results suggest that a break in inflation expectations takes place anywhere from twelve to four years in four of the seven inflation targeting countries considered in the present study, namely Australia, Canada, Finland, and New Zealand.[25] The delay does appear to be somewhat

---

[21] Via interpolation in the form of a cubic function.

[22] U.S. Greenbook data are available only until the end of 1993 while forecast data for Finland and New Zealand from their respective central banks are not available prior to the adoption of inflation targets in these countries.

[23] Other forecasts that have been examined include those from Consensus Economics, the U.S. Survey of Professional Forecasters, the U.S. Blue Chip Consensus Forecasts, as well as forecasts from the IMF. This list is, by no means, exhaustive. Many of these forecasts tend to be averages of some kind from surveys and may therefore be affected by the number and changes in respondents over time. For applications that use these forecasts see, for example, Batchelor (1998), Gavin and Mandal (2001), Johnson (1998; 1999), and Romer and Romer (2000).

[24] The loss function, not be to confused with the loss function of the central bank in making policy (see Chapter 4), reflects an assessment of the "quality" of the forecast.

[25] Interestingly, breaks in forecasts published by the Reserve Bank of New Zealand (and the U.S. Greenbook vis-à-vis the OECD) occur later than in competing forecasts. Again, however, data limitations make it difficult to draw firm implications from these results. Also, see Romer and Romer (2000).

shorter than in other countries where earlier tests detected a break in the inflation process in the early 1990s such as in Denmark, Germany, the Netherlands, and the United States. In these countries, a significant change in the process driving inflationary expectations occurs between four and seven years following a similar change in the process driving actual inflation rates. To the extent that some countries considered in Table 2.2 saw a change in inflation in the late 1980s, and none in the 1990s, the delay between effects of policy changes on actual versus expectations of inflation is potentially even longer. Note that three inflation targeting countries, the United Kingdom, Sweden, and Spain, are included in this category. However, it bears repeating that limitations in the forecast data make it difficult to draw firm conclusions. Nevertheless, the sluggishness evident in changes in the process driving inflation forecasts, and the apparent improvement in the speed of change following the adoption of inflation targets, is consistent with earlier evidence and with the notion that inflation targeting does have a measurable impact on expectations. Of course, the tests are silent about the mechanisms that can produce such results. We consider the issues again in later chapters of this study.

It is also noteworthy that the inflation forecast data from the OECD suggests that there is a discrepancy between official announcements of changes and changes in the persistence of inflation forecasts. Hence, while a structural break in inflation forecasts is apparent one to two years following the end of Bretton Woods for Canada, Japan, and the United Kingdom, no similar relation is detected for the remaining G7 countries. Indeed, breaks in inflation forecast persistence are more likely to be related to political events (for example, as in France and Germany) or other major economic events (for example, as in the United States). Some of these have already been discussed and we shall consider others later in this study (especially in Chapter 4).

Caveats

Along with greater central bank autonomy comes the recognition that not all factors that contribute to inflation require an immediate response by a central bank. In particular, it is now widely agreed that the first round effects of a "supply shock," for example in the form of higher energy prices, ought to be ignored by the monetary authorities, that is, so long as expectations of inflation are not permanently affected. The implication then is that not all movements in inflation warrant a response by a central bank. Therefore, monetary authorities are generally at pains to repeat that "supply side shocks" to inflation, as they are generally referred to, are outside the inflation control mandate. It is interesting that whereas "supply shocks," these are reflected in the most volatile components of an aggregate price index such as food, energy, and certain types of taxes (for example, indirect taxes) and give rise to the concept of "core" inflation, are nowadays viewed as an ingredient in policy discussions that ought to be eschewed, it was not always the case. Indeed, as we shall see, proposals for "good" conduct in monetary policy throughout the first half of the twentieth century focused on the desirability of targeting certain commodity price movements as these were believed to be highly indicative of the overall change in the purchasing power of money.[26] Such schemes were never implemented in practice in part because of measurement problems that now preoccupy today's policy makers but also because it was felt that the public might not be convinced of their usefulness or appropriateness as a target for monetary policy. Critics included von Hayek (1931) who complained that such proposals ignored the sources of changes in such prices (that is, relative prices versus aggregate price changes; change in productivity). Other critics pointed to what, in modern parlance, might be called the policy horizon for proposals that aimed at targeting some price index. "Irving Fisher's plan depends on using a price index as a guide but a price index is not a scientific thing. It only shows the average of a number of changes in prices. His contention is that the prices of all commodities move up or down together. Over a long period and in chaotic conditions like the present this may occur. It is certainly not true over short periods . . ." (Public Records Office 1933).[27]

Some of the foregoing concerns have not entirely disappeared in current discussions about "headline" versus "core" inflation. Indeed, the public continues to be more concerned about overall inflation than with "core" inflation. This presents a difficulty for central banks that target inflation since they must persuade the public when it is or is not appropriate to respond to a rise in inflation.[28] It is in part for this reason that the manner in which a central bank communicates with the public can

---

[26] As reflected, for example, in the great American economist, Irving Fisher's recommendation that U.S. monetary policy adopt the "commodity dollar" standard.

[27] The quote is from a memo written by an official in the U.K. treasury, dated October 25, possibly H.D. Henderson, dealing with an evaluation of U.S. monetary policy and proposals for change.

[28] Although this aspect of inflation control responsibilities has only been formally recognized in the New Zealand case. Also, see Chapter 7.

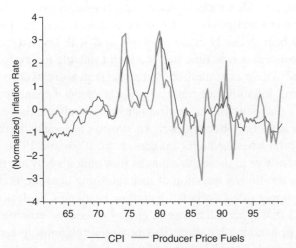

Figure 2.3 Inflation in the CPI and Energy Prices: United States, 1961–1999 (*Note*: The vertical axis shows the annual percent change in either the CPI or in energy prices. Data are quarterly.)

have important repercussions on expectations and markets' perceptions about the performance of monetary policy in general, and the central bank in particular. Recognition of the role of communicating monetary policy decisions has grown in recent years, as we shall see (also see Blinder, Goodhart, Hildebrand, Lipton, and Wyplosz 2001; Siklos 1999c; Siklos and Bohl 2001). Other than the fact that a central bank response to a supply shock worsens the macroeconomic problems facing an economy, the other difficulty posed by supply shocks is that the prices they directly influence are considerably more volatile. Figure 2.3 illustrates by plotting the CPI inflation rate for the United States and the inflation rate in the United States produces price index for fuel oils, a commonly used proxy of supply side influences on domestic prices. It is immediately apparent that energy prices are more volatile, though the differences are more readily apparent beginning around the mid-1980s than throughout the entire sample considered. A similar story holds for the other countries in the present study.[29] Ideally, we would like to extract

---

[29] I was able to compile data on energy prices – usually an index of fuel and electricity costs at the producer or consumer levels – for thirteen of the twenty countries considered for the period since 1969. Definitional changes and other gaps make it difficult, however, to rely too heavily on the data. More details about the data are available at http://www.wlu.ca/~wwwsbe/faculty/psiklos/centralbanks.htm. Also, see Deutche Bundesbank (2000b).

the impact of supply-side shocks on underlying consumer prices. The difficulty for a long-run analysis of central bank policies is that the relevant data have only been recently made available and, with few exceptions, are neither consistent across time nor are they available for more than a few countries.[30] There exist methods to extract a measure of core inflation from overall inflation but these are highly model dependent and may not reflect the views of the central banks themselves. Also, as the relevant issues have only become well known to economists in recent years, it is doubtful whether policy makers in the 1960s and 1970s were necessarily as sensitive to these questions as they undoubtedly are today. Finally, there is the thorny question of distinguishing between first and second round supply-side effects on overall or headline CPI. It is clear from Figure 2.3 that a persistent rise in energy prices, for example, can presage a rise in headline inflation. This potential relationship renders the exclusive focus on "core" inflation still more difficult to explain.[31]

Although measuring losses in purchasing power by resorting to some variant of the CPI is customary, one could argue that reliance on broader indexes might be desirable. The GDP deflator is probably the broadest index of prices available. Most analysts (Haldane 1995b; Leiderman and Svensson 1995) conclude, however, that the relatively infrequent publication of the GDP deflator (usually available quarterly only), and the considerable lags before its publication (up to three or four months versus usually one month for the CPI) hampers the central bank's ability to respond in a timely fashion to shocks.[32] In addition, the GDP deflator includes many more prices of goods and services than in the so-called representative basket consumed by a household. As a result, measures

---

[30] For example, one widely used source for international data, namely the OECD's *Main Economic Indicators*, only began to report core CPI in the mid 1990s. The IMF's *International Financial Statistics* still only reports underlying CPI inflation. Some individual central banks (for example, United States, Canada, New Zealand, United Kingdom) report core CPI but long time series are not available. For study that highlights the dangers of relying on the core inflation concept, see Laidler and Aba (2000).

[31] Numerous instances of this kind of problem exist among inflation targeting countries but nowhere is this more apparent than in New Zealand where, on a few occasions, most recently in 2000, the inflation target was breached. This prompted the central bank to issue a press release to underline the fact that the reserve bank can "... ignore the impact of these on-off 'shocks' to the inflation rate only if we New Zealanders do not use them as an excuse to start a more generalized and enduring increase in the inflation rate." See http://www.rbnz.govt.nz/news/nr000802.htm.

[32] A table showing the release lags for the CPI (and the unemployment rate) confirms the great advantage of the index in terms of timeliness. The table is available at http://www.wlu.ca/~wwwsbe/faculty/psiklos/centralbanks.htm.

of GDP inflation may be more sensitive to changes in relative prices and in the composition of output over time than the CPI.[33]

Alternatively, the index used might incorporate asset prices, as suggested by Goodhart (1995). Serious consideration was given to the possibility of including them in New Zealand (Mayes and Chapple 1995). The key problem with asset prices is in identifying changes stemming from the reallocation of financial portfolios as opposed to changes due to the public's or the market's perception that the relative price of future consumption has changed.[34] In addition, the economics profession's difficulty with forecasting asset price inflation also makes it impractical at present to incorporate them in the target. Here too, however, there are recent developments that might lead to a different treatment of the role of asset prices in monetary policy in the future. Stock and Watson (2001) exhaustively review the old and new evidence on the predictive performance of asset prices for key macroeconomic aggregates. While their results are inconclusive they do report success at using combinations of asset prices. Goodhart and Hofmann (2000a; 2000b; 2000c) also report some success in this area and emphasize the role of housing prices in particular. Asset prices do play a role in the analysis in Chapter 4 where we report estimates for a model that a central might use in forecasting, for example, future inflation. This may or may not be satisfactory relative to a target for asset prices, but the approach does at least recognize that they matter and that their movement can potentially threaten economic performance.[35]

---

[33] Increasingly, countries are adopting the "Chain Fisher" index to measure GDP (for example, Australia, the United States, Canada). The data used in this paper are not based on chain-weighted indexes and this fact potentially has implications for some of the inferences made throughout this study. In particular, the sum of chained values for each component of real GDP does not equal the value for the real GDP aggregate. For more details, see http://www.statcan.ca/english/concepts/chainfisher/bibliography.htm. Also, see Fortin (1990) and Shapiro and Wilcox (1996).

[34] Despite this well-known problem this did not prevent several central banks, most notably Canada and New Zealand, from using a Monetary Conditions Index (MCI) as indicator of the stance of monetary policy (also see Chapter 3). See Reserve Bank of New Zealand (1996c; 1996d). The usefulness of such an index is dependent on, among other things, real versus portfolio shocks affecting a small open economy, a point recognized by Freedman (1999) and Smets (1997). Also see Siklos (2000a).

[35] The tension between an explicit recognition of asset prices and the practical difficulties associated with their measurement is widely recognized by the central bankers. "In many countries, central banks are charged with promoting financial stability. . . . However, unlike a target for inflation, it is difficult to quantify financial stability, and therefore it is not easy to know when asset prices threaten that stability" (Bank for International Settlements (2000: p. 66)). Former Governor of the Bank of Japan, Yasushi Mieno, put

Interest Rates

It was commonplace from the 1950s through the 1980s to assume that a monetary aggregate is the preferred instrument of monetary policy. Other than for the apparent breakdown in the links between monetary aggregates and economic variables likely to be included in the central bank's objective function, there is, in theory at least, little to choose between an interest rate or a monetary aggregate as the instrument (for example, McCallum 1989). Nevertheless, there is an important caveat to this interpretation, namely that the adoption of a monetary targeting framework has possibly important, implications for the volatility of inflation and output outcomes (Svensson 2000). Although monetary targeting as a strategy for the conduct of monetary policy fell out of favor in the 1980s (Bernanke and Mishkin 1992) it is part and parcel of the monetary strategy of the European Central Bank (1998). Nevertheless, these instruments of monetary policy were considered for this study and rejected.

Narrow or broad monetary aggregates, which include the liabilities of the commercial banking system, are clearly not controlled by the central bank within the one-quarter sampling frequency generally used in this study. In many countries, fluctuations in interbank clearings, banking crises, and seasonality mean that even the monetary base is not fully under central bank control in the short term. Studying the monetary base would also require considerably more institutional knowledge of all changes in reserve requirements or reserve accounting procedures in each country than is practical for the kind of study considered here.

Using the level or the rate of change of the exchange rate as a measure of monetary policy across countries was also rejected. There is no adequate model of the "normal" exchange rate, from which to assess the tightness of policy. Although central banks often manage exchange rate intervention, governments generally choose the exchange rate regime (also see Chapters 4 and 6). The importance of the exchange rate

it in the following terms: "Of course, monetary policy should not be aimed at asset price stability. Yet we cannot ignore asset prices ... given that any large fluctuation can have a serious impact on financial systems. I think the question still remains on how we should treat asset prices in formulating monetary policy" (Mieno 1994: p. 251). Finally, Alan Greenspan points out that "We no longer have the luxury to look primarily to the flow of goods and services ... There are important – but extremely difficult – questions surrounding the behavior of asset prices ..." (Greenspan 1996). For a general discussion of the relevant issues, see Cecchetti, Genberg, Lipsky, and Wadhwani (2000) and Fuhrer and Moore (1992).

varies with the openness of the economy, making intercountry comparisons difficult. Since international influences are controlled for, the domestic short-term interest rate (see Chapter 4) may also give some information about the desired exchange rate. Moreover, the connection between central banking policies and the exchange rate regime plays an integral part of the analysis to follow. Therefore the signal-to-noise ratio on the stance of monetary policy is viewed as being highest for an interest rate instrument. Also, individuals, interest groups, and politicians are likely to focus on interest rate behavior, and not the state of money supply growth, in evaluating central bank or government actions (also see Bernanke and Blinder 1992).

Nevertheless, there are a few practical problems with interest rates as an instrument as well. Interest rates are not always comparable across time or across countries. For example, the U.S. Fed funds rate is clearly a long-standing instrument of policy in the United States (for example, see Friedman 2000; Goodfriend 1991) but few comparable measures exist for the other countries over the same time span. Accordingly, the chosen interest rate was governed by three factors:

1. an interest rate that is directly influenced by monetary policy decisions and is, whenever possible, market determined;
2. maturity of the underlying instrument in question to match the quarterly time span of the data used extensively in this study;
3. availability over a sufficiently long time span to permit inclusion in formal statistical analyses.

Table 2.6 lists the definitions and available sample for the interest rates to be used throughout this study. Also shown are the definitions for the long-term interest rate series to be considered later as a potential indicator of future inflation.

Figure 2.4 shows a selection of interest rates for four countries. Two of them, namely Japan and Germany, are generally considered to have stellar reputations for their inflation record. The two remaining countries, Belgium and Italy, are considered to have relatively poor inflation and fiscal records. It is immediately clear that while interest rate movements at times parallel each other, especially during the 1990s, as well as broadly reflecting inflation differentials between these same countries, there is also a considerable amount of diversity in interest rate behavior, both in the levels and in their volatility over time. The kind of broad regime identification used to describe inflation does not seem to

Table 2.6. Interest Rate Definitions

Country	Short-Term (Sample)	Long-Term (Sample)
Australia	Money market rate (1967:1–1998:4)	10 years Government bonds (1970:1–1999:4)
Austria	Bank accepted bills (1969:3–1999:4)	Government bonds (1960:1–1999:4)
Belgium	Treasury certificates (1957:1–1998:4)	Government bonds (1960:1–1999:4)
Canada	Treasury bill rate (1957:1–1999:4)	10 years or more long-term government bonds (1957:1–1999:4)
Denmark	Interbank rate (1967:1–1999:4)	Long-term government bonds (1960:1–1999:4)
Finland	Call money rate (1971:1–1998:4)	Yield on public bonds (1969:1–1999:4)
France	Call money rate (1957:1–1998:4)	Yield on bonds guaranteed by the government (1957:1–1998:4)
Germany	Call money rate (1957:1–1998:4)	Yield on listed government securities (1957:1–1999:4)
Ireland	Call money rate (1971:1–1998:4)	15 years yield on government bonds (1957:1–1999:4)
Italy	Interbank rate (1971:1–1998:4)	Yield on government bonds (1957:1–1999:4)
Japan	Call money rate (1960:1–1999:4)	Government bond yield (1966:4–1999:3)
Netherlands	Call money rate (1960:1–1998:4)	Central government bond yield (1957:1–1999:4)
New Zealand	Bank bills (1984:3–1999:4)	Yield on government bonds (1960:1–1990:4)
Norway	Call money rate (1963:1–1999:4)	6–10 years yield on government bonds (1957:1–1999:4)
Portugal	Interbank deposit rate (1981:1–1998:4)	Yield on government bonds (1960:1–1999:4)
Spain	Call money rate (1973:2–1998:4)	2 years or more long-term government bonds (1978:2–1999:4)
Sweden	Treasury discount notes (1963:1–1999:4)	Yield on long-term government bonds (1957:1–1999:4)
Switzerland	Eurodeposit rate (3 month) (1975:1–1999:4)	Yield on confederation bonds (1957:1–1999:4)
United Kingdom	3 month Interbank loans (1960:1–1999:4)	Yield on government bonds (1957:1–1999:4)
United States	Fed funds rate (1957:1–1999:4)	Yield on long-term government bonds (1969:1–1999:4)

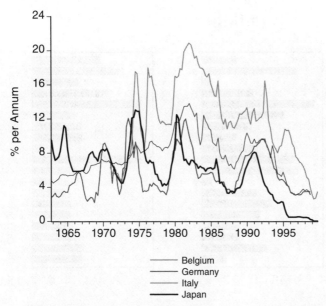

Figure 2.4 Selected Indicators of Short-Term Interest Rates, 1963–1999*
(* Definitions are provided in Table 2.6.)

apply as readily to the interest rate experience, with the possible exception of the international phenomenon of the reduction in interest rates
in the 1990s. There will be more on this period in monetary history in
Chapters 4 and 7.

While Figures 2.1 and 2.3 are instructive they do mask some important developments with implications for the interpretation of monetary
policy over the last four decades. Figure 2.5 provides a series of bar charts
showing average inflation rates and interest rates for nineteen of the
twenty countries in this study since the 1960s.[36] Although the 1960s are
often heralded as a decade of low inflation, fifteen of nineteen countries
in the sample experienced average inflation rates that exceeded 3%,
normally considered to be the threshold for acceptable inflation in
current policy discussions. By contrast, the inflation record in the 1970s
and 1980s is very similar across countries.[37] Turning to the interest rate

---

[36] Portugal is omitted because usable interest rate data began in the 1990s only.
[37] Indeed, a scatter plot of average inflation in the 1980s against average inflation in the
1970s for the nineteen countries in Figure 2.5a reveals a fairly close fit (though not a
one-to-one fit, at least statistically speaking).

(a) Inflation

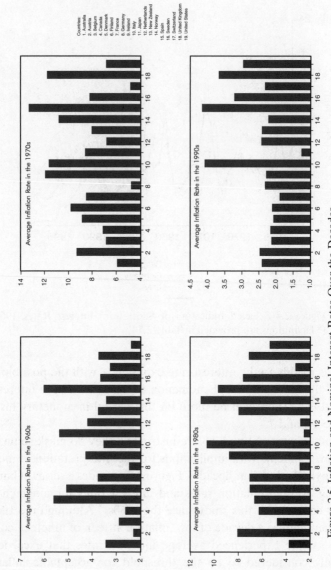

Countries:
1. Australia
2. Austria
3. Belgium
4. Canada
5. Denmark
6. Finland
7. France
8. Germany
9. Ireland
10. Italy
11. Japan
12. Netherlands
13. New Zealand
14. Norway
15. Spain
16. Sweden
17. Switzerland
18. United Kingdom
19. United States

Figure 2.5 Inflation and Nominal Interest Rates Over the Decades

62

(b) Nominal Interest Rates

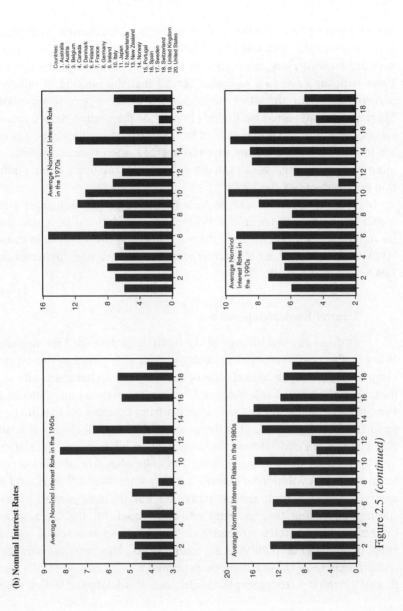

Figure 2.5 *(continued)*

63

record, Figure 2.5b shows the striking result that, for countries with available interest rate data since the 1960s (twelve of nineteen countries), nominal interest rates are higher in the 1990s on average than in the 1960s with the exception of Japan. Recall that the ranking of inflation performance over the same decades goes in the opposite direction. Therefore, as suggested by Taylor (1998a) for the United States, monetary policy in the 1990s may indeed have improved, assuming the figures are interpreted as indicating that the average interest rate response to inflation is more aggressive than even during the relatively benign inflation environment of the 1960s.[38]

Indeed, more formal tests suggest that average inflation rates were higher in the 1980s than in the 1970s. Similarly, one can conclude that mean inflation rates across countries are lower in the 1990s than in the 1960s while mean nominal interest rates are, on average, higher in the 1990s than in the 1960s.[39]

Central Bank Independence

Is there any significance in the analysis of data for each decade? What is the reasoning behind such an approach? This is the typical sampling frequency used in studies of the relationship between statutory measures of central bank independence on macroeconomic outcomes. Presumably, the intention was to abstract from business cycle influences on inflation and economic growth but, as we shall see, the timing of statutory changes on central bank laws, as well as other issues, raise some questions about this approach. Since the main objective of this study is to analyze the evolution of central banking since World War II, and to uncover not only what central banks do but the role played by the statutes governing their actions, one must confront the tremendous impact, in policy circles especially, of the numerous indexes of central bank independence published in recent years. The most notable and comprehensive of these is the one proposed by Cukierman (1992) and, flawed though it is (for example, see Banaian, Burdekin, and Willett 1998;

---

[38] Without stretching the point too much, the "slope" of the relationship between average interest rates and inflation rises steadily over the decades from a value of less than one to a value of one in the 1980s, indicative of a constant real interest rate on average, to a slope value of well over one in the 1990s.

[39] A t-test (value 2.58, significance level .014) rejects the equality of 1970s and 1980s inflation. The t-test for equality of 1960s and 1990s inflation is 3.99 (.0003) while the equality of 1960s and 1990s nominal interest rates is also rejected (t = 3.35 (.0022)).

Eijffinger and DeHaan 1996; Forder 1998), it endures as an indicator of the degree of statutory autonomy enjoyed by a wide variety of central banks around the world. Interestingly, Cukierman (1992: p. 378) gives a rather weak justification for the decennial choice of periods to analyze:

> The time period considered covers the four decades, starting in 1950 and ending in 1989. It is divided into four subperiods: 1950–9, 1960–71, 1972–9, and 1980–9. They correspond to the dollar standard period, the period of convertibility with the dollar, the period of the two oil shocks, and the period of disinflation and the debt crisis.

As a broad characterization of the events, Cukierman's choice is certainly adequate.[40] However, there are a number of reasons why one should raise questions about his choice of time periods. First, as noted earlier (for example, Table 2.1), the chosen periods bear little relation to the dates of actual major changes in central banking legislation in several countries. Second, the choice of samples in some cases does not fit the rough characterization of episodes of inflation and interest rates considered in Figures 2.1 and 2.5. Third, as will be shown in Chapter 4, there is considerable diversity across countries, most notably, in the dating of the end of exchange rate regimes. Fourth, there may be some value in allowing the data to speak for themselves regarding changes in monetary policy regimes. Finally, as noted earlier, despite the choice of samples, there are virtually no changes in *any* of the elements that make up Cukierman's index across most of the decades considered. Nevertheless, the data in Figure 2.5 do suggest some interesting phenomena that can be explained by adopting the decade-by-decade approach, as noted in the discussion surrounding Figure 2.5. Despite this, we are left wondering: To what purpose are the different samples, at least insofar as the countries in our sample study, concerned?

Figure 2.6 shows four scatter plots that illustrate the relationship between measures of central bank independence and inflation in the 1980s versus the 1990s.[41] As discussed previously, the 1990s represent the only decade when substantial reforms to the statutes of central banks

---

[40] It is also interesting to note that followers and critics of Cukierman's index have tended to use data by decade rather than the actual definiton in Cukierman. The practice of using data for the period 1960–9, 1970–9, 1980–9, 1990–9 is followed here though none of the conclusions to be described as follows are materially affected if we use precisely the sample definitions in Cukierman (1992). Also, see Mangano (1998).

[41] Revisions and other modifications to Cukierman's original index are discussed later in this section.

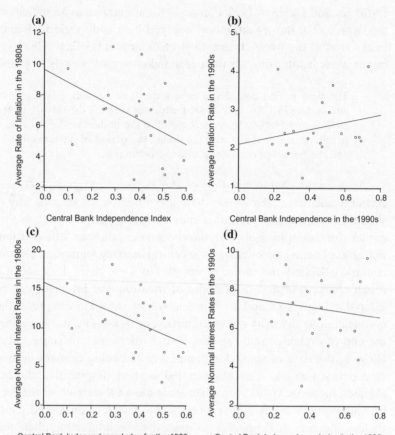

Figure 2.6 Central Bank Independence and Monetary Policy Outcomes (*Source*: See Table 2.7.)

were enacted in a majority of the countries under study. Moreover, all index values were revised upward indicating more independence vis-à-vis government, in line with the policy prescription that more autonomous central banks deliver lower average inflation rates. Indeed, the negative inflation–central bank independence relationship is apparent in the 1980s *before* policy makers in the industrial world instituted reforms (Figure 2.6a). By the 1990s, as shown in Figure 2.6b, the situation is reversed with the revised indexes pointing to *higher* average inflation among central banks with greater autonomy. Has something gone wrong? First, a comparison of parts a and b of Figure 2.6 reveal that, although the sign of the correlation has changed, average inflation rates are practically lower everywhere than they were in the 1980s (also see Figure 2.5). Second, as pointed out previously, central bank independence rose in all the countries considered regardless of past inflation performance. As a result, the index of the 1990s reflects the historical experience with inflation in the 1980s (and perhaps the 1970s), and is no doubt partly explained by the slow pace of change in the statutory relationship between central banks and governments previously alluded to. In fact, the more independent central banks in the 1990s also delivered lower inflation, on average, in the 1980s (not shown). Either enhanced autonomy has delivered little in the way of changing the rankings in inflation performance or the impact of such changes will only be felt in future years or even decades.

Parts b and c in Figure 2.6, however, do reveal that more autonomous central banks deliver lower average nominal interest rates in *both* decades. Whether this is the result of lower expected inflation in countries with more independent central banks remains, of course, to be seen.[42]

As noted previously, some have been increasingly critical of qualitative measures of central bank independence. Despite the criticisms, they are useful in the sense that they point to the difficulties of reconciling institutional measures of central bank behavior with economic performance. Since Cukierman's (1992) index is perhaps the best known, and certainly the most detailed, this measure will continue to be used in the present study alongside the suggested revisions and updates.

As discussed previously, there are reasons to believe that Cukierman's index may contain some inaccuracies for the 1980s. To my knowledge, the index has not been extended precisely as originally specified, into the 1990s.[43] Table 2.7 presents both the revised 1980s index as well as the index for 1990s. Note that Portugal was omitted from Cukierman's original list, but is added here. In addition, an index for the

---

[42] This result need not be inconsistent with the notion that central banks that deliver lower inflation, and possibly lower real interest rates, are also more aggressive at raising nominal interest rates to forestall future inflation. The resulting increase in nominal interest rates may instead be shorter lived.

[43] Cargill, Hutchison, and Ito (2000: Table 4.3) present an estimate of the weighted index of Cukierman, Webb, and Neyapti (1992 for Japan of 0.39 (after 1998) which is slightly higher than the 0.36 estimate produced here). Also, see Banaian, Burdekin, and Willett (1995).

Table 2.7. Updating and Modifying Cukierman's (1992) Central Bank Independence Index

Country	(1) 1980s	(2) 1980s revised		(3) 1990s
		(a)	(b)	
Australia	.31	.42		.31
Austria	.58	.59		.58
Belgium	.19	.12		.19
Canada	.46	.51		.46
Denmark	.47	.39		.47
Finland	.27	.45		.27
France	.28	.45	.25	.28
Germany	.66	.74	.57	.66
Ireland	.39	.72	.51	.39
Italy	.22	.41		.22
Japan	.16	.38		.36
Netherlands	.42	.38	.51	.42
New Zealand	.27	.29		.69
Norway	.14	.27		.26
Portugal	.33	.35		.52
Spain	.21	.10		.73
Sweden	.27	.40		.47
Switzerland	.68	.50		.68
United Kingdom	.31	.26		.53
United States	.51	.27	.45	.51
ECB	N/A	N/A	N/A	.81

Column 1 from Cukierman (1992:Table 19.3), and based on data in Appendix (not shown) using Cukierman's (1992) coding. Column 2a based on mean of term of office, who appoints CEO, provision for dismissal, monetary policy formulation, conflict resolution, and CB's objective. Column 2b recodes provision for dismissal for France, Germany, Ireland, Netherlands, and the United States; recodes CB's objectives for Ireland; recodes conflict resolution and monetary policy formulation for the United States. The Appendix is available at http://www.wlu.ca/~wwwsbe/faculty/psiklos/centralbanks.htm.

newly created European Central Bank (ECB) is also added.[44] Suffice it to note that the discussion surrounding the relationship between inflation and central bank independence in the 1980s is sensitive to the construction of the index. In particular, the negative relationship reported

---

[44] Bini Smaghi and Gros (2000) report an index they refer to as an "elaboration" of Cukierman's index and arrive at an index value of 0.91 (op. cit., Table 5: p. 127). However, they resort to a weighted index that produces the higher index value. Most observers have used the unweighted index since it does not appear that the weights themselves can convincingly be defended in any economic sense.

earlier only emerges when the revised index is used and not the original one published by Cukierman.

Real Economic Performance

One of the most debated questions about central bank performance concerns the attention paid by the monetary authorities to real economic factors. Most economic models (for example, see Chapter 4) and texts continue to regard output performance, as measured by real GDP growth, as the primary indicator of real developments in the economy. In particular, the output gap is regarded as a useful and straightforward summary of factors likely to contribute to inflation. Central banks themselves have or are investing considerable efforts at estimating proxies for this variable (for example, Claus, Conway, and Scott 2000; Dupasquier, Guay, and St-Amant 1999; Orphanides, Porter, Reifschneider, Tetlow, and Finan 1999) but there is, as yet, no widespread agreement on the best measure to employ in practice. In addition, while central bankers have long referred to capacity utilization data to indicate aggregate demand pressures, the output gap is a fairly recent addition to the arsenal of central bank indicators of pressures on inflation. Perhaps just as important, however, is the fact central bank statutes do not directly mention output performance as such but instead tend to refer to some employment objective. Consequently, the unemployment rate is an indicator that is more likely to warrant comment or reaction by central banks than the latest output gap figure. Needless to say, using unemployment rates solves some problems with the use of output gap type measures but creates others. In particular, series covering a long enough time span are not, strictly speaking, comparable across countries. This may or may not be a difficulty since central banks would be, in any event, called upon to respond to employment conditions as measured locally, as opposed to some measure that attempts cross-country comparability. In addition, unemployment rate data are highly seasonal in raw form, with some countries making the data available only in seasonally adjusted form. There is, a priori, no reason to believe that the filters used to seasonally adjust the data are common across countries thereby creating additional difficulties.

Figures 2.7 and 2.8 illustrate some of the aforementioned indicators of real economic performance. Output gaps plotted in Figure 2.7 for the G3 countries reveal some broad comovements in business cycle activity, but there are also some noticeable differences across time. In particular,

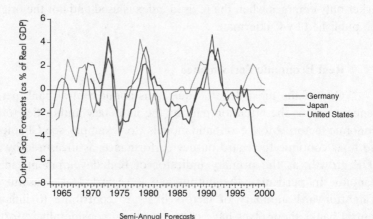

Semi-Annual Forecasts

Figure 2.7 Output Gap in the G3 Countries, 1964–2000 (*Note*: Data do not always begin in 1964 due to limitations in the available time series. *Source*: OECD. Also, see text for details about definition of the series.)

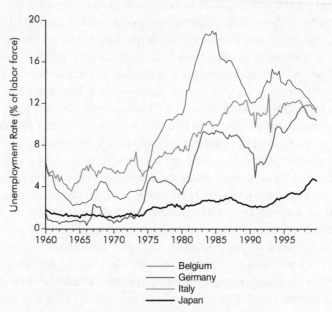

Figure 2.8 Selected Unemployment Rates, 1960–1999

recessions and recoveries appear sharper for Germany and Japan than for the United States.

Figure 2.8 illustrates the wide range of unemployment rate experiences in a selection of countries. Once again, the time series properties differ substantially across countries and, prima facia at least, reveal greater differences in economic performance than are revealed by the output gap data. Whether one time series is relatively more informative than another about central bank behavior remains to be seen, and we return to this question in Chapter 4.

Just as the output gap requires the estimation of some potential level of output, unemployment rates must be adjusted for the fact that structural factors imply a level of unemployment consistent with stable inflation. In principle, estimation of trend unemployment[45] across countries and across time requires a considerable amount of country-specific institutional data (for example, degree of unionization, generosity of unemployment insurance programs, minimum wage data, and so on) outside the scope of this study.

One can, of course, rely on the atheoretical measure used to create output gaps, implement the Phillips curve-based techniques outlined in a recent symposium on the question (Symposium 1997), or use a measure that is based on the well-developed relationship between oil prices and the macroeconomy (Murchison and Siklos 1999). Figure 2.9 illustrates the impact of selected measures for the case of the German unemployment rate. Figure 2.9a illustrates that the atheoretical H-P filter is sensitive to the data endpoints and, therefore, to the chosen sample (see Cogley and Nason 1995; Hodrick and Prescott 1997; and Orphanides and van Norden 1999). Figure 2.9b, in turn, compares deviations from trend unemployment using the H-P filter (based on the full 1960–99 sample) and a measure derived from the presumed long-run relationship between oil prices and the unemployment rate.[46] Comovements between the two

---

[45] In preference over the term *natural* unemployment since a statistical device is employed for its derivation. For additional discussion on related issues see, for example, Staiger, Stock, and Watson (1997a; 1997b).

[46] The cointegrating or long-run relationship is written

$$u_t = a_0 + a_1 OIL_t + \varepsilon_t$$

where u_t is the unemployment rate at time, OIL is the energy price index, also at time t, and ε_t is then the estimate of deviations from trend unemployment under cointegration (see Murchison and Siklos 1999). I also considered the case, in line with the possibility of an asymmetric relationship between oil and the real economy (for example, see Hooker 1999), of an asymmetric relationship between u_t and OIL_t of the form

$$u_t = a_0' + a_1' OIL_t + \varepsilon_t$$
$$\Delta \varepsilon_t = \rho_1 I_t \varepsilon_{t-1} + \rho_2 (1 - I_t) \varepsilon_{t-1} + \ldots + v_t$$

where $I_t = \begin{cases} 0 \; if \; \varepsilon_{t-1} \geq \tau \\ 1 \; if \; \varepsilon_{t-1} \leq \tau. \end{cases}$

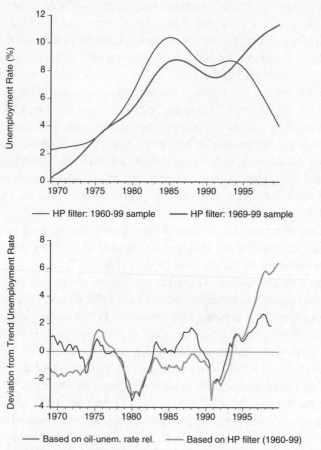

Figure 2.9 Measuring Deviations from Trend Unemployment: Germany, 1969–1999

are broadly similar except in the early 1970s and the second half of the 1990s. It is, of course, unclear which is the best proxy for deviations from some underlying equilibrium unemployment rate. Although yet another characterization of "shocks" in output or unemployment will be con-

---

I_t is an indicator function that takes on a value of 1 when ε_{t-1} exceeds some threshold τ and is zero otherwise. A finding that $\rho_1 \neq \rho_2$, in statistical terms, is an indication that a form of threshold cointegration holds for the relationship between u_t and OIL_t. While some countries (for example, Ireland and Italy) showed evidence of asymmetric effects it was not sufficiently strong or widespread to apply this formulation to the vast majority of the countries in our sample. For additional details about the test, see Enders and Siklos (2001).

sidered and implemented in the next chapter, the measure derived from the unemployment-oil prices relationship appears to suitably describe business cycle influences after 1969 while, for the 1960–8 period, the H-P filter is used owing to data limitations on energy prices.[47]

CENTRAL BANKS AND CONFLICTS WITH GOVERNMENT

One of the objectives of the present study is to ascertain how governments interact with central banks and the role played by institutional versus purely economic, political, or statutory factors. The potential influence of political and legal factors has previously been discussed so the present section concentrates on economic sources of conflict.

One obvious source of conflict is from fiscal policy. It is conceivable that markets interpret a worsening fiscal stance over time as necessitating some form of central bank reaction via higher interest rates, in the form of a risk premium,[48] perhaps temporarily. A serious difficulty is obtaining quarterly data for a wide variety of countries about the stance of fiscal policy for a sufficiently long time span. Data on the net borrowing requirements at the quarterly frequency, and for a sufficiently long time span, are available for only nine of the twenty countries in our study.

Another potentially promising source of conflict between monetary and fiscal authorities is linked to the stage of the business cycle. There is considerable anecdotal evidence for several countries (for example, Capie, Fischer, Goodhart, and Schnadt 1994; Dean and Pringle 1995; Marshall 1999; Muirhead 1999, to name just a few) that a conflict with the monetary authority is more likely during a recession than during an expansion. While the dating of recessions and expansions is well

---

[47] Another possibility that was explored is to estimate an output gap via the estimation of structural vector autoregressions (SVAR; also see Chapter 4). Limitations of this approach are well known (for example, see Enders 1995: pp. 341–2). The appendix to this chapter (not shown) compares one of the measures of the output gap shown in Figure 2.9 (the H-P filter generated proxy) with one generated via an SVAR of real GDP growth and the unemployment rate.

[48] There is, of course, the well-known debate of government borrowing crowding out private sector borrowing via higher interest rates and the reaction to such notions in the form of the Ricardian equivalence hypothesis which refutes any straightforward links between fiscal policy and interest rates. See, for example, Barro (1990). In what follows no particular stand is taken on the above questions. Instead, the possibility is entertained that a worsening fiscal position may lead to a short-term premium being built into interest rates. This view is not incompatible with the views linking interest rates and fiscal policy just described.

developed for the United States, for other countries (for example, Artis, Kontolemis, and Osborn 1997; Kim, Buckle, and Hall 1995), we must rely on proxies that attempt to replicate the U.S. National Bureau of Economic Research (NBER) reference cycle methodology. As a result, we are able to compile recession dates that are roughly comparable for ten of the twenty countries in our data set.

Figure 2.10 illustrates for the United States and Germany the fiscal policy and recession indicator proxies. There appears not to be any straightforward link between the stage of the business cycle and fiscal stance, as measured by a smoothed measure of net central government borrowing as a percent of GDP.[49] Based on the measure of loose and tight fiscal policies developed in Alesina and Ardagna (1998), virtually every episode of loose fiscal policy was coincident or followed a recession.[50] Moreover, although there have been recessions in every decade since the 1950s, episodes of loose fiscal policy occurred in the 1970s through the 1990s in almost every country for which we also have recession data. Finally, the vast majority of countries experienced loose fiscal policy around the time of the first oil shock of 1974–5 but generally not in the aftermath of the second shock of 1979–80. Nevertheless, the time path of key macroeconomic aggregates, most notably inflation, differs substantially across countries, as we have seen (also see Parkin 1986).

In general, one would expect the stage of the business cycle to be a more meaningful indicator of the likelihood of a conflict than pure fiscal measures. In addition, the recession indicator would be potentially useful for another reason, namely to capture the role played by the international transmission of business cycles. Our sample includes at least three powerful economies whose business cycle influence, in the area of monetary policy especially, goes well beyond their borders. Indeed, recession indicators are highly correlated between the United States, Canada, Australia, and New Zealand, as well as between Germany and France. But the correlations are far from perfect or constant through time. For example, business cycle activity between the United States and Japan was highly correlated in the 1970s but the correlation was non-existent in the 1990s. It is conceivable that these correlations may, in a limited sense, reflect choices made by the central banks.

---

[49] The relevant data have been tabulated for other countries but are not shown here to conserve space. See http://ww.wlu.ca/~wwwsbe/faculty/psiklos/centralbanks.htm.

[50] A separate table (not shown) is available listing episodes of loose fiscal policy and recession dates for Australia, Belgium, Canada, France, Germany, Japan, Netherlands, Switzerland, the United Kingdom, and the United States.

(a) United States

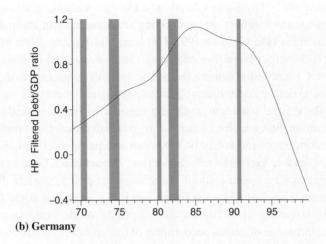

(b) Germany

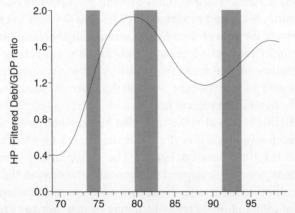

Figure 2.10 Indicators of Fiscal Stance and Recession Dates for Select Countries, 1969–1999 (*Note*: The shaded areas represent periods of recessions. Data source is provided in the text. Also see http://www.wlu.ca/~wwwsbe/faculty/psiklos/centralbanks.htm and Deutsche Bundesbank (1998b) for German data.)

CREDIBILITY AND REPUTATION OF MONETARY POLICY

The focus on the credibility of monetary policies involves a search for the "commitment technology" best suited to deliver credible policies. It is this line of reasoning that led to the advice that an open economy with poor credibility should opt for limited flexibility in the exchange rate vis-à-vis a country with demonstrated credible monetary policy credentials. The advantages of "tying one's hand" are obvious so long as the stipulated exchange rates reflect the underlying fundamentals in the participating economies (De Grauwe 1992; Giavazzi and Pagano 1988; Melitz 1988). If, on the other hand, the exchange rate is permitted to float, this choice is not sufficient to characterize the type of monetary policy in place. An alternative commitment technology is then necessary, such as providing the central bank with sufficient autonomy to achieve either an implicit or an explicit goal for inflation. The point that deserves emphasis is that the conduct of monetary policy is not adequately defined via the fixed versus flexible exchange rate distinction. In particular, floating rates requires that one be specific about the strategy of policy, namely defining the nominal anchor of monetary policy. If the answer is some form of inflation targeting then this requires de facto or de jure – we will explore the influence of each – recognition of the autonomy and accountability of the central bank.

Ultimately, credibility is determined by the perceived inconsistencies between existing fiscal and monetary policies. However, it is extremely difficult to assess the role of such factors empirically because the degree of incompatibility may pose a serious problem only if it is large enough to create tensions arising from the statutory arrangements between a central bank and its government. As noted earlier, these are relatively rare, though often landmark, events.

The credibility issues at stake may also be sketched using a variant of existing models of credibility (for example, Drazen and Masson 1994; Flood and Isard 1989; Masson 1995).[51] The credibility of a monetary policy regime is assumed to depend on the trade-off between the number of objectives that define central bank independence and the credibility of the current inflation objective (which may or may not be explicit). In

---

[51] Of course, the root of the credibility problem does not lie with financial variables alone as is the focus below. Indeed, Masson's model deals with policy makers facing a trade-off between inflation and unemployment. Whether the sources of credibility are more general than those outlined below remains to be seen, however. Masson does not consider the potential role of independent versus more dependent central banks as is done here. Finally, even if the credibility question is a more general one, the arguments and evidence below suggest that some countries have more credible policies because their policy actions are focused on a few well-understood actions, such as central bank independence or inflation targets. In contrast, other countries lose credibility because they focus on trade-offs, such as the one between inflation and unemployment, which are poorly understood, nonexistent except in the short run, or unstable over time. Also see Siklos (1997b) for another application of this model and additional details.

what follows we ignore the potential distinction between de facto and de jure central bank autonomy. Let $\pi - \pi^*$ represent the deviation of actual (π) from some targeted inflation rate (π^*). Deviations in this magnitude will be assumed to be determined, broadly speaking, (1) by a change in perception about how autonomous the central bank is; (2) by an unobservable shock (τ) that puts pressure on the policy makers to decide whether to sacrifice central bank autonomy for a larger deviation in inflation from the target; and (3) in recognition of the fact discussed earlier that inflation is highly persistent, the lagged value of the inflation differential term. We can write such a model as follows:

$$(\pi - \pi^*)_t = \sqrt{\alpha}[-(\Delta cbi_t) + \tau_t + \alpha(\pi - \pi^*)_{t-1}] \tag{2.5}$$

where Δcbi_t measures the change in de facto, as opposed to de jure, central bank independence. All other terms have been defined. Policy makers act according to a loss function. For each period, such an objective function might look like the following (also see Chapter 4).[52]

$$L_t = \mu(\pi - \pi^*)^2 + \theta(\Delta \tilde{y}_t)^2 \tag{2.6}$$

Deviations from targeted inflation are penalized, as is instability in the output gap $(\tilde{y})$, with weights μ and θ, respectively.[53] Governments that place a lower priority on central bank independence will display higher values for θ than for μ, and vice-versa for governments intent on minimizing inflation variability. If we let L_t^π represent loss under an inflation targeting regime, and L_t^c be the loss under a regime where the government effectively controls central bank policies, then the choice depends, of course, on whether $L^\pi > L^c$. In particular, the results in Masson (1995) can be used to show that, in the present context, control over central bank policies will be preferred if the (unobservable) shocks are larger than a linear combination of the parameters of the model, the size of changes in central bank independence, and the degree of

---

[52] Following the usual practice, the loss function is not specified for a multiperiod horizon. Notice also that symmetry is assumed in the costs-benefit calculus of deviations in inflation from the targeted value. This need not be the case. For simplicity, I ignore the possibility of asymmetry here, though the issue may be an important one in the context of inflation targets (see, for example, Ball and Mankiw 1994 and Siklos 1997a) or interest rate behavior (Enders and Siklos 2001).

[53] Notice that L_t is specified in terms of changes in the output gap. Walsh (2001) argues that one interpretation of a policy whereby the central bank precommits to a regime that is optimal relies on changes in the output gap to deliver better social outcomes.

persistence in the inflation differential term.[54] Since only the central bank term is controllable by government, and the other terms are assumed to be exogenous, the public's determination of the likelihood of flexibility in the current regime must be assessed. In Masson (1995), it is a function of the public's assessment of whether a government is "weak" (that is, prone to interfering with central bank policies) or "tough" (that is, determined to maintain the current independent stance toward the central bank) and the probability that either weak or tough governments will change policies. In general, however, the size of Δcbi_t gives meaning to the concept of credibility. Specifically, if ε is the public's assessment of the probability that the government allows Δcbi to change de facto (is "weak"), and ρ^I is the probability that a government of a particular type will emphasize more central bank independence (that is "tough," or conservative, or not imminently facing election), while ρ^{II} represents the same probability but for type II government ("weak," liberal, or facing election soon), then

$$E_{t-1}\Delta cbi_t = \left[\rho_t^I \varepsilon_t + \left(1 - \rho_t^{II}\right)\varepsilon_t\right]\Delta cbi_t \tag{2.7}$$

In Equation 2.7, while ρ^I is observable, ε_t is not. Therein lies the source of the credibility problem. The term ε is specified as depending on the degree of independence the central bank enjoys, or specific covariates that identify the room to maneuvre within the existing institutional arrangement. It is here that we see the potential need to differentiate between countries or regions or the world and the role of political and institutional factors.

THE FISCAL AND MONETARY POLICY NEXUS: DO WE NEED A CENTRAL BANK AT ALL?

A central bank with a mandate beyond settling and facilitating payments, or acting as the lender of last resort, is largely a creature of the twentieth century. But as the twentieth century ended economists, and even politicians, became increasingly convinced that the central bank's role in the stabilization of output or unemployment was limited. If not, activist monetary policy might make matters worse by making both inflation and output more volatile than they need be. In other words, the twentieth century began with central banks following a rule, namely the Gold Standard, then through an era of activism as central banks, by now

[54] The condition $L_t^c < L_t^\pi$ holds if $\tau_t > [(a + \theta)\,\Delta cbi_t]/2a - (\Delta cbi_t) - \alpha(\pi - \pi_{t-1})]$.

creatures of central governments, sought to choose their preferred point on the Phillips curve, back to an era where discretion was downplayed and the central bank's functions were seen, once more, as being limited.[55]

As a result, at the beginning of the twenty-first century, it is reasonable to ask: Whither central banking? It should be noted that there are a couple of forces at work that have prompted the question being posed. One is technological, namely the development and growth of electronic transactions and forms of money. Although the developments rightly raise the question of the rationale for central banks it is not one that directly concerns the present study. Rather, questioning the existence of central banking arises here since, if monetary policy does nothing of consequence for the real economy as many central bankers have endlessly pointed out in recent years, then why bother with a central bank at all? Moreover, if democratic accountability is a concern (for example, Fischer 1995; Stiglitz 1997) then why go through the tortuous process of designing an institution that is both autonomous and accountable? Should any legislation effectively recognize that central banks do nothing real?

Textbook descriptions of the natural rate hypothesis certainly lend credibility to the argument that central banks need not be separate institutions at all. Nevertheless, there is one overarching reason for the continued existence of a central bank and to preserve its autonomy. This has to do with the monetary authority's role in helping ensure the stability of the financial system, and acting as a bulwark against the temptation by the central government to exploit an opportunity to try to improve monetary policy in a manner that would have a detrimental impact on the economic welfare of the nation. In other words, an autonomous central bank, structured to deliver an adequate strategy for monetary policy (see Chapter 7), is able to be more farsighted than governments that need to be reelected every few years. As we shall see, this gives rise to a form of disciplined discretion on the part of central banks. Disciplined, because the focus of policy is on inflation, and discretion because no rule is able to deliver good policies and stable financial systems all the time.

Finally, democratic accountability is a fine and laudable goal but, in principle, it can and does conflict with the "welfare of the nation"

---

[55] The evolutionary aspect of monetary policy strategies was also emphasized in Chapter 1 and is a recurring theme throughout this study. Readers may also be interested in Woodford (1999a) for a description and assessment of the evolution of thinking about macroeconomics more generally in the twentieth century.

principle enshrined in most legislation governing central banks. Moreover, the point of emphasizing notions of accountability and transparency is precisely to clarify democratic accountability within a framework of disciplined discretion (see Chapter 3). A separate institution with a suitable structure, therefore, is a reasonable response to the differences with which governments discount the future relative to the general public and financial markets in particular.

SUMMARY

Cross-country data require some explanation before they can be used in the type of comparative exercise undertaken in this study. The construction and availability of data can differ markedly across countries, so it is useful to spend some time describing the basic data. The chapter provides a broad description of the available time series and qualitative information about central banks for twenty countries, and it outlines the connection between monetary and fiscal policies and various measures of economic performance. Reputation in policies is proxied by the degree of persistence in inflation while credibility can be proxied by the speed with which inflation changes, the behavior of policy makers across partisan types, or in anticipation of looming elections. The relationship between forecasts of inflation and actual inflation is also considered. Tentatively, it is demonstrated empirically that policy changes do matter, and that the behavior of actual time series can differ significantly from some of the proxies for inflation expectations.

The chapter also reviews, and comparatively assesses, existing qualitative measures of central bank autonomy in a manner that has, heretofore, not been done in a systematic fashion. An important objective of this chapter, therefore, is to provide a discussion and an analysis of the evolution of views about the role of central bank autonomy and the place of the central bank in government during the second half of the twentieth century. A reconsideration of the empirical evidence reveals both the dangers and, despite much recent evidence to the contrary, the proper role and value of such data in a study of central bank performance. A historical perspective is offered throughout by tracing the development of inflation persistence and the potential role played by institutional factors especially.

3 | Central Bank Personalities and Monetary Policy Performance

INTRODUCTION

Although the major theme of this book is the interaction between policies and institutions, monetary policies have often been interpreted as the outcome of a decision by the head of the central bank. Indeed, a widely accepted notion, popularized, if not originally formulated, by Friedman (1962), is the "extraordinary importance of accidents of personality" (op. cit.: p. 234). The spate of books published over the last few decades (for example, Greider 1987; Marsh 1992; Marshall 1999; Mayer 2001; von Furstenburg and Ulan 1998) to name but a very few) on the apparent symbiosis between personalities and policies certainly lends credence to Friedman's view. Examples from economic history, however, suggest that while personalities can at times matter more than the institutions they lead, it is the intersection of personalities with infrequent crises that gives rise to the hypothesis. Perhaps this is what Friedman intended by the term *accidents*.

This chapter begins by asking in what sense personalities can and do matter. The analysis is carried out at various levels. First, it is argued that Friedman's hypothesis is largely anecdotal and that it is difficult to find strong evidence in the series that matters to a central bank, or in the evaluation of the conduct of monetary policy, namely inflation, for the predominance of personalities in explaining central bank performance.

Of course, personalities can influence monetary policy performance in a manner that could not have been anticipated by Friedman. Technology, the proliferation of data, and the globalization of financial systems have increased the focus on the role of financial data available at very high frequency. Large daily movements in exchange rates and interest rates has thrust central bankers into a position where they are expected to comment, and possibly react, to every development in financial markets. As we shall see, this creates pitfalls for central bankers who are, after all, responsible for objectives that can only be meaningfully measured over the medium term, but not the very short term. One response to these developments is the growing importance of disclosure in central bank operations.

LEGACIES OF THE PAST

Prior to World War I central banking was still in its infancy in most industrial countries. Many took on the role as lenders of last resort following prolonged economic crises, notably the Great Depression, and were in any event, often constrained by the rigors of the gold standard. In addition, central banking in the first thirty or so years of the twentieth century was dominated by the activities of the Bank of England and the U.S. Federal Reserve. Indeed, central bankers, notably Montague Norman of the Bank of England and Benjamin Strong of the U.S. Federal Reserve (New York), buoyed by the growing influence of central banks over monetary policy,[1] came to view interference by political authorities as a nuisance and sought, through central bank cooperation, to circumvent the decisions of the political authorities.

If one examines the working relationship between governments and the major central banks at the time, disagreements generally would not be aired in public. Moreover, central banks did not, as a rule, interpret their role as consisting of communicating with the public on a regular basis or explaining their policies. The strictures of the gold standard, and the laissez faire ideology of central banks concerning their role in the maintenance of financial stability did not lend themselves to attaching much importance to a communications strategy toward the public. Central banks, whether in law or in practical terms, were very much an instrument of the state, even if their autonomy was recognized as desirable. However, the desirability of government control over the central bank can vanish at times of crisis. Indeed, whether governments actually impose their will on the central bank is often a function of the nature of the crisis and the personality in question.

---

[1] As accounts of the early history of major central banks point out, see Toniolo (1988), clashes between the treasury and the central bank have often contributed to redefine the latter's responsibilities over the conduct of monetary policy.

It seems clear that the notion of central bank autonomy from government was originally intended to prevent frivolous abuses of influence over the monetary authority's power to lend money to the treasury. It can be argued that, at times, central bank autonomy was intended as an extension of the autonomy of the treasury from the rest of government.[2]

Finally, one must not loose sight of the fact that central banks' views of the transmission mechanism owed much to the views of bankers whose focus was on the role of credit in influencing economic activity. The influence of monetary policy on the price level was considered secondary or unimportant (Siklos 1999a). In the aftermath of World War II the relative importance attached to credit creation was enshrined in the policy of providing "cheap" credit, which amounted to the setting of interest rates at below market clearing levels. It is only by the mid to late 1950s that the meaning of central bank independence, the role of monetary policy, and its primacy in influencing the nation's price level, came to the fore once again.

FRIEDMAN'S HYPOTHESIS

Friedman's views of the role of an independent monetary authority are simply stated: ". . . the extent to which a system of this kind is really a system of rule by man and not by law and is extraordinarily dependent on the personalities involved" (Friedman 1962: p. 235).

It is not difficult to find examples throughout the history of central banking in the twentieth century of personalities putting their stamp on monetary or central bank operations. Marshall (1999) outlines the considerable influence of a group of central bankers on the policies and on the ultimate design of the European Central Bank. Deane and Pringle (1995) note that the change in policy from interest rate control to reserves targeting by the U.S. Federal Reserve was entirely associated with the personality of Paul Volcker and his mandate to reduce the inflation rate that had reached extraordinarily high levels by U.S. historical standards.[3] Sicilia and Cruikshank (2000) devote an entire volume to how the words and actions of U.S. Fed Chairman Alan Greenspan move

---

[2] More modern parallels of this phenomenon can be found in the disagreements between the Finance Ministry and the Bank of Japan. Also see, in this connection, Cargill (1989), Cargill, Hutchison, and Ito (2000), Miller (1996), and Walsh (1997).

[3] In Volcker and Gyohten (1992: ch. 6) it would appear that it was the crisis of inflation that led to importance of the personality in charge of the Fed and not the other way around.

markets, among several recent books on his life and tenure at the U.S. Federal Reserve.[4] Von Furstenberg and Ulan (1998) offer a largely hagiographic account of the battle for disinflation beginning in the 1980s, led by a representative group of central bankers. Toniolo (1988) is another collection of articles about the importance of personalities over policies in central banking circles but, with a few notable exceptions previously discussed, the studies do not generally conclude that the rule of men dominates the rule of law. Goodhart (1988) is a more sober assessment of the *natural* evolution of central banks that owes much to the development and growing sophistication of the financial system, the increased involvement of governments in the economy, and the recognition that inflation needs to be low and stable to enhance economic growth. Blinder's (1999) retrospective, on his time as a central banker at the U.S. Federal Reserve, also heavily emphasizes the role of policies over personalities (also see Blinder 1998a; 1998b). As we shall see, both empirical evidence and case studies suggest that Friedman's hypothesis holds only in a limited sense.

It is not so much personalities that matter, although they can in times of crisis as noted earlier, but the extent to which the state, de jure or de facto, permits the central bank to follow a particular course of action. Anticipating a portion of the description of the U.S. experience that follows, it is worth recalling, by way of illustration, that when President Nixon and Fed Chairman (and personal friend) Arthur Burns crossed swords over monetary policy matters, disagreements and misunderstandings arose due to differences over the place of the Fed in government and the importance of the inflation problem. The former issue was in no small part facilitated by the absence of clear monetary policy objectives (a de jure problem); the latter stemmed from the incompatibility of economic and political objectives at the time (a de facto question). Nixon, perhaps surprisingly, coming from a Republican President, believed that "Inflation has never defeated an Administration – but recession has" (Reeves 2001: p. 166). The notion of the "right-wing" politician seemed to be turned on its head. Later, frustrated by the de facto independence of the Fed as it attempted to fight large wage settlements and looming high inflation (in early 1970), Nixon uttered

---

[4] Curiously, while the analysis points out several instances where Greenspan's words or actions move the stock market down there is no explanation of Greenspan's possible role in the generally sharp upward trend (until 2000) in stock prices since he became chairman.

"When we get through, this Fed won't be independent if it's the only thing I do in office" (op. cit.: p. 187) The foregoing also illustrates that crises have a political dimension though, in the discussion that follows, the focus is on the performance of central bankers under these conditions.

The chosen course of monetary policy will be dictated by the prevailing economic ideology and is reinforced by the tremendous growth in central bankers' (and markets') abilities to digest, analyze, and look ahead to the consequences of central bank actions. This development is further facilitated by the current emphasis on central banks being accountable for monetary policy outcomes while governments, perhaps jointly with the central bank, are held accountable for selecting the monetary framework.

The alternative to a "rule of men" is not, historically, the "rule of law" but rather the rule of institutions that evolve over time, often dictated by singular economic events or large shocks. Since policy regimes have changed more frequently than the rule of law governing central bank actions, a central bank viewed only through the filter of the rule of men is only a small part of the story of central banking, especially in the second half of the twentieth century.

CEOs OF CENTRAL BANKS

A possible corollary of the view about the primacy of personalities over policies is that central bank governors ought to either outlast their political masters or, at the very least complete their term of office as scheduled and be reappointed despite policy differences with the government, perhaps owing to the force of their personality. There are, however, a number of potentially insurmountable difficulties with any attempt to conduct such a test in a statistical framework.[5] First, as emphasized earlier in this chapter, the personality aspect of central banking is more apparent at times of crisis than as a feature of the entire *term* of a particular central bank CEO. Second, it is likely that all but the most serious disagreements between governments and central banks are kept private

---

[5] The problem is less acute in the case of developing countries where, by custom, the political primacy of the government over the central bank is a fact of life. Indeed, it is in part this kind of consideration that allows Cukierman (1992) to find a connection between the turnover rate of central bank governors and the degree of central bank independence. Also, see Cukierman, Kalaitzidakis, Summers, and Webb (1993), and Cukierman and Webb (1995; 1997).

and tend to spill over into the public domain only when an economic crisis either looms or is under way. One is reminded of a former governor of the Bank of England who, when asked: "Do you feel your bank has the right to defy the government?" replied, "Oh, yes, we value that very highly – and wouldn't think of exercising it" (Bach 1949: p. 1183). In the case of the Bundesbank where, for historical reasons (discussed as follows), defiance of government is considered to be a realistic possibility, these events took place on rare and in especially stressful economic situations.

Third, there are potentially several reasons for not reappointing a governor other than policy disagreements. Some CEOs may simply wish to leave for personal reasons. Others may disagree with the future direction of the government and may not wish to be reappointed, not because of past disagreements, but owing to a potential future conflict with the government. Additionally, some central bankers, including ones with "forceful" personalities, may be offered more attractive opportunities outside their own central bank. Finally, there may be institutional provisions in central banking legislation that either prevents reappointment (for example, as in the case of the European Central Bank) or where there is no provision for regular appointments (for example, Italy). Also, if the term of office does not coincide with the political cycle there may be additional slippage preventing turnover when deemed politically appropriate.

Similarly, it may be difficult to associate any election or partisan change in government with the turnover of the CEO at the central bank because the event that might precipitate a turnover need not coincide, of course, with election timing. Moreover, as has been pointed out already, partisan attitudes toward monetary policy need not be as sharply defined as the proxies developed to measure such differences.

Table 3.1 summarizes some key information about the average tenure of central bank CEOs roughly since exchange rates floated, as well as since approximately the end of World War II.[6] A separate column indicates the length of the term of office as laid out by statute, as well as whether it is renewable or not. Omitting cases where the term is indefinite, the tenure of about half of the CEOs exceeds the statutory minimum and, in the remaining cases, the differences are small. Indeed, a test cannot reject the null hypothesis that the difference between actual

---

[6] A separate file, available at http://www.wlu.ca/~wwwsbe/faculty/psiklos/centralbanks. htm, provides a listing of CEO names and terms of office.

Table 3.1. The Tenure of Central Bank CEOs

Country	Samples	Average Tenure (years)	Statutory Tenure (years)
Australia	Full	8.50	
	Post 75	6.25	7R
Austria	Full	5.33	
	Post 75	5	5R
Belgium	Full	7.86	
	Post 75	6.25	5R
Canada	Full	7.86	
	Post 75	8.33	7R
Denmark	Full	13.75	
	Post 75	12.50	I
Finland	Full	7.86	
	Post 75	6.25	7
France	Full	6.38	
	Post 75	5	6R
Germany	Full	7.30	8R
	Post 75	6.25	
Ireland	Full	6.88	
	Post 75	6.25	7R
Italy	Full	10	
	Post 75	8.33	I
Japan	Full	5	
	Post 75	4.20	5R
Netherlands	Full	13.50	
	Post 75	8.33	7
New Zealand	Full	6.88	
	Post 75	6.25	5R
Norway	Full	9	
	Post 75	8.33	6R
Portugal	Full	5	
	Post 75	4.20	5R
Spain	Full	6	
	Post 75	6.25	6NR
Sweden	Full	7	
	Post 75	6.25	6
Switzerland	Full	7.57	
	Post 75	6.25	6
United Kingdom	Full	8.50	
	Post 75	8.33	5
United States	Full	9.20	
	Post 75	6.25	4R
European Central Bank	1999–	N/A	8NR

Average tenure is found by taking the number of governors who served during the 1975–99 period divided by 25 (length of the sample). A CEO whose term began before 1975 but whose term ends after 1975 is counted if more than half the statutory term remains from 1975 on. The same consideration was used for CEO whose term continues past 1999. The full sample begins in 1945, except for Australia, France, Germany (1949), Austria (1968), Italy, Portugal (1960), Netherlands, Norway (1946), Spain (1970), Sweden (1951), Switzerland (1947), and the United Kingdom (1949).
R = explicitly renewable; I = indefinite term of office; NR = nonrenewable term. Otherwise, whether term is renewable or not is not explicitly laid out in the legislation. N/A = not available.
Source: Individual central banks. See http://www.wlu.ca/~wwwsbe/faculty/psiklos/centralbanks.htm.

and statutory measures of CEO tenure is zero. A variety of regressions where either average tenure, or the deviation of actual average from statutory length of the term of office, was regressed on inflation, the output gap, unemployment rates, the number of elections or partisan changes in government, the degree of federalism, and even the volatility of inflation, interest rates, and the output gap, were considered. While some evidence was found that the average term of office, since exchange rates were permitted to float in much of the industrial world, exceeded the statutory minimum in countries where output exceeds its trend, the greater the degree of federalism, and the lower the degree of central bank independence, the results were not especially robust to various changes in the specifications considered. While this result does not mean that personalities do not matter, it does suggest that the impact of personalities on central bank performance does not appear to be reflected in the rate of turnover of central bank CEOs in any meaningful statistical sense.

A slightly different perspective on the personalities question is to examine the record of inflation under each CEO. Table 3.2 shows the results of a simple regression of each country's inflation rate on a measure of foreign inflation and a dummy variable for each CEO's term of office. Assuming that there is some "unavoidable" or long-run underlying inflation rate in each country, proxied by a five-year moving average of inflation,[7] the regressions ask whether a CEO's term of office resulted in inflation above or below some unavoidable level. In addition, higher or lower than average foreign inflation – either in the United States or Germany – is permitted to influence domestic inflation performance. "Inflation fighters" are CEOs who presided over reductions in average inflation, while CEOs soft on inflation were in charge when inflation was rising above the average.

We focus on the broad features of the table only and discuss only the salient results. First, virtually all CEOs deemed to be "soft" on inflation presided over their central banks around the time of the first oil price crisis (especially 1973–4). A few also presided over the second OPEC oil price shock (1979–80).[8]

Second, many of the "inflation fighters" are a product of the period since the second half of the 1980s. As a result, they are an international

---

[7] Other variants were tried with little impact on the conclusions.
[8] Also notable as a standout in the "soft" on inflation category is Schlesinger of Germany who led the Bundesbank through the period of German Economic and Monetary Union.

Table 3.2. Central Bank CEOs and Inflation Performance[1]

Country	Inflation Fighters[2]	Soft on Inflation[2]	Foreign Inflation Effect[5]
Australia	[1990–6][4] Fraser* [1997–] Macfarlane*	[1969–74] Philips*	0.25
Austria	[1979–88] Koren*		0.71
Belgium	[1976–82] Strycker* [1983–9] Godeaux*	[1972–5] Vandeputte*	0.51
Canada	[1988–94] Crow		0.70
Denmark	—	—	0.55
Finland	[1985–92] Kullberg*		0.75
France	[1985–7] Camdessus* [1988–93] Larosière*	[1961–9] Brunet [1975–9] Clappier*	0.80
Germany	[1960–9][3] Blessing* [1977–9] Emminger* [1994–8] Tietmeyer*	[1970–6] Klasen* [1991–3] Schlesinger*	0.30
Ireland	[1981–6] O'Cofaigh* [1987–93] Doyle*	[1969–75] Whitaker* [1994–] O'Connell*	1.20
Italy	[1979–92] Ciampi*		1.11
Japan	[1965–9] Usami* [1975–9] Morinaga*	[1970–4] Sasaki*	0.68
Netherlands	[1982–95] Duisenberg*	[1960–6][3] Holtrop* [1996–] Wellink	0.80
New Zealand	[1982–4] Wilks* [1989–] Brash*	[1968–77] Low*	0.00
Norway	[1985–93] Skaanland*	[1970–84] Wold*	0.32
Portugal	[1985–91] Tavares* [1994–9] Fernandes*	[1966–74] Barbosa* [1975–80] Lopes*	0.00
Spain	[1978–84] Rendueles* [1985–93] Jimenez* [1994–] Rojo*	[1970–5] Palma* [1976–7] Letona*	0.00
Sweden	[1982–93] Dennis* [1994–] Backstrom*	[1973–5] Wickman* [1976–8] Nordlander*	0.55
Switzerland	[1988–96] Lusser*	[1984–7] Languetin	1.19
United Kingdom	—	—	1.00
United States	[1979–87] Volcker*	[1960–9][3] McMartin* [1970–7] Burns*	n/a

[1] Regression estimates based on quarterly data from the expression: $(\pi_{it} - \bar{\pi}_i) = \alpha(\pi_{it}^* - \bar{\pi}_i^* + \beta$ **GOV** $+ \varepsilon_t$, where, π_{it} = annual inflation at time t in country i, $\bar{\pi}$ = five-year moving average of inflation in country i, π^* = foreign inflation rate; United States for Australia, Canada, Germany, Japan, New Zealand, and the United Kingdom. Otherwise, Germany is the foreign inflation rate. No foreign inflation rate used in estimates for the United States. **GOV**$_{it}$ = dummy variable set to 1 when a particular CEO in office, 0 otherwise.
[2] An inflation fighter is one whose term of office results in $\beta_K < 0$; a CEO soft on inflation results in a $\beta_K > 0$. Otherwise, β_K is insignificant. β_K is estimate of β for CEO K.
[3] Term of office actually began before 1960.
[4] In all cases term of office is shown on an annual basis. Last name of each CEO is listed.
[5] The figures are the estimated coefficients for α. All are statistically significant at least the 5% level, except when $\hat{\alpha} = 0.0$ is shown.
* Indicates that CEO impact on inflation larger than foreign inflation effect (that is, absolute value of $\beta_K > \alpha$).

phenomenon and not the product of just a few countries' experiences. Third, whether U.S. or German inflation rates are above or below average has a significant impact on the performance of domestic inflation. However, as indicated in the table, the foreign impact is smaller than the domestic effect associated with a particular CEO. Moreover, the fact that the "exceptional" CEOs presided at a time when exchange rates were floating suggests that a "made at home" inflation rate is possible. Indeed, the fact that few CEOs from the 1960s and early 1970s show up in the table other than, most notably, the U.S.'s CEO, is consistent with the notion that inflation during this period was made elsewhere. This is just another way of stating that exchange rate regime considerations play a pivotal role in central bank performance.

CASE STUDIES

As noted previously, and despite the foregoing discussion, there is a strong presumption among some that personalities at the helm of a central bank do matter. Cecchetti (2000), for example, complains of a "cult of personality" surrounding the current chair of the Federal Reserve, Alan Greenspan, due to the role of the FOMC's chair as "first among equals." No doubt the perceived spectacular success of monetary policy during the 1990s also enters into the equation. Bopp (1944: pp. 271–2) noted over a half century ago that ". . . a single individual may dominate a central bank so completely that the history of the institution for a period can be written accurately only with reference to that individual's life." Whittlesey (1970: p. 219) later concurs by adding

> A notable feature of central banking in the twentieth century has been the extent to which the current scene, here and abroad, has been dominated by a few outstanding personalities.

An alternative way of delving into this topic further is to consider a few selected countries and to explore the interplay between personalities and policies. The object of the exercise is to further examine the degree to which the notion that the personalities versus policies debate is critical to our understanding of what monetary policy is all about, namely the control of inflation. As we shall see, personalities have more to do with the response to a particular financial or economic crisis and need not, therefore, set the tone for the entire term of a CEO.

As is true of all case studies, they are selective but, hopefully, instructive. While not a substitute for more formal evidence of the kind discussed earlier and to be presented in the following chapter, it is hoped that the examples considered point to the difficulties with the "personalities" approach to studying central bank behavior.

The United States is chosen first because it is the case that largely prompted Friedman (1962) to formulate his hypothesis. The Fed, and the holders of the chairmanship of the FOMC in particular, have probably prompted the writing of more books and articles than possibly for any other central bank. The second case considered is that of Canada for it illustrates a critical avenue through which personalities can matter, namely via the absence of well-defined means for resolving conflicts between a central bank and the government. The third case to be examined is that of Germany because it also illustrates how institutional design shifts the emphasis, in general and at times of crisis, away from the personalities toward policies.

These cases cover what, I believe, are the essential ingredients of the debate about personalities versus policies. Other illustrations can no doubt be added, from other countries. Indeed, such examples have already been referred to, and others will follow in the remainder of this study. Nevertheless, the three cases examined are viewed as representative of the experience in industrial countries.

The Fed and the Tension between Personalities and Policies[9]

Some authors have pointed out that, prior to 1935, the regional structure of the Fed, built into the original Federal Reserve Act, prevented any personality from dominating monetary policy. Chandler (1958; 1971), for example, argues that the New York Fed emasculated the Federal Reserve Board and this allowed the personality of Benjamin Strong, then governor, to dominate Fed policies during the 1920s. It is also tempting to conclude that, unlike present-day discussions, fiscal policy did not matter much prior to 1945. However, both Meltzer (2001) and Wueschner (1999) describe how the Fed's monetary policy, largely deter-

---

[9] The U.S. case is somewhat different from other countries' experiences since the Fed must formally answer to Congress and, more indirectly, to the president. Congressional versus presidential effects on monetary policy are highlighted by, among others, Alesina, Cohen, and Roubini (1997, ch. 4) for the post-World War II era. Also, see Romer and Romer (1996). For the purposes of a cross-country study of the kind conducted here we limit the amount of institutional detail though other factors influencing central banks and their development are indirectly captured via some of the qualitative variables considered (for example, degree of federalism, type of government, and so on). Also, see Burdekin and Willett (1991).

mined by Benjamin Strong's views, dominated the discussion though President Herbert Hoover's fiscal policy eventually triumphed. Roberts (2000), in reviewing the role of Strong in policy matters, also concludes that flawed policies, not personalities, produced the Great Slump.

Friedman and Schwartz (1963) argue that the errors that exacerbated the Great Depression might not have taken place but for the personality and influence of Benjamin Strong. Eichengreen (1992a; 1995) is equally critical of Strong and his commitment to the Gold Standard. On the other hand, Wheelock (1991) shows, with equal persuasiveness, that Fed policies were consistent during the 1920s and 1930s, and that a combination of faulty interpretation of economic events and common beliefs about the efficacy, or lack thereof, of monetary policy among a majority of the members of the Federal Reserve Board can explain what, in retrospect, appear to have been bad monetary policy decisions. Indeed, the first twenty years of the Fed's existence was spent by the institution, and the Federal Reserve Board, defining itself and its authority. Timberlake (1993), for example, chronicles how the vagueness, or lack of specificity, in the Federal Reserve Act was exploited by the Board to enhance its power (also see Wicker 1993), either via the control of discount rates or through the use of open market operations. Moreover, the first years of the Fed's existence, especially 1914–20, were devoted to fending off intervention by the secretary of the treasury who sat as an ex-officio member of the Board (see Sylla 1988 and Wicker 1993).

This type of interference can be said to have continued at least until the Fed-Treasury Accord of 1951 that clarified still further the functions of the Fed not specifically dealt with in the Banking Act of 1935. Indeed, Mayer (2001: p. 83) calls the Fed-Treasury Accord the "... most important moment in the history of central banking, the first stirring of the idea that a central bank could be an instrument of governance separate from the legislature that created it and the executive that appointed its leaders." Until the Accord then, as Chandler remarks, Board decisions "frequently turned on the presence or absence of the ex-officio members of the Board" (Chandler 1971: p. 146). About the only thing that is clear about Fed actions during the years leading up to the Great Depression was the tenacity with which Board members held to the real bills doctrine. For example, in the 1923 Annual Report the Fed states:

> The Federal Reserve is a system of productive credit for either investment or speculative purposes. Credit in the service of agriculture, industry, and trade may be described comprehensively as credit for productive use. The exclusion of the use of Federal Reserve Credit for speculative

and investment purposes and its limitation to agricultural, industrial, or commercial purposes thus clearly indicates the nature of the tests which are appropriate as guides in the extension of Federal Reserve credit.

From the perspective of the history of central banking, how important were the personalities at the Fed? After all, as Meltzer (2001: ch. 7) points out, the dominant view among authorities in the Fed, at least until the early 1950s, was that monetary policy was ineffective.

The Banking Act of 1935, the Fed-Treasury Accord of 1951, and the Monetary Control Act of 1980 provide convenient dividing points to organize the discussion and to ascertain spheres of influence. The six governors, as they were then called, who preceded Marriner Eccles, did not generally play the role of central actors in monetary policy as have Paul Volcker or Alan Greenspan in more recent times. As noted earlier, this was partly due to the institutional set-up of the Fed which did not define lines of authority precisely. An equally important factor was the views of Fed Board members who, more often than not, hesitated about the degree of action or inaction in matters of monetary policy. This attitude was fostered by political interference, especially from the likes of Senator Carter Glass, one of the framers of the Federal Reserve System, who effectively blocked clarification of Fed objectives (Chandler 1971). But there was also considerable ambivalence within the Fed about the desirability of a single central bank. Many, including Strong, worried that a more centralized institution would actually increase political interference. Therefore, the members of the Board of Governors of the Fed, and the chair in particular, were reluctant to initiate action or press the Fed's role in public as long as its political masters did not define that role with more precision. The debacle of the Great Depression is also relevant as the Fed was seen as ineffective. Indeed, it is instructive to consider Eccles' definition of central bank independence. As we shall see, it stands in sharp contrast with the concept of central bank independence as interpreted in the German context.

> [T]he kind of independence a central bank should have was an opportunity to express its views in connection with the determination of policy, and that after it had been heard it should not try to make its will prevail but should cooperate in carrying out the program agreed upon by the Government . . ." (Meltzer 2001: ch. 7, n. 23).

It is also instructive to consider that, during the early years of its existence, when the financial system was relatively unsophisticated, the Fed was reluctant, except perhaps once, to rely on "moral suasion" as a regular tool of monetary policy. This too mitigated the influence of personalities over politics in the United States and, on balance, suggests a similarity of views among the early governors of the system (and the drawing of wrong lessons from the past).

Another important consideration was that Board chairmen were always appointed from the outside and, in the early years, had little training in domestic or international finance. Charles Hamlin, for example, a key Board governor and its first chairman, was a lawyer by training. Governor Harding is another case in point. As Friedman argues, "he had a limited understanding of monetary affairs, and even less backbone" (Friedman 1962: 234). Even Benjamin Strong and Marriner Eccles, both with experience in commercial banking, nevertheless had to learn the business of central banking on the job. Occasionally, the problem was that, in the early years of the Fed's history, the chair was able and knowledgeable but the Board was weak, at a time when the regional federal reserve banks exercised greater power. This was true of Eugene Meyer's tenure. He became governor under crisis conditions in 1930. A further consideration was the personal and working relationship between the president of the United States and the chair of the Board of Governors of the Federal Reserve about which more is discussed as follows.

The corollary to the hypothesis about the potential importance of personalities in central banking history, outlined earlier, becomes more evident when we consider the aftermath of some of the defining events in U.S. economic history. First, of course, is the Great Depression, the growing desire to centralize the powers of monetary policy in the hands of the Board of Governors in Washington, and the greater role of fiscal policy in overall economic affairs. Both found a champion in Marriner Eccles who, as Timberlake put it, permitted the "rule of men" to spread at the Fed (Timberlake 1993). Indeed, Eccles was instrumental in the eventual Fed-Treasury Accord (see Hyman 1976) that, in a sense, formalized the Fed's independence, and his position played a role in Truman's decision not to reappoint him in 1948 (although, significantly, he remained a Board member until 1951).

The potential influence of personalities is also reinforced by the fact that it is the CEO who briefs and discusses monetary affairs, and economic policy more generally, with the president. Two examples illustrate the importance of this feature of Fed operations. Hamlin, the first Board chairman, feared the close connection between Eugene Meyer and both the president (Herbert Hoover) and his secretary of the treasury (Ogden Mills), as well as fearing Meyer's connections with the New York

Fed, clearly the dominant regional federal reserve bank at the time (Memoranda 1984; Pusey 1974).

Another example, from more recent history, is the on-again off-again relationship between Arthur Burns and Richard Nixon during the turbulent years that saw the end of Bretton Woods, the oil price shocks, and wage and price controls. It seems quite clear, according to Woolley (1984; 1995), that Burns thought, or hoped, that he had a significant influence on economic policies (see Wells 1994) even though Nixon's own attitude toward Burns was, at times, hostile, in part because of the influence of the secretary of the treasury on Nixon's views (also, see Hetzel 1998). Of course, as Mayer (2001: p. 183) points out: "It would never have occurred to Richard Nixon that the Federal Reserve Board was really independent of the White House." Indeed, Nixon remarked, at the swearing-in ceremony for Burns in 1970 "I respect his independence. However, I hope that independently he will conclude that my views are the ones that should be followed" (Maisel 1973: p. 107).

But a close working relationship between a Fed chairman and a president has its drawbacks since it permits the Board chairman, appointed by the president, to "campaign" as it were for reappointment. It is unclear, however, whether the length of the Board chairman's term can, by itself, indicate anything about the degree to which administrations over time got the monetary policy they wanted. Apparently, in defending his record, Governor Harding (1916–22) called attention to the fact that a different policy (that is, other than a real bills doctrine) might have led to the loss of his position (Friedman 1962: p. 234). This is due perhaps to Section 10 of the original Federal Reserve Act of 1913. It stipulates that, in areas where there is conflict between the Fed and the secretary of the treasury, the latter would prevail (see Walsh 1981: p. 12). However, it is interesting to note that only one chairman exceeded the four-year term of a president (Harding) before the Second World War while after 1945, all chairmen since Eccles, with the exception of McCabe and Miller, exceeded the length of the presidential election cycle. This in spite of controversies and disagreements with the administration over economic policy in general, and discount rate policies in particular. Figure 3.1 plots the inflation rate and highlights the terms of office of FOMC chairmen since 1960.[10]

---

[10] Siklos (1999a) conducts a longer run formal and informal analysis of the development of key macroeconomic aggregates since the formation of the Fed. For reasons already outlined, the post Fed-treasury accord is perhaps more relevant to the issues considered in this chapter.

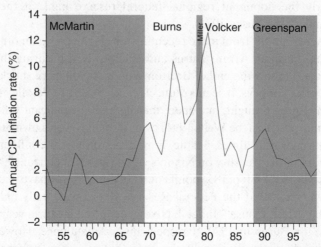

Figure 3.1 Inflation and the FOMC Chairmen, 1952–1999 (*Note*: For McMartin and Greenspan plot does not show inflation during their complete term of office. CPI inflation is measured on an annual basis on the vertical axis.)

Recent discussions about the personalities who chaired the Federal Reserve Board have occasionally centered around Paul Volcker's term in office. He was perhaps one of the most experienced central bankers to rise to the head of the Fed, and, like some of his predecessors, was appointed in 1979 at a time of crisis, this time when inflation had reached double digits (over 13% in the CPI on an annual basis). However, what distinguishes his term from that of many former office holders is that he interpreted his mandate as a signal to achieve a specific policy objective, namely a sharp reduction in inflation, and he exploited the opportunity given to him (also see Bernanke and Mishkin 1992). The fact that estimates of macroeconomic conditions do not appear to indicate Volcker's term to be "above" average in terms of inflation performance may be explained by the fact that it took some three years for inflation to come under control (thus taking up about half his term in office), and he had to contend with the Reagan deficits, as well as an international debt crisis. Moreover, the credit control policies of 1980, and the problems caused by extensive financial deregulation and innovation, also made the task of inflation reduction and the resumption of economic growth difficult to achieve. His own surprise at his selection (Volcker and Gyohten 1992: p. 165), and the resistance he faced within the FOMC about increases in the discount rate, reinforced his views about why markets were cynical about the Fed and inflation, and therefore precipitated in his mind the need for some dramatic policy initiatives to break inflationary expectations.[11]

Many of the benefits and the prestige conferred on the Fed would accrue to Volcker's successor, Alan Greenspan, appointed following Volcker's announcement that he did not wish to be a candidate for another four-year term as Fed chairman.[12] Nevertheless, the Fed's reaction to the October 1987 stock market crash, when it provided the financial system with abundant liquidity, gave Greenspan the opportunity to put his stamp on leadership at the Fed, and to enhance both the institution's credibility and reaffirm its independence. This episode enabled Greenspan (and the Fed) to focus on the goal of low inflation, as a reading of the Fed's semiannual monetary reports to Congress makes abundantly clear.

Despite several legislative attempts to do so, a formal requirement to have the Fed focus on price stability alone has yet to pass and be signed by any president, possibly because the last vestiges of moral suasion practiced by the executive branch since the Fed's creation might effectively disappear. Of course, it is also unclear the extent to which the Fed itself would wish to become accountable for as Hawtrey long ago surmized: "If they cannot avoid taking decisions, then conformity with a few easily understood shallow empirical concepts will enable them to face criticism" (Hawtrey 1970: p. 247). More accountability would also deprive the Fed from claiming the potency of monetary policy when convenient. As Friedman put it, based on his reading of the Board of Governors Annual Reports:

> In years when things are going well, the report emphasized that monetary policy is an exceedingly potent weapon and that the favorable course of events is largely the result of the skilful handling of this delicate instrument by the monetary authority. In years of depression, on the other

[11] Indeed, one of the estimated "breaks" in inflation expectations occurs around the 1979–82 period. See Chapter 2.

[12] It should not be forgotten that while the Fed chairman is *primus inter pares*, appointments to the FOMC Board are made by the president. Consequently, voting on Fed funds rate changes can, on rare occasions, go against the chair. This happened in 1986, when Volcker was chair. President Regan was able to put into office a sufficient number of supporters to apparently go against Volcker's recommendation against lowering the discount rate. In this connection see, for example, Havrilesky (1991; 1993).

hand, the reports emphasize that monetary policy is but one of many tools of economic policy, that its power is highly limited, and that it was only the skilful handling of such limited powers as were available that averred disaster (Friedman 1962: 233).

A less churlish view would simply argue that, as creatures of government, central banks cannot avoid for long the objectives and policies of governments in a democracy. As Paul Volcker put it, "Central banks are human institutions. Like other institutions, how they are led and how they are staffed makes a difference for policy in both a technical sense and in the larger sense of its overall coherence" (Volcker 1994: p. 22).

Hence, it appears that any predominance of personalities over policies may be primarily a feature of pre-World War II history, the result of a combination of the lack of clarity about the duties of a central bank vis-à-vis the government, and supported by a preference for private or informal relationships consistent with imprecision about the respective boundaries between fiscal and monetary policies (for example, see Wood 1939). The history of changes in Federal Reserve legislation (for example, see Siklos 1999a: Table 8.1) confirms the evolving role of the Fed and the fact that specification of broader economic goals was a feature of the post-World War II period. For example, this is reflected in subsidiary legislation, such as the Full Employment Act of 1946, and later in the Full Employment and Balanced Growth Act of 1978, also known as the Humphrey-Hawkins bill, which amended the 1946 legislation.[13]

There is an important sense, however, in which it is tempting to think of personalities as being more important than policies in the U.S. experience. It is important to underline the many attempts by the U.S. Congress to more clearly define the objectives of the Fed. Most notable are the numerous, varied, and ultimately, failed attempts throughout the twentieth century to make the Fed more accountable for its performance. As noted previously, this reflects the need felt by lawmakers once the Fed was established, to fill gaps in the statutory role of the Fed as it evolved into an institution that was more central to the performance of economic policy in general. Indeed, an early version of the Federal

---

[13] The Act specified a goal of zero inflation but directs the board of governors of the Fed to report semiannually on its objectives and plans and review economic conditions in light of administration and congressional plans and goals. The Act has since expired so what came to be known as the Humphrey-Hawkins Report has, since July 2000, been called the Monetary Policy Report.

Reserve Act in 1913 contained a provision that the central bank should be used to promote a stable price level (Willis 1923). The first attempt to fine tune the Fed's statutory objectives took place during the 1920s, at hearings of the Committee on Banking and Currency of the House of Representatives.[14] Following the sharp deflation and inflation of the early 1920s, a proposal was made to enshrine price stability as the primary task of the Federal Reserve. Benjamin Strong was the most prominent critic of the idea and won over supporters of the bill, including Professor Irving Fisher, who was one of the principal advocates of stable purchasing power. Strong believed that price stability was too narrow an objective for a central bank (Sproul 1947: pp. 71–2).

The Great Depression of the 1930s once again produced attempts to force the Fed to stabilize prices via statute. The so-called Goldsborough bill (HR.10517, HR.11499, and S.4429) proposed stability in commodity prices.[15] Although the bill was approved by the House, the legislation was subsequently defeated in the Senate (also see Harris 1933; Miller 1921).

The Fed-Treasury Accord mentioned earlier, and the problems of providing credit in a looming inflationary environment in the post-war economy, once again led to a congressional report (Douglas Senate subcommittee report of 1952) that specifically outlined – but did not quantify – the need for the Fed to have a specific "mandate" in order for the institution to be seen as being "accountable" for its actions. Efforts to better define the Fed's statutory responsibilities were then spurred by the high inflation of the 1970s and early 1980s, culminating in a series of attempts at legislating inflation targets, in line with the growing practice abroad. Although the current chair of the FOMC, Alan Greenspan, placed considerable importance on the concept of price stability as far back as 1988, the Federal Reserve Accountability Act of 1993 failed to pass amid fears that it signaled political interference in central bank

[14] The hearings proposed to amend section 14(d) of the Federal Reserve Act to the effect that the Fed shall set the discount rate "... with a view to accommodating commerce and promoting a stable price level for commodities in general. All the powers of the Federal Reserve shall be used for promoting stability in the price level" (*Federal Reserve Bulletin*, May 1926: p. 308).

[15] The proposal was to mandate that "It shall be the duty of the Fed to raise the price level, until full employment ... shall have been achieved, and until the price level shall at least reach the all-commodity index of 100 as established by the Department of Labor for the year 1926 ... Thenceforth such price level shall be standardized and maintained at a variation not to exceed 2 percent above or below the standard reached" (Hearings of the Committee on Banking and Currency, 75th Congress, 3rd Session; Patman-Stock hearings 1938: p. 168).

affairs instead of a clear mandate.[16] However, by 1999, legislation was again put forward to require the Fed to meet inflation target objectives, this time with the apparent consent of Alan Greenspan (Joint Economic Committee 1999). Hence, to the extent that skepticism continued to exist about "rules rather than persons" (Simons 1936), this permitted, in principle, the emergence of personalities over policies in views about central banking.

It is probably closer to the truth then to state, as former Fed chairman Paul Volcker wrote: "It is only when things go poorly that the central bank becomes prominent" (Volcker 1990: p. 64). In other words, it is only at times of crisis that the combination of central banking and the personality at its head become pivotal. Combined with the perception of the continuing lack of clarity in Fed objectives it is not surprising that, as Alan Greenspan (1996) stated: "Despite waxing and waning over the decades, a deep-seated tension still exists over government's role as an economic policy maker." While it is unclear whether the Fed chairman was referring only to the fiscal or monetary authorities, his remarks suggest the need for both tools of economic policy to be finely balanced, a difficult task, especially in times of crisis.

The Bank of Canada and the Directive

Canada's experience with central banking is, of course, briefer than the Fed's but it too has undergone an evolution marked by the personalities at its head. Figure 3.2 shows the evolution of inflation in Canada under six governors.

Graham Towers was the Bank of Canada's first governor and a commercial banker by profession. While he supported the concept of central bank autonomy, he also adhered to the idea that the government has final authority over the conduct of monetary policy. Given that his tenure at the Bank of Canada overlapped with the war, there naturally arose a need to finance extraordinary government expenditures during this period. Following the war, there was the problem of retiring the large accumulated debt left in its wake, although the problem would be passed on to his successor, James Coyne. Towers believed that, rather than

---

[16] "If accountability is achieved by putting the conduct of monetary policy under the close influence of politicians subject to short-term election cycle pressures the resulting policy would likely prove disappointing over time" (Hearing before the Committee on Banking, Finance, and Urban Affairs, H.R. 163rd Congress, October 13, 1993: p. 16).

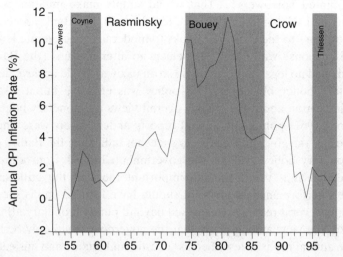

Figure 3.2 Inflation and the Governors of the Bank of Canada, 1952–1999 (*Note*: For Towers and Thiessen, plot does not show inflation during their complete term of office. Data are annual.)

become entirely subservient to the treasury, or initiate conflict with the government, as was the case in the United States, discretion was the better part of valor. He, therefore, fully subscribed to the view of the finance minister who, in 1936, indicated that "while the Bank should resist temporary gusts of public fancy, it must in the long-run show responsiveness to public opinion and be responsible to government" (Report of the Royal Commission 1964: 534). This sentiment echoed the report of an earlier commission that led to the creation of the bank, to the effect that a central bank ". . . is at the same time an instrument and a force. As an instrument it is the means by which the State – which must necessarily retain ultimate sovereignty in matters affecting the currency – can give effect to the national policy" (Royal Commission on Banking and Currency in Canada (1933: par. 207).

The concentration of banking assets among relatively few chartered banks, and the origins of the Bank of Canada as a creature of commercial banking concerns, provided an opportunity to apply the policy of moral suasion. This is reflected in the culture of the Bank that, while adhering to the function of lender of last resort, was very reluctant to make advances except under extreme circumstances. As the 1956 Annual Report put it, "it is clear that the central bank cannot provide relief to disappointed borrowers ... That would simply make inflation worse" (Cairns and Binhammer 1965: p. 165). Instead, the Bank argued that "suggestions" to the chartered banks to moderate or accelerate lending, or "discussions" with securities dealers to alter margins (the Bank of Canada had no legal authority to do so on its own), could achieve desired monetary policy objectives. This policy was effective but it also left little indication about the Bank's overall views on monetary policy. As Gordon (1961) points out, annual reports under Towers were uninformative and the governor made few speeches indicating the Bank's stand on monetary policy vis-à-vis the government. Indeed, from a modern perspective, it is ironic that an important focus of the criticisms of Coyne's performance as governor should have focused on his speeches which, in several respects, trespassed beyond purely monetary affairs. It was still the view among many that the governor should only be heard via the annual reports, described as "caustic, ambiguous, and misleading" (Hanright 1960), and not seen in public. Between June 1957 and October 1959, Coyne made no speeches at all (Young 1961). Nevertheless, at a time when there was a growing divergence between the policies enacted and contemplated by the government of the day and the Bank of Canada, the governor felt it was his duty to explain himself in public. The controversy owed more to the difficulties in the statutory relationship between the government and the central bank than to mistakes about the appropriate stance of monetary policy (Siklos 2002, but see Gordon 1961, and Howitt 2001).

Although the policy of moral suasion would continue well into the 1960s, the rise of James Coyne to the governorship in 1955 would usher one of the defining moments in the bank's history. Faced with the conversion of Victory Bonds into short-term Treasury bills, the bank was concerned that fiscal policy was too easy and that a sound monetary policy required some tightening (Annual Report of the Governor 1959 and 1960). Figure 3.3 shows the evolution of inflation and interest rates in Canada and the United States during the second half of the 1950s. As inflation rates fell steadily from 1957 to 1959 nominal interest rates rose, after temporarily falling in 1958 in both countries, but the spread between the two countries' interest rates widened until 1959. Inflation rates were very similar in both countries throughout. Note that the Canadian dollar floated during this period, with Canada earning a reputation as a "maverick in international circles" (Powell 1999: pp. 42–3). The same figure does not highlight a difficulty that central bankers would eventually recognize, namely the need to smooth interest rate changes.

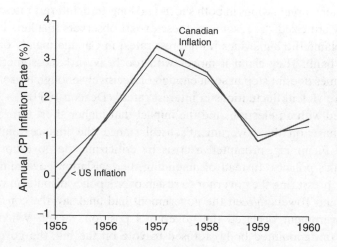

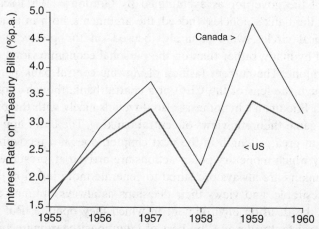

Figure 3.3 Inflation and Interest Rates in Canada and the United States, 1955–1960

Interest rate volatility was a relatively new phenomenon at the time. After all, since the 1940s, interest rates were typically set, if not directly, certainly indirectly, by government. Canada, having borne the brunt of considerable international criticisms about floating the exchange rate, then chose in 1956 to link the key lending rate, called the bank rate, to fluctuations in the Treasury bill rate. The resulting change in "regime," apparently not adequately explained by the Bank of Canada, and the consequent larger swings in both short- and long-term interest rates were severely criticized. "..., some of these expert observers [bankers in the main] blame the big swings [in interest rates] in Canada mainly on the central bank. They claim it moves with too heavy a hand sometimes, other times doesn't step in soon enough or decisively enough to iron out the more violent fluctuations in interest rates" (Deacon 1960).

Faced with an election, and the impact that higher short-term rates would have on the government's fiscal stance, the finance minister, Donald Flemming, prompted a crisis by criticizing the governor and the bank's policies. Instead of amending the legislation governing the bank or pressuring the governor to resign over a policy dispute, in which Coyne and Towers agreed the government had final say, the conservative government declared the governor's position vacant. When the Senate (an appointed body) refused to vote on the bill, the governor resigned (Rymes 1994).

Coyne's experience led to a rare outpouring of debate over the competence of the governor as exemplified by Gordon's (1961) scathing attack on the bank's policies. Indeed, the arguments, both in academic and political circles, were squarely focused on the policy in place supported by many, rather than on the personal economic views of the governor alone. The current fashion of viewing central bank performance through the lens of the CEO of a central bank, though rooted in history via Friedman's hypothesis, also dovetails nicely with the preeminence of game-theoretic views of central banking. The latter approach, discussed at greater length in the next chapter, does not recognize the process by which monetary policy actions are arrived at, presumes that central bankers are always pressured to generate more inflation than is socially desirable, and views their decisions as always optimal, conditional on the decision environment in which they operate. But if the decisions are faulty, despite the best of intentions regarding economic performance, how else can one explain both the parallel developments in inflation across countries noted in the previous chapter, and the failure of central bank CEOs with impeccable "conservative" central banker credentials to keep inflation rates from rising above desirable levels?[17]

---

[17] This criticism of the game-theoretic approach is increasingly shared by economists who either bemoan the lack of sufficient attention to the role of institutions, politics, or the process of implementing monetary policy. This is a recurring theme throughout this study. While the essential ingredients of the arguments appear in Howitt (2000), Johnson and Siklos (1994; 1996), McCallum (1997a), Sargent (1999), and Siklos (1995; 1997a; 1999a), also make similar points in a forceful and cogent fashion.

This was certainly true of Coyne's next two successors at the helm of the Bank of Canada.

Coyne's successor, Louis Rasminsky, previously the deputy-governor, clarified the bank's position in the wake of the Coyne affair. Henceforth, the bank would be responsible for monetary policy and, in the event of a conflict with the government over monetary policy, it would require that the minister issue a directive that would compel the bank to follow the government's wishes. The statement, issued in 1961, became enshrined in the 1967 version of the Bank of Canada Act. The "directive," as it has often been called, not only gave the bank more independence, by forcing the minister of finance to publicly air disagreements with the bank over monetary policy, but it increased its accountability by clearly spelling out its ultimate responsibility over monetary policy.[18]

While Rasminsky's successor, Gerald Bouey, presided over problems similar to those facing his U.S. counterpart, Arthur Burns, his performance was equally mixed. An accountant by training, his tenure is notable for the "Saskatoon manifesto" and the "strategy of gradualism" that was adopted in its wake whereby the bank, using monetary targeting, would gradually reduce money growth and, therefore, inflation. The failure of this policy (though inflation did fall substantially toward the second half of his tenure), on both technical and policy grounds, provided Bouey's successor with the opportunity to move the Bank of Canada in an entirely new direction.

The crisis in inflation that affected the United States also affected Canada but, by the time John Crow became governor in early 1987, the fight over inflation had seemingly been won. As deputy-governor, he experienced both the stagflation that monetary policy wrought, and he also set out to guarantee the gains from lower inflation. The thrust of the bank's policy was first outlined in a public lecture in 1988 in which, without hesitation, he outlined the goals of monetary policy:

> Monetary policy should be conducted so as to achieve a pace of monetary expansion that promotes stability in the value of money. This means

---

[18] Ominously, Coyne anticipated his own experience with conflict when, five years prior to the Coyne affair, he stated that "if government of the day were sufficiently displeased with the bank or the management of the bank, they could put in motion steps which would bring about a change in management. At some stage in that process, if the government were so determined as to make a real issue of it, a public issue presumably, the governor would have to resign" (Neufeld 1958: p. 13). Indeed, the position of the Bank vis-à-vis the government would be clarified under Rasminsky by the Act of 1967 but resignation would not be explicitly mentioned in the legislation.

pursuing a policy aimed at achieving and maintaining stable prices. (Crow 1988: p. 4)

Laidler and Robson (1993) argue, however, that it was not until explicit inflation targets were agreed to between the Bank and the Finance department, as outlined in the federal Budget of 1991 (but not in the Bank of Canada Act), that some form of price stability (in reality low and stable inflation) was agreed upon (Laidler and Robson 1993: ch. 7).[19] The political feelings toward price stability were also, no doubt, facilitated by international concerns over Canada's rising debt and the growing fraction of the debt held by foreigners. It was, therefore, a fiscal crisis, rather than a purely monetary one, which led to greater harmony between the bank and the federal government's policies.

When the newly elected liberal government chose not to reappoint Crow in 1993 it was not so much because of a disagreement over the desirability of low and stable inflation but in part perhaps because of the governor's insistence that zero inflation be included in the target range of acceptable inflation rates, instead of the original 1–3% target range. The fact that the deputy-governor, Gordon Thiessen, was appointed in 1994 signaled some continuity in the "price stability" policy, as did the agreement to extend the 1–3% inflation targets first to 1998, and renewed once more in 2001 under the new governor, David Dodge. Ultimately, however, the fiscal constraints that emerged under the previous government tightened further and so, in effect, left the incoming government with little choice but to pursue existing monetary policies. This is evidenced by public statements of the governor, as well as by emphatic statements about the importance of meeting the inflation targets (Bank of Canada 1995). Again, what emerges from all this is the search for good monetary policy rather than the preeminence of particular personalities.

The "Directive" in International Perspective

The importance of the Coyne-Rasminsky Directive cannot be underemphasized for it brought into the open the need to formally clarify the relationship between the central bank and government. It is also perhaps less well known that the questions that came to a head in

---

[19] Bernard Bonin's recollections on this score (2000) also underscore the importance of John Crow's insistence that the government commit to inflation targets that were seen to be feasible and, therefore, credible. Bonin was senior deputy-governor at the Bank of Canada (1994–9), and deputy-governor (1988–93). Also, see Howitt (1993), Johnson (1990), and Thiessen (2000a).

the Canadian case were discussed and handled in a variety of forms in other countries approximately at the same time. After all, as has been noted previously, the tension between the state and the central bank is indicative of the debate about how much autonomy a central bank should have. Nor is this tension particularly a phenomenon either of the post-World War II era or of the twentieth century more generally.[20] It is also somewhat ironic that the impetus to include a government directive in central bank statutes was probably to ensure *less* not *more* central bank independence. History, as the Canadian episode attests, would prove that such directives would have altogether the opposite effect.

Likely the first piece of postwar legislation that formally enshrined the power of the treasury to issue a "directive" is contained in the Bank of England Act of 1946 (sec. 4; Aufricht 1967: vol. I, p. 186). However, the directive[21] was vague and, in fact, was viewed as placing the Bank of England firmly in the role of a subordinate of the state (Gregory 1955: p. 18). The subsequent Radcliffe Committee of 1959 would underline the case against independence in the following terms:

> ... it seems to us that it either contemplates two separate and independent agencies of government of which each is capable to initiating and pursuing its own conception of what economic policy requires or else assumes that the true objective of a central bank is one single and unvarying purpose, the stability of the currency and the exchanges ... [and is] both too limited in scope and incapable of achievement without corresponding action on the part of the central government. (Radcliffe Committee 1959, p. 273)

Elsewhere, in the case of Belgium in 1939 (art. 29; Aufricht 1967: vol. II, p. 65),[22] the directive need not be made public nor was it necessary

---

[20] Writing about the Bank of England in the nineteenth century, Schuster (1906: p. 8) points out how government requirements to raise money via the central bank can be both a source of conflict and difficult to resist. Hence, as we shall see, the necessity of clarity in central bank–government relations, "Each extension of these privileges [to the Bank of England] ... was the result of some pecuniary accommodation, and an institution so dependent on the government of the day for the continuance of valuable rights was little able, as Mr. Richards observed, to withstand the cajolings of Ministers."

[21] See Aufricht (1967: vol. 1, p. 186): "The Treasury may from time to time give such directives to the Bank as, after consultation with the governor of the Bank, they think necessary in the public interest." Incidentally, the connection between the Bank of England's directive and the concerns that transpired around the time of the creation of the Bank of Canada, is no accident. Key figures in the Royal Commission that led to the formation of the Bank of Canada came from the City of London." See Neufeld (1958: p. 6, n. 2).

[22] See Aufricht (1967: vol. 2, p. 65): "The Minister of Finance shall have the right to control all the Bank's operations."

to justify its invocation. In Australia, a 1937 Royal Commission into Money and Banking felt that policy conflicts should be resolved by Parliament *not* the government (Linklater 1992). In the event, the Reserve Bank Act of 1959 placed ultimate responsibility for monetary policy performance on the government but the dispute settlement mechanism did not allow public disclosure until the matter was put in front of Parliament.[23] There was apparently no consideration given to elaborating the circumstances that might lead to a conflict. However, it was presumed that, as long as the government had a sufficient majority in Parliament, it should be able to carry out its intended policy and take full responsibility for its actions.[24] In Ireland, the original statutes of the Central Bank Act of 1942 reflected the belief, at least according to one former governor, that a directive ought to allow interference in the Central Bank of Ireland with as little justification as possible.[25]

In New Zealand the Reserve Bank Act, revised in 1939, 1950, 1960, and the changes consolidated with the Act of 1964, specified that the Reserve Bank of New Zealand (RBNZ) was to support the economic policies of the government with the proviso that ". . . the Bank was to be required to give effect to any resolution of Parliament to monetary policy."[26]

There are other models defining the relationship between the state or the government and the central bank but the Netherlands Bank Act of 1948 comes closest perhaps to what may have inspired what eventually became known as the Coyne-Rasminsky Directive.[27] The crucial element in the Dutch version of the directive is the publication of the central bank's objections to government interference, and the reasons for the actions taken.[28] This directive provides, along with the Canadian

---

[23] See Aufricht (1967: vol. 1, pp. 55–6). Section 11 contains the description about how differences of opinion on questions of policy are to be resolved.

[24] From Giblin (1951: p. 344, author's italics): "In cases in which it is clear beyond doubt that the differences are irreconcilable, the government should give the Bank an assurance that it accepts full responsibility for the proposed policy and *is in a position to take, and will take*, any action necessary to implement it."

[25] "The central bank thus began its career with a governing statute and an attitude towards monetary matters on the part of the political parties that would have greatly hampered it in any efforts to restrain an inflationary growth of bank credit" (Moynahan 1975: p. 462).

[26] See Hodgetts (1992: p. 234) and Quigley (1992: p. 210).

[27] Coyne had earlier recommended the directive idea to the government. See Rymes (1994: p. 354). The actual directive was apparently originally sketched on the back of an envelope by Rasminsky, according to Muirhead (1999: p. 176).

[28] See Aufricht (1967: vol. II, p. 471, art. 26).

version, by far the clearest indication not only where the ultimate responsibility for monetary policy lies but emphasizes the fact that the central bank and the government must both take responsibility for monetary policy. The notion of dual responsibility, the central bank for monetary policy "... in the ordinary course of events ...," and the government for the ultimate objectives of monetary policy, would become central to the development of monetary policy in the 1990s, and in the adoption of inflation targets in particular.

Table 3.3 provides a compendium on the nature of directives in monetary policy for the twenty countries examined in this study. Roughly half the countries have or had explicit override provisions in the area of monetary policy. Of these countries with override provisions, appeal is usually to the finance minister and, to a lesser extent, to a board of the central bank or to the legislative body. Six central banks allow a conflict to be made public by the government (typically via the legislative body), and in no instance is the conflict made directly public by the central bank. However, even where there exists a directive, it is clear that the ultimate responsibility for monetary policy rests with government. Given the risks posed by such conflicts it is instructive that none has ever been formally issued. Far from suggestive of the irrelevance of such legal devices, the directive clarifies, up to a point, the ultimate responsibilities for monetary policy and codifies the obvious fact of life of conflict between the monetary and fiscal authorities. Perhaps this gives rise to what the former governor of the Bank of Canada, Louis Rasminsky, who was instrumental in having the directive concept incorporated into the 1967 revision to the Bank of Canada Act, meant when he stated in his Per Jacobsson lecture (Rasminsky 1966: p. 51) that "... the meaning of independence of the central bank is not an independence *from* government, it is an independence *within* government" (italics in original).

The Bundesbank and the Preeminence of Policy

Whether it is the autonomy granted to the Bundesbank, as reflected in the 1957 legislation,[29] the memory of earlier bouts of hyperinflation or high inflation, or citizens' trust in the central bank over the government, Germany has, relative to the other countries considered in

---

[29] For the sake of brevity we omit the important role of the predecessor of the Bundesbank, the Bank Deutscher Länder in 1948. See, for example, Berger (1997) and Lohmann (1994).

Table 3.3. Government Directives in Monetary Policy: A Compendium

Country	Explicit Government Override of Monetary Policy Permitted (year introduced)	Appeal and Resolution Procedures of Central Bank Decisions					
		Appeal Process				**Resolution of Conflict**	
		Minister Responsible	Legislative Body	Central Bank Board	None	CB To Follow Prescribed Policy	Conflict Made Public by CB Gov't
Australia[1]	Yes (1959)	X				X	X
Austria[2]	No (1955)				X		
Belgium⊥[3]	Yes (1939)				X		
Canada[4]	Yes (1967)				X	X	X
Denmark[5]	No (1936)			X			
Finland⊥[6]	Yes (1925)				X	X	
France⊥[7]	Yes (1945)	X				X	
Germany⊥[8]	No (1957)				X		
Ireland⊥	Yes (1942)[9]				X		
Italy⊥	No (1936)[10]				X	X	
Japan[11]	No (1957) Yes (1997)			X			
Netherlands[12]	Yes (1948)			X			
New Zealand[13]	Yes (1964) Yes (1989)	X (1989)	X (1964)			X (1964, 1989)	X (1989)
Norway	No (1982) Yes (1985)[14]	X (1985)	X (1985)				X (1985)
Portugal⊥	No (1931)				X		
Spain⊥	Yes (1962)[15] No (1995)[16]				X (1962)	X (1962)	
Sweden	Yes (1934)[17] No (1988)[18]		X (1934)			X (1934)	
Switzerland	No (1953)				X		
United Kingdom	Yes (1946)[19] Yes (1998)[20]	X (1946)			X (1998)	X (1946)	X (1998)
United States	No (1973)				X		
ECB[21]	No (1999)				X		

[1] "The Treasurer may . . ., by order, determine the policy to be adopted . . ." (part II, 10 (4); Aufricht 1967, vol. I, p. 7).

[2] " ". . . unless expressly otherwise provided by statutory enactment, no appeal may be lodged against decisions of the Bank" (art. 7; Aufricht 1967, vol. II, p. 5).

3 "The Minister may ... give to the Governor a written directive concerning monetary policy ... and the Bank shall comply with that directive" (sec. 14, Bank of Canada Act, 1967).

4 "The Minister of Finance should have the right to control all the Bank's operations" (art. 20; Aufricht 1967, vol. II, p. 65).

5 "All matters of special importance which may be considered to be outside the domain of daily business ..." (sec. I.4; Aufricht 1967, vol. II, p. 117).

6 "The administration and management of the Bank are subject to review by the Bank Supervisors of the Diet in accordance with these regulations and instruction drawn up for them by the Diet" (art. 15; Aufricht 1967, vol. II, p. 149).

7 "Upon information from the Minister of Finance, the Council of State shall take cognizance ... of disputes concerning its internal policy ..." (art. 95; Aufricht 1967, vol. II, p. 185).

8 "The members of the Federal Government ... may make motions. At their request the taking of a decision shall be deferred, but for not more than two weeks" (sec. III, art. 13 (2); Aufricht 1967, vol. II, p. 256).

9 "The Minister may ... consult and advise with him in regard to the execution and performance by the Bank of the general function and duty imposed on the Bank ..." (part II, 6 (2); Aufricht 1967, vol. II, p. 362).

10 The governor " ... shall make proposal to the Minister of the Treasury concerning changes in the discount rates and in the interest rates on advances." (art. 25; Aufricht 1967, vol. II, p. 429). A board of governors that reports to the government can dismiss the governor and it is conceivable that this can be over a matter dealing with monetary policy. No explicit appeal mechanism is provided in the legislation.

11 "It shall be the duty of the Policy Board to formulate, direct and/or supervise ... other basic monetary policies ..." (art. 13–2; Aufricht 1967, vol. I, p. 426). The 1997 law stipulates that "The Minister of Finance ... [may] request that the Board postpone a vote on monetary matters until the next Board meeting of this type." (BOJ Law 1997, art. 19 (3)).

12 "Our Minister ... will give to the Governing Board, after the Bank Council has been heard, the directives required ..." (art. 26 (1); Aufricht 1967, vol. II, p. 471).

13 From RBNZ Act 1989 (section 12 (6)): "The Minister shall ... publish a copy of the order in the Gazette."

14 "Before the Bank makes any decision of special importance, the matter shall be submitted to the ministry" (sec. 2, Act of 24 May 1985 on Norges Bank and the Monetary System).

15 " ... the Minister of Finance, shall issue to the Bank of Spain ... the directives to be compiled with at each stage in the specific implementation of monetary and credit policy ..." (art. 9; Aufricht 1967, vol. II, p. 613).

16 " ... the Bank shall not take instructions from the government or the Economy and Finance Minister, ..." (Preamble, Law of Autonomy of the Banco de España 1994).

17 "The Directors may not receive instructions in the regional administration of the Riksbank from anyone except the Riksdag ..." (art. 32; Aufricht 1967, vol. II, p. 668).

18 "Members of the Executive Board may not seek nor take instructions when they are fulfilling their monetary policy duties" (ch. 3, art. 2, The Sverges Riksbank Act 1988: p. 1315).

19 "The Treasury may from time to time give such directives to the Bank as, in consultation with the Governor of the Bank, they think necessary to the public interest" (art. 4 (1); Aufricht 1946, vol. I, p. 186).

20 "The Treasury may by notice in writing to the Bank for the purposes of section 11–1(a) what price stability is to be taken to consist of, or what the economic policy of Her Majesty's Government is to be taken to be" (sec. 12, Bank of England Act of 1998).

21 " ... neither the ECB, nor a national central bank, ... shall seek or take instructions ... from any government from Member State or from any other body" (art. 7, ch. III, protocol to the Maastricht Treaty of 1992).

⊥ These countries became part of the European Monetary Union (EMU) on January 1, 1999 thereby coming under the jurisdiction of the ECB.

Sources: Individual central banks and http://www.wlu.ca/~wwwsbe/faculty/psiklos/centralbanks.htm.

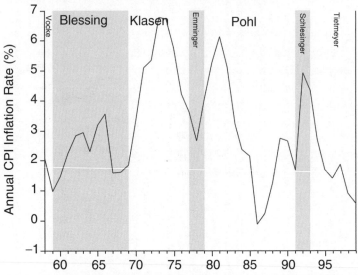

Figure 3.4 Inflation and the Presidents of the Bundesbank, 1958–1999

the present study, an unparalleled reputation for having provided auton-omy to the Bundesbank. These forces have contributed to the German experience being viewed as a role mode for other central banks. Figure 3.4 plots inflation in Germany since the passage of the landmark Bundesbank Law of 1957.

There exists a rich literature, of course, describing the actual behavior and performance of the Bundesbank. Recent comprehensive references include Kennedy (1991), Deutsche Bundesbank (1995; 1999), Heisenberg (1999), and Frowen and Pringle (1998). The objective of the present section is to explore some of the salient features of recent monetary policy experience in Germany relevant to the question of personalities versus policies.

Marsh's (1992: pp. 171–2) comment about the reputation of the Bundesbank nicely summarizes how policies have, for the most part, dwarfed personalities throughout the Bundesbank's history. "The loyalty which Bundesbank presidents may occasionally feel towards the Chancellor in Bonn is subordinate to greater allegiances. The reputation of the Bundesbank, and the course of sound money, at all time takes precedence."

Three features of the laws governing the Bundesbank stand out in the present discussion. First, until the European Central Bank came into being in 1999, the federal government could request that the Bundesbank defer, but not overturn, a monetary policy decision it disagreed with. This power has never been formally invoked.[30] Thus, while the Bundesbank is "independent of instructions" from the federal government (Deutsche Bundesbank Act: sec. 12), it is expected to "support the general economic policy" of the same government. No doubt such wording raises the possibility of conflict between the federal government and the Central Bank Council (CBC), the body responsible for carrying out monetary policy in Germany. Nevertheless, the politicians at the time, who understood the dangers inherent in establishing this kind of relationship between the Bundesbank and the political authorities, felt that institutional structures to avoid such conflicts could not be adequately designed (Kennedy 1991; Wahlig 1998). This is reflected in the legislation's emphasis on "cooperation" (art. 13(1)), and the federal government's limited ability to, at most, temporarily delay a decision of the Central Bank Council (art. 13(2)). However, the legislation is silent about how a conflict is eventually resolved (Lohmann 1994). A primary reason is that legislators apparently understood that conflict would be rare and that both the government and the central bank would be forced to come to terms with what might be at stake in the event of a conflict. In the case of government this meant the loss of public support. For the Bundesbank, it implied a potential reduction of autonomy in the event of government interference and a certain loss of reputation.[31]

Second, there is formal recognition that the Bundesbank expected to provide advice to the federal government on "monetary policy matters of major importance" (Deutsche Bundesbank Act: sec. 13). The advisory role of the monetary authorities, while not surprising, is generally more informally established at other major central banks (for example, the U.S. Federal Reserve). While fear of the loss of autonomy may be one reason, it could also be argued that such a formal arrangement actually enhances independence by permitting a form of "moral suasion" to operate in both directions. Indeed, more than one former president of

---

[30] Although Pöhl's resignation in 1991 comes close, at least in spirit, since he disagreed with the exchange rate conversion between the East German ostmark and the Deutschemark (DM). Also, see Berger and Schneider (1997).

[31] "These regulation[s] (determining relations between the Bundesbank and the government) may turn out to be uncomfortable in individual cases. But generally it must be assumed that the government and the Bundesbank will act in accordance with one another and that unavoidable differences of opinion will be settled . . . so that real cases of conflict which could lead to postponment of important Bundesbank measures will be rare" (Marsh 1992: p. 174).

Bundesbank (for example, Tietmeyer 1998a; 1998b) considers this aspect to be an important one in understanding the relationship between the federal government and the central bank.[32]

The third relevant element in the Bundesbank's institutional role is the federal structure of German politics. While some authors have recently stressed this feature (for example, Kennedy 1991; Lohmann 1998; 2000; Vaubel 1997), it remains an underemphasized aspect of the German experience. It is widely believed, for example, that the appointment process of boards at central banks can lead to partisan-like behavior by the monetary authority, at least in the U.S. experience (for example, Havrilesky 1993). There is also some evidence for this type of influence in Germany monetary policy (Alesina, Cohen, and Roubini 1992; Frey and Schneider 1981; Johnson and Siklos 1996; Vaubel 1997). The problem is that a majority of the Bundesbank's CBC consists of appointments made at the Länder level[33] while the remaining members, including the Bundesbank president, are nominated by the federal government. Even if the president is considered "primes inter pares," much like the chair of the U.S. Federal Reserve Board, and the Directorate preeminent in monetary policy decision making, there is at least the potential for conflict within the CBC, and this aspect of the relationship between the Bundesbank and the political authorities may, at times, be decisive.[34] The foregoing considerations suggest that rivalry between the Bundesbank and the federal government, reflected in electoral or partisan considerations, is a notable feature of German monetary policy.[35]

---

[32] Neumann (1999: p. 277) produces the following quote from the 1972 Bundesbank Annual Report: "this means that the Bundesbank . . . can approach the Federal Government on its own initiative, and must do so if it considered, in its duty-bound judgement, advice . . . to be called for." Also, see Issing (1993) and Maier and de Haan (2000).

[33] To be more precise, the presidents of the Länder Central Banks are nominated by the Bundesrat (Legislature) and are appointed by the president of the Federal Republic. See Deutsche Bundesbank (1995).

[34] The CBC meets less often than the Directorate and the latter is considered closer to the conduct and operations of monetary policy. Consequently, Directorate members "face" politicians frequently while the Länder representatives are somewhat more removed from political aspects of monetary policy decision making. Lohmann (1998) goes into more detail in explaining the differences between the U.S. and German institutional arrangements at this level, as well as reviewing the literature on partisan and electoral influences on the Bundesbank. Also, see Richter (1999).

[35] Again, there is a large literature detailing various episodes that highlight the tension between the federal government and the Bundesbank. Several of the most notable references are in Siklos and Bohl (2001), but also see Berger and Schneider (2000) and references therein.

While statutory aspects of the Bundesbank law help underscore the primacy of policies over personalities one should not lose sight of the fact that since World War II Germany has predominantly operated under a fixed exchange rate regime of some kind. The exchange rate was fixed, first, vis-à-vis the U.S. dollar in the Bretton Woods era, and later against other European currencies under the European exchange rate mechanism. But here too the statutes of the Bundesbank are somewhat distinct from legislation in other countries. The Bundesbank law, while not giving authority to the Bundesbank to choose the exchange rate regime, or the exchange rate value as such, does provide the central bank with the authority to conduct "foreign exchange transactions and transactions with other countries" (art. 7.3; Aufricht 1967: vol. II, p. 253). This aspect of the legislation further reflects the desire on the part of the originators of the law to define the fine line between responsibilities that foster co-operation versus ones that can lead to conflict between the government and the Bundesbank, as happened in the 1970s with the creation of the Exchange Rate Mechanism and, again, at the time of German Economic and Monetary Union.

Another set of influences that are unlike ones experienced by central banks outside Europe was the push for monetary integration and eventual monetary union across Europe. The so-called convergence requirements restricted to some extent the freedom of both the Bundesbank and the German government, in the area of monetary policy, but with the result that policies became all the more important for the Bundesbank especially, as it sought to influence in a crucial manner the institutional design of the European Central Bank.

Drawing Some Conclusions

Political scientists and economists are divided about the role of personalities and politics in the history of central banking. A reader who examines only the previous section of this chapter would surely be tempted to conclude that personalities matter a great deal in the post-World War II history of central banking. By contrast, someone interested only in the econometric analysis of time series would be rather less sanguine about the importance of either personalities or politics (for example, as in Chapter 2, but also see Chapter 4). Instead, it would appear that a few defining events have more to do with the path taken by macroeconomic time series than with either the CEOs of the central banks considered in this chapter, or with electoral and partisan politics.

Is there then a conflict of sorts between the data and history? I would argue that this is not the case. Academic authors (for example, Kettl 1986) who place a great deal of weight on the role played by the CEO (in this case of the Fed), as do more popular histories of the Fed (for example, Deane and Pringle 1995 or Greider 1997), are quick to point out that, more often than not, the interests of the politicians merge with those of the central banks by virtue of necessity, and the realization that their interests are eventually common ones. When disagreements do arise, they tend to produce defining moments in the history of the central bank.

It is also interesting to note that the tremendous interest shown toward personalities at the helm of central banks is more of a U.S. phenomenon perhaps because, in the case of the Bank of Canada, the great issue of who is responsible for monetary policy, and what are its objectives, were more or less eventually settled early on. The only occasion when a dispute between the government and the central bank arose was when the rules of responsibility were not sufficiently clear. In this respect, the Fed, in the sense of Goodhart (1988), has benefited from a longer "evolutionary" period than the Bank of Canada. Moreover, and again unlike the Fed, the Bank of Canada was not born out of a crisis but out of political need (Bordo and Redish 1990). What then is the source of a possible conflict between the historical and statistical evidence?

If one were to hazard a guess, part of the problem is that many economists are wedded to the Barro-Gordon (1983) view, wherein the inflation bias of governments arises because of the inconsistency of optimal plans that can only be resolved through central bank independence. However, a growing body of empirical evidence suggests that this is not the correct way to think about what central banks do, be they independent de jure or de facto. Central banks, especially in the post-World War II era, at times behave more like each other than their statutes would lead us to believe (also see Howitt 2000).

This brings us to the next vital question about central banking in North America and elsewhere. If, despite the institutional differences between central banks, overall macroeconomic performance is, broadly speaking, similar, are institutional arrangements irrelevant? This is certainly a possibility. Posen (1995) argues that opposition to inflation from the financial sector in particular, and financial wealth holders more generally, impose the necessary and sufficient discipline on central banks to maintain low and stable inflation. Bordo, Jonung, and Siklos (1997) point out that the common development of institutional change in the financial sector is one of the principal determinants of similarities in business cycles since the late nineteenth century in at least five industrialized countries (Canada, the United States, the United Kingdom, Sweden, and Norway).

One element in the debate about the role of institutional factors, and the role of financial sector opposition to inflation, revolves around the role of the central bank in supervising the financial system. Goodhart and Schoenmaker (1995), Grilli, Masciandaro, and Tabellini (1991), and Di Noia and Di Gregorio (1999) review the arguments in favor and against the separation of central banking and banking supervisory functions. Suffice it to say that promotion of financial sector stability (see the following section) is a prime argument in favor of combining the two functions while the conflict of interest problem, stemming from the central bank's lender of last resort function, is the main argument for assigning the supervisory function to a separate agency. As shown in Table 3.4 there have been relatively few changes in the assignment of responsibility for supervision of the banking sector over the past few decades.

This explains perhaps why correlations suggesting that inflation and central bank independence are, respectively, positively and negatively related with whether the central bank is assigned the task of banking supervision are significant only when inflation rates are averaged over decades. Indeed, Table 3.5 shows the results of simple regressions of the kind presented in the literature, except that here we consider the trivariate connection between inflation, central bank independence, and whether supervision is a responsibility of the central bank. The negative connection between central bank autonomy and inflation discussed in Chapter 2 holds until the 1990s when it appears that inflation is higher on average when the central bank is given the task of supervising the financial system. Central bank autonomy, as such, is no longer relevant. How robust are these results? As will be argued in the following section, while the search for "monetary salvation" (Fischer 1994) has focused on price stability and central bank autonomy, reflecting the concerns and experiences of the 1970s and 1980s, the 1990s led to a growing interest in the central bank's role as a guarantor of financial stability.

Table 3.4. Responsibility for the Banking Supervision Function

	1960s and 1970s	1980s	1990s
Australia	Central bank	Shared	Central bank[4]
Austria	Finance Ministry	Finance Ministry	Finance Ministry
Belgium	Separate Commission	Separate Commission	Separate Commission
Canada	Inspector of Banks	OSFI[1]	OSFI[1]
Denmark	Finance Inspectorate	Finance Inspectorate	Finance Inspectorate
Finland	Bank Incorporate	Bank Incorporate	Finance Sup. Agency
France	Banking Commission	Shared	Shared[2]
Germany	Fed. Banking Sup. Office[5]	Fed. Banking Sup. Office	Fed. Banking Sup. Office
Ireland	Central bank	Central bank	Central bank
Italy	Central bank	Central bank	Central bank
Japan	Shared	Finance Ministry	Finance Ministry
Netherlands	Central bank	Central bank	Central bank
New Zealand	Central bank	Central bank	Central bank
Norway	Bank Inspectorate	BISC[2]	BISC[2]
Portugal	Central bank	Central bank	Central bank
Spain	Central bank	Central bank	Central bank
Sweden	Bank Inspection Board	Fin. Sup. Authority	Fin. Sup. Authority
Switzerland	Fed. Banking Comm.	Fed. Banking Comm.	Fed. Banking Comm.
United Kingdom	Central bank	Central bank	Central bank[3]
United States	Shared	Shared	Shared
ECB	n/a	n/a	Member States

[1] Office of Superintendent of Financial Institutions.
[2] Banking, Insurance, and Securities Commission.
[3] Until 1997, thereafter Financial Service Authority.
[4] Transferred to Australian Presidential Regulation Authority since 1998.
[5] The Bundesbank effectively claims a role in the supervision process, via section 7 of the Banking Act, in the form of financial sector surveillance. See "The Deutsche Bundesbank's Involvement in Banking Supervision," *Deutsche Bundesbank Monthly Report* 52 (September 2000): 31–44.
n/a = not applicable.
Sources: individual central banks, Aufricht (1967), Committee to Review the Functioning of Financial Institutions (1980), Di Noia and Di Gregorio (1999), Goodhart and Shoenmaker (1995), Grilli, Masciandaro, and Tabellini (1991), and Masciandaro (1993a; 1993b).

THE THREAT TO MONETARY POLICY IN THE TWENTY-FIRST CENTURY: FINANCIAL INSTABILITY

There is another dimension along which the issue of personalities versus policies manifests itself. Next to the threat of loss of independence from conflict with the political authorities lies the equally powerful threat from financial instability. An obvious reason, of course, is that central banks have long been viewed, first and foremost, as lenders of last resort. The importance of this function began to subside over the past two

Table 3.5. Inflation, Central Bank Independence, and Banking Sector Supervision

			1980s		
Coefficient Estimate	**1960s**	**1970s**	**(a)**	**(b)**	**1990s**
Central Bank Independence	–2.17	–9.21	–8.11	–4.24	1.18
	(1.57)	(2.98)*	(3.43)+	(3.68)	(0.95)
Central Bank Supervision	0.41	0.14	0.77	1.09	0.69
	(0.50)	(0.95)	(1.10)	(1.21)	(0.31)+

Inflation is the rate of change (first log difference), averaged over each decade, in the CPI. Other details are provided at http://www.wlu.ca/~wwwsbe/faculty/psiklos/centralbanks. htm. Sample omits Portugal and the ECB due to data limitations. For 1980s (a) uses Cukierman's (1992) original index values while column (b) uses the adjusted index. See Chapter 2. Central bank supervision is a dummy variable taking on the value of one when the central bank alone supervises the banking system or shares in the duties with other agencies and is zero otherwise. Also see Table 3.2 for institutional details. Standard errors are in parenthesis.
* Signifies statistically significant at the 1% (+ at 5%) level.

decades especially as the impact of technological developments and financial innovations made their way across the industrial world. Curiously, these developments have created new tensions for central banks, once again potentially raising the profile of the personalities over policies debate. These tensions have not been fully resolved but, as this is written, it is becoming apparent that attention to policy design, as opposed to the role of central bank personalities, is at the forefront. But, as with other aspects of central bank behavior, there is a fine line between the two views. Hence, while the apparent importance of the lender of last resort function appears to have receded, and central banks turn their attention to the macroeconomic consequences of their actions, the threat of financial instability has not. Instead, it is the tools believed to be appropriate in handling such crises that have changed, and these appear once again to have thrust central banking personalities to the forefront. This development, rather than the personalities charged with implementing them, is a noteworthy feature of the 1990s especially, and whose consequences have not yet been fully played out.

Financial market innovations since the 1980s have greatly increased interest in the properties of high-frequency data. Stimulated by the search for greater arbitrage opportunities, which have been created or facilitated by innovations in computer technology, central banks are now able to monitor and, if they choose, react daily to developments influencing financial markets in particular.

Central banks in several industrialized countries are responsible for maintaining some form of price stability. To do so, monetary policy makers tend to use information that is released relatively infrequently (for example, CPI inflation, GDP growth). Moreover, the lags in the effects of monetary policy are long and variable, while those for other forms of central bank intervention in financial markets (for example, changing the overnight interest rate band) are very short. As a result, there can be a conflict between being too concerned about daily developments in financial markets and attaining a specific monetary policy objective. This is a problem alluded to in Zelmer (1996) based on case studies. The implication then is that there is a risk that monetary authorities may develop "myopia" or "tunnel vision" and overreact to what appear to be random or inexplicable events from the perspective of overall monetary policy objectives.

History is replete with examples of policy makers who appeared to be short sighted, triggered by the misinterpretation or ignorance of the available evidence. Friedman (1992), for example, points out that innocuous policy moves whose full consequences were not considered can have disastrous economic effects. Taylor (1999) suggests that frequent changes in U.S. monetary policy regimes over the last century reflect a lack of understanding of what constitutes a set of rules consistent with "good" monetary policy practices. Other recent examples of myopia or tunnel vision include coordination failures throughout the 1970s among central banks and governments in the industrialized countries (Volcker and Gyohten 1992), and, arguably, the failure to anticipate the magnitude of the Mexican and Asian financial crises of the 1990s (Fischer 1998; General Accounting Office 1996). It should be pointed out, however, that when authorities focus on a specific event this need not always be a symptom of bad policy making or shortsightedness. For example, the U.S. Federal Reserve Board reacted to the stock market crash of 1987 with what were generally regarded as the right signals, even if the event was a singular one with unclear long-term consequences for monetary policy. What may seem like a myopic response to some may not be so from the broad macroeconomic perspective.

There is much interest in the properties of high-frequency data. For example, Granger, Ding, and Spear (1997), reveal that high-frequency data show long memory and other intriguing properties. However, it is unclear to what extent the testing procedure can explain the results, whether the available samples are too short, or if the tests used to gauge the properties of the data are inappropriate, or even whether the sampling frequency plays some role. As well, conventional measures of volatility or risk, such as variance, or models with generalized autoregressive conditional heteroscedasticity (GARCH), may actually proxy some of the hidden features or structure in the data (such as non-linearity), instead of the underlying risks in asset markets which are, arguably, of more immediate concern to the monetary authorities.

Policy makers seeking to understand the implications of high-frequency data for the conduct of monetary policy ask: Since information is supplied to the market apparently more frequently, should this necessarily elicit more frequent responses? Why should central bankers care about daily fluctuations in, say, the exchange rate, interest rates, or stock prices, if these are unlikely to have permanent economic effects or thwart central bank policies?

A couple of reasons explain the tension between taking the long view on policy questions and the need to be seen as being responsive to frequent shocks that may, or may not, have lasting economic consequences. First, central banks are viewed as the guardians of the stability of the financial system and, as such, may be expected to react to news that might influence financial markets. Consequently, one would expect central bank announcements and interventions to be more precise or perhaps less frequent, possibly to counter the "noise" of high-frequency information. A second explanation for central banks' interest in high-frequency information is the fear that one small event, whether "rational" or not, can trigger a financial crisis and threaten the stability of the financial system (as in the "irrational exuberance" statement made by U.S. Fed Chairman Alan Greenspan in December 1996). Policy makers fear that one small event can be enough to warrant monitoring and responding to high-frequency data. Indeed, it is becoming apparent that, just as defining more precisely the boundaries between the central banks and the government became central issues in the 1980s, developments in financial markets would place the role of financial stability at the forefront of central bank concerns.

Table 3.6 highlights the view that statutory recognition of the role of financial sector stability, either explicitly, or via mechanisms to ensure a minimum of "systematic risk,"[36] has grown in the 1990s. Whereas only

---

[36] Defined as the risk that a financial disruption in one sector of the economy can have similar effects in other sectors of the economy.

Table 3.6. Central Banks and The Role of Financial Stability

	Statutory Recognition?		
	1960s and 1970s	1980s	1990s
Australia	No	No	Yes[11]
Austria⊥	No	No	No
Belgium⊥	No	No	No
Canada	No[1]	No	Yes[12]
Denmark	Yes[2]	Yes	Yes
Finland⊥	Yes[3]	Yes	Yes[6]
France⊥	No	No	Yes[5]
Germany⊥	No	No	No
Ireland⊥	No	No	No
Italy⊥	No	No	No
Japan	No	No	Yes[7]
Netherlands⊥	No	No	No
Norway	No[4]	No	No
Portugal⊥	No	No	No
Spain⊥	No	No	Yes[8]
Sweden	No	No	Yes[9]
Switzerland	No	No	No[13]
United Kingdom	No	No	Yes[14]
United States	No	No	No
ECB	n/a	n/a	Yes[10]

[1] "... mitigate by its influence fluctuations in ... prices."

[2] "... safe and secure currency system ..."

[3] "... maintain stability and security in the monetary system."

[4] Article 10 permits the Bank, after approval from Parliament (Storting) to issue notes in excess of the permitted limit in the event of a "... serious financial crisis."

[5] Security of the payments system.

[6] "... the reliability and efficiency of the payment system and overall financial system ..." (art. 3, Bank of Finland, Legal Provisions).

[7] "... maintenance of an orderly financial system" (art. 1.2, Bank of Japan Law of 1997).

[8] "to promote the smooth functioning of the payments system" (art. 7.3(d), Law of Autonomy of the Banco de España 1994).

[9] "... the Riksbank shall promote a safe and efficient payment system" (art. 2, Sveriges Riksbank Act of 1988).

[10] "to promote the smooth operation of payments systems" (art. 3.1, Protocol on the Statute of the European System of Central Banks and of the European Central Bank).

[11] "The Reserve Bank is responsible for maintaining the stability of the financial system" (http://www.rba.gov.au/about/ab-finan.html).

[12] While financial stability is not, strictly speaking, part of the Bank of Canada's mandate, the Payment Clearing and Settlement Act of 1996 provided a role for the Bank of Canada in reducing "systemic risk."

[13] The Federal Commission of banks is primarily responsible for the efficiency and supervision of the banking sector. Price stability is believed to be most conclusive to bringing about financial sector stability. See http://www.snb.ch/f/snb/index.html and click on "Stabilité du système financier."

[14] "The Bank's second core purpose is to maintain the stability of the financial system ..." See http://www.bankofengland.co.uk/links/settframe.html.

⊥ Member States of the ECB.

Sources: See notes 1–10, Goodhart and Shoenmaker (1993), and Aufricht (1967).

two central banks formally recognized such concerns in the 1960s through the 1980s, sixteen of the twenty countries in our sample did so, directly or indirectly, by the end of the 1990s. It should be emphasized that financial stability, narrowly defined in terms of systemic risk, has not been accorded the same place in the statutes of central banks. However, as has been pointed out in the previous chapter, legislation alone does not a central bank make. Moreover, changes in central banking legislation are often a lagging indicator of the relative importance the monetary authorities place on a particular issue in their sphere of influence.

Varieties of Shortsightedness in Monetary Policy

Central bankers exhibit myopic behavior when they become overwhelmed by high-frequency data and lose sight of the consequences of their actions. Alternatively, they can appear to have tunnel vision when they focus exclusively on a particular problem and ignore the possible consequences of their actions. Both are types of shortsighted behavior that manifests itself in many different ways, not all necessarily linked to the existence of high-frequency data.

Myopic central bank policy focuses too much on day-to-day events that may not have a lasting effect on the overall objectives of monetary policy. For example, monetary policy objectives might be defined via an inflation control target. Assuming that day-to-day news events have, at most, a temporary effect on price level movements, a central bank that is overly responsive in some fashion, may be seen as myopic.

It is clear from many central bank publications that policy makers' vision – and here I include the fiscal authorities as well – of what constitutes good monetary policy has converged considerably in the last few years (also see Chapter 7). Inflation control is typically viewed as the ultimate objective of the monetary authorities. Some (for example, Fortin 1996) might interpret this as a form of tunnel vision because they see the statutory mandate of the central bank to be much broader than just inflation control. They view inflation targets, for example, as a sign of a lack of concern for the real side of the economy (the so-called "inflation nutter," coined by Governor of the Bank of England Eddie George). However, this presupposes some well-defined trade-off between the two. Needless to say, that is a controversial question.

If high-frequency data contain more up-to-date information about current and anticipated economic activity, then central banks would be excessively shortsighted if they ignored this type of information.

Similarly, when institutions such as the International Monetary Fund or the Bank for International Settlements, partly as a result of their historical or perceived mandates, pressure or force policy makers to pay too much attention to the specific aspect of economic performance, such as the current account balance, the budget deficit, or the capital adequacy of banks, this is also tantamount to tunnel-vision policy making. Other warning signals that may be present in high-frequency data (for example, as in the exchange rate) can easily be ignored or underestimated. Yet another manifestation of tunnel vision occurs when the central bank fails to consider the impact of policy shocks on large versus small firms. The extensive body of literature dealing with channels of monetary policy transmission is relevant here. There has been a revival of interest in this topic, as a result of greater experimentation with different types of monetary regimes (Mishkin 1995).

Central banks may show tunnel vision or myopia by reacting too quickly to some news events, as opposed to too often, without allowing time for sober economic analysis to confirm whether the impact on some stated policy objective could be great enough to breach an inflation goal or other policy target. However, central banks have been forward looking longer than much of the empirical literature on central bank reaction functions gives them credit for.[37] And because they are aware of the inaccuracies and measurement biases inherent in several macroeconomic aggregates, central bankers do not mechanically apply simple rules to monetary policy. They rely on many proxies or leading economic indicators as well as informal information-gathering techniques. To generate inflation forecasts, they use a "portfolio" of models (see Longworth and Freedman 1995 for a Canadian illustration). The reason is that myopic behavior can be less stabilizing than pure foresight. To see why this might be the case, assume, as in Johnson and Siklos (1996) and elsewhere, that monetary policy is governed by forward-looking behavior of the following type:

$$R_t = \theta(E_t \pi_{t+k} - \pi^+), \tag{3.1}$$

where R is the policy instrument, here assumed to be a short-term interest rate, π is the inflation rate, π^+ is either the inflation forecast or the

---

[37] As we shall see in the next chapter, what is crucial is how central banks interpret historical data. This provides clues about how they translate forward-looking behavior into action. In what follows, I draw upon some of the material in Siklos (1999c).

inflation target. Now, I will incorporate (3.1) into a simple macro model of the form:

$$\pi_t = E_t\pi_{t+1} + \Phi\tilde{y}_{t-1} + \upsilon_t, \tag{3.2}$$

$$y_t = -\delta(R_t - E_t\pi_{t+1}), \tag{3.3}$$

where $\tilde{y}$ can represent either deviations from the natural rate of output (as in a Taylor-type rule; see Clarida, Gali, and Gertler 1998), or unemployment (as in Johnson and Siklos 1996). Equation 3.2 is a standard expectations augmented Phillips curve. Together with Equation 3.3, it forms a conventional aggregate demand supply model of the economy. Consider first a policy rule or reaction function in which the monetary authorities are forward looking so that

$$\pi_t = E_t\pi_{t+1} + \delta\pi^* - \delta(\phi - 1)E_{t-1}\pi_t + v_t \tag{3.4}$$

Assuming $\theta > 1$, this leads to a stable solution. The basic intuition is that, in the event of a positive shock (that is, $v_t > 0$), the nominal interest rate increase is *greater* than the rise in inflation so that the real interest rate also rises. This, of course, leads to a dampening of future or *expected* inflation, offsetting the original positive shock. Now consider the case of the *myopic* policy maker who reacts to *any* deviation from the stated or explicit inflation objective. Such a rule would be written:

$$R_t = \chi(\pi_t - \pi^+). \tag{3.5}$$

This leads to the following reaction function, after rewriting Equation 3.5 in reduced form:

$$\pi_t = E_t\pi_{t+1} - \delta\chi\pi_{t-1} + \delta E_{t-1}\pi_t + \delta\chi\pi^+ + \varepsilon_t. \tag{3.6}$$

It can be shown that there are two solutions in this case. One is the "bubble" or explosive solution; the other is the stable solution, but one that introduces oscillatory behavior in the inflation process. Clearly, myopia is to be avoided under these circumstances. There is nothing in the foregoing example, of course, to suggest that myopia is the result of the presence of high-frequency information. However, a central bank that reacts as in Equation 3.4 by frequently adjusting the target for, say, overnight interest rates may be showing signs of shortsighted behavior.

Myopic behavior might also be the outcome of a misunderstanding about, say, sources of price changes in a market economy. For example, some, such as Johnson and Keleher (1996), have argued that central banks should focus their attention almost exclusively on the behavior of commodity prices as a reliable guide to inflationary pressures. Observations on these series are available more frequently than for the CPI, which again suggests that policy makers are missing an opportunity to monitor high-frequency data. While central banks do not entirely ignore such information, it is doubtful that they are guided only by fluctuations in these prices. The relationship between these prices and the overall objectives of monetary policy is still not well understood, given that there are many other equally useful signals of future inflation performance. Hence, a form of myopia occurs when the central bank's information set is deliberately restrictive.

A variation on the restricted-information-set theme brings to mind yet another form of myopia. Since policy objectives, formal or not, are stated in terms of the *levels* of some aggregate, the *volatility* of time series, more apparent in high-frequency data, may not be taken fully into account by policy makers. Part of the reason might be the difficulty of distinguishing "meteor showers" from "heat waves" (Engle, Ito, and Lin 1995). The latter originates from the impact of volatility outside of the domestic market, while the former effect is country or market specific. Another explanation is that perhaps the consequences of volatility are not well understood.

The exigencies of dealing with the tremendous increase in information flows serves to enhance the role played by communication by central bank officials. Improving the public's understanding of central bank policies need not, of course, be centered on the pronouncements of the CEO but rather on the nature and quality of the information published by the monetary authorities, a topic to be examined in greater detail in Chapter 6. Nevertheless, recent events and publication of reactions to them by central bank officials (for example, as described in Siklos 1999c) can easily create the erroneous impression that the words of central banks matter more than the policies they follow. In fact, more likely than not, it is the need for consensus about the future direction of monetary policy rather than the express wishes of a particular personality, and the lessons learned from past experiences at conducting personality-centered monetary policy, that leads to a deemphasis of personalities over policies.[38]

---

[38] This is certainly evident in the U.S. case as evidenced by the statements of the FOMC (the so-called policy directives). See, for example, Cecchetti (2000), Edison and Marquez (1998), Friedman (2000), Friedman and Schwartz (1993), and Thornton and Wheelock (2000). This view is also characteristic of the German experience (Siklos and Bohl 2001).

SUMMARY

The notion that central bank behavior can be defined by the personalities at the head of the central bank (the CEO) is generally attributed to Friedman (1962). This chapter argues that Friedman's hypothesis is largely a product of the early history of central banks, notably in the United States and the United Kingdom in particular. While the personality of the CEO matters, it is more likely to be the case that events around some crisis determine the degree of autonomy a central bank enjoys and the influence of personalities. Indeed, it is difficult to find any reliable statistical evidence supporting the notion that the term of office of a particular central bank governor or president is significantly related to the main variables of interest to a central bank. An historical description provides some insights into why this might be the case. Case studies, most notably, from the United States, Canada, and Germany are used to illustrate the main points of the argument. In particular, it is argued that of critical important is the clarity of the relationship between the central bank and the government, especially in times of crisis.

Perhaps the most significant development in central banking in the late twentieth century has been the increased focus on the availability of information at very high frequency. As a result, the traditional emphasis on medium- and long-term objectives in monetary policy can conflict with the arrival of information with greater frequency that can jeopardize the stability of the financial system. It is, therefore, natural to ask the extent to which central banking today versus the past should be concerned with financial market developments. Again, the historical dimension suggests that this is not a new concern of central banks but that it has reappeared in a new form. Empirical evidence suggests that the availability and use of high-frequency data makes it all the more important for central banks today to convey the appropriate information to governments and the public. The recent focus on the roles of accountability and disclosure in central banking, is the subject of Chapter 6. Hence, despite the movement to ostensibly simplify and clarify the main objectives of monetary policy, there is the danger that central banks can develop "tunnel vision." This problem can manifest itself in many forms and has given rise to a resurgence of interest in the personalities at the head of central banks. The evidence, however, suggests that the renewed emphasis on personalities is somewhat misplaced.

4 | Econometric Analysis of Central Bank Behavior: An Evolutionary Approach

INTRODUCTION

The quantitative study of central bank behavior has a long history. Introduced in the heyday of trust in fine tuning, functions describing how central banks react to economic conditions, called *reaction functions*, were intended to convey the belief that a central bank or government could achieve a set of economic goals by solving an optimal control problem. Political or institutional considerations did not matter initially since policy makers were assumed to have the requisite instruments at hand to optimally achieve desired objectives.

Until recently, and other than general dissatisfaction with the concept of fine tuning[1] born out of the stagflation of the 1970s, two other rather technical issues led economists to shy away from estimating reaction functions for a time. These were the temporal instability of estimates and the inability of standard functions to reveal policy makers' preferences. By contrast, political scientists never lost their enthusiasm for the approach as their concerns primarily dealt with political influences on the macroeconomy in general. The ability to separately identify the preferences of the central bank or government from those of the public was considered secondary, perhaps because the State and the central bank were not viewed as separate institutions as such.

Recently, reaction functions have been interpreted, as we shall see, as a device to reflect rules like behavior apparently adopted by several

---

[1] The intellectual stimulus is often traced to Lucas' (1976) critique of econometric policy evaluation, supplemented with the Lucas-Sargent-Wallace policy ineffectiveness proposition.

central banks.[2] Some of the earlier technical problems remained but economists overcame, to some extent, their displeasure with the reaction function approach thanks in part to several important developments in the econometric analysis of time series. No doubt the long economic expansion of the 1990s also contributed to the feeling that, while fine tuning as originally conceived was out of the question, a credible and clear set of monetary policy rules could deliver low and stable inflation rates and be most conducive to guaranteeing good economic performance. Central banks were now viewed as "forward looking," in part because economic theory had convinced policy makers that this was a desirable approach.[3] Moreover, the "technology" of implementing monetary policy improved sufficiently[4] to allow central banks to resort more frequently to interest rate changes in anticipation of signs of higher future inflation instead of taking a wait-and-see attitude that was believed to describe how interest rate policies were previously implemented.

The present chapter devotes some space to tracing the evolution of central bank reaction functions and how they are put into use in quantifying the behavior of monetary authorities. Reaction functions can enlighten us about the evolution of central bank policies over the past few decades. Next, the idea that there exists a paradox between econometric estimates and prior beliefs about the connection between institutions, politics, and the implementation of monetary policy is developed. A possible explanation stems from difficulties in measuring and interpreting how policy actions and political and institutional considerations interact.

---

[2] McCallum (2000a) considers the rules versus discretion debate in the analysis of monetary policy to be a meaningful one. Hence, inflation targets are not rules since the central bank's objective function has not been announced. Svensson (1997a; 1997b; 1999b), however, considers inflation targets to represent rules – like behavior. The approach followed here is less interested in the rules versus discretion debate, not because it is uninteresting, but because the historical and empirical description of central banks so far considered in this study suggests that central banks have always sought to marry rules within some framework that permits some discretion. We return to some of the questions raised by this debate in Chapter 7.

[3] See Sack and Wieland (2000) for a straightforward description and references. Desirability here refers to the central bank implementing changes in interest rates on an infrequent basis. A variety of arguments for this type of behavior has been put forward, some of which are considered later in this chapter. Also, see Wieland (2000a; 2000b). Woodford (2000) points out the dangers of interpreting central bank policies solely in terms of forward-looking behavior.

[4] Along with improvements in the clarity and openness in central bank operations. The issue is taken up in greater detail in Chapter 6.

The next chapter pursues these issues in greater detail. Technical details are kept to a minimum but cannot be avoided entirely.

The remainder of the chapter lays the foundation for an empirical study that attempts to begin sorting out the connection between reputation, credibility, monetary policy interdependence, and the interaction between monetary policy and interest rate behavior. The premise is that inflation is the fulcrum of monetary policy. A corollary, therefore, is that monetary policy actions are central to the control of inflation. While politicians do not directly control the instruments of monetary policy there exist a variety of ways through which indirect control can be exercised.

VARIETIES OF REACTION FUNCTIONS

In its most basic form a typical reaction function builds upon the concept of a (quadratic) loss function. The latter reflects the notion that the monetary authority is thought to manipulate an instrument under its control more vigorously the further away the goal variables of interest are from their desired values. This approach permits the constrained optimization problem to be solved and reflects the choices to be made by some governing authority in attaining a particular objective.[5] The paradigm of loss minimization, based on an objective function constrained by some model of the economy, was pioneered by Frisch and Tinbergen, but it was Reuber (1964) who initiated what came to be known as the reaction function literature. Whose welfare is maximized or loss minimized? The focus lies usually on "policy makers" or "authorities" but it is only fairly recently that the respective responsibilities of the political and monetary authorities has become an issue. Initially, the central bank was viewed as entirely a creature of the State.[6] More recently, the fiscal or political authorities are ignored so that the loss function in discussions of monetary policy outcomes is the one faced by the central bank alone.

---

[5] The quadratic loss function is the most widely used one in economics both because of its simplicity and the fact that it accords with our intuition concerning the costs of making forecasting or policy judgment errors. However, it is far from clear that this is the only way or even the best way of thinking about how economic models or forecasts ought to be evaluated. See, for example, Granger (1999) for an assessment of the main alternatives.

[6] Lohmann (2000) makes an interesting point by suggesting that economists have given insufficient attention to the "audience" in the monetary policy arena.

Motivated by a desire to exploit what is believed to be a (short-run) trade-off between inflation and output, or unemployment, the monetary authorities, presumably acting at the behest of the political authorities, have an incentive to exploit the trade-off because they are presumed to act taking expectations of inflation as given.

Tradition and common sense dictate that inflation, and some measure of economy-wide performance, such as real GDP, should be salient features of a central bank's loss function. Typically, such an objective function might be written as

$$L_t = \frac{1}{2}\left[\delta(\pi_t - \pi^*)^2 + \lambda(y_t - y^*)^2\right] \tag{4.1}$$

where π_t and y_t are, respectively, measured inflation in consumer prices and (the log of) real GDP, while π^* and y^* are the targeted or notional values for inflation and output.[7] Squared deviations emphasize the importance of larger departures from notional values and are, therefore, viewed as being more "costly" than smaller ones. The coefficients δ and λ are, respectively, the weights placed on the inflation and output objectives. Equation 4.1 presumes that inflation and the output gap are the only influences on central bank behavior. There need not, of course, be a limit to the types of macroeconomic variables that could conceivably enter into the central bank's loss function. In particular, a concern for interest rate and the exchange rate movements come immediately to mind (see, for example, Collins and Siklos 2001; Favero and Rovelli 2000; Leitemo 1999; Rudebusch and Svensson 1999). However, in what follows, and other than for comments about the implications of extensions to the basic function in Equation 4.1, it shall be assumed that output and inflation are the dominant influences on central bank actions.

---

[7] Normally, specifications such as Equation 4.1 do not include a "weight" on the inflation objective in large part because of the specification of the short-run trade-off between inflation and the output gap, that is, the aggregate supply curve, otherwise called the expectations augmented Phillips curve, namely

$$y_t - y = \theta + (\pi - \pi^e) + \varepsilon$$

where θ is the natural or long-run output growth and ε are other unaccounted for shocks to aggregate supply. Aggregate demand is, by contrast, driven by a quantity-theoretic relationship, namely

$$\pi = m + \upsilon + \xi$$

where m is the growth rate in some measure of the money supply, υ is the rate of change in velocity and ξ are the uncontrollable factors affecting inflation.

While L_t applies to the monetary authorities, the loss function principle can just as easily apply to the political authorities. This is where issues of central bank independence potentially play an important role. For example, an autonomous monetary authority can pursue L_t independently of political or fiscal objectives so that the weights placed on the inflation and output objectives primarily reflect the beliefs of the monetary authorities. Whether the solution that best guarantees autonomy is via the legislative route or through other means has, as we have seen, preoccupied policy makers, among others, for decades. Several interesting questions then stem from disagreements over the relative importance attached to inflation versus output objectives. Indeed, as we shall see, attributing outcomes of policy actions to central bank motives are highly problematic if it is unclear whether Equation 4.1 applies to the government, the central bank, or both. Even if we abstract from this problem, the path followed by π and y (and perhaps even that of π^* and y^*) are not independent of the structural relationships driving economic activity. We return to this issue below. Also, in the discussion that follows, we ignore whether there are any substantive differences between some legislated or formally announced values for π^* as opposed to some goal known only to the central bank. Whether such considerations matter is also examined separately.

A number of other technical considerations stem from the specification of Equation 4.1 and it is best to leave out the details here.[8] Suffice it to say that the goal of policy is minimize Equation 4.1 subject to the choices of π^* and y^*. Moreover, the problem is an intertemporal one so that L_t needs to be minimized in a dynamic setting over some time horizon. The resulting time inconsistency problem is now well known,[9] as are the remedies, in theory, to these problems. These include the appointment of a conservative central banker (Rogoff 1987), or the redesign of the central banking institution to ensure that time consistent inflation rates are delivered (for example, Cukierman 1992). The concern here is how the notion of a loss function leads to an estimable characterization of central bank behavior in the form of a reaction function.

---

[8] A number of recent articles cover the relevant issues with varying degrees of technical detail. For example, see Brunner (2000); Clarida, Gali, and Gertler (1999); Evans and Kuttner (1998); Freeman, Williams, and Tse-Min (1989); Goodhart (1999); and Romer (1995: ch. 9).

[9] Made explicit by Calvo (1978) and Kydland and Prescott (1977). Also, see Fischer (1990).

Characterizing the Reaction Function

From the outset the reaction function approach was meant to discover in an objective fashion, how a central bank uses the instruments of monetary policy at its disposal to attain certain economic objectives. Who sets these priorities? The usual presumption is that, in the short run, the monetary authorities set these in the context of the statutory constraints or objectives placed on the central bank. After all, it is the monetary authorities that control the instruments of monetary policy. The reaction function approach eventually ebbed and economists zeroed in instead on institutional determinants of central bank behavior. It is likely, however, that a proper reaction function represents a mixture of what the monetary authorities actually do as well as what they are legally expected to do.

Consider then, in slightly more formal terms, the specification of the reaction function. The central bank has at its disposal, a set of instruments (the vector $\mathbf{I}$) that react to the variables (the vector $\mathbf{X}$) describing the state of the economy. If institutional or political factors are ignored, for the time being, a simple way of expressing this relationship is to write

$$\mathbf{I}_t = A_0 + A(L)\,\mathbf{X}_t + u_t \tag{4.2}$$

where $\mathbf{I}_t$ and $\mathbf{X}_t$ are both vectors, $A(L)$ is a distributed lag operator, A_0 is a constant term, and u_t is a residual vector capturing a number of factors that are deemed uncontrollable from the econometricians' perspective. Equation 4.2, therefore, represents a system of equations describing the structural relationship between the instruments of monetary policy and relevant economic time series that are the concern of the authorities. Note the timing of the relationship between the left-hand and right-hand side variables. For example, some have suggested that central banks enjoy an informational advantage over the public so that, in principle, data are available right up to the time instruments are set.

To some extent the significance of this issue lies with the data frequency used in the empirical analysis. After all, Equation 4.2 is the econometrician's view of the problem of how central banks set instrument levels. Nothing is implied about the length of time between t and $t-1$ that is appropriate for analysis. Not all data are immediately available in several countries even, for example, at the quarterly frequency. More importantly, even if information is available at time t there is little reason to believe that central banks will act on it. Caution, or the unwillingness to act on the latest information to prevent one from being perceived as overreacting, support this view.[10] There is also a signal extraction problem since a particular datum might be a convolution of business-cycle and seasonal factors, among others to be considered below. In addition, there is the question of data revisions. For some key variables, such as output and monetary aggregates, the significance of revisions is likely to be important. For others, such as interest rates and prices, data revisions are perhaps less important.[11]

Over and above these considerations it must be the case that the reputation and credibility of central bank actions must also play a role in whether the latest economic data influence current policy settings. Would a central bank hurt its reputation or risk its credibility by acting on advance information about the current state of the economy? This is all the more relevant since one must bear in mind that, as Milton Friedman said long ago, monetary policy lags are long and variable. Hence, the signal to noise ratio for current observations is likely to be rather different than for past observations.[12] Unless its reputation or credibility are perfect there are no independent means for the public to assess the usefulness of judgements based on data received between $t - 1$ and t, unless t is too large, say one year, which is not really relevant to the situation considered in the present study. This is an aspect not generally mentioned in discussions about the specification of reaction functions. Instead, caution is said to rule when instead what may be at stake in the process is the central bank's reputation or credibility. For the time being, we abstract from the question whether the central bank has an informational advantage over the public between period $t - 1$ and t. Since Equation 4.2 is in structural form, contemporaneous values of $\mathbf{X}_t$ influence $\mathbf{I}_t$. A more practical form of Equation 4.2 for estimation

---

[10] Several authors have argued that central bankers are, as a group, cautious. Early explanations of this phenomenon focused on the role of uncertainty facing policy makers in evaluating the current state of the economy (Brainard 1967). This notion has been revived recently (for example, see Goodhart 1999 and Sack 1998 and references therein). Another strand of the literature argued that central bankers are, by nature, a secretive group, prone to judging their actions in a favorable light ex post facto (for example, Friedman 1962). Also, see Rudebusch (2000).

[11] Even in the case of prices, data revisions of the kind that revisit how the index is constructed, as opposed to the arrival of new or better information, can have a major impact on the evolution of key indicators to central banks. Hence, in recent years, statistical agencies have migrated from the fixed-weight index (that is, one that used current year quantities at base year prices, or vice-versa) to the chain-weighted index (that is, one that essentially uses the geometric average of the two fixed-weight methods).

[12] Indeed, Siklos and Bohl (2001) confirm this to be the case, at least for German data.

purposes[13] is to allow past values of $\mathbf{X}_t$ to determine the setting of the vector of instruments so that

$$\mathbf{I}_t = B(L)\,\mathbf{X}_{t-1} + \mathbf{v}_t \tag{4.3}$$

where $B(L)$ are the reduced form coefficients incorporating the economists' view of the central bank's information set and, therefore, the policy makers' weights on achieving its objectives. In line with a loss function of the kind outlined in Equation 4.1, $\mathbf{X}_{t-1}$ would include deviations in inflation from some targeted, forecasted, or notional value, as well as the output gap. But this was not always so.

Early reaction functions, beginning with Reuber (1964) and, later, Abrams, Froyen, and Waud (1980) typically assume that $\mathbf{I}_t$ is represented by an interest rate or a monetary aggregate. $\mathbf{X}_{t-1}$ is then proxied by unemployment or lagged money growth levels, perhaps in deviation form from some desired level, the latter of course being unobservable, inflation, and possibly a measure of exchange rate movements. Other than the fact that estimates of $B(L)$ do not permit inferences to be drawn about central bank preferences for reasons already alluded to, early reaction function research (for example, Christian 1968; Havrilesky 1967) quickly seized on their temporal instability. In addition, what is or is not included in $\mathbf{X}_{t-1}$ can also greatly influence reaction function estimates (Khoury 1990).

Two other aspects of early reaction function estimates are noteworthy. First, estimates overwhelmingly rely on specifications relevant to the U.S. experience. This is perhaps to be expected owing to the availability of data over a longer time span in the United States relative to most countries. In addition, the most popular proxy for $\mathbf{I}_t$ in Equation 4.3, namely the Fed funds rate in the U.S. context, has remained unchanged for over forty years. No other industrial country can match the United States for longevity in terms of having a consistent candidate as an instrument of monetary policy without any obvious discontinuities.[14] As will become apparent later in this chapter, data related questions are an important, but often neglected, consideration in the study of central bank behavior.

---

[13] Readers interested in the technical reasons for this step and other related issues examined in this chapter should consult, for example, Enders (1995: ch. 5) or Hamilton (1994: ch. 11).

[14] That is somewhat of an exaggeration. It is perhaps better to state that the definition of the Fed funds rate has always been the instrument of choice at the Fed as discussions of the Volcker years, for example, make clear.

A second feature of many reaction functions estimated by economists is the failure to consistently consider any role for direct political influence on the conduct of monetary policy. Again, this might appear to be an understandable development. Since the U.S. Federal Reserve is viewed as being independent of instructions from politicians,[15] a political business cycle originating with monetary policy actions should not be apparent in the data. Yet, there is plenty of justification in believing that political economy considerations do matter, as has been repeatedly pointed out in this study. We return to this question below.

Identifying the Central Bank's Preferences

As noted previously there was a considerable gap from the time when dissatisfaction with reduced forms of the kind in Equation 4.3 led economists to abandon the estimation of reaction functions, and their recent return to prominence in the academic literature. Another prime consideration is the strong likelihood that the elements of X and I are not devoid of feedback. That is, while Equation 4.3 presumes that changes in the output gap, or in deviations of inflation from its target, prompt changes in the instrument of monetary policy, it will also be the case that changes in the latter lead to future changes in the variables in the central bank's objective function. Consequently, it would seem preferable to estimate Equation 4.3 treating all variables as endogenous.

One way of dealing with the simultaneity between I and X is via the specification and estimation of vector autoregressions (VAR). These can be used to characterize both the central bank's information set and the interrelationship with the instruments of monetary policy. While the VAR approach is a sensible way of viewing the econometric relationship between variables of interest there remains the crucial question of deciding which variables to include as part of the central bank's information set. Even if researchers agree on the contents of X_t the resulting estimates do not have an economic interpretation in terms of a structural model. That is not, strictly speaking, true as the order in which the variables appear in the model dictate the prior restrictions placed implicitly on the structural model. For example, if researchers argue that changes in I_t always take place prior to changes in X_t then one can presume that I_t affects all the elements of X_t but not vice-versa. Unfortunately,

---

[15] This represents a feature, as noted earlier, of the historical development of the Federal Reserve and not guaranteed by statute.

however, such restrictions are precisely the ones that may not be confidently known, in light of the foregoing discussion, to truly identify the structural parameters of the model. There is, however, another, less widely acknowledged presumption, namely that the economic model is a version of the one that the central bank uses. In addition, even if all agree, both inside and outside the central bank, about the appropriateness of the restrictions being imposed to recover the structural parameters from Equation 4.3, central bank decision making is surely not based alone on estimates from a single model nor will the parameters remain unchanged over time. The approach to be outlined later in this chapter is, I believe, more realistic. Nevertheless, it must always be borne in mind that any alternative approach that seeks to make gains in one area may result in other drawbacks, as we shall soon see.

A popular way around the problem of identifying structural relations then is to estimate a structural VAR. Essentially, this requires the imposition of restrictions on the VAR such as, for example, permitting monetary policy actions to have only temporary effects but no long-run effects on, say, the output gap or deviations from some trend measure of the unemployment rate. In terms of Equation 4.3, for example, a structural VAR of this kind would be written as follows:

$$\mathbf{X}_t = \delta_X + \delta_{XX}\mathbf{X}_{t-1} + \delta_{XI}\mathbf{I}_t + B_X(L)\mathbf{Z}_{t-1} + \upsilon_t^X$$
$$\mathbf{I}_t = \delta_I + \delta_{IX} + \delta_{II}\mathbf{I}_{t-1} + B_I(L)\mathbf{Z}_{t-1} + \upsilon_t^I \qquad (4.4)$$

where $\mathbf{I}, \mathbf{X}, B(L)$ and ψ are as defined previously, and δ_I and δ_X are constant vectors. $\mathbf{Z}_{t-1}$ combines all the variables in the system (that is, $\mathbf{X}_t$ and $\mathbf{I}_t$) so that, unlike Equation 4.3 where $\mathbf{I}$ was a function of $\mathbf{X}_{t-i}$ alone, here $\mathbf{X}_t$ is also a function of $\mathbf{I}_{t-i}$, $i \geq 1$. Finally, δ_{IX}, δ_{XX}, δ_{II}, and δ_{XI} are coefficient matrices.[16] Note that the equation describing how the economy evolves, namely the first equation of the system, precedes the equation describing the reaction function of the central bank for reasons already noted. Next, to estimate Equation 4.4 one generates a reduced-form version of the system, namely:

$$\mathbf{X}_t = \delta_X^* + B_X'(L)\mathbf{Z}_{t-1} + \mu_t^X$$
$$\mathbf{I}_t = \delta_I^* + B_I'(L)\mathbf{Z}_{t-1} + \mu_t^I \qquad (4.5)$$

Since $\mathbf{Z}_{t-1}$ is known at time t, the μ represent the impact of new information between $t - 1$ and t. From Equations 4.4 and 4.5 then we can

---

[16] Where the diagonal elements of δ_{II} and δ_{XX} are zero since both are contemporaneously related to the left-hand side variables in Equation 4.4.

relate the structural errors (that is, υ^I and υ^X) to the reduced-form errors as follows:[17]

$$\mu_t^X = \delta_{XX} + \mu_t^X + \delta_{XI}\mu_t^I + \upsilon_t^X$$
$$\mu_t^I = \delta_{IX} + \mu_t^X + \delta_{II}\mu_t^I + \upsilon_t^I \qquad (4.6)$$

Clearly, in order to identify the structural model (i.e., the δ_{ij} i,j = I,X), restrictions must be imposed. As noted earlier this can either be accomplished via a specific ordering of the variables (i.e., **X** first and then **I**) or by using economic theory to form linear combinations of the δ_{ij} i,j = I,X to generate the required number of restrictions.

Early in the VAR literature (around the mid 1980s) the identification problem was solved by ranking the elements of $\mathbf{I}_t$ and $\mathbf{X}_t$ (that is, the variables in $\mathbf{Z}_t$) so that the variable thought to be the most "exogenous" entered last.[18] This approach can appear somewhat ad hoc, as pointed out above, since it is implicit in the earlier reaction function estimation methodology. Consequently, a number of identification schemes have been proposed. Nevertheless, all identification procedures have in common the notion that "nonpolicy" variables (that is, the elements of $\mathbf{X}_t$) do not contemporaneously respond to monetary policy actions (as proxied by $\mathbf{I}_t$). The reason, of course, is the presumption of lags in the effect of monetary policy. Ultimately, however, all such identification schemes must rely on an assumption about the central bank's model of the economy and how it conducts monetary policy. But, as has already been pointed out, central bank actions are based on a variety of considerations including estimates from some model. Moreover, existing identification procedures, of which several types exist (for example, see Bernanke and Mihov (1996; 1998); Enders (1995: ch. 5); Favero and Rovelli (2000); Hamilton (1994: ch. 11); Sack (1998), to name a few), suggest that there is far from universal agreement about an "ideal" scheme.[19] Instead, a different approach is proposed below which seems

---

[17] Since Equations 4.4 and 4.5 are transformations of each other we can equate them to obtain Equation 4.6.

[18] In other words, the innovations in the VAR are likely correlated. The so-called Choleski decomposition simply attributes the common component to the variable according to the order in which it enters the VAR. See, for example, Enders (1995: ch. 5).

[19] In essence, the difficulty is that the observer has to estimate a "restricted" versus an "unrestricted" path for the instrument under the central bank's control. The "restricted" estimates convey the path of the instrument under different assumptions about how much weight a central bank places on inflation versus output objectives. In other words, the restricted estimates proxy the "rule" followed by a central bank while the unrestricted estimates also contain effects not directly related to policy makers' preferences.

to better describe the flavor of how monetary policy actions might be quantified.

The reaction function approach presumes that it is desirable for the central bank to adopt an activist policy. Note also that activism, as represented by changes in the instruments of monetary policy over time, reflects either some kind of information advantage of the central bank over the private sector, or differences between the private sector and the authorities about the driving forces behind economic activity. After all, central banks are presumed to act on the basis of how they see the future. There is no reason for the monetary authority and the private sector to see the future the same way (that is, expectations may be heterogeneous). Discretion then need not refer to the central bank attempting to exploit some presumed macroeconomic trade-off or practice fine tuning as such. Rather it arises out of the responsibility handed to the central bank to maintain control over inflation within an implicit or explicit range in an uncertain environment.

Discretion in the Form of a Rule

The combined response to the developments considered so far has been the search for rules not of the purely mechanistic variety but where the central bank is expected to react to inflation or output shocks. Indeed, the type of policy rules contemplated in the 1990s are best viewed as guiding principles for how central banks have behaved, that is, providing information about the *sign* of the response to shocks to the elements of a reaction function with only a general idea of the *size* of the central bank response to such shocks. This is the spirit of the so-called Taylor (1993) rule, according to which a central bank, the U.S. Federal Reserve serves as the archetypical example, endeavors to maintain an equilibrium real interest rate of 2%, is assumed to have an implicit inflation rate target of 2%, over some specific time horizon (viz., one year), and places equal weights on inflation and output gap shocks.[20] One such "rule" is written (omitting time subscripts for the time being for simplicity)

$$R = \bar{\pi} + .5(y - y^*) + .5(\pi - 2) + 2 \qquad (4.7)$$

where R is the instrument of monetary policy, namely a nominal interest rate, $\bar{\pi}$ is an average inflation rate over some time horizon, and all other

---

[20] The choice of 2% targets for the real interest rates and inflation are based on a mixture of historical and practical experience.

variables have previously been defined.[21] Equation 4.7 is a rule in the sense that it is meant to describe the (average) response of a central bank to the variables in its objective function. It is also important in understanding Equation 4.7 to ask how the central bank takes account of private sector expectations. Otherwise Equation 4.7 is not, strictly speaking, a rule but comes closer to becoming a discretionary form of monetary policy. An expression such as Equation 4.7 describes in some sense how central banks ought to behave and not necessarily how they actually behave.[22]

Specifications such as Equation 4.7 raise questions similar to ones posed in response to dissatisfaction with early estimates of the kind of reaction functions discussed previously. However, the emphasis in the present study is on practical issues with the specification and estimation of reaction functions and not especially in the theoretical questions raised by this approach to researching central bank behavior. That is, the practical issues with these types of reaction functions are sufficiently important to be considered in their own right. We consider some of the most important ones in turn. First, interest rate data are serially correlated for a number of reasons. In the U.S. case there is a target for R and, combined with partial adjustment to shocks for reasons outlined previously, this provides some justification for the view that the current interest partly responds to its own lags. In other words, central banks practice interest rate smoothing.

Next, a specification such as Equation 4.7 is backward looking, that is, retrospective, and therefore ignores, at least directly, a role for expectations that, as noted earlier, are crucial. We can obtain an estimable form for Equation 4.7, first, by expressing the rule in regression format and, second, by explicitly incorporating the interest rate smoothing feature of central bank behavior. The latter phenomenon can be expressed, for example, as

$$R_t = (1-\alpha)R_t^* + \alpha(L)R_{t-1} \qquad (4.8)$$

where $\alpha(L)$ is a distributed lag function capturing persistence in interest rate movements, R_t^* is the target for the instrument of monetary policy,

[21] McCallum (1999) also develops a similar rule based on the growth rate of the monetary base as the instrument of monetary policy.

[22] Though Taylor's implementation of Equation 4.7 with U.S. quarterly data over the 1987–92 period produces a reasonable fit relative to the actual evolution of R, namely the Federal funds rate. Also, see Hetzel (2000); Judd and Rudebusch (1998); Kozicki (1999); McCallum (2000b); and Orphanides (2000).

exclusively represented by an interest rate measure. Note that, according to Equation 4.8, if the current interest rate target rises by 100 basis points (that is, 1 percentage point) current interest rate settings are adjusted only gradually (that is, by a factor $(1 - \alpha)$) toward the desired target, other things being equal. Now, generalize rule Equation 4.7 so that central bank reactions to inflation and output gap shocks are estimated from the data, and the equilibrium real interest rate is also estimated from the data but is assumed to be constant within the sample period considered. This amounts to replacing R_t^* in Equation 4.8 with a version of Equation 4.7 with time subscripts now added resulting in

$$R_t = (1-\alpha)[\rho^* - (\beta-1)\pi^* + \beta\pi_t + \gamma(y - y^*)_t] + \alpha(L)R_{t-1} + \varepsilon_t \quad (4.9)$$

where ρ^* is the equilibrium real interest rate, ε_t is a residual term, and all other terms have previously been defined. To obtain Equation 4.7 on average, set $\rho^* = 2$, $\pi^* = 2$, $\beta - 1 = .5$, and $\gamma = .5$. As before many right-hand side variables are endogenous so that they are correlated with the error term ε_t and, hence, are not appropriately estimated via ordinary least squares.[23] Consequently, reaction function estimation might proceed via instrumental variable estimation whereby time series are chosen such that they are correlated with the variables of interest (that is, π_t, π^*, and $(y - y^*)_t$) but uncorrelated with the error term.[24] Obvious choices include lags in the variables of interest, since they can be viewed as exogenous, although little effort is made in the existing literature to document how good the correlation is with the variable for which it acts as the instrument. Other candidates include lags in commodity prices, growth rates in some monetary aggregate, or the slope of the yield curve. Although economic theory gives us good reasons to believe that each one of these instruments is correlated with the variables of interest in Equation 4.9 there are also grounds to be skeptical about their validity. The link between money growth and inflation, in particular, has been questioned for some time as being unstable (for example, see Feldstein and Stock 1996; Siklos and Barton 2001; and references therein), and grave doubts have been expressed about the appropriateness of any

---

[23] All right-hand side variables in Equation 4.9 determine R_t, including ε_t which captures all other omitted factors. Hence, if ε_t and any of the remaining variables are correlated, ordinary least squares is inappropriate.

[24] The Generalized Methods of Moments (GMM) approach is currently popular in part because the technique does not require the complete specification of the model and its probability distribution. However, estimation is quite sensitive to the specification of the instrument set. See, for example, Mátyás (1999).

monetary aggregate as an instrument in the context of implementing monetary policy (Svensson 1999a). Similar doubts can be raised about the links between the yield spread and either future inflation or future economic activity. Even if these issues are somewhat less problematic for U.S. data the evidence is either mixed or, at best, suggests only *some* predictive ability.[25]

While the phenomenon of interest rate smoothing has been known to exist there has been relatively little effort to document its relative importance nor how it has possibly evolved over time. As we shall see, there are considerable differences across countries and across time in the significance of this feature of interest rate behavior. Indeed, there is a certain lack of clarity about the most plausible explanation for interest rate smoothing. Several arguments, each one convincing up to a point, have been put forward to rationalize interest rate smoothing. They are:

1. *The maintenance of reputation.* A central bank that changes interest rates too frequently runs the risk of being viewed as overreacting unnecessarily in the face of constant shocks, thereby giving the impression that it is less than fully competent at managing monetary policy. In principle, however, more openness about how decisions are taken ought to temper both the frequency and reputational problems associated with this argument.

2. *Consensus decision making implies fewer policy changes.* As we have seen, however, the role of a committee of experts in influencing decisions about the appropriate stance is a fairly recent, and welcome, phenomenon. In contrast, interest rate smoothing is a long-standing feature of the data.

3. *Frequent changes in interest rates are unsettling to financial markets.* This is a powerful argument, not unrelated to others being considered here. In the face of numerous shocks, and the uncertainty surrounding whether these are transitory or of a permanent nature, a central bank is better off in reputational terms, to reduce the frequency of reversals in interest rate increases that might follow "aggressive" policy making (also see Goodhart 1999). A corollary argument, of course, is that frequent policy

---

[25] A selective survey would include Bernard and Gerlach (1996); Bonser-Neal and Morley (1997); Estrella and Mishkin (1997; 1998); Haubrich and Dombrosky (1996); Hess and Porter (1993); and Siklos (2000d).

actions can threaten the soundness of the financial system, an important concern of central banks (see Chapter 3).

4. *The nature of expectations.* Central banks have been accused of being too timid in the context of models where expectations of inflation are assumed to be adaptive, and the underlying structural relationship describing the economy is invariant to policy choices (for example, Ball 1999; Rudebusch and Svensson 1999). If, instead, expectations are formed rationally markets will expect small interest rate changes to be followed by subsequent small changes in the same direction. Indeed, a series of small policy moves can stabilize inflation and output to a greater degree than sudden aggressive instrument setting behavior (for example, Levin, Wieland, and Williams 1998).

5. *Data are revised and are, in any event, observed with error.* This issue was first discussed in Chapter 2 and, indirectly, plays a crucial role in the development of the reaction function estimates presented in this study. Orphanides (1998) has argued that the interpretation of central bank performance is significantly affected according to whether initial data as opposed to final estimates are used in the analysis.[26] While it is impractical and, indeed, extremely difficult to construct real-time data sets for a cross section of twenty countries below an alternative is suggested which amounts to roughly the same thing. In particular, good conduct in monetary policy requires caution not for the sake of caution but, preferably, reliable indicators of the future course of economic activity. Consequently, the most recent data will be less decisive in setting policy than previous observations because these will play a more decisive role in influencing expectations. Part of the reason may have to do with the persistence in expectations that effectively places a small weight on the newest observation, in addition to the problem of noise in the latest data. Nevertheless, as Bernanke and Boivin (2000) point out, the type of series used in generating a forecasting model as well as its size matters more than whether real time versus revised data are employed.

6. *Changing parameters in the model describing the transmission process of monetary policy.* It was pointed out in preceding

---

[26] There are signs already that the choice of vintages of data may not be as serious a limitation as was previously thought. See, for example, Croushore and Evans (2000).

chapters that the concerns of policy makers have not remained constant over time. Moreover, the ability and flexibility of central banks to react to shocks has also evolved over time. Both of these considerations would influence the makings of the model used for policy analysis, another feature of the empirical study presented below. While one might expect model uncertainty to temper the aggressiveness of policy settings, for many of the same reasons that have been indicated above, this need not always be the case.[27]

7. *Inflation and output stabilization are not the only goals of monetary policy.* Reducing interest rate volatility may be an additional objective of the central bank. The reasoning here cannot, of course, be separated entirely from the role of expectations or the frequency of interest rate changes considered above. Central banks affect short-term rates but long-term rates only indirectly via the impact of their policies on expectations. Consequently, the most effective way for a central bank to conduct policy is by responding to infrequent but major shocks and essentially ignoring small shocks (for example, see Woodford 1999b).

It should be clear that all of the foregoing explanations of interest rate smoothing are not mutually exclusive. Moreover, in most cases, the presumption is that the smoothing is a deliberate action of policy makers. Little allowance has been made for the possibility that central banks with credible inflation targets, supported by other institutional mechanisms to guarantee success in meeting the targets, generate stability of inflation expectations and, thence, smooth interest rates even in the face of seemingly large but transitory shocks. At the time of writing, the Asian crisis of 1997–8 represents one such example. Note, however, that one cannot disassociate the institutional framework from its impact on expectations in the presence of large shocks. To be sure, it is in part the lack of institutional support, together with the state of knowledge about the transmission process that contributes significantly to this outcome. It is but one illustration of the changing face of central banking.

---

[27] For example, Tetlow and von zur Muehlen (1999) show that more aggressive central bank reactions are called for when there exists model uncertainty and the monetary authority wishes to prevent against a worse case scenario (either spiraling inflation or deflation).

THE POLICY PARADOX

There is a strong presumption in the reaction function literature that central banks are adequately described as reacting to just a few variables.[28] Putting aside many of the technical issues discussed in the previous section, there is considerable skepticism about them since this approach gives the impression that fine tuning is possible, or at least, that monetary policy decision making can be summarized via simple models. Indeed, the notion that Taylor rulelike functions can explain much of the U.S. monetary policy experience since at least the 1970s underemphasizes the significant evolution of central banks as institutions, their changing ability to forecast future economic outcomes, as well as changes in political pressures on monetary policy.[29] Once again whether this is due to the belief that the U.S. Federal Reserve eventually implements the policy it wants, so other considerations in a central bank's reaction function are secondary, is unclear. Yet, ironically, nowhere is the literature on the political pressures on monetary policy as well developed as in the U.S. experience. Indeed, analysts of monetary policy, in the United States and elsewhere, are always quick to point out the political angle in attempting to decipher monetary policy actions. Nevertheless, it is curious that the "modern" reaction function literature formally ignores the political dimension. We return to this issue now.

At a more fundamental level, again abstracting from some of the relevant technical considerations, and even if we accept that central banks can be depicted as institutions which react solely to inflation and output performance relative to some benchmark, there remains the problem that the chosen instruments of monetary policy do not react to its determinants as quickly as the reaction function methodology would have us believe.

As discussed earlier, central bank uncertainty about the true state of the economy is one explanation. However, it is not generally modeled in estimated reaction functions, even though its theoretical implications are well known, except by adding some rather ad hoc term to capture what is essentially persistence in central bank decision making. This approach

---

[28] Bernanke and Boivin (2000) is a recent contribution that questions this presumption. Also, see Boivin (1999).

[29] Aspects germane to the history of the U.S. Fed have been documented by several authors. See, for example, Greider (1987); Havrilesky (1993); Wicker (1966); and Woolley (1984).

is meant to capture the notion that central bankers are a cautious lot in the face of uncertainty and, consequently, react slowly and gradually when they decide to take action. Next, there is growing recognition that the actual information set of the central bank is considerably larger than existing reaction function estimates permit. Data and sample span limitations represent a formidable constraint on the researcher to greatly expand the information set although it is unclear that, in doing so, model reliability and forecast quality would necessarily improve. Nevertheless, with few exceptions, the possibility that I_t contains more than one variable is also ignored. Yet, it should be clear by now that central banks not only use more than one instrument but, indeed, that these instruments have changed over time in most industrial countries.

An additional lacuna in many existing estimates of central bank reaction functions is the downplaying of the significance of exchange rate regimes. Clearly, not only do theoretical considerations suggest that central bank reactions are affected by such considerations but the history of central bank cooperation, if not coordination, would also lead one to conclude that international influences on central bank behavior also exist.

Macroeconomic analysis has invested considerable resources over the past three decades at least in attempting to model the role of reputation and credibility in understanding not only policy makers' behavior but in assisting with institutional design. As we have already seen, some central banks have earned a considerable reputation in the conduct of monetary policy. Others have sought, through a variety of means, to earn the necessary credibility where reputation did not exist, or was insufficient to successfully carry out particular policies. Neither reputation nor credibility are constants so the presumption that each reaction of I_t to changes in X_t as in, say, Equation 4.3 can be assessed independently of the state of these variables is, as a practical matter, an unsatisfactory approach.

Finally, as noted previously, reaction functions that ignore politics and the institutional framework also seem to fly in the face of the widespread belief that these considerations matter greatly to our understanding of central bank behavior.

The foregoing suggests a paradox of the kind implied by Woolley (1983; 1984), namely that political factors, while admittedly important, have not conclusively altered the narrow view of how central bank reaction functions ought to be constructed. The bottom line is that attempts to model central bank reactions have been frustrated in part by the fact that implementation of monetary policy is a subtle exercise. Moreover, it is arguably the case that the central banks of today are more forward looking than two decades ago but that is, to a large extent, precisely because our ability to model economic activity has improved, as have the techniques used to analyze economic time series. Consequently, reaction function estimates are a useful tool not because they are meant to summarize the entire process of monetary policy formation and implementation but because they enable analysts, and other interested observers, to offer a fair portrayal of the essentials of the making of monetary policy.[30]

NEW ESTIMATES OF CENTRAL BANK REACTION FUNCTIONS: SPECIFICATION AND ECONOMETRIC CONSIDERATIONS

As noted in earlier sections, existing estimates of central bank reaction functions suffer from a number of drawbacks. This section outlines an alternative strategy for the specification and estimation of such reaction functions. Arguably, elements of the estimation approach outlined below may be found in the literature. However, it is the elaboration of a strategy that begins by asking how central banks may have implemented monetary policy over time through to the various pressures, both institutional and political, faced by them that represent a departure from much of the existing literature.

Motivation

The objectives of the proposed estimation strategy are six-fold:

1. To produce a realistic quantification of the shocks a central bank might respond to over time.

Previously, it was argued that central bankers react to shocks based on forecasts of the future course of the economy as opposed to the shocks generated from typical structural VARs.

---

[30] The following extract from Mayer (2001: p. 180) is instructive about the decision-making process in the senior echelons of the U.S. Federal Reserve: "Preston Martin commented that in his time as vice-chairman, in the mid-1980s, the staff economists at the Fed were preparing great macroeconomic models of the economy . . . He asked Edward M. Gramlich, a sitting governor, . . . whether those models are still on tap . . . 'I prefer little models myself,' he said."

2. To incorporate the notion of caution in central bank reactions to these same economic shocks.

While there is considerable evidence that central bankers are cautious, as reflected in the gradual changes in the interest rates under their control, it is not immediately clear how to quantify caution. Certainly one manifestation of this caution is typically captured by permitting some form of persistence in interest rate movements.[31] Lags in interest rate movements are the obvious mechanism to capture such persistence. Nevertheless, persistence alone seems inadequate to capture the caution of central banks that typically argue that uncertainty, not necessarily well captured by lags in the variables of interest, represents the driving force behind cautious behavior. Caution in policy making comes in many forms, and it is far from straightforward to deal with the issue in an econometric setting. This leads to the third element in the estimation strategy.

3. To incorporate the possibility that central banks might react not just to economic shocks but to uncertainty regarding future economic prospects.

Central bankers rely on, among several pieces of information, forecasts from one or several models that its economic research units maintain. A prime reason for this type of behavior is that it reflects not only the inherent uncertainty about the future economic outlook but also uncertainty around existing forecasts. In other words, even if central bankers and individuals demand a point forecast for key macroeconomic variables of interest, there is uncertainty around the specific forecast between decisions taken by the central bank. Therefore, it is conceivable that caution may be exercised by a central bank because forecast uncertainty is greater even if other variables in the reaction function might suggest action is desirable. Put differently, these considerations provide a measure of the risks of reacting to certain economic shocks when the point forecast might suggest otherwise. As discussed in the previous chapter, however, the central bank must walk a fine line between caution in the face of greater forecast uncertainty and loss of credibility if markets perceive central banks as weakening their resolve, say, to fight inflation. This is where the roles of communication with the public and

---

[31] Whether such persistence captures caution, or is simply a feature of how the economy functions, is debatable (see Sack 1998; Rudebusch 1998).

transparency in central bank operations can also become relevant (also see Chapter 6).

4. To recognize that the econometrician's information set and the one used by the central bank and markets need not coincide.

It has long been assumed that the econometrician does not possess the same information as does, say, private sector forecasters or the central bank. While inclusion of lagged values is the usual vehicle used in a central bank reaction function as a way out of this dilemma, it is argued here that there are at least two alternative avenues open to the econometrician not heretofore adequately exploited. First, central banks are no doubt interested also in the forecasts of others since this has a bearing on the issue of the credibility of monetary policy. Second, it is doubtful that most central banks act completely independently of other central banks at all times.

Third, a desirable ingredient in good monetary policy is the quality of the forecast, not the size or the degree of overlap in information sets across those who prepare such forecasts. On the other hand, models are inherently incomplete, and so a model that can produce a good forecast today might break down in subsequent periods. However, it is doubtful that even a model that consistently produces superior forecasts will influence policy makers if it cannot be framed in terms of a believable set of economic hypotheses, for example, as in the case of a purely mechanistic forecast that forecasts the future solely by extrapolating from the past. Although such a model might forecast well, the outcome purely represents a feature of the time series in question and says little about *how* the forecast was prepared. Presumably, policy makers require some economic frame of reference in order to assess or act on a forecast. In addition, it is also possible that the less superior forecast, though relatively more firmly grounded in economic principles, also produces less uncertain forecasts. To a very limited extent, one can think of the distinction made by Rudebusch and Svenson (1999) between a rule purely based on a loss function of the kind discussed earlier, and central bank behavior based on source information set at the time decisions are made. The latter is a more feasible way of conducting policy while the former is far more mechanistic and less likely to actually portray what central banks actually do.

5. To recognize that the reaction function estimation practice of econometricians can only tell part of the story about what makes a central bank react to shocks and other events.

There are three reasons for this problem. One has already been discussed, namely that even if data for the most recent period is indeed immediately available to the central bank it may not be treated on an equal footing with earlier data likely since revised and available in the form a final estimate.

Proper quantification of central bank reactions also requires considerable data over a sufficiently long span of time. It is unlikely that estimates over a full sample chosen by the researcher will adequately describe central bank reactions since the estimates will be based on data the central bank could not possibly have had when policy decisions were taken. Hence, to the extent that this is feasible, one must attempt to evaluate central bank behavior based on the information actually available to a central bank when policy decisions were made.

Second, if we are to replicate central bank actions we need to be mindful of the fact that the "technology" available to estimate the shocks faced by a central bank, used as inputs into the reaction function, has not remained constant. Not only were issues of stationarity, and structural breaks, unknown or less well understood, say, in the 1960s than today, but model complexity or size, as well as the frequency of revisions to existing forecasts will have changed owing to changing cost considerations and improvements in the techniques used to generate such forecasts. Indeed, strictly speaking, one must also consider the possibility that the practice of econometric policy evaluation was considerably downgraded, if not ignored, in the aftermath of the Lucas critique (for example, see Sargent 1999). As can be imagined, it is extraordinarily difficult to deal with such problems in an empirical setting. Nevertheless, at the very least, such considerations should lead one to carefully consider both the size and degree of complexity of the chosen econometric model.

6. To attempt to identify the preferences of central bankers, as opposed to the parameters describing the underlying structural relationships that prevail in the economy.

Earlier discussion highlighted an important difficulty with existing reaction functions, namely that coefficient estimates can represent a mixture of coefficients from a structural model of the economy and the preferences of the monetary authority. One solution is to evaluate from the loss function Equation 4.1 the optimal response to shocks (via first order conditions). These are assumed to describe the preferences of central bankers (see, for example, Favero and Rovelli 2000). While this approach certainly solves one problem it leaves another one unresolved for while the central bank may have instrument independence and autonomy, the elected government has ultimate authority over desired values for π and y, and may even be thought of as having a similar loss function of its own for electoral reasons. Consequently, either we identify politicians' preferences separately from those of the central bank or adopt a simpler approach, if only because of data limitations in measuring the stance of fiscal policy in a cross-country setting. An approach, as we shall see, is to assume, for reasons stated already, that the central bank's optimal response is a function of the forecasts of an economy's future outlook, conditional on the degree of caution exercised in carrying out its policies. We then compare actual versus the desired interest rate implicit in the forecasts and other considerations directly affecting central bank behavior to identify central bank preferences. Finally, as these preferences are likely to be influenced by political pressures on monetary policy, the resulting estimates are further conditioned on assumptions about how such political pressures are thought to have a bearing on central bank behavior.

To be sure, it is highly unlikely that all of the aims of the estimation strategy will be fully realized. Nevertheless, the attempt is to at least broaden our understanding, in a quantitative setting, of the main features that drive instrument-setting behavior of central banks. It should also be added that any attempt to explore actual central bank behavior in a cross section of countries acts as an additional constraint in how elaborate the model of the central bank can be and still result in useful policy conclusions.

Specification of the Forecast Function

The proposed estimation approach proceeds in essentially two steps. In the first stage, a forecasting model is specified that is used as a key input into the decision-making process about changing interest rates. In the second stage a central bank reaction function is specified that permits estimation of the key forces, economic and noneconomic, that drive the main instrument of the central bank.

The first stage assumes that central banks are forward looking in the sense that a forecast is made of the variables in its objective function, namely inflation and output, or unemployment. As argued previously, the forecasting phase must incorporate a number of key features meant to replicate the quantitative and, to some extent, qualitative aspects of forecast preparation. First, there are lags in obtaining several key pieces of economic data. Moreover, most data are noisy and subject, therefore, to considerable revision that cloud the accuracy and usefulness of any forecast. Further, central banks generate forecasts conditional on a number of exogenous factors that are, of course, given. Fifth, central bank forecasting models are large and are no doubt idiosyncratic, that is, tailored to their particular economic and structural circumstances. It is, of course, impractical to attempt to replicate precisely the forecasting process in a cross section of central banks. However, our objective is to describe what central banks actually do and not necessarily the forecasts presented to decision makers (that is, staff projections; see Chapter 7). The latter, as had been noted by many (for example, Baltensperger 1999; Blinder 1999; Freedman 1995) represent only one input into the actual decision to change the setting of the instruments of monetary policy. Consequently, a forecasting model, sensibly structured, provides a useful benchmark with which to evaluate monetary policy decisions. Moreover, since the effectiveness of any monetary policy is largely dependent on its credibility and the latter is, at least partly, a function of private sector expectations relative to those of the central bank it is highly likely that the forecasts of others will also be incorporated into the central bank's information set.

Next, the central bank must confront the question of how to revise its forecasts. Part of the decision hinges on the quantity of available data since forecast accuracy will undoubtedly be influenced by this consideration.[32] However, in the event of a regime shift or other notable economic event, the distant past may become less useful in forecasting the future. Moreover, lengthening the span of data used in preparing forecasts implies that the most recent observation has less weight in current decisions than might otherwise be the case or experience which central bank actions suggests. Three alternatives were considered in the current study. One is to fix the length of the sample but update the sample as new observations come in. In this fashion the information set rolls through time. The principal drawback, of course, is that this imposes limitations on the number of parameters that a given model can estimate with reasonable precision. An alternative is to assume that the forecasting variable can be expressed as a function of random variables, not

---

[32] For a given sample, as the number of estimated parameters grows, precision in coefficient estimates is lost and they can become inconsistent in the statistical sense. Too many lags for a given sample, however, and estimates become increasingly inefficient. Parsimony limits model size, thereby limiting the number of hypotheses that can be tested.

all necessarily observed. The so-called state space representation (for example, see Harvey 1989; Kim and Nelson 1999) is a flexible means that permits parameters to be estimated in a time-varying fashion using the Kalman filter. Finally, again following a suggestion by Harvey (1993), we can maintain observations from the distant past but impose the additional restriction that the control bank weights observations in a geometric fashion so that memory from the distant past is lost at an increasingly faster rate. After some experimentation a variant of the first alternative is reported below in part because it appears to be the most suitable way to proceed on econometric grounds in a cross-sectional context.

Finally, even if we allow for sufficient flexibility in how a given data set is exploited, there remains the question of whether the information set is constant through time. Central banks may not always have been as forward looking as is commonly thought to be the case today. In addition, constraints on its ability to set the instruments of monetary policy may have been impaired over time due to institutional rigidities or other, at least partly, exogenous considerations such as the type of exchange rate regime in place. We account for these considerations in two ways. First, if we accept that central banks were less willing and able to be forward looking prior to, say, the abandonment of the Bretton Woods system of pegged exchange rates, then we can arbitrarily constrain the number of parameters to be estimated. This also has the virtue of making forecast accuracy less important in the Bretton Woods period than in the period since, again a reasonable view owing to the fact that so much of monetary policy decision making was effectively subject to U.S. Federal Reserve actions or, depending on the countries involved, affected by decisions of the German Bundesbank. A second avenue through which we can permit a change in the "technology" of forecasting is by varying the number and type of exogenous influences on the forecasting model. Thus, for example, the maintenance of pegged exchange rates under the Bretton Woods system would enhance the role of foreign exchange reserves relative to the period of floating exchange rates. Similarly, the increase in capital flows since the collapse of Bretton Woods, combined with the relaxation of regulations in the tracking of cross-border financial assets, would eventually increase the relative importance of the maintenance of financial stability as a desirable outcome of good monetary policy. We can summarize the forecasting specification more formally as follows. Let $\mathbf{W}_{t|ER}$ represent a vector of exogenous variables conditional on the exchange rate regime (ER) in place. Based on earlier arguments we arbitrarily change the information set the central bank uses to forecast the future along these lines. Now, as described previously, let $\mathbf{X}_t^*$ represent the latest forecast of the variables in $\mathbf{X}_t$, that is, of the variables in the central bank's objective function (see, for example, Equations 4.4 and 4.5) which determine the instrument setting outcome of monetary policy decisions. The vector of instruments and the variables in the central bank's information set having already been defined, we can proceed to write the forecast function as

$$\mathbf{X}_t^* = \delta_{0t} + \delta_{1t}(L|ER)\mathbf{X}_{t-1} + \delta_2(L|ER)\mathbf{W}_{t|ER} + \delta_3(L|ER)\mathbf{I}_{t-1} + r_t \quad (4.10)$$

The * indicates that the central bank's notional setting for the vector $\mathbf{X}_t$, namely $\mathbf{X}_t^*$, is obtained from a forecast based on lagged values of the endogenous variables in its objective function characterized by the vector $\mathbf{X}_{t-1}$, and conditional upon the contemporaneous value for the exogenous vector of variables $\mathbf{W}$. Lagged values of the instrument $\mathbf{I}_t$ (that is, the interest rate) are also used to generate forecasts for $\mathbf{X}_t$. The vector r_t then represents the forecast errors.[33] Note that the forecasting function permits coefficients (for example, δ_{0t}) in the central bank's objective function to be time varying. For simplicity, time-varying estimates or the parameters on the exogenous factors, namely $\mathbf{W}$ and $\mathbf{X}_t^*$ are not permitted. However, the lag structure for both the endogenous and exogenous variables is allowed to differ as between the Bretton Woods and post-Bretton Woods periods. The contents of the exogenous vector $\mathbf{W}$ are also permitted to differ, again as between the two exchange rate regimes considered. Table 4.1 summarizes the contents and specification of the forecast function. We assume that all central banks generate forecasts on the basis of Equation 4.10 although, as we shall see, their reactions to such forecasts can, of course, differ. For the moment then we omit a subscript identifying the country in question.

Finally, and again for simplicity, we assume that the principal instrument of monetary policy is an interest rate (we consider other instruments in Chapter 7). A market-determined short-term interest rate is chosen as the central bank's instrument of monetary policy. A second choice was the central bank discount rate where no market-determined rate was available for the whole sample. The central bank is assumed to

---

[33] We could also make the setting of $\mathbf{X}^*$ conditional on private sector forecasts. This possibility was considered. However, it was deemed preferable to either use private sector forecasts as an alternative to model generated forecasts in the actual reaction function estimates or as an instrument for central bank forecasts. See the following.

Table 4.1. Elements in the Central Bank's Forecast Function

		Content (lag[a])	
Vector	**Definition**	**Bretton Woods (BW)**	**Post-Bretton Woods (PBW)**
I	Instrument of monetary policy	Interest rate	Interest rate
X	Central bank "loss" function	1. Inflation $(t-k-1)$ 2. Output gap or deviation from trend unemployment $(t-k-1)$	1. Inflation $(t-k'-1)$ 2. Output gap or deviation from trend unemployment $(t-k'-1)$
W	Exogenous factors affecting forecasts	1. Foreign exchange reserves $(t-k)$ 2. World interest rate $(t-k-1)$	1. Real exchange rate $(t-k'-1)$ 2. Stock market prices $(t-k')$ 3. Oil prices or commodity prices $(t-k')$ 4. World interest rate $(t-k'-1)$

[a] Lags refers to the length of the lags in the VAR used to generate the forecasts, such that $k < k'$ owing to the relative lengths of the Bretton Woods and post-Bretton Woods samples.

achieve its desired average interest rate within a quarter. Other monetary instruments were considered as possibilities for this study but were rejected. Narrow or broad monetary aggregates that include the liabilities of the commercial banking system are clearly not controlled by the central bank within the sampling frequency used here. In most countries, fluctuations in interbank clearings, bank crises, and seasonality mean that even the monetary base is not fully under central bank control in the short term. The short-term interest rate is, however, generally comparable across countries.[34] Individuals, interest groups, and politicians are likely to focus on interest rate behavior, and less so on the state of money supply growth, in evaluating central bank or government actions (see also Bernanke and Blinder (1992)). Using the level or the rate of change of the exchange rate as a measure of monetary policy across countries

---

[34] If a credit allocation process were in operation a shortage of credit would increase the interest rate in the market-determined sector. This was one of the considerations for relying on a market-determined interest rate for the post-war sample considered in this study.

was also rejected. There is no adequate model of the exchange rate, from which to assess the tightness of policy.[35] Although central banks often manage exchange rate intervention, governments choose the exchange rate regime. The importance of the exchange rate also varies with the openness of the economy, making inter-country comparisons difficult. In any event, the influence of world interest rates on the domestic short-term interest rate is considered, and this may also give some information about the desired exchange rate via the uncovered interest rate parity hypothesis.

The bottom line then is that both economic reasoning and empirical experimentation by a large number of authors has led to the conclusion that an interest rate is adequate as a proxy for the main instrument of monetary policy actions.[36]

Specification of the Reaction Function

Forecasts from the vector **X** represent a key input into a central bank's decision about whether to change current instrument settings.[37] In addition, however, reaction functions, as noted earlier, must incorporate the following features believed to describe central bank behavior. They are caution in changing the principal instrument of monetary

---

[35] The Bank of Canada has published an equation that characterizes real exchange rate movements reasonably well (see Amano and van Norden 1993; Murray 2000). However, it is fundamentally driven by the impression that Canada is a commodity-based economy. It is doubtful that this equation could be successfully applied to all the countries in our sample. In addition, Siklos (2001) augments loss function (Equation 4.1) to incorporate exchange rate deviations from some targeted value and conclude that it does not improve reaction function estimates for Canada or the other countries considered in this study. The main difficulty is in empirically identifying the level of an exchange rate target in several countries.

[36] Readers will readily notice that the forecasting VARs are specified in levels. There exists an important literature (for example, see Enders 1995: ch. 5) that debates whether the variables in a VAR need to be stationary. The view taken here is that stationarity is an uncontroversial assumption except possibly for the interest rate. Moreover, once a trend or a structural break of some kind (as implied by the earlier discussion, also see Table 4.1) is permitted individual series did not appear to contain a unit root. The conclusion also extends to the panel setting, an important feature in the empirical analysis to be presented below.

[37] It is conceivable that a central bank would also rely on past forecasts of I_t in the reaction function. However, to the extent that lags in X_t^* contain elements of past values of I_t, together with the assumption that the central bank is able to set I_t to its desired value within the quarterly span of data considered, such an addition would be superfluous.

policy, uncertainty surrounding the risks of missing internal forecasts, allowance for shocks due to contemporaneous changes in the instruments of monetary policy in other countries, recognition of political pressures on monetary policy[38] and, finally, account of the influence that the overall "framework" for monetary policy may have a separate impact on how domestic monetary policy is conducted.[39]

Deriving a reaction function is simplified somewhat by assuming that the central bank can attain the desired or targeted value of its principal instrument within each quarter. This implies $\mathbf{I}_{t-1}^* = \mathbf{I}_{t-1}$. Next, if we assume that the central banks aim for a constant long-run equilibrium interest rate then a reaction function incorporating forward-looking behavior on the part of the central bank predicts that desired *changes* in the instrument of policy evolve according to[40]

$$\Delta\mathbf{I}_t^* = \mathbf{I}_t^* - \mathbf{I}_{t-1}^* = \mathbf{I}_t^* - \mathbf{I}_{t-1} = \Phi_1(\mathbf{X}_t - E_{t-1}\mathbf{X}_t) + \Phi_2 E_t\Gamma_t + \psi_t \qquad (4.11)$$

where $(\mathbf{X}_t - E_{t-1}\mathbf{X}_t)$ are the expected deviations in inflation and output or unemployment from their forecasted or targeted values.[41] As in the Taylor rule literature, $\phi_\pi > 0$ must hold if the central bank responds to an anticipated inflation by raising nominal interest rates.[42] In the case of an unemployment shock one predicts that $\phi_u < 0$. The vector Γ_t summarizes the other forces that can influence the setting of the instrument of policy.[43]

---

[38] Such as whether the central bank targets inflation explicitly, the de jure level of autonomy of the central bank, or other such institutional considerations.

[39] We leave until Chapter 7 a more complete discussion of what constitutes a monetary policy "framework." However, the specification of variables will make it clear the type of characteristics considered important in this context.

[40] The methodology of Clarida, Gali, and Gertler (1999); Clarida and Gertler (1997); and McCallum and Nelson (1999), can also be used to arrive at the reaction function specification below, except for several notable differences to be discussed. Essentially, the kind of reaction function usually estimated of late requires an IS type of relationship and a price-adjustment function. The output gap is thus expressed in terms of the deviation from the potential level of output. We use the first difference form in part because of the nonstationarity in interest rates for some sample but also because the present study is more interested in how central breaks change instrument settings in response to innovations in economic activity and other political or institutional considerations.

[41] E_{t-1} is the conditional expectation of $\mathbf{X}_t$ given the information available up to and including time $t - 1$.

[42] It is anticipated that $\phi_\pi > 1$ may not hold at all times though such a condition must eventually hold so that inflation shocks produce a stabilizing response in nominal interest rates via a rise in the real interest rate.

[43] Note that expectations are now conditional on information available at time t. The reason is given in the following text.

It is further assumed that these forces enter linearly into the reaction function. Hence, we write

$$\Gamma_t = \varsigma_1\sigma_t^2 + \varsigma_2\Delta R_t^W + \varsigma_3\Lambda_t + \varsigma_4 D_t + \varsigma_5\kappa_t$$

$$\varsigma < 0, \varsigma_2 > 0, \varsigma_3 \overset{>}{_<} 0, \varsigma_4 \overset{>}{_<} 0, \varsigma_5 < 0 \qquad (4.12)$$

The variable σ_t^2 captures the uncertainty surrounding the underlying risks associated with estimates of shocks from inflation, unemployment or output, proxied by an estimate of the conditional variance of interest rate changes.[44] ΔR_t^W represents the contemporaneous change in the world interest rate which proxies surprises in the setting of the instruments of monetary policy relevant to the small open economy in question. The term Λ_t represents the political forces on monetary policy. As explained earlier these are proxied by a variety of electoral and partisan variables meant to capture the possibility that the government's weighting of the relative importance of inflation and output shocks need not be the same as those of the government. The variable D_t captures constraints on instrument setting behavior stemming from the presence or absence of a "framework" for monetary policy (viz., inflation targeting, target zone exchange rate system). Finally, κ attempts to measure the role of caution in changing the instrument of monetary policy.

Below Equation 4.12 are the anticipated signs for each term. A central bank more concerned with interest rate volatility may make fewer changes to interest rates in order to better anchor inflationary expectations.[45] Otherwise, the coefficient ζ_2 measures the response of domestic interest rates to world interest rates. There are at least three exchange rate regimes in our sample. After roughly 1978, and until late 1992, many European countries operated under a quasi-fixed exchange rate system (Snake, Exchange rate mechanism) with remaining countries operating under a largely managed float regime where the amount of management varied widely. Prior to 1973, under the Bretton Woods system, pegged but adjustable exchange rates were the rule. The size of

---

[44] The use of conditional variances reflects the fact, as noted earlier in this study and in this chapter, that central banks may also be concerned with interest rate volatility. The resulting reaction function is known as an ARCH in mean, or ARCH-M, specification. See, for example, Enders (1995: ch. 3) and Hamilton (1994: ch. 21).

[45] Greater risk of inflation is likely to be positively correlated with inflation volatility. A reduction in interest rate changes in the face of higher interest rate volatility could then signal a reduction in the future risks of inflation. A large literature linking inflation levels and volatility has emerged since at least Friedman's Nobel Lecture (1977). See, for example, Grier and Perry (1998).

ζ_2, of course, depends on the exchange rate regime in place. The sign of the political and institutional factors depend on their particular specification. For each of the specifications we ask: Do the political or electoral variables help explain the behavior of the monetary authorities beyond their reaction to the other variables in the reaction function? If so, there is some evidence that the monetary authority is influenced by political forces and is, in this sense, less autonomous than a monetary authority not influenced by political events.

Two types of political influences are considered. In the first type, Λ_t is a dummy variable active around elections. In the Nordhaus (1975) model, everything else being equal, we should find that a dependent central bank would reduce interest rates in the months before an election to aid in the re-election of the governing party. This is implemented with a dummy (*Eprior*) equal to 1 in the election quarter and in the two previous quarters. For a politically motivated, less-independent central bank the coefficient on such a dummy should be negative. A second dummy variable (*Etmp*), equal to 1 in the election quarter and in the two previous quarters and equal to -1 in the two subsequent quarters, was also considered. A politically motivated central bank may defer an increase in interest rates until after an election. This variable partly handles the issue of a preelection fiscal expansion, if such an expansion raised inflation and lowered unemployment, since the politically motivated central bank would try to defer the necessary interest rate increases. A significant positive sign on this variable would capture the temporary nature of the election-oriented monetary policy. The election dummy *Etmp* is distinguished from the election dummy *Eprior*, since the latter variable assumes the election effect is permanent. A zero or a significant positive sign on either election dummy is evidence of independence, while a negative sign on either is evidence of dependence. Experimentation with versions of these variables active for different numbers of more quarters did not impact the conclusions.

The second type of political influence considered focuses on the political preferences of the party in power. Alesina and Roubini (1990) argue that a switch from a right-wing to a left-wing government would be associated with expansionary monetary policy.[46] A dummy representing this

---

[46] The definitions of "right wing" and "left wing" follow Alesina, Cohen, and Roubini (1992; 1997) and Alesina and Roubini (1990). A general difficulty with the specification of both versions of the political dummy variables is that previous studies do not use a statistical criterion to determine how long the dummies should remain active. If, for example, monetary policy acts with long and variable lags, then existing specifications may be misspecified. Also, see Persson and Tabellini (1994; 1997) and Faust and Irons (1999).

switch measures, given past unexpected inflation and unemployment, whether a new left-wing government lowers nominal interest rates. If a new right-wing government dislikes inflation more than its left-wing predecessor, monetary policy will be tightened and interest rates increased.[47] A dummy variable, *Drpt2*, takes on a value of +1 in the election quarter and two (four) quarters after the election of a new right-wing government (we also specified variables four and eight quarters in length with no effect on the conclusions). The variable is set equal to −1 for the same time period following the election or appointment of a new left-wing government. Consequently, the reaction of interest rates to a right-wing party is positive since such a government (+1) would want to raise interest rates if the central bank were dependent while a left-wing government (−1) would prefer lower interest rates with a dependent central bank, other things being equal.

One complication is the fact that, in several of the countries in our sample, election timing is endogenous. The case in which a dependent central bank reduces interest rates before an election and the case where an election is called because, say, of a series of interest rate reductions are then observationally equivalent. An additional problem is that an autonomous central bank may agree with a right-wing or a left-wing government about the necessity to raise or lower interest rates if the shocks in Equation 4.11 warrant such a reaction. In other words, a politically influenced central bank may raise or lower interest rates more than is warranted, given the other determinants in the reaction function, so political effects are evaluated conditional on the fundamentals in the reaction function.[48] We return to the endogeneity issue in the discussion of the empirical results.

Considerations of fiscal policy can also produce complications. In the case of partisan changes, if a new left-wing government expanded fiscal policy, and if the central bank accommodated the expansion so that interest rates did not rise, a zero coefficient on the partisan dummy

---

[47] A central bank could be viewed as being (somewhat) independent if the interest rate change is less than "desired" by politicians. Unless we have a model of national interest rates by, say, political party we cannot, strictly speaking, measure degrees of independence.

[48] It is tempting to add an interaction term. However, it is unlikely that a central bank will share its internal forecast with government. To the extent that the finance ministry generates its own internal forecasts, or relies on private sector forecasts, there might be some room for the kind of interaction effects contemplated here. Such a possibility was not, however, implemented in the estimated specifications.

is evidence of dependence. A negative coefficient could, in principle, reflect a fiscal contraction by a newly elected right-wing government. Nevertheless, it is important to recognize that this issue may not be of much practical importance, since it is difficult to imagine actual changes in fiscal policy enacted within a quarter of a new government taking office.[49]

A second test of the partisan model considered is more straightforward and perhaps more telling. Reaction functions are estimated separately where, in one sample, the data are taken from the period where the left-wing government is in power. In a separate sample we use data only from the period when the right-wing government is in power. If the coefficients of the reaction function are significantly different by partisan regime, then this may be viewed as substantial evidence in favor of the joint hypothesis that the central bank is influenced by the party in power and that the two parties do in fact have different preferences over their response to the forecast errors in inflation and unemployment. If the coefficients do not differ significantly, it is not possible to know which part of the joint hypothesis is rejected – either the central bank is independent or the political parties do not differ.

Finally, there is the matter of whether de jure forms of central bank autonomy might have an independent influence on central bank decisions to change interest rates. One can certainly imagine that an autonomous central bank can be relatively more aggressive in the face of unexpected inflation or may even place relatively greater weight on inflation over output or unemployment in the loss function. But it is equally possible that an autonomous central bank is constrained from

---

[49] Drazen (2000a) reviews the evidence since the survey of Alesina (1988; 1989) but concentrates largely on the U.S. experience. He advocates the view that fiscal policy is the driving force behind partisan political cycles in the monetary policy as the passive action in the process. It is far from clear that the evidence presented in his study is applicable to countries other than the United States. In addition, it is largely assumed that relevant monetary impulses are measured via money growth. The issues referred to above in this connection are largely ignored, as is the complication of the lags between changes in money growth and interest rates. Finally, it is never clearly explained in what sense the monetary authority is "passive" as questions of the role of the autonomy of the central bank are not directly addressed (see, however, Drazen 2000b for more details on the relevant issues). Nevertheless, as noted earlier (see Chapter 2), making the connection between fiscal and monetary policy more explicit is a valuable addition to existing theoretical constructs. The empirical evidence presented as follows considers the impact of fiscal policy (based on a measure described in Chapter 2) on monetary policy. Also, see Alesina and Rosenthal (1995) and Alesina and Sachs (1988).

overreacting either to protect its autonomy or precisely because autonomy has permitted the central bank to focus on long-term stability and not to react to every wiggle in inflation. As with political factors then, a subsample of central banks that have experienced significant changes in de jure autonomy is chosen and reaction functions are again estimated separately where in one sample the data are taken when autonomy was low while, in a second sample, de jure autonomy is uniformly high. If the coefficients of the reaction function are significantly different then this suggests that de jure autonomy affects interest rate determination of central banks.

The analysis of central bank behavior outlined so far suggests that central banks change the instruments of monetary policy gradually, if not incrementally. If we assume that an interest rate represents the principal instrument of policy then caution would suggest that a future change is less likely the more recent an interest rate change and the larger the change. As noted previously, a simple way to deal with this problem is to add a lagged dependent variable – since there is only one instrument assumed – in order to capture persistence in interest rate changes (R). In other words, one can write

$$\varsigma_5 \kappa_t = \varsigma_5 \Delta \mathbf{I}_{t-1} = \varsigma_5 \Delta R_{t-1}$$

For simplicity, we assume that the decision to raise or lower the interest rate is a symmetric one though, in the empirical analysis, the possibility of asymmetric responses is also contemplated. In addition, since an interest rate change by the central bank is intended primarily to influence future expectations of inflation and output or unemployment, it is conceivable that the central bank will be more aggressive if past changes in the instrument have the desired effect on expectations. Consequently, caution may be a function not so much according to whether there has been a change in the instrument setting in the previous period but the size and timing of the last change, its impact on private forecasts, and the likelihood that this would require additional change to ensure that the central bank meets its objectives. Therefore κ_t could be interpreted in a probabilistic fashion to indicate whether the probability that a central bank will be less cautious and change interest rates (in either direction). While some evidence was found to indicate that changes in private sector forecasts of inflation and output, and the length of time since the last discount rate change increased the probability of a change in the discount rate, the statistical evidence was largely inconclusive.[50] Hence, the lagged dependent variable is retained in the reaction function estimates presented below.

So far the reaction function has been discussed for essentially the "representative" central bank. There is nothing wrong, in principle, with estimating separate reaction functions for each country in the data set. Indeed, such estimates already control, in a limited fashion, for the impact of the world economy on domestic economies. But there are virtues in taking one step further and asking whether better account of the reactions of central bankers to economic shocks, institutional, and political determinants can be taken by estimating reaction functions in a panel setting, especially since the number of data points for particular regimes and policy frameworks are potentially too few to permit adequate testing of some of the hypotheses of interest. In addition, as noted in Chapter 2, several important institutional characteristics that are likely to influence central bank behavior vary little through time but considerably across countries. With the panel approach, however, we are able to exploit cross-country differences. This would appear to be especially important under the circumstances because, as Siklos (1999b) and others have pointed out, it remains to be determined to what extent similarities or differences in inflation behavior across countries are evident in the data. Moreover, electoral, or partisan, goals in small open economies may also be influenced by events in the rest of the world. Therefore, the estimated models are of the fixed effect variety with constant slopes. The fixed effects are country-specific dummies to control for cross-country differences in interest rate movements.[51]

---

[50] One of the specifications considered was of the form

$$\kappa_t = \chi_0 + \chi_1 DUR_t + \chi_2 \Delta \ln DR_t + \chi_3 \Delta \pi_{t-1}^f + \chi_4 \Delta y_{t-1}^f + \chi_5 \{DUR_t \cdot \Delta \pi_{t-1}^f\}$$
$$+ \chi_6 \{DUR_t \cdot \Delta y_{t-1}^f\} + e_t$$

where DUR is the duration, in quarters, since the last change in the central bank's discount rate, $\Delta \ln DR_t$ is the log difference in the discount rate, $\Delta \pi_{t-1}^f$ and Δy_{t-1}^f is the previous period's change in the private sector's forecast of inflation and output or unemployment, respectively. Taking log differences in the discount rate treats a given discount rate change at low interest rates differently than the same absolute change at higher interest rates. Finally, κ is a 0–1 dummy that is active in quarters when there is an interest rate change, and zero otherwise. The longer the time that has elapsed since the last interest rate change, or signs that private sector expectations of inflation and output or unemployment rise conditional on all the other factors already considered, are likely to reduce caution and trigger a discount rate change.

[51] Note that the panel does not contain a lagged dependent variable that can create statistical problems in some situations (Hsiao 1986).

EMPIRICAL EVIDENCE

Some Stylized Features of the Data

Although broad features of the data were described in Chapter 2, Table 4.2 summarizes for each of the twenty countries in the study mean inflation, interest rate, unemployment, and output developments for the full Bretton Woods (BW) and post-Bretton Woods (PBW) samples. The table highlights both some of the stark differences over time in the main measures of macroeconomic performance as well as some of the potential limitations of sample selection. The post-Bretton Woods era marks the widespread adoption of floating rates, at least among the major industrialized countries. In any event, it is generally thought that the period since the first oil price shock especially represents an era where policy makers seemed to be keen on placing a domestic slant on monetary policy. Nevertheless, the PBW sample reveals that average inflation rates were higher in eighteen of twenty countries considered, though in the case of Germany and Switzerland, the differences are marginal at best. Consequently, even if inflation is thought of as being largely made at home in the PBW, a remarkable number of countries chose higher inflation. The higher inflation rates are also reflected in nominal interest rates that are not only higher on average in the PBW in fourteen of fifteen countries with data covering both periods, but are also more volatile, as measured by the standard deviation. It is also the case that the average unemployment rates are higher under the floating regime in all nineteen countries with data covering the BW period serving as the basis for comparison. Turning to the unemployment rate, we find that they are higher in the PBW period. Of course, the data do not consider the possibility that structural or trend unemployment may also have changed over time, a feature to be considered in the empirical study below. Nevertheless, the broad parallels in inflation, interest rate, and unemployment rate behavior as between the BW and PBW samples is notable. In Chapter 2 other features of the unemployment rate experience, both adjusted and unadjusted for underlying economic factors, were also discussed.

Finally, the data for the output gap reflect the nature of their construction, that is, they reveal that over a forty-year period countries, on average, operated at capacity. In contrast, most countries operated below capacity in the PBW period though seven countries

Table 4.2. Summary Statistics for Inflation, Unemployment, and Interest Rates: The Bretton Woods Divide

Country	Inflation (π)			Interest Rates (R)			Unemployment (U)			Output Gap (y)		
	60–99	BW	PBW	60–99	BW	PBW	60–99	BW	PBW	60–99	BW	PBW
Australia	5.61	3.46	6.69	9.08	5.04	9.77	5.94	1.81	7.53	0.00	.091	-0.046
(74Q1)	(4.05)	(2.51)	(4.24)	(3.84)	(0.81)	(3.73)	(3.09)	(0.42)	(1.99)	(2.22)	(2.46)	(2.09)
Austria	3.88	3.83	3.86	6.08	4.77	6.39	3.89	2.66	4.48	0.00	0.19	-0.06
(73Q1)	(2.06)	(1.35)	(2.29)	(2.08)	(0.61)	(2.19)	(1.88)	(0.50)	(2.01)	(1.90)	(1.68)	(1.97)
Belgium	4.18	3.27	4.58	7.50	5.85	8.32	9.71	3.40	12.75	0.00	0.10	-0.05
(73Q1)	(2.89)	(1.35)	(3.28)	(2.53)	(0.83)	(2.68)	(5.39)	(0.91)	(3.75)	(4.14)	(0.33)	(4.62)
Canada	4.58	2.67	5.18	7.29	4.54	8.24	7.67	5.03	8.59	0.00	-.008	.002
(70Q2)	(3.14)	(1.32)	(3.30)	(3.54)	(1.52)	(3.43)	(2.35)	(1.33)	(1.89)	(1.90)	(1.45)	(2.01)
Denmark	5.82	5.74	5.86	6.32	4.76	6.66	6.45	1.24	8.19	0.00	0.46	-0.07
(73Q1)	(3.48)	(2.29)	(3.91)	(2.32)	(0.61)	(2.42)	(3.78)	(0.43)	(2.63)	(4.92)	(4.72)	(4.97)
Finland	6.03	5.14	6.43	11.98	—	11.98	6.12	2.16	7.73	0.00	0.25	-.019
(73Q1)	(4.16)	(2.55)	(4.65)	(4.46)		(4.46)	(5.01)	(0.88)	(5.11)	(2.72)	(3.67)	(2.66)
France	5.33	5.03	5.78	7.74	6.02	8.99	6.25	1.47	8.89	0.00	0.49	-0.06
(74Q1)	(3.64)	(2.55)	(4.26)	(3.34)	(2.69)	(3.30)	(4.27)	(1.01)	(2.77)	(1.44)	(0.70)	(1.49)
Germany	3.11	3.00	3.15	5.47	4.28	6.07	5.20	0.95	7.25	0.00	0.11	-0.047
(73Q1)	(1.82)	(1.27)	(2.02)	(2.47)	(1.82)	(2.54)	(3.73)	(0.46)	(2.75)	(2.05)	(2.30)	(1.94)
Ireland	6.88	5.97	7.47	11.10	8.95	11.36	10.49	6.50	12.64	0.00	0.00	-0.13
(74Q4)	(5.42)	(2.80)	(6.26)	(5.14)	(3.68)	(5.24)	(4.51)	(0.81)	(4.21)	(9.66)	(3.11)	(11.86)
Italy	7.55	3.91	9.37	12.19	5.47	12.71	8.29	5.28	9.74	0.00	-0.15	0.07
(73Q1)	(5.43)	(1.93)	(5.69)	(4.33)	(0.46)	(4.05)	(2.80)	(0.71)	(2.21)	(2.51)	(2.96)	(2.30)
Japan	4.39	5.57	3.86	6.08	7.84	5.24	2.13	1.29	2.54	0.00	0.17	-0.08
(73Q1)	(4.10)	(1.49)	(4.24)	(3.16)	(1.96)	(3.29)	(0.85)	(0.16)	(0.74)	(2.09)	(2.34)	(1.98)
Netherlands	4.05	4.26	4.00	5.79	4.22	6.22	5.10	0.87	6.75	0.00	—	0.00
(71Q2)	(2.63)	(1.98)	(2.84)	(2.70)	(2.09)	(2.79)	(4.02)	(0.41)	(3.55)	(1.43)		(1.43)

165

Table 4.2 (continued)

Country	Inflation (π)			Interest Rates (R)			Unemployment (U)			Output Gap (y)		
	60–99	BW	PBW	60–99	BW	PBW	60–99	BW	PBW	60–99	BW	PBW
New Zealand	6.97	4.54	8.11	11.72	—	11.72	3.47	0.21	5.14	0.00	—	0.00
(73Q3)	(5.14)	(2.43)	(5.67)	(5.83)		(5.83)	(3.50)	(0.21)	(3.21)	(3.30)		(3.30)
Norway	5.59	4.74	5.97	10.03	6.69	11.27	2.40	1.07	3.05	0.00	-0.06	0.01
(73Q1)	(3.13)	(2.34)	(3.36)	(4.65)	(1.93)	(4.76)	(1.80)	(0.31)	(1.87)	(2.67)	(0.30)	(2.67)
Portugal	10.52	4.71	13.11	12.83	—	12.83	6.21	—	6.21	0.00	—	0.00
(73Q1)	(7.63)	(2.57)	(7.71)	(4.84)		(4.84)	(1.55)		(1.55)	(3.40)		(3.40)
Spain	8.35	6.31	9.26	12.65	—	12.65	13.83	2.84	15.05	0.00	-0.15	0.01
(73Q1)	(3.80)	(1.88)	(0.18)	(5.13)		(5.13)	(2.40)	(0.67)	(2.23)	(1.40)	(2.30)	(1.33)
Sweden	6.30	4.36	5.71	8.99	5.54	8.99	3.70	1.65	3.03	0.00	-0.57	0.07
(73Q1)	(3.80)	(1.88)	(0.18)	(2.12)	(1.54)	(2.12)	(2.40)	(0.67)	(2.23)	(2.12)	(2.53)	(2.07)
Switzerland	3.40	3.35	3.41	3.17	—	3.17	1.07	0.02	1.48	0.00	0.44	-0.08
(73Q2)	(0.73)	(1.12)	(2.57)	(2.29)		(2.29)	(1.61)	(0.02)	(1.73)	(2.67)	(2.16)	(2.75)
United Kingdom	6.63	4.50	7.49	7.25	5.60	7.97	5.52	2.06	7.02	0.00	-0.12	0.05
(72Q2)	(4.82)	(2.06)	(5.84)	(3.33)	(1.33)	(3.67)	(3.35)	(0.53)	(2.92)	(1.99)	(1.46)	(2.17)
United States	4.43	2.86	5.07	6.54	4.45	7.46	6.00	4.91	6.48	0.00	-0.16	0.07
(72Q2)	(2.89)	(1.69)	(3.03)	(3.19)	(1.85)	(3.24)	(1.49)	(1.04)	(1.41)	(2.05)	(1.83)	(2.13)

Data begin in 1960:1 and end with 1999:4, unless otherwise noted below. Australia: R (69:3), U (64:1); Austria: R (67:1); Denmark: R (67:1); Finland: R (75:1), U (62:1); Ireland: R (71:1); Italy: R (71:1); New Zealand: R (84:3); Norway: R (63:1); Portugal: R (81:1), U (83:2); Spain: R (73:2), U (70:1); Switzerland: R (75:4). Unemployment data for Switzerland in the Bretton Woods period may not be comparable to the post-Bretton Woods sample, see Johnson and Siklos (1996). Data for interest rates for Austria, Belgium, Denmark, Finland, France, Ireland, Italy, Netherlands, Portugal, and Spain end in 1998:4 due to the start-up of the ECB. Output gap is GDP growth less H-P filtered GDP growth with a smoothing parameter of 4800. Data begin in 1960:1 and end in 1999:4, unless otherwise noted below. Australia (ends 99:3), Denmark is industrial production (begins 69:1), Belgium is industrial production, France (begins 71:1), Ireland is industrial production (ends 98:3), Netherlands (begins 78:1), New Zealand (begins 83:2), Norway (ends 98:4), Portugal (begins 78:4), Spain (begins 71:1), Sweden (begins 70:1), Switzerland (begins 66:1). BW = Bretton Woods; PBW = post-Bretton Woods. The date under each country's name marks the beginning, as dated by the IMF, of the post-Bretton Woods period. Standard deviations are shown in parentheses.

did manage slightly higher than trend output since the early 1970s.[52]

Table 4.3 gives a flavor of the degree to which central banks are cautious in changing the stance of monetary policy. For each country, changes in the discount rate[53] are examined and the fraction of time the discount rate is left unchanged or increases and decreases are limited to half a percentage point are tabulated. These calculations are shown for both the full sample as well as for the decade of the 1990s. There are a number of interesting features in the table. First, in twelve of the twenty countries studied here central banks became less reluctant to change the discount rate in the 1990s than in the full sample.[54] An important exception is the United States where the fraction of the time the Fed funds rate was left unchanged is slightly higher (though not significantly so) in the 1990s. In this sense central banks have became less cautious. However, caution is represented not only by whether a central bank changes the discount rate but also by the size of such changes when they are deemed necessary. By this metric, in seven countries, central banks became more reluctant to increase the discount rate (including the United States) while essentially nineteen of twenty countries implemented reductions in the discount rate. There is some evidence of asymmetries in discount rate changes and this feature of interest rate behavior is explored in the more formal empirical analysis below. Finally, if we consider changes in the discount rate that range anywhere between a reduction to an increase of half of a percent we find that, in a slight majority of countries, this fraction has risen over time. In several

---

[52] As explained in Chapter 2, the technique used to construct trend output is sensitive to the end points of the sample. Experimentation with separate filtering of output for the BW and PBW samples yielded different results of course. However, for the sake of comparability, the BW and PBW calculations are based on the filter applied to the full sample.

[53] Note that these are not the same interest rates as are used in the empirical analysis conducted later in the chapter. See Chapter 2 for the list of interest rates used to estimate central bank reaction functions discussed earlier. For the purposes of Table 4.3 the IMF's definition of the discount rate is used.

[54] An important difficulty in interpreting the data is that, with the possible exception of the United States and Germany, institutional factors have led to changes in the mechanism by which the central bank changes the discount rate. In some countries official discount rates as such have been abandoned. As a result, whereas central banks typically changed the discount rate arbitrarily by a fixed amount in the 1960s, for example, it is more likely that by the 1990s the discount rate has a floating element to it (within a range under the central bank's control). Consequently, institutional reasons alone would explain some of the reduction in the fraction of time the discount rate is left unchanged.

Table 4.3. Caution in Interest Rate Movements

	No Change		0 < Change ≤ .5		−.5 < Change < 0		Total		Number of Runs[3] (% of Full Sample)	
Country[2]	Full Sample	1990s	Full Sample	1990s	Full Sample	1990s	Full Sample	1990s	Increase	Decrease
Australia	22.43	50.00	16.82	0.00	17.76	7.70	57.01	51.70	24	19
Austria	73.55	58.33	5.81	11.11	10.97	25.00	90.33	94.40	22	23
Belgium	45.75	52.94	10.46	14.70	16.99	23.53	73.20	91.17	25	21
Canada	22.64	10.00	16.35	10.00	16.35	20.00	55.34	40.00	8	25
Denmark	64.78	45.00	4.41	17.50	9.44	15.00	78.63	77.50	14	35
Finland	81.94	69.44	0.00	0.00	6.47	22.22	88.41	91.66	0	21
France	81.20	NA	1.70	NA	6.84	NA	89.74	NA	0	20
Germany	63.87	61.11	5.81	8.34	10.97	22.45	80.65	91.90	11	32
Ireland	28.10	44.12	11.11	8.82	22.22	32.35	61.43	85.29	24	23
Italy	66.45	41.67	3.23	5.56	7.74	16.67	77.42	63.90	0	12
Japan	66.04	75.00	13.21	0.00	1.89	7.50	81.14	82.50	0	32
Netherlands	53.55	44.44	12.27	19.44	12.26	25.00	78.08	88.88	26	32
New Zealand	54.09	5.00	5.66	15.00	9.43	30.00	69.18	50.00	11	20
Norway	69.18	52.50	3.77	7.50	8.81	17.50	81.76	77.50	0	29
Portugal	65.81	16.67	3.23	2.78	8.39	25.02	77.43	44.47	0	35
Spain	42.58	13.89	7.74	11.12	14.19	38.90	64.51	63.91	25	34
Sweden	56.60	35.00	6.29	10.00	12.58	15.00	75.47	60.00	10	25
Switzerland	74.21	72.50	3.14	0.00	12.58	17.50	89.93	90.00	40	24
United Kingdom	32.70	35.00	9.43	25.00	12.59	12.50	54.72	72.50	20	31
United States	60.38	65.00	14.46	12.50	12.57	17.50	87.41	95.00	22	21

Percent[1]

[1] The figures show the percent of the sample with changes in the official discount rate in the ranges shown in the column headings.

[2] Samples are as follows: Australia (69:4–96:2), Austria (60:2–98:4), Belgium (60:2–99:4), Canada (60:2–99:4), Denmark (60:2–99:4), Finland (60:2–98:4), France (60:2–89:1), Germany (60:2–98:4), Ireland (60:2–98:4), Italy (60:2–98:4), Japan (60:2–99:4), Netherlands (60:2–98:4), New Zealand (60:2–99:4), Portugal (60:2–98:4), Spain (60:2–98:4), Sweden (60:2–99:4), Switzerland (60:2–99:4), United Kingdom (60:2–99:4), United States (60:2–99:4). For the United Kingdom the bank rate is replaced by the minimum lending rate (1981:3–1995:4) and then the repo rate (1996:1–1999:4). See http://www.bankofengland.co.uk/mfsd/index.htm. For the Netherlands, the fixed advance rate is used for the period 1994:1–1998:4. See http://www.statistics.dnb.nl/indexuk.html.

[3] The figures show the percent of increases or decreases in the discount rate within the [−0.5, +0.5] interval that occurred in consecutive quarters in a given year. If consecutive changes in discount rates occurred on the last quarter of one year and the first quarter of the following these instances were also counted.

countries large changes in the discount rate are a rare event. Although we have discussed the role and motivation for interest rate smoothing we have not specifically made the distinction, except empirically, between successively small changes in interest rates versus large one-time interest rate changes made more infrequently. The results in Table 4.3 suggest that there may be costs and benefits in implementing one type of interest rate change versus the other and such decisions may be influenced by whether the central bank in question has an explicit and credible inflation target (or possibly an implicit target but one that is credible) or a vaguely stated inflation objective not backed by a reputation for delivering good inflation outcomes. We do not pursue the matter further empirically (see, however, Siklos 2002b). Some recent theoretical work has made some progress on these questions (see, for example, Eijffinger, Schalling, and Verhagen 1999).

Reaction Functions for Individual Countries

Table 4.4 presents selected estimates of reaction function Equation 4.11. As is clear from the earlier discussion in this chapter, a large number of potential reaction function estimates were considered. The estimates chosen for discussion reflect a selection based on seeking estimates that are both well behaved in a statistical sense as well as ones that yield coefficient estimates consistent with theoretical predictions. Results are clearly sensitive, in particular, to how proxies for central bank expectations of inflation and unemployment are formed but not overly so.[55] Therefore, while the representativeness of the results is, to an extent, dependent on the observer's judgment, the choices reflect some remarkable *cross-country* patterns that cannot be summarily dismissed since the selection was made on a country-by-country basis and not by examining consistency across countries.

In fifteen of twenty countries, central banks appear to respond to forecasts made a year ahead rather than to one-step-ahead forecasts. In a sense this result is not surprising in light of the earlier discussion of cautious policy making by central bankers for, as illustrated in Figure 4.1 in the case of Germany, four-step-ahead forecasts are not only more accurate but are much smoother than the one-step-ahead forecast.

---

[55] The volume of results is far too large to present in its entirety here. In part for reasons discussed in Chapter 2 and in the description of the results in Table 4.2 results using the output gap are not shown. See, however, Siklos (2001).

Table 4.4. Baseline Reaction Function Estimates[1] Dependent Variable: ΔI_t

Country	Cumulative Impact[2]		Political Impact[3]	Institutional Impact[4]	Foreign Impact[5]	Policy Persistence/Caution[6]	R^2
	Inflation	Unemployment					
Australia[7]	0.198 (4.79)	-.054 (.09)	-0.201 (.260)	4.15 (2.25)⊥	0.269 (.113)@	-0.014 (2.25)	.18
Austria	0.143 (.079)⊥	-0.551 (.304)⊥	-0.327 (.164)@	32.05 (12.15)*	0.129 (.041)*	-0.015 (.111)	.35
Belgium	0.062 (5.53)@	-.009 (.037)	-0.074 (.131)	-0.525 (1.83)	0.108 (.034)*	1.53 (.438)*	.23
Canada	0.038 (.590)	-0.192 (6.752)*	0.224 (.164)⊥	1.06 (2.80)	0.845 (.097)*	-0.199 (.100)@	.78
Denmark	0.115 (.041)*	0.035 (.135)	-0.043 (.302)	-1.57 (2.80)	0.166 (0.54)*	-0.067 (.153)	.15
Finland	0.687 (12.59)*	0.514 (2.37)	2.91 (2.60)⊥	2.74 (1.66)⊥	0.025 (.264)	-0.219 (.136)	.52
France	0.095 (3.07)⊥	0.005 (.001)	-0.128 (.541)	-0.91 (.80)	0.215 (.075)*	0.102 (.183)	.39
Germany	0.193 (.116)⊥	-0.302 (28.29)*	0.077 (.295)	0.632 (1.790)	0.160 (.066)*	0.065 (.100)	.37
Ireland	-0.018 (0.01)	0.016 (0.21)	-0.034 (.124)	2.218 (.86)*	-0.003 (.039)	0.280 (.408)	.49
Italy	0.024 (.354)	-0.43 (3.04)⊥	-0.718 (.671)	1.50 (1.11)⊥	0.378 (.109)*	0.245 (.105)@	.38
Japan	0.108 (30.30)*	-0.615 (4.24)@	0.283 (.248)⊥	-0.431 (.56)	-0.079 (.07)	1.573 (.51)*	.48
Netherlands	0.078 (.70)	0.049 (.09)	-0.715 (.346)@	0.494 (7.69)	0.303 (.124)*	0.043 (.088)	.35
New Zealand	0.133 (.058)@	-0.055 (0.33)	0.106 (.148)	-0.97 (.81)⊥	-0.03 (.027)	-0.03 (0.09)	.65
Norway	-0.011 (2.21)	-0.654 (3.76)@	0.139 (.073)@	0.468 (0.420)⊥	-.0002 (.015)	-0.119 (.093)	.23
Portugal	-0.05 (1.30)	0.012 (.70)	0.200 (.168)⊥	n/a	0.331 (.160)@	-0.243 (.195)	.53
Spain	0.113 (.047)@	0.092 (43.96)*	-0.177 (.072)*	0.244 (.176)⊥	0.000 (.027)	0.532 (.094)	.46
Sweden	0.023 (2.87)⊥	-0.211 (1.01)	-0.172 (.102)⊥	0.718 (.398)⊥	-0.002 (.014)	0.267 (.157)⊥	.21
Switzerland	0.066 (2.70)⊥	-0.024 (.030)	-0.242 (.114)@	-1.215 (.767)⊥	-0.046 (.055)	0.068 (.090)	.15
United Kingdom	0.191 (6.55)*	-0.610 (2.04)	-0.019 (.335)	-1.726 (1.211)⊥	0.072 (.119)	0.022 (.090)	.19
United States	0.19 (3.60)@	-0.61 (6.36)*	-0.259 (.176)⊥	5.534 (3.42)⊥	n/a	0.129 (.089)	.28

[1] All estimates are based on (4.10) to generate forecasts for inflation and unemployment. The reaction function is (4.11). Estimates of the constant not shown.

[2] Three lags for $\phi_t = [\phi_\pi, \phi_U]$ were estimated and the sum of the coefficients are shown. In parentheses, the χ^2 test statistic for the null hypothesis that the sum of coefficients is different from zero is given.

[3] Political impact is a dummy variable capturing electoral or partisan influences. The table below provides the details for each country.

Country	Political Variable	Country	Political Variable	Country	Political Variable	Country	Political Variable
Australia	EPRIOR	Austria	DRPT2	Belgium	DRPT2	Canada	DRPT2
Denmark	DRPT2	Finland	EPRIOR*	France	DRPT2	Germany	DRPT2
Ireland	DRPT2	Italy	DRPT2	Japan	EPRIOR	Netherlands	EPRIOR
New Zealand	DRPT2	Norway	DRPT2	Portugal	EPRIOR	Spain	DRPT2
Sweden	DRPT2	Switzerland	ETMP	United Kingdom	EPRIOR	United States	ETMP

[4] Cukierman's (1992) measure of central bank independence until 1989. For the 1990s, as described in Chapter 2.

[5] The contemporaneous change in the U.S. Fed funds rate.

[6] One lag in the dependent variable.

[7] The type of VAR generated forecast used differs by country. The table below provides the details while the text describes the type of forecasts.

Country	Type of Forecast	Country	Type of Forecast	Country	Type of Forecast	Country	Type of Forecast
Australia	1 step (BW, PBW)	Austria	4 step (Full)	Belgium	4 step (Full)	Canada	4 step (Full)
Denmark	4 step (Full)	Finland	1 step (BW, PBW)	France	4 step (Full)	Germany	4 step (Full)
Ireland	4 step (BW, PBW)	Italy	4 step (Full)	Japan	1 step (Full)	Netherlands	1 step (Full)
New Zealand	4 step (BW, PBW)	Norway	4 step (BW, PBW)	Portugal	4 step (BW, PBW)	Spain	4 step (BW, PBW)
Sweden	4 step (BW, PBW)	Switzerland	4 step (Full)	United Kingdom	1 step (BW, PBW)	United States	1 step (BW, PBW)

* signifies statistically significant at 1%; @ 5%; ⊥ 10% level of significance.

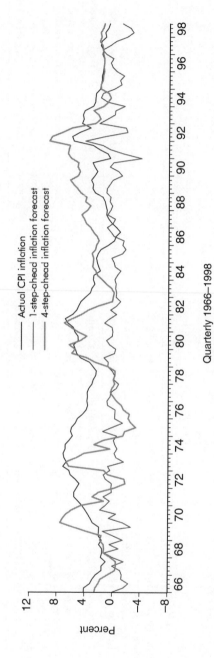

Figure 4.1 Varieties of Inflation Forecasts: Germany

Consequently, less frequently revised forecasts capture the smoothness of interest rates that characterizes central bank actions. Also, in half of the countries, the model whose structure is constant throughout the entire sample (see Table 4.1) was chosen while, for the remaining ten countries, separate forecasting models were estimated for the BW and PBW samples. It is instructive that the latter group of countries include Australia, Finland, Ireland, New Zealand, Spain, Sweden, the United Kingdom, and the United States, all of whom underwent from an historical perspective, at least significant changes in policy regimes over the sample considered. Arguably, other countries experienced similar changes but these may have manifested themselves in ways not captured by the forecasting models considered. Moreover, in thirteen of twenty countries central banks react positively to accumulated shocks in inflation while only eight central banks react at all, and negatively as expected, to unemployment shocks.[56]

Beyond these results there are three other notable features in the results that are essentially ignored in much of the literature on central banking. First, in a majority of countries (eleven of twenty) a proxy for electoral or partisan effects on interest rates policies is significant. In some instances (that is, Finland, Japan, Netherlands, and Portugal) the electoral variable that is active prior to an election is significant while, in the case of Switzerland and the United States, interest rate changes appear to be deferred until after the election. Indeed, for the latter two countries, election-oriented monetary policy is temporary and the negative sign suggests some dependence for both central banks considered traditionally to be among the most autonomous. For the countries with significant prior election effects, only the Netherlands' central bank shows signs of dependence. The remaining central banks in this list, including the Bank of Japan, show signs of independence. In the remaining countries where political effects are relevant (that is, Austria, Canada, Norway, Spain, and Sweden) the impact is of the partisan variety. Nevertheless, except for Canada, "right-wing" governments place pressure on central banks to reduce interest rates. Interestingly, all but Canada are European countries where the left-right distinction is not as clear cut as in, say, the North American context. It is conceivable that right-wing governments deliver lower interest rates via expectations of lower inflation while, in Canada, right-wing governments raise interest

---

[56] In general, the flavor of the results is not much different if we replace unemployment rate shocks with output gap shocks.

rates as a means of fighting against higher inflation rates inherited from left-wing governments. It should also be noted that, for countries where none of the political variables were found to be statistically significant, including Australia, New Zealand, Germany, and the United Kingdom, these central banks show signs of political independence.

There is, however, another sense in which central banks can signal their autonomy, namely via the degree of institutional independence. The results in Table 4.4 show that central bank autonomy has a significant impact in eleven of twenty countries considered. In most of these cases, autonomy has permitted the relevant country's central banks to raise interest rates.[57] This is the case for Australia, Austria, Finland, Ireland, Italy, Norway, Sweden, and the United States. It is noteworthy that several of these countries gained more independence beginning in the 1980s and 1990s where institutional independence was used as one device to reduce inflation rates from historically high levels. For the remaining countries with a statistically significant institutional impact on interest rate determination the relevant coefficient is negative. It is noticeable that New Zealand and the United Kingdom are included in this list, for greater autonomy was granted at the same time as disinflation was underway (see Chapter 2) suggesting that autonomy permits lower interest rates via the credibility route. For other central banks, independence can serve as a device to permit necessary increases in interest rates as a counterpoint perhaps to political pressure (for example, as in the U.S. case). A more focused measure of the manner in which institutional features of government-central bank may have influenced interest rate changes is now considered.

The reaction function estimates also reveal that interest rates set abroad, most notably in the United States, have a significant impact on interest rate changes in half of the countries considered. All, with the exception of Germany, are of the small open variety and confirm the findings of Johnson and Siklos (1996) and, indirectly, support the relative importance of exchange rate regime considerations (also see the following). Indeed, as a result of the additional conditioning factors included in the reaction functions, there is considerably less persistence in inter-

---

[57] There is a significant difficulty with the interpretation of the size of the institutional impact coefficient for it is unclear what, say, a 0.10 increase in the index of central bank independence – recall that the index ranges from 0 to 1 – means as far as the value of the change in the degree of autonomy enjoyed by a central bank.

est rate changes than might be expected. Statistically significant lagged interest rate changes are significant in only five countries.[58]

Figure 4.2 displays the interest rate paths for each individual country based on the model forecast together with the actual interest rate. There are at least three notable features in cross-country patterns. First, forecasts appear more volatile than the actual interest rates until at least the 1990s. To the extent that policy settings are influenced by such forecasts, this suggests that central bankers are indeed more cautious than would be predicted from model estimates. Second, to the extent that the interest rate paths reveal the degree to which central banks follow rules like behavior, the plots indicate that they were somewhat less likely to do so in the 1970s and the 1980s than in the most recent decade. Finally, the plots clearly reveal diversity in the experiences faced by the individual central banks. Yet, as will become more apparent as follows, the sources of pressure to respond to economic shocks that afflict individual economies are roughly similar. Diversity arises in part because of institutional and political constraints on central bank behavior. Whether the interest rate behavior displayed in Figure 4.2 suggests that different policy advice might have been appropriate in the past is unclear for at least two reasons. The estimated reaction functions may or may not be optimal and, in any event, they have not been subjected to a robustness test of the kind advocated by McCallum (1988). That is, it is not clear whether the same set of interest rate paths would have been generated if different paradigms had been considered. Nevertheless, the results do reveal that, in a forecasting sense, there has been some evolution over time in how interest rates might have been set.

Extensions to Basic Reaction Function Estimates

Several features of interest rate and central bank behavior more generally warrant, however, alternative specifications of reaction function (Equation 4.11). Tables 4.5 to 4.9 consider some of these extensions. Table 4.5 considers the role of asymmetries in interest rate changes as well as fiscal policy effects on interest rate determination.[59] In roughly

[58] Persistence is positive for all the relevant cases, except Canada, suggesting that an increase is followed by further increases. In Canada's case, an increase is partially reversed in the next quarter.

[59] To economize on space, readers are asked to consult the notes to these tables that indicate how the results in Table 4.4 are affected by changes to the baseline reaction function specification.

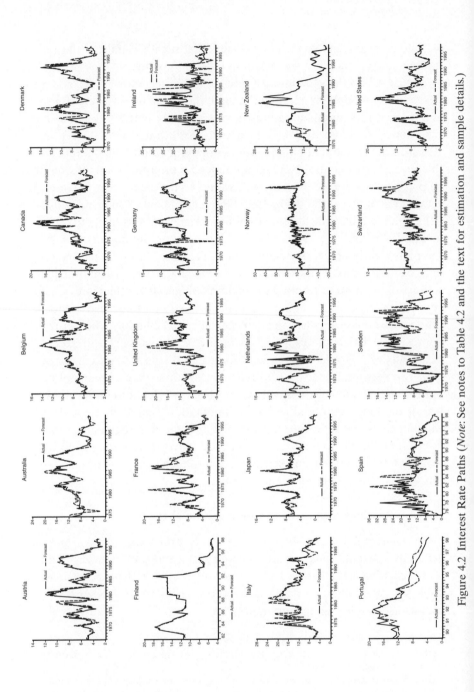

Figure 4.2 Interest Rate Paths (*Note*: See notes to Table 4.2 and the text for estimation and sample details.)

Table 4.5. Extensions to the Baseline Reaction Function Estimates[1]

Country	Asymmetric Interest Rate Changes[2]		Fiscal Pressures Index[3,4]
	Positive	Negative	
Australia	−0.038 (.216)	0.0001 (.184)	0.55 (.30)⊥
Austria	−0.079 (.238)	−0.008 (.181)	0.10 (.066)[5]
Belgium	−0.181 (.153)	0.464 (.148)*	−0.146 (.172)
Canada	−0.172 (.087)*	−0.226 (.192)	1.95 (.632)*
Denmark	0.189 (.173)	−0.438 (.331)	0.131 (.122)
Finland	−0.920 (.200)*	0.225 (.156)	0.90 (.313)*
France	−0.266 (.270)	0.302 (.201)	1.08 (.255)*
			[*LVAU*: −2.54 (.99)*]
Germany	0.306 (.178)⊥	−0.317 (.281)	0.68 (.258)*
Ireland	−0.844 (.131)*	0.377 (.126)*	2.077 (.367)*
Italy	0.049 (.154)	0.456 (.181)*	0.452 (.309)[6]
			[*LVAU*: .823 (6.333)]
Japan	0.135 (.170)	0.264 (.107)*	−0.083 (.073)
Netherlands	−0.200 (.119)⊥	0.482 (.171)*	1.091 (.297)*
			[*LVAU*: 16.359 (7.353)@]
New Zealand	−0.064 (.147)	−0.122 (.150)	0.565 (.499)
Norway	−0.173 (.124)	−0.155 (.120)	0.128 (.051)*
Portugal	−0.429 (.208)@	−0.348 (.198)⊥	−0.310 (.152)@
Spain	0.545 (.092)*	0.507 (.094)*	0.440 (.124)*
Sweden	0.276 (.163)⊥	0.258 (.156)⊥	0.098 (.093)@
			[*LVAU*: 0.470 (.387)]
Switzerland	−0.239 (.161)	0.414 (.175)@	0.312 (.161)@
			[φ_π = 0.005 (.007)]
United Kingdom	0.125 (.133)	−0.327 (.219)	1.288 (.55)@
			[*LVAU*: .156 (1.425)]
United States	0.322 (.141)@	−0.074 (.146)	0.670 (.287)@
			[*ETMP*: −.192 (.176)]

[1] See notes to Table 4.4. Samples differ owing to fewer observations for fiscal pressure index series. Samples are as follows:

Country	Sample	Country	Sample
Australia	75.2–99.1	Austria	70.2–97.2
Belgium	78.2–98.4	Canada	80.1–95.3
Denmark	71.2–98.4	Finland	82.4–98.4
France	70.1–98.4	Germany	70.1–98.4
Ireland	71.1–98.4	Italy	72.2–98.4
Japan	70.1–98.4	Netherlands	77.1–98.4
New Zealand	84.3–99.4	Norway	67.2–98.4
Portugal	91.1–98.4	Spain	78.2–98.3
Sweden	70.2–98.4	Switzerland	75.4–98.4
United Kingdom	70.1–98.1	United States	68.1–98.4

[2] When $\Delta R_t > 0$ the change is recorded as being positive; a negative value is recorded when $\Delta R_t < 0$.

[3] This is the index introduced in Chapter 2 and discussed more fully in Chapter 5 (see especially Equation 5.2). The index assumes that there are three sources of pressure on fiscal policy. They are recessions, the deficit/surplus to GDP ratio, and the long-short interest rate differential.

[4] Estimates presented in Table 4.4 are unaffected unless otherwise indicated in the column.

[5] Significant at 14% level.

[6] Significant at 15% level.

half the countries, interest rate increases are either reversed or lead to additional interest rate increases. Notably, the Bundesbank and the U.S. Federal Reserve show evidence of gradual interest rate increases.

In contrast, in almost every case where the coefficient on negative interest rate changes is significant, a decrease is followed by additional future decreases. Hence, it appears that, in almost half of the cases, central banks reduce interest rates gradually but may not increase them in the same fashion.

The second modification to the basic reaction function considers adding the fiscal pressure index first mentioned in Chapter 2 (also see Chapter 5). In sixteen of twenty countries sampled a rise in fiscal pressure, implying an increase in the deficit or in an expectation of inflation via rising government borrowing, signals higher interest rates. Far from indicative of "passive" monetary policy, the results reveal the importance of a connection between fiscal and monetary policies noted earlier in the study. The table also reveals that, in several cases, the addition of the fiscal proxy acts as a substitute for institutional independence (as in Italy, Sweden, and Switzerland), political independence (as in the United States), or economic independence (as in Switzerland).[60] In these instances, the fiscal measure renders the relevant coefficients insignificant. In two cases (France and Netherlands) the fiscal variable complements institutional independence. It should be noted that the difficulties discussed in Chapter 2 in measuring fiscal effects on monetary policy means that one ought to be careful in interpreting the results. Nevertheless, the evidence presented is highly instructive about the variety of channels through which pressures on monetary policy can manifest themselves.

Table 4.6 considers in greater detail the potential for partisan effects in monetary policy by separately estimating reaction functions for "right-" wing and "left-" wing regimes. The results presented in the table focus exclusively on instances where the partisan distinctions are empirically meaningful. As shown in Table 4.6, thirteen of twenty countries display significant partisan differences. Moreover, in six of the countries (Australia, Germany, New Zealand, Spain, the United Kingdom, and the United States) right-wing governments indeed appear to place pressure on central banks to raise interest rates while placing no weight on the unemployment objective (with the exception of Spain). The situation is a little more clouded in the case of left-wing governments. While several

---

[60] For Italy at least, this corroborates the views of Fratianni and Spinelli (2001) on the influence of fiscal policy on central bank behavior.

Table 4.6. Reaction to Inflation and Unemployment Shocks under Separate Partisan Regimes: Selected Estimates[1]

Country	"Right" Wing		"Left" Wing	
	Inflation	Unemployment	Inflation	Unemployment
Australia	0.150	0	—	—
Austria	—	—	0	–0.652
Belgium	—	—	0	–0.184
Canada	—	—	0.150	0
Denmark	—	—	0	–0.290
Finland	—	—	0.370	0
Germany	0.190	0	–0.058	0
Ireland	—	—	0	–1.20
New Zealand	0.200	0	—	—
Norway	—	—	0	–0.461
Spain	0.610	–3.90	–0.54	0
United Kingdom	0.350	0	—	—
United States	0.204	0	0.243	–0.781

[1] See Table 4.4 for details of reaction function estimates. Reaction function (4.11) was separately estimated for periods where only "right-" wing or "left-" wing governments were in power. Sum of coefficients on inflation and unemployment show that both were statistically significant, at least the 10% level of significance or differ from the results presented in Table 4.4. When no results are shown the conclusions in Table 4.4 are unaffected.

such governments place more pressure on central banks to emphasize the unemployment objective (as in Austria, Belgium, Denmark, Ireland, New Zealand, Norway, Spain, and the United States) not all central banks in such an environment ignore inflation entirely (Canada and the United States).

Finally, Table 4.7 considers the potential role of interest rate volatility in reaction function estimates. For almost half of the countries considered, greater volatility tempers interest rate changes in all countries where the variance term is statistically significant, as predicted. There is some evidence then that interest volatility indeed separately enters many central banks' reaction functions. Moreover, although the proxy is conditional on the assumed model, the results do suggest that many central banks do react differently to periods of turbulence versus periods of calm. Whether the chosen approach best reveals the nature of central bank concerns over interest rate volatility remains, however, to be seen. Nevertheless, explicit consideration of the role of interest rate volatility

Table 4.7. Extension to the Baseline Reaction Function Estimates: The Impact of Interest Rate Volatility[1]

Australia	−0.756 (.189)*
Austria	0.229 (.348)
Belgium	−0.711 (.267)
Canada	0.267 (.168)
Denmark	−1.094 (.166)*
Finland	−6.798 (11.090)
France	−0.267 (.176)
Germany	.170 (.187)
Ireland	−3.623 (.019)*
Italy	−4.423 (4.651)
Japan	−2.145 (.611)*
Netherlands	−.131 (.163)
New Zealand	−0.756 (.113)
Norway	−0.459 (.574)
Portugal	−3.419 (22.01)
Spain	6.693 (8.705)
Sweden	−0.337 (.074)*
Switzerland	−0.526 (.264)@
United Kingdom	−0.388 (.206)⊥
United States	0.167 (.163)

[1] See Table 4.4 for details about the reaction function estimation approach. The coefficient estimate shown is for Φ_{σ^2} from (4.11) or ζ_1 in (4.12), that is, the estimate of the ARCH-M coefficient. Bollerslev-Wooldridge robust standard errors are shown in parenthesis.

is not typically a feature of existing reaction function estimates found in the literature.

A further extension of the reaction function estimates consists in asking how private sector forecasts of inflation and unemployment (or the output gap) influence the results.[61] Table 4.8 considers whether the set of available inflation forecasts is unbiased, as well as whether private forecasts dominate the VAR-based forecasts discussed earlier, or vice-versa, in a statistical sense (also see Chapter 7).[62] Results are clearly mixed in that while there is considerable evidence that many forecasts

[61] The term *private sector* is meant to convey the notion of forecasts other than by the central bank. While *The Economist* forecasts are prepared by the private sector, OECD forecasts would be more accurately referred to as forecasts by a government agency. In a couple of cases (not shown) we also used central bank forecasts (Finland and New Zealand).

[62] The notes to Table 4.9 provide additional details.

Table 4.8. Testing Forecast Dominance and Encompassing[1]

		Unbiasedness		Dominance — Private[2]		Dominance — VAR[3]		Forecast Combination	
Country	Type of Forecast[4]	(1)	(2)	(1)	(2)	(1)	(2)	(1)	(2)
Australia	1	1.65 (.20)		1.91 (.38)		35.26 (.00)		125.38 (.00)	
	4	0.86 (.35)		0.39 (.82)		47.76 (.00)		118.78 (.00)	
	1 Full	0.12 (.73)		10.86 (.004)		35.20 (.00)		164.25 (.00)	
	4 Full	10.42 (.001)		22.66 (.00)		341.37 (.00)		215.52 (.00)	
Belgium	1	1.61 (.20)		4.47 (.11)		62.15 (.00)		133.39 (.00)	
	4	4.71 (.03)		1.95 (.38)		947.52 (.00)		121.72 (.00)	
	1 Full	5.35 (.02)		2.57 (.28)		92.29 (.00)		124.56 (.00)	
	4 Full	4.36 (.04)		13.81 (.001)		98.96 (.00)		176.66 (.00)	
Canada	1	1.36 (.24)	2.67 (.10)	0.68 (.71)	231.69 (.00)	88.98 (.00)	104.91 (.00)	246.51 (.00)	1279.55 (.00)
	4	0.36 (.55)	49.54 (.00)	0.65 (.72)	57.17 (.00)	375.38 (.00)	468.02 (.00)	246.26 (.00)	604.94 (.00)
	1 Full	2.01 (.16)	7.80 (.01)	8.16 (.02)	515.58 (.00)	38.52 (.00)	62.80 (.00)	305.55 (.00)	2376.94 (.00)
	4 Full	0.36 (.55)	2.03 (.15)	5.41 (.07)	139.15 (.00)	359.39 (.00)	226.99 (.00)	283.87 (.00)	933.86 (.00)
Finland	1	10.38 (.001)		37.95 (.00)		61.04 (.00)		5.55 (.06)	
	4	7.71 (.01)		34.57 (.00)		54.40 (.00)		6.27 (.04)	
	1 Full	11.01 (.00)		39.52 (.00)		36.95 (.00)		4.04 (.013)	
	4 Full	17.09 (.00)		42.93 (.00)		54.35 (.00)		7.75 (.02)	
France	1	2.83 (.09)	0.02 (.89)	7.00 (.03)	127.78 (.00)	57.48 (.00)	169.20 (.00)	232.32 (.00)	2283.30 (.00)
	4	6.21 (.01)	11.32 (.00)	9.09 (.01)	15.12 (.00)	2420.83 (.00)	693.08 (.00)	246.83 (.00)	1192.04 (.00)
	1 Full	6.66 (.01)	0.10 (.75)	16.79 (.00)	127.51 (.00)	34.15 (.00)	138.551 (.00)	300.16 (.00)	2280.70 (.00)
	4 Full	2.07 (.15)	0.08 (.78)	2.00 (.37)	27.21 (.00)	54.39 (.00)	196.55 (.00)	197.69 (.00)	1304.89 (.00)

Table 4.8 (*continued*)

Country	Type of Forecast[4]	Unbiasedness (1)	Unbiasedness (2)	Private[2] (1)	Private[2] (2)	VAR[3] (1)	VAR[3] (2)	Forecast Combination (1)	Forecast Combination (2)
Germany	1	1.10 (.29)	0.00 (.99)	0.61 (.74)	197.11 (.00)	62.46 (.00)	56.34 (.00)	41.22 (.00)	395.50 (.00)
	4	1.87 (.17)	19.59 (.00)	6.98 (.03)	104.16 (.00)	227.17 (.00)	561.21 (.00)	55.78 (.00)	246.18 (.00)
	1 Full	1.13 (.29)	0.06 (.80)	2.25 (.33)	277.03 (.00)	29.05 (.00)	56.14 (.00)	50.63 (.00)	534.67 (.00)
	4 Full	0.59 (.44)	0.73 (.39)	1.09 (.58)	123.61 (.00)	72.24 (.00)	104.76 (.00)	47.84 (.00)	281.28 (.00)
Italy	1	0.12 (.72)	0.06 (.81)	1.93 (.38)	50.01 (.00)	95.77 (.00)	164.10 (.00)	502.25 (.00)	1799.35 (.00)
	4	0.41 (.52)	8.96 (.002)	5.37 (.07)	39.75 (.00)	903.86 (.00)	868.05 (.00)	557.94 (.00)	1717.63 (.00)
	1 Full	0.00 (.99)	0.06 (.81)	2.70 (.26)	56.87 (.00)	59.01 (.00)	139.08 (.00)	514.74 (.00)	1881.15 (.00)
	4 Full	4.40 (.04)	3.35 (.07)	12.29 (.002)	39.58 (.00)	323.25 (.00)	613.25 (.00)	670.09 (.00)	1715.47 (.00)
Japan	1	0.15 (.70)	5.03 (.02)	1.78 (.41)	68.41 (.00)	115.54 (.00)	306.27 (.00)	141.99 (.00)	1193.40 (.00)
	4	0.06 (.81)	30.95 (.00)	5.37 (.07)	109.02 (.00)	499.19 (.00)	977.72 (.00)	200.72 (.00)	1672.13 (.00)
	1 Full	0.06 (.81)	3.72 (.05)	0.07 (.97)	75.24 (.00)	102.66 (.00)	220.47 (.00)	132.96 (.00)	1238.91 (.00)
	4 Full	0.33 (.56)	0.10 (.75)	4.72 (.09)	87.25 (.00)	165.08 (.00)	788.14 (.00)	157.50 (.00)	1431.40 (.00)
Netherlands	1	0.06 (.81)		6.21 (.04)		49.70 (.00)		58.21 (.00)	
	4	5.38 (.02)		7.18 (.03)		1590.90 (.00)		55.65 (.00)	
	1 Full	1.49 (.22)		2.82 (.24)		36.96 (.00)		50.10 (.00)	
	4 Full	3.72 (.05)		6.91 (.03)		125.73 (.00)		59.09 (.00)	
New Zealand	1	0.58 (.45)	0.09 (.76)	6.70 (.04)	5.43 (.07)	131.12 (.00)	60.61 (.00)	141.66 (.00)	24.33 (.00)
	4	0.06 (.81)	0.93 (.34)	0.59 (.74)	4.11 (.13)	132.88 (.00)	33.76 (.00)	115.61 (.00)	22.30 (.00)
	1 Full	0.70 (.40)	0.14 (.71)	37.10 (.00)	31.32 (.00)	61.94 (.00)	21.47 (.00)	251.43 (.00)	64.44 (.00)
	4 Full	0.17 (.68)	0.50 (.48)	1.30 (.52)	1.95 (.08)	256.32 (.00)	38.74 (.00)	122.17 (.00)	18.95 (.00)
Spain	1	1.86 (.17)		9.97 (.01)		141.11 (.00)		539.01 (.00)	
	4	4.19 (.04)		32.83 (.00)		1968.87 (.00)		857.17 (.00)	

Dominance

Country	Forecast							
	1 Full	0.15 (.70)		0.73 (.70)		148.58 (.00)		410.45 (.00)
	4 Full	.001 (.98)		0.96 (.62)		90.36 (.00)		413.70 (.00)
Sweden	1	16.92 (.00)		4.45 (.11)		605.79 (.00)		587.04 (.00)
	4	6.73 (.01)		4.76 (.09)		201.97 (.00)		592.43 (.00)
	1 Full	17.09 (.00)		4.43 (.11)		969.57 (.00)		586.70 (.00)
	4 Full	15.25 (.00)		5.81 (.05)		468.94 (.00)		610.85 (.00)
Switzerland	1	4.34 (.04)		10.52 (.01)		91.99 (.00)		491.46 (.00)
	4	5.85 (.02)		9.98 (.01)		119.33 (.00)		454.91 (.00)
	1 Full	10.71 (.001)		14.63 (.00)		119.41 (.00)		509.92 (.00)
	4 Full	9.42 (.002)		9.32 (.01)		154.11 (.00)		447.00 (.00)
United Kingdom	1	0.07 (.79)	5.22 (.02)	19.93 (.00)	114.80 (.00)	121.50 (.00)	298.13 (.00)	180.04 (.00)
	4	0.46 (.50)	38.04 (.00)	0.23 (.89)	68.30 (.00)	103.70 (.00)	1981.09 (.00)	92.47 (.00)
	1 Full	1.60 (.21)	8.28 (.00)	26.65 (.00)	134.30 (.00)	38.10 (.00)	299.20 (.00)	208.75 (.00)
	4 Full	1.66 (.20)	1.82 (.18)	4.06 (.13)	43.99 (.00)	259.67 (.00)	566.94 (.00)	112.22 (.00)
United States	1	6.73 (.01)	0.03 (.87)	3.79 (.15)	92.31 (.00)	245.20 (.00)	198.62 (.00)	236.78 (.00)
	4	4.45 (.03)	0.47 (.49)	2.49 (.29)	12.71 (.00)	524.59 (.00)	816.94 (.00)	226.76 (.00)
	1 Full	3.59 (.06)	0.39 (.53)	3.85 (.15)	122.37 (.00)	190.16 (.00)	198.02 (.00)	237.22 (.00)
	4 Full	4.17 (.04)	1.46 (.23)	7.48 (.02)	14.37 (.00)	196.39 (.00)	425.17 (.00)	265.19 (.00)

[1] The test results in the table are based on Chong and Hendry's (1986) encompassing test of the form $x_t = a_0 + a_1 x_{1t}^f + a_2 x_{2t}^f + u_t$, where x_t is the actual value of the series of interest (here inflation), and x_{1t}^f and x_{2t}^f are two competing forecasts. If the null hypothesis that $a_0 = 0$ cannot be rejected then the forecasts are said to be (mean) unbiased. If $a_1 = 1, a_2 = 0$, or $a_1 = 0, a_2 = 1$ then the nulls that x_{1t}^f encompasses x_{2t}^f and x_{1t}^f, respectively, cannot be rejected. If the null that $a_1 \neq 0, a_2 \neq 0$ cannot be rejected then some combination of forecasts is preferred. The encompassing tests are F-statistics with significance levels in parenthesis. For unbiased the t-statistics is given, again with significance level in parenthesis.

[2] "Private" forecast is from The Economist, as described in Chapter 2 in Column 1. In Column 2 forecasts from OECD are used (for the G7 countries only).

[3] VAR forecasts are as described in this chapter.

[4] Type of forecast is as described in the text.

are unbiased there is no obvious pattern to the results. In addition, while there is extensive evidence that VAR forecasts do not encompass private sector forecasts there is also similar evidence that, perhaps unsurprisingly, some (linear) combination of forecasts is ideal, at least in a statistical sense.[63] The difficulty, of course, is in how to best combine such forecasts. Further, it is doubtful that central banks use external forecasts exclusively in preference to internal assessments of the future course of the economy. Ideally, some measure of the impact of heterogeneous expectations on central bank decision making would be considered as a separate component of its reaction function. This extension is not feasible in the present context. Instead, as will be argued as follows, it is preferable to view Equation 4.11 with private sector forecasts substituting for model-based expectations, as an indicator of how outsiders view the process of interest rate change determination. If this interpretation is accepted, the results in Table 4.9 are indeed instructive. To conserve space we show estimates of Equation 4.11 using OECD forecasts for the G7 only.

For Italy, Japan, and the United Kingdom, private forecasts suggest a reduction in interest rates in the face of positive inflation shocks. For the remaining central banks there is no response to inflation shocks. The Bank of Canada is assumed to respond negatively to unemployment shocks as expected. However, the coefficients are much larger than those presented in Table 4.4. Moreover, there is no discernible impact from central bank autonomy to interest rate setting behavior while, with the exception of Italy, a looming election brings about a reduction in interest rates. The Canadian reaction to the election of a right-wing government is the same as that found in Table 4.4, but once again, the coefficient is twice as large suggesting that the Bank of Canada at least is susceptible to more political pressure if reactions are based on private forecasts of economic activity than model-based ones. The role of foreign interest rates and interest rate persistence are broadly consistent with model-based forecasts used in reaction function estimates.

Cross-Country Reaction Function Estimates

Attempting to evaluate the role of institutional factors in a reaction function raises a number of practical problems, as noted earlier. In

---

[63] Makridakis, Wheelwright, and Hyndman (1993) are proponents of forecast combination while Clemen (1989) argues that forecast combination reflects the capitulation of model-based forecasts to the process of seeking improvements in forecast performance. Also, see Croushore (1996) and Romer and Romer (2000).

Table 4.9. Baseline Reaction Function Estimates Using Alternative Forecasts: OECD Forecasts for the G7[1]

Country	Cumulative Impact		Political Impact[2]	Institutional Impact	Foreign Impact	Policy Persistence/Caution	R^2
	Inflation	Unemployment					
Canada	-0.063 (1.43)	-0.880 (4.44)@	0.425 (.197)@	3.3122 (3.003)	0.852 (.066)*	-0.192 (.058)*	.60
France	0.096 (.600)	-0.248 (1.028)	-3.808 (2.230)⊥	-0.7471 (.650)	0.254 (.084)*	0.129 (.084)	.18
Germany	0.024 (.175)	-0.213 (1.13)	-1.240 (.604)@	3.333 (3.066)	0.214 (0.067)*	0.162 (.081)@	.21
Italy	-0.179 (4.46)@	0.076 (.266)	1.635 (.798)@	0.383 (1.194)	0.306 (.086)*	0.275 (.083)*	.23
Japan	-0.158 (12.13)*	-0.672 (.164)	0.227 (.152)	-0.308 (.568)	-0.026 (.058)	0.301 (.074)*	.28
United Kingdom	-0.161 (2.84)*	-0.023 (.008)	0.117 (.295)	-1.333 (1.171)	0.086 (.110)	-.012 (.085)	.07
United States	0.094 (.829)	-1.864 (12.11)*	0.074 (.201)	3.104 (3.037)	n/a	0.138 (.084)⊥	.22

[1] Reaction function (4.11). Also see notes to Table 4.4.
[2] Political Impact Variables are as follows: Canada *DRPT2*; France *EPRIOR*; Germany *EPRIOR*; Italy *EPRIOR*; Japan *EPRIOR*; United Kingdom *EPRIOR*; United States *EPRIOR*.

particular, key indicators of central bank autonomy, or its principal components (see Chapters 2 and 7) change little over time and reflect primarily *cross-country* differences in central bank independence. Moreover, the estimates presented for individual countries reveal that there are important common features in central bank reactions to both economic shocks and the institutional and international economic environments. These considerations suggest that one ought to investigate reaction function in a panel setting.[64] Table 4.10 then investigates what can be learned by pooling data for all the central banks in the sample. A total of eight cases are shown and it is notable that, in every single case, the fixed effects model was rejected. Consequently, it was not necessary to estimate a separate intercept for each country.[65] Other than using the panel for all twenty countries in the study, the other cases seek to identify differences across country groupings and institutional arrangements. For example, Column 3 considers the countries that formed European Monetary Union (EMU) in 1999, while Columns 4 and 5 distinguish between countries that fixed their exchange rates or floated them for a considerable period of time since 1980 (also see Chapters 2 and 7 for exchange rate arrangement definitions). The final four columns consider potential differences between countries with a high degree of central bank autonomy versus countries that had little independence but gained considerable autonomy over the period in question. Finally, we consider the impact of perhaps the single most distinctive characteristic of central banking in the 1990s, namely the push for central bank accountability. Although details are relegated to Chapters 6 and 7 suffice it to say that the growing de facto, if not de jure, autonomy among central banks has come at a "price," namely greater responsibility for delivering good monetary policy outcomes. An index of accountability, to be described in greater detail in Chapter 6, attempts to capture the essential notion that greater accountability enhances both central bank autonomy and performance.

Estimates for the full panel (Column 1) reveal that the twenty countries, as a group, respond to positive inflation shocks but are relatively

---

[64] This is another angle of the exploration of central bank behavior that has not been widely taken up in the literature. For an exception, see Siklos (2001).

[65] In other words, conditional on the other variables in the panel version of the reaction function, cross-section estimates are common to all countries in the particular grouping shown. The alternative of permitting cross-sectional variation over time, namely the so-called random effects model, was not considered, as the key inputs into the reaction function already reflect changing economic circumstances through time.

more sensitive to unemployment shocks. There is less persistence in interest rate changes than is commonly believed while central bank independence does not independently contribute to changing interest rate levels. As a group, inflation targeting countries have lower nominal interest rates but it is worth recalling (see Chapter 2) that inflation control objectives were adopted at a time when disinflation was under way. Nevertheless, as suggested earlier, it is conceivable that such a device in effect captures a reduced risk of future inflation that is reflected in nominal interest rates. Turning to the results in Column 2 we see that this "principal component" of central bank independence also has a beneficial impact on interest rates.[66] Indeed, the inflation targeting dummy becomes insignificant. As we shall see (but also see Chapter 2), an inflation targeting policy contributes importantly to clarifying the government–central bank relationship when there is conflict.

Next, the case of EMU countries is examined. Interestingly, as a group, European central banks did not respond to inflation shocks, only to unemployment shocks. The impact of inflation targeting is considerably larger among the European countries than in the full panel.[67] To the extent that the Bundesbank's reaction to inflation shocks, in particular (see Table 4.4), is at odds with those of several other EMU members (most notably Ireland, Italy, and the Netherlands) we have a little bit of evidence supporting Germany's concerns over enshrining strict price stability safeguards in the Maastricht Treaty.

Columns 4 and 5 reinforce the earlier suspicion and findings that the exchange rate regime is an important element in understanding how central banks react to shocks. As expected, countries on a fixed regime are sensitive to external interest rate changes but benefit, in the form of lower interest rates, from greater central bank autonomy. Also interesting is the finding that among the central banks that opted out of the fixed regime for a time[68] (that is, Italy, Finland, and Sweden) they were able to reduce their interest rates relative to the remaining countries in the panel. Moreover, note that while central banks in a floating rate regime react to inflation shocks, the same is not true of fixed regime countries.

---

[66] Using the definitions for conflict resolution outlined in Chapter 2, no index could be assigned for the decades of the 1960s to the 1980s for Ireland, Italy, and Sweden. Setting the index to zero for those three decades did not affect the conclusions but doing so is, strictly speaking, inappropriate.

[67] The significance of the inflation targeting dummy does not disappear with the inclusion of the conflict resolution variable though this necessitates omitting Ireland and Italy from the panel.

[68] This is captured by the "control" variable listed in Table 4.10.

Table 4.10. Pooled Cross-Section Time Series Estimates of Reaction Functions[1]

Independent Variables	(1) All 20 Countries	(2) Countries with Conflict Resolution Procedures[2]	(3) EMU Countries[3]	(4) Floating Exchange Rate Countries	(5) Fixed Exchange Rate Countries	(6) Countries with high CBI	(7) Countries that Increased CBI in the 90s	(8) The Role of Accountability in the 1990s
Inflation shocks	0.031 (13.28)*	0.054 (2.36)[11]	0.034 (1.76)	0.074 (2.35)[12]	−.005 (.004)	0.068 (.947)	0.025 (.170)	0.043 (51.6)@
Unemployment shocks	−0.173 (27.06)*	−0.217 (41.67)*	−0.172 (25.81)*	−0.292 (10.61)*	−0.154 (27.52)*	−0.114 (1.710)	−0.249 (2.84)⊥	−0.075 (13.97)*
Lagged dep. variable	0.070 (.040)⊥	0.131 (.095)⊥	0.046 (.062)	0.005 (.060)	−0.026 (.068)	0.217 (.092)@	0.151 (.088)⊥	0.143 (.081)⊥
Change in U.S. int. rate			0.203 (.017)*		0.112 (.019)*			
CBI[4]	−0.012 (.028)		−0.017 (.038)	−0.088 (.076)	−0.117 (.034)*	−0.063 (.050)	0.215 (.194)	0.023 (.070)
Inflation targeting[5]	−0.166 (.045)*	−0.044 (.040)	−0.305 (.083)					0.500 (.037)
Conflict resolution		−0.176 (.023)*						
Political impact[6]						−0.284 (.289)	−0.337 (.173)@	
Accountability[7]								−0.237 (.061)*
Control variable[8]				.328 (.427)	−.267 (.064)*			
Sample	1966:2–1994:4	1966:2–1999:4	1966:2–1998:4	1980:1–1999:4	1980:1–1999:4	1980:1–1999:4	1980:1–1999:4	1990:1–1999:4
R^2	.02	.06	.05	.13	.03	.10	.12	.04
N[9]	20	17	10	7	13	3	4	20
T[10]	2300	637	1087	544	935	224	188	728
Countries omitted (o) or included (i)	(i) All	(o) Ireland, Italy, Sweden	(i) 10 EMU countries	(i) Australia, Canada, Japan, New Zealand, Switzerland, United Kingdom, United States	(o) Floating countries	(i) Germany, Switzerland, United States	(i) New Zealand, Spain, Sweden, United Kingdom	(i) All

[1] Panel estimates via feasible generalized least squares that corrects for cross-section heteroskedasticity. Heteroskedasticity standard errors are given in parenthesis, except for coefficients on inflation and unemployment shocks. Also, see Table 4.3 for description of significance levels symbols. Reaction function (4.11) is estimated with the sum of contemporaneous and two lagged shocks for inflation and unemployment.

Column No.	Type of Forecast
1	1 step (BW, PBW)
2	1 step (BW, PBW)
3	1 step (BW, PBW)
4	4 step (Full)
5	1 step (BW, PBW)
6	1 step (Full)
7	1 step (BW, PBW)
8	1 step (Full)

[2] The same type of forecast is used for all countries.

[3] See Chapter 2 for more details of the construction of the conflict resolution variable.

[4] Austria, Belgium, Finland, France, Germany, Ireland, Italy, Netherlands, Portugal, Spain. CBI = central bank independence index; see Table 4.4 and Chapter 2.

[5] A dummy variable set to 1 for inflation targeting countries, namely Australia, Canada, Finland, New Zealand, Sweden, and the United Kingdom. Adding Spain does not affect the conclusions but was omitted from the estimates.

[6] See Table 4.4 for definitions. In every case the partisan dummy *DRPT2* is used.

[7] Accountability is an index whose construction is detailed in Chapter 6. It is defined in the same manner as the CBI index so that the higher the value of the index the more accountable is the central bank.

[8] A dummy variable set to 1 when a floating exchange rate country temporarily switches exchange rate regimes. See Chapter 2. In the case of floaters Australia (1983–4), New Zealand (1983–5), and the United Kingdom (1991–2) temporarily drop floating rates. In the case of fixers, Finland (1996–9), Italy (1993–), and Sweden (1994–6) drop the fixed rate type regime.

[9] Number of cross sections (countries).

[10] Number of observations in the pooled sample.

[11] Significant at the 12% level.

[12] Significant at the 13% level.

189

In addition, central banks in floating rate regimes are more sensitive to unemployment shocks than their counterparts in fixed rate regimes.

Next, we consider the differences between countries with historically autonomous central banks (Germany, Switzerland, and the United States) versus ones that had little autonomy in the 1980s but obtained considerably more independence in the 1990s (New Zealand, Spain, Sweden, the United Kingdom). Again, some interesting features emerge. Countries that provided little autonomy to their central banks until the 1990s are more prone to partisan political pressure than their counterparts with historically independent central banks. Moreover, countries that did not historically grant independence to their central banks are prone to react only to unemployment shocks (in the appropriate manner) but not at all to inflation shocks. The reaction to unemployment shocks, however, is quantitatively larger than most of the estimates shown in Table 4.10. Indeed, the best reflection of the benefits of central bank autonomy is captured by the conflict resolution variable which is found to be significantly negative.[69]

Finally, Table 4.10 shows the impact in the 1990s of demands for more central bank accountability. To the extent that greater central bank accountability improves institutional credibility and performance this is seen as translating into lower interest rates. The arguments linking these variables are developed in more detail in Chapters 6 and 7.

While the statement "one size fits all" may not, strictly speaking, be an accurate description of reaction function estimates presented here, there are clearly a number of important common features in how central banks change interest rates that seem to be adequately captured by the panel approach.[70] Perhaps more interestingly, however, are the differences among groups of countries that operate under different exchange rate regimes and institutional arrangements. The panel estimates high-

---

[69] Central bank independence was also found to be negative, but is significant only at the 18% level.

[70] Space limitations prevent discussion of a number of technical issues dealing with the estimation of panels. Although some details are provided in the table, a couple of additional points need to be mentioned. First, the dependent (and relevant independent) variables are in first differences to avoid possible biases in panels with a lagged dependent variable. Such differencing can create additional problems that were considered but proved not to be significant in the present application. See Arellano and Bond (1991); Nickell (1981); and Pesaran, Shin, and Smith (1997) for further discussion of the issues. Second, the panels are unbalanced but to the extent that the explanations provided here, and in Chapter 2, are adequate, this need not create additional difficulties. Nevertheless, there is at least the potential for biases in coefficient estimates that are not fully corrected.

light a role for central bank–government relations that cannot be so readily ascertained at the level of individual country estimates.

SUMMARY

The essence of a quantitative analysis of central bank behavior is captured by the reaction function. This function summarizes the response of central banks to a variety of economic and noneconomic shocks. A major difficulty lies in determining the extent to which both the shocks and the reactions to such shocks, in the form of interest rate changes, reflect the calculations and preferences of the central bank as opposed to those of governments and markets more generally. In this chapter it is suggested that central banks act as if they respond to shocks that are forecasted from some econometric model. Two sets of models were specified with different information sets in order to capture changes in economic structure in the countries considered and the relative noisiness of more recent data relative to earlier vintages of the same data. Next, it is argued that there exist at least three other "pressures" on monetary policy: political pressure arising from elections or partisan changes in government, institutional pressure arising from statutory features that describe central bank–government relations, and international pressures that stem from policy decisions abroad.

Briefly, estimates reveal that central banks for the most part do react to positive inflation shocks and unemployment shocks by, respectively, raising and lowering nominal interest rates. In addition, there is plenty of evidence that central banks are not immune to political, institutional, or international pressures. Moreover, while there is some persistence in interest rate changes, it is not as large as the existing literature suggests because most reaction functions ignore the variety of influences on monetary policy.

Other evidence was marshaled to show not only that fiscal policy appears to directly influence the setting of interest rates by central banks but also that interest rate volatility may indeed play a separate role in the monetary authority's loss function. A difficulty with reaction function estimates for individual countries is that they fail to fully exploit the potential impact of institutional factors such as the type of exchange rate regime and the slow changing nature of government–central bank relations. Accordingly, a series of panel reaction function estimates were also presented. These clearly show the important function of institutional characteristics in explaining central bank behavior. The cross-section estimation approach also reveals the significant role played by exchange rate and inflation targeting regimes. There is also some evidence that central banks in certain groups of countries, such as the countries forming the European Monetary Union, react somewhat differently than the rest to the various sources of influences on monetary policy behavior.

Having demonstrated the important role of institutional factors we proceed to explore a more recent series of milestones that have affected central banking in the last two decades. Accountability, disclosure, and inflation targeting reflect new pressures on central bank performance with origins in monetary history that can be traced to events that took place over previous decades.

5 | Contrasting Quantitative and Qualitative Assessments of Central Bank Behavior and the Evolution of Monetary Policies

INTRODUCTION

It is apparent from the results so far that there is a gap between the qualitative and econometric evidence. The former predicts not only that central banks can be fairly easily classified according to the degree of statutory autonomy enjoyed vis-à-vis government but that there is also a clear empirical connection between their independence vis-à-vis government and average inflation performance.[1] By contrast, the econometric evidence would lead one to conclude that central banks in the industrial world are not as different as the qualitative evidence implies. This chapter attempts to provide explanations for the conflicting evidence. It is argued that certain elements in the measurement of central bank behavior are difficult to quantify, are imperfectly measured, or have evolved over time in a manner that is not easily reconciled by the two approaches.

This possibility was already discussed in Chapter 2. Moreover, while the exchange rate regime clearly matters, it appears to matter less than would be suggested by the attempts to refine existing classifications in relation to textbook descriptions. Of course, as we have seen in Chapter 2, dating a change in policy regimes is a tricky matter. Conflict between official dates and ones estimated via econometric methods rest in part on how fast individuals' expectations respond to actual changes in the

---

[1] Brumm (2000) is one of the latest in a series of attempts at examining the notion of a statistical link between inflation and central bank independence, based on an analysis of covariance structures for data from the 1948–72 and 1973–84 periods. Although CEO turnover rates are included there is no other distinction made between industrial and nonindustrial countries in the data set. Also, see Forder (2000) and Hadri, Lochwood, and Maloney (1998).

variables of interest. In addition, until recently, exchange rate regime considerations rarely figured as an explicit feature of the statutory relationship between the central bank and governments.

There is also considerable difficulty in applied work in incorporating the role of fiscal policy, in part because of data related issues, and also because there need not be a simple or predictable link between fiscal and monetary policies. Finally, and perhaps just as important, qualitative measures of central bank behavior are about what a central bank is expected to do, and this need not always coincide with what the monetary authority actually does, as interpreted by the reaction function approach.

Nevertheless, the econometric and qualitative evidence compiled for this study appear to be converging in a manner of speaking, especially in the 1990s. There is once again a shared, and strongly felt, belief among policy makers in industrial countries about the desirability of low and stable inflation combined with sound fiscal policies. There continue to be disagreements, however, about the desirability of central bank intervention in foreign exchange markets, and the degree to which the major central banks especially should be seen to coordinate their policies, as well as the role of the exchange rate regime in this context. Whether these developments signal a different era of sorts is unclear but it is certainly not entirely new. The 1960s also represented a watershed in the degree of commonality in views about what constitutes good monetary policy. Back then, however, the pillar upon which the similarity of views rested was the exchange rate and the balance of payments, whereas today shared opinions rest on the inflation rate. Similarly, expert opinion during the 1920s rested on the support for the gold standard, also an exchange-rate–based pillar. The danger then is that such common perceptions can be misplaced. For example, Keynes, and others, felt strongly that the exchange rate was seriously misaligned when Britain was considering a return to the Gold Standard at the old parity in 1925. Nevertheless, prestige, and a sense that the Gold Standard was a "knave-proof" regime, led to a return to the pre-World War I monetary arrangement. As described by Eichengreen (1992a), the failure of coordination among countries whose economic fortunes were tied together by the exchange rate anchor, and an almost slavish adherence to the ideology of the Gold Standard, combined to create a jarring end to that policy regime but not until the economic damage was done. More important then than a consensus for or against a particular regime is a strategy that is based on experience, flexibility in the event of unexpected shocks, and an institutional design that can best facilitate good economic outcomes.

What appears to have led to the current state of affairs regarding central bank policies in particular, and attitudes toward monetary policy in general, is the confluence of two separate forces. First, there is society's recognition of the high costs of excessive inflation.[2] The difficulty, of course, has been to agree on what exactly constitutes "excessive" since the empirical (negative) correlation between economic activity and inflation has been difficult to pin down with precision or confidence.[3] Second, there is now fairly widespread agreement that a form of "disciplined discretion,"[4] and not mechanical rules-based central bank policies, work best.

The remainder of this chapter is organized as follows. First, we discuss the probable sources of differences between the econometric and qualitative evidence on central bank behavior presented so far. Next, we describe how monetary policy in the major industrial countries evolved since the 1960s via experimentation to the current growing shared belief in the desirability of policies aimed at controlling inflation. Finally, it is suggested that the current state of affairs may be viewed as the triumph not so much of central banks or politics but of policies. We may, therefore, have reached a time that could fulfill Bopp's (1944) expressed wish for the United States over a half century ago when he hoped ". . . that a shift in emphasis for insistence upon rights, sovereignty, and

---

[2] ". . . the change in attitude of the majority of ordinary people about inflation has been the most important change during my period in office" (Erik Hoffmeyer, Governor of the Central Bank of Denmark from 1965–95 (Hoffmeyer 1994: p. 7)). An influential survey (Shiller 1997) also confirms this to be true for the United States at least. It is also clear that the public believes a central bank has an impact on inflation. For example, a survey by the Bank of Canada conducted in 1999 (Compas Inc. 1999) concluded that the public perceives the Bank of Canada to have "some" or a "great deal" of effect on the price of goods and services.

[3] Arthur Burns, the Fed chairman who presided over a bout of high inflation, at least by U.S. standards (1979–7) once declared, "No country that I know of has been able to maintain widespread economic prosperity once inflation got out of hand (*U.S. News and World Report*, June 10, 1974: p. 20). The difficulty is that some influential analyses (for example, Bruno and Easterly 1998) suggest that the threshold beyond which inflation is harmful to economic growth exceeds 10% and may be as high as 30%.

[4] Laubach and Posen (1997) coined the term but the concept was well known to central bankers, among others. Consider, for example, the comments by the former governor of the Bank of Italy, Carlo Ciampi (1979–92) who, in the early 1980s, commented ". . . it would be inappropriate to renounce the contributions that the discretionary actions of central banks can make, even when this action is set within an operational framework expressed in terms of a quantitative objective" (Ciampi 1983: p. 12).

independence to comprehensive duties and responsibilities . . ." (p. 277). This, together with improvements in the understanding of the role of the central bank, is perhaps another distinguishing characteristic of the present state of affairs over conditions that dominated in previous decades.

RECONCILING THE ECONOMETRIC AND QUALITATIVE EVIDENCE

As noted earlier, a striking feature of the recent econometric evidence dealing with central bank behavior is the deemphasis on political and international sources of pressure on monetary policy. This is partly understandable since the central bank most frequently under the microscope, namely the U.S. Federal Reserve, can be thought of as fairly autonomous in setting the stance of monetary policy. Yet, there is also extensive evidence that political pressures on monetary policy are significant and persistent. Without it one could not properly understand the evolution of U.S. monetary policy (Timberlake 1993; Wicker 1993; and Woolley 1984, are some examples). The same is true of the Bundesbank, also frequently mentioned as belonging to the group of most autonomous central banks in the world. Yet, there is considerable evidence of political pressure on the Bundesbank, as well as pressures from abroad. The latter is in the form of U.S. monetary policy actions, or the state of economic policy more generally elsewhere within the European continent where Germany has long played a lead economic role.[5]

An additional factor that distinguishes the econometric from the qualitative evidence is the emphasis in the former type on economic shocks central banks are thought to react to. In contrast, the qualitative evidence focuses on what central banks are expected to do, and also capture political economy considerations at the time legislation was enacted and, to a limited extent, how these evolve over time.

In a fundamental sense then the two types of evidence are at cross purposes. The reaction function approach typically fails to consider the political economy of central banks, while the qualitative evidence ignores the subtleties of central bank behavior reflected in their actual response to economic shocks not readily captured in any statute. Moreover, the qualitative evidence cannot adequately come to grips with the *dynamics* of the political economy of central banking. Since the fundamental

---

[5] A recent example is the collection of papers in de Haan (2000).

premise of each type of evidence is rather different one might well ask whether reconciliation of the different findings is necessary or even possible?

The necessity to reconcile the evidence stems from the separate impact each strand of the literature has had on policy making and policy makers. The qualitative evidence has certainly given the impression, if not the impetus, to grant greater de jure autonomy to several central banks. This is true even though advocates of the idea do not claim a firm causal relationship between autonomy and inflation or economic performance more generally. Nor has it ever been made clear why statutory autonomy, as such, is more important than, say, some clearly specified quantified inflation objective, together with a governance structure that ensures clarity of purpose and accountability to governments and the public. One reason, of course, is that statutory independence is viewed in this literature as representing a *sufficient* condition to deliver good monetary policy, and appears to solve the "credibility" problem associated with a government that promises no inflation surprises, but is not bound by institutional constraints that would conditionally enter into individuals' expectations of inflation. Moreover, the qualitative literature is unable to agree on a set of core elements or conditions that deliver the desired autonomy which can then be translated into low and stable inflation performance. As a result, the evidence sends mixed messages about the robustness of the connection between de jure autonomy and the quality of monetary policy being delivered. Finally, the qualitative evidence gives the impression that the credibility problem can be solved easily and is all that needs to be addressed. It is, however, becoming increasingly apparent that credibility is enhanced and facilitated via accountability, and transparency measures or, rather, that the legal framework as such can and should take a back seat to how central banks and, by implication, governments ought to communicate with the public both the possibilities and limitations of economic policies.

Ordinarily the econometric evidence has not explicitly considered the role played by the institutional structure in delivering a particular kind of monetary policy (exceptions were noted in Chapter 4; also see de Haan 2000: ch. 2). Since the qualitative approach strongly suggests that institutions do matter, it would seem desirable to assess the relative merits of this type of evidence. Indeed, recent attempts to show that the same reaction function fits the data for several industrial countries point to a literature that has lost sight of the fact that, over the last few decades at least, central banks appear to differ substantially in their performance, for example as measured by inflation outcomes. Hence, the typical central bank loss function is either misspecified or cannot adequately deal with the various pressures on central banks in the face of repeated economic shocks. In other words, the econometric evidence is founded on a specific-to-general modelling strategy that rejects institutional factors and considers the elements of the central bank's loss function described earlier to represent an adequate description of central bank behavior. Therefore, a minimalist approach is taken that asks whether and how central banks respond to real and nominal shocks in deciding on the stance of monetary policy.[6]

To be fair, the econometric approach is hampered by the lack of agreement about the variables that can adequately capture institutional influences on central bank actions, not to mention difficulties in constructing consistent data sets of roughly the same quality in a cross-country setting. Nevertheless, the failure to address the issue of how institutional influences might be brought into the empirical analysis is an important lacuna of the reaction function literature.[7]

There is also an additional reason an attempt should be made to reconcile the econometric and qualitative strands of the central banking literature. Even if we accept the standard specification of the central bank loss function as a reasonable, though incomplete, description of what a central bank does, and by all accounts such a consensus among economists does exist, actual reaction function estimates must also contend with a number of technical issues that bring this approach into conflict with the notion that institutional aspects also matter.

First, of necessity, the shocks a central bank is believed to respond to must originate from estimates from some underlying, possibly structural, model. Even if all agree on the size and restrictions needed to identify the shocks of interest, the fact is that central banks do not, as a rule, rely

---

[6] Collins and Siklos (2001) estimate reaction functions for the dollar bloc countries (United States, Canada, New Zealand, and Australia) and conclude that, despite the adoption of comparable inflation targeting regimes, central banks in each of these countries react, at least part of the time, differently to common type shocks over the 1988–2000 period.

[7] I have not mentioned another potential conflict between the two approaches to the measurement of central bank behavior, namely the possibility that qualitative measures focus on "long-run" aspects of central banking while reaction functions highlight "short-run" behavior. If this is the case then why are politicians, who write central bank legislation, acting in such a forward looking manner when they are assumed to be shortsighted? Moreover, reaction functions are specified with some explicit underlying long-run relationships in mind such as, for example, the inability, in equilibrium, to exploit any trade-off between inflation and output growth. As these issues are not central to the arguments being made here they are not pursued any further.

on single estimates in deciding the appropriate stance of monetary policy. This is precisely an area where the underlying reaction function approach may be enriched via the addition of institutional factors.

Second, some of the reaction function literature has not been sufficiently sensitive to external, and largely institutional, events that affect how a central bank responds to shocks over time. Instead, the criticism leveled against the literature has been couched mostly in technical terms as a failure to properly address the possibility that estimated relationships change over time. Again, sensitivity to institutional considerations would point to the role of the exchange rate regime on the one hand, and monetary policy regimes more generally, as candidates to improve upon existing reaction function estimates, as opposed to placing the blame squarely on the estimation technique.[8]

Third, it has been argued that policy makers' views of the structure of the economy changes over time either because of factors outside their control, or because some large shock forces a reassessment of the existing ideology. In a sense then, just as a one size fits all model may be unsatisfactory, unless institutional considerations are brought to bear in the empirical analysis, the same is true of the underlying structure of the model *over time*.

It should be emphasized that there are circumstances under which explicit recognition of the role of institutional factors is not crucial. For example, if the object of the analysis is a clearly identifiable policy regime, and one that is sufficiently long enough to conduct a sensible econometric investigation, then one can reasonably assume that institutional considerations are held constant. Note, however, as demonstrated in chapter 2, that there is no certainty in dating the beginning or ending of policy episodes.

Having discussed the desirability of attempting to reconcile two fundamentally different approaches to the analysis of central bank behavior, there remains the question of whether the practical possibility of reaching reconciliation is feasible. In general, the answer is a guarded yes.

If the 1990s indeed mark a convergence of sorts in beliefs about the desirability of low and stable inflation, together with the institutional

---

[8] There is also the related issue of whether the reaction function approach adequately mimics central bank behavior when much of the literature assumes, implicitly, that the central bank has more economic information than it could possibly have had when setting interest rates. This issue was dealt with separately in the previous chapter.

safeguards to ensure the proper location of accountability, as well as sufficient transparency in central bank operations, then, much as Goodhart's law[9] would predict, institutional considerations would no longer be relevant even though these were critical to the outcome. At the same time, and somewhat ironically, the emergence in the 1990s of shared viewed about what constitutes sound monetary policy may instead have produced a reversal of sorts in Goodhart's Law. In other words, once central banks and governments jointly accepted the desirability of low and stable prices then, far from producing a breakdown in the link between inflation and interest rate actions, the relationships that explain central bank behavior became more similar across countries.

If the object of the investigation is, as the title of the book suggests, an attempt to analyze the changing face of central banking then it ought to be possible, as was shown in the previous chapter, to show that institutional factors do matter. However, it was also noted that it appeared difficult to pin down which type of institutional factors appear to matter most. The choice of the exchange rate regime is an important consideration and its effects are, at times, identifiable while, at other times, they are difficult to pin down. Measures to enhance central bank autonomy, accountability, and transparency are imperfect and, while the improvements in measurement to be suggested here do help (see Chapter 6), there is clearly room for improvement. The point is that, unless an econometric model that contains proxies for institutional change is able to "encompass"[10] a competing model that omits such factors, we cannot reject the "institutionalist" hypothesis out of hand.

THE EMERGENCE OF COMMON FEATURES IN MONETARY POLICY: THE TRIUMPH OF POLICIES?

The results of the previous chapters, though largely suggestive, point to "defining" moments, crises, or stresses that are associated with changes that can be regarded as "institutional" in nature with a potentially profound impact on central bank behavior. If this view is accepted, is there

---

[9] Refers to Charles Goodhart's idea that any policy aimed at controlling an aggregate economic variable will (eventually) render such control ineffective.

[10] The term *encompassing* is used as in Hendry (1995, part III) and refers to a statistical property of a model that is pitted against another model. Essentially, when one model encompasses another it provides a relatively better statistical representation of the underlying phenomenon being investigated.

anything else to distinguish the various regimes from each other? If so, what are the implications for the conduct of monetary policy?

It has been noted by some that the adoption of policy regimes may perhaps be cyclical in nature or, alternatively, that there is an important "learning" component involved in decision making within a particular policy regime (for example, Howitt 2000; Sargent 1999). For example, it was argued earlier that the desirability of central bank autonomy is not a phenomenon new to the post-World War II era. By contrast, the push toward greater accountability and transparency in central banking is a fairly new development.[11]

The evolution of exchange rate arrangements is another illustration of possible cyclical behavior in the adoption of policy regimes. Giovannini (1993), for example, views the evolution of the choice between fixed and floating exchange rate regimes during the twentieth century in this fashion.

The evidence so far, together with the evidence cited earlier in connection with the evolution of regimes prior to and since World War II, suggests that, ultimately, politics (and, possibly, personalities) were also a factor rather than the inherent qualities alone of the policies being adopted. This might, at least in part, explain why policies are adopted and then abandoned for a time. For example, the choice of exchange rate regimes has generally been firmly in the hands of the politicians. Even here the matter is not perhaps as clear cut as might be expected. Table 5.1 provides information about statutory responsibilities in the realm of exchange rate arrangements. Since virtually no changes were made in the relevant statutes between 1950 and 1990 the table is subdivided according to the situation prior to and since 1990.

Approximately the same number of central banks laws (six) have either no provision or the question of who sets the exchange rate regime rests solely with government. There is a slight increase, from one to three,

---

[11] Though this is not unheard of. The description of tensions between the Fed, Congress, and the executive clearly centered over accountability and transparency issues even if such terms were not frequently used. The same can be said to have been true for the Bank of Canada. But, as Neufeld made clear over four decades ago, the state of knowledge simply made it impractical for central banks, let alone their political masters, to support or encourage such developments. "The prestige of the Bank [of Canada] might be further enhanced if the public had a greater understanding of its policies . . . but a fuller interpretation of the excellent but bare statistics which are currently being compiled might conceivably do much more good than harm. The Bank might well take an even more active interest than it has so far in providing the material necessary for an intelligent public opinion on monetary matters" (Neufeld 1958: p. 19).

Table 5.1. Central Banks and the Exchange Rate Regime

Country	None or Government 1950–89	90s	Intervention/ Management of Reserves 1950–89	90s	Setting Exchange Rate/Regime 1950–89	90s	Joint Responsibility with Government 1950–89	90s
Austria			√[3]	√[3]				
Australia							√[1,2]	√
Belgium	√[4]	√						
Canada			√[5]	√				
Denmark	√	√						
Finland			√[6]	√				
France			√[7]	√[19] (1993)				
Germany							√[8]	√ (until 1999)
Ireland			√[9]	√				
Italy			√[10,11]	√				
Japan	√			√[20] (1998)	√ (1998)			
Netherlands							√[12]	√ (until 1999)
New Zealand		√[21] (1989)	√[18]					
Norway		√[22] (1985)	√[13]					
Portugal			√[14]	√				
Spain			√[15]					√[23] (1994–8)
Sweden			√[16]					√[16]
Switzerland	√[24]						√[25] (1978)	
United Kingdom	√	√						
United States	√		√[26]					
ECB					N/A	√[17]		

[1] Part II 8, Aufricht (1967: vol. I, p. 7).

[2] Part V 31(g), Aufricht (1967: vol. I, p. 11).

[3] Chapter 1, article 2(3), Aufricht (1967: vol. II, p. 4) and Federal Act on the Oesterrechische Nationalbank (1984), article 47(1).

[4] Chapter III, articles 17, 18, Aufricht (1967: vol. II, p. 69).

[5] Article 18, Aufricht (1967: vol. I, pp. 93–5).

[6] Article 11, Aufricht (1967: vol. II, p. 149).

[7] Article 141, Aufricht (1967: vol. II, p. 193).

[8] Articles 4 (and footnote 4), 13(1), Aufricht (1967: vol. II, pp. 252, 255–6).

[9] Article 7(a), Aufricht (1967: vol. II, p. 362).

[10] Article 41(6), Aufricht (1967: vol. II, p. 435).

[11] Article 27, Aufricht (1967: vol. I, p. 431) may be viewed as an escape clause permitting foreign exchange intervention.

[12] Articles 9(1) and 26(1), Aufricht (1967: vol. II, pp. 466, 471).

[13] Article 15(d), Aufricht (1967: vol. II, p. 504).

[14] Articles 4(3), 20 (par. 2), Aufricht (1967: vol. II, pp. 544, 547–8).

[15] Article 2, Aufricht (1967: vol. II, p. 611).

Notes to Table 5.1 *(continued)*

[16] Articles 14 and 2, Aufricht (1967: vol. II, pp. 665, 663). Under the new legislation (Riksbank Act of 1999), "... responsibility for general issues of exchange rate policy rests with the Government, which also decides the exchange rate system. Before deciding the exchange rate system, the Government shall consult with the Riksbank. The implementation of the exchange rate system laid down by the Government is decided by the Riksbank" (available at http://www.riksbank.com/default.asp).

[17] Articles 20, 23, 2, 3 and Maastricht Treaty article 111. Available at http://www.ecb.int; and European Central Bank *Collection of Legal Instruments* (June 1998–May 1999), p. 96. In force since January 1, 1999.

[18] Reserve Bank of New Zealand Amendment Act (1960) and Reserve Bank Act of 1964.

[19] Article 2, Loi No. 93, 980 du 4 août 1993.

[20] Article 2, Bank of Japan Law; and articles 15(5).

[21] Articles 17 and 18, RBNZ Act specifies that intervention is subject to a directive from the Minister.

[22] Norges Bank Act 1985, section 4.

[23] Chapter II, article 5(a), and articles 11, 12 Law of Autonomy of the Bance de España, 1994.

[24] 1953–77, Aufricht (1967: vol. II), Central Bank Law, 1953.

[25] Article 2.2, Loi sur la Banque nationale.

[26] The preamble to the Federal Reserve Act mentions that the Fed was established, for among other tasks, "... for other purposes." While this could include foreign exchange intervention or even the choice of exchange rate regimes, major decisions in this sphere appear to rest with the Administration.

Year legislation enacted shown in parentheses where necessary. Otherwise, see Chapters 1 and 2 for additional statutory details.

N/A signifies not applicable.

in the number of central banks that are responsible for setting the exchange rate and/or the exchange rate regime. Moreover, the situation prior to 1990 suggests that a majority of central banks (eleven of twenty) were able to intervene in foreign exchange markets with differing levels of discretion. After 1990, fewer central banks actively resorted to foreign exchange intervention. Of course, since Japan and the European Union are among the group of countries that effectively delegated responsibility to the central bank over the choice of the exchange rate regime, this marks an important shift since they effectively represent eleven of the twenty central banks considered in this study. In any event, there is a definite movement toward clarification over who has responsibility for exchange rate issues.

Therefore, so long as there are fairly precise and quantifiable domestic objectives for monetary policy, political motives have, if indirectly, had a significant impact on monetary policy performance.[12] The ideology of the moment helps dictate then whether it is politically acceptable for a country to tie its hands economically with the fortunes of others via the

---

[12] Included among the political aspects would be the degree of international policy coordination, a crucial element in explaining the severity of the Great Depression, and its aftermath, as well as economic policy in recent decades. See Eichengreen (1992a) and Volcker and Gyohten (1992).

choice of exchange rate regimes, irrespective of the degree of statutory autonomy enjoyed by its central bank.

The stagflation of the 1970s and 1980s, together with dissatisfaction over the desirability of government or central bank intervention in foreign exchange markets[13] also contributed to a significant shift in emphasis away from the ideology of policy coordination, via the exchange rate, toward setting domestic and quantifiable inflation goals. Together with the greater central bank accountability and transparency this has the advantage of tying policy makers' hands by delivering "good" monetary policy in a form that can be understood by the public while providing sufficient flexibility to allow the central bank to avoid having to react to each and every shock that inevitably hits an economy. There is no need with such arguments to necessarily bring in the role of credibility as such, though one could argue that the flexibility of inflation objectives is more credible than the flexibility inherent in any announced exchange rate objective. The key difference then is that an inflation objective helps clarify the responsibilities of the central bank vis-à-vis government.

It is also abundantly clear (also see Mahadeva and Sterne 2000) that the adoption of inflation type goals has spread quickly since the early 1990s. The growing consensus over the desirability of such a monetary policy strategy is significant for it also marks a shift toward considerably less dependence of monetary policy on politics, though it need not completely eliminate it, than on the policies used to attain a particular inflation objective. It is not so much that central banks have triumphed, as Volcker (1990) once observed, but that the appropriate location of responsibility for monetary policy and its outcome that has triumphed.

A HALF CENTURY OF EXPERIMENTATION

In a variety of contexts (for example, foreign exchange rate speculation, balance of payments crises) economists have been asking whether critical factors or leading indicators exist to explain the onset of a "crisis." To be sure, the approach that constructs an index of leading or coinci-

---

[13] Schwartz (2000) points out the general futility of government foreign exchange market intervention. There is, in addition, a large literature dealing with technical aspects of foreign exchange market intervention by central banks and the limitations of such policies. See, for example, Edison (1993) and Sarno and Taylor (2001).

dent type indicators is problematic. First, such indicators do not follow directly from some structural economic model (for example, see Weber 1995). Second, indexes of this kind are subject to problems of aggregation bias that can distort the true sources of an economic crisis (for example, see Siklos 2000c). Yet, at the same time, economists have been taught that each policy regime can render irrelevant or, at the very least, reduce the usefulness of econometric estimates based on data from an earlier regime. Nevertheless, sensible indicators have their uses in helping us understand the impact of economic policies.

Given the conflict that exists between the different strands of the literature on central banking, and the apparent adoption of a sequence of monetary policies since World War II, it is useful to delve further into the possibility that indicators point to the last half century as being one of experimentation.

While fully cognizant of the limitations of any indicator or index the objective of the present section is modest. A broad summary of the findings is provided in Table 5.2. It gives the timing of exceptionally large shocks originating from three sources to be described in greater detail below. They are: exchange rate or interest rates, fiscal policy, and political pressure. The overall evidence can be summarized as follows. First, countries experiencing more frequent sources of economic "stress" do not necessarily change monetary policy regimes more frequently. Second, it is difficult to temporally disentangle pressure on the exchange rate regime from pressure on fiscal policy. Third, to the extent that oil price shocks confound the analysis, these emerge more clearly as pressures on fiscal policy than as pressures on either the exchange rate or political pressure indicators considered. Fourth, although periods of economic "stress" that are catalysts for change take place occasionally during the 1990s, "large" shocks are predominantly a feature of the 1970s and 1980s. Indeed, the first half of the 1970s and 1980s were stressful eras for virtually all countries in our sample. The frequency, magnitude, and distribution of shocks does suggest why the period since 1960, in particular, can be characterized as one of experimentation.

Exchange Rate Pressure

Eichengreen, Rose, and Wyplosz (hereafter ERW; 1996a; 1996b) propose an indicator of speculative pressures on a currency. Some criticisms of their approach have already been noted. Essentially, their index is a weighted average of three factors believed, in theory, to have a

Table 5.2. Timing of "Large" Economic Shocks by Source

Country[4]	Decade	Exchange Rate or Interest Rate[1]	Fiscal Policy[2]	Political Pressure[3]
		(Dates: Year.Quarter)		
Austria	1960s	1968:2		1965:3–1966:2
	1970s	1971:4	1970:1–2	
			1973:2–4	
	1980s	1981:3–4	1979:4–1981:4	1983:1–2
			1982:2	1986:3–1987:1
	1990s	1992:3–1993:1	1989:1–1994:1	1999:3–4
			1998:4	
Australia	1970s	1971:4–1973:4	1974:1–3	1974:1–2
				1975:3
	1980s	1982:4–1983:2	1982:2–1983:1	
		1985:2–1986:4	1985:4–1986:1	
			1989:4	
Belgium	1960s	1968:2		
	1970s		1978:2–4	1976:2
	1980s	1981:3–1982:2	1980:4	1985:2–4
		1986:2	1982:2	
			1983:3	
			1987:2	
	1990s			1993:4
Canada	1960s	1968:2		
	1970s	1971:1		1975:2
	1980s	1987:4–1989:1	1980:1	
			1980:4–1982:2	
			1986:1	
	1990s	1992:4–1993:1	1989:1–1990:4	
Denmark	1960s	1968:2		1964:4–1965:1
	1970s		1970:1–3	1971:1–3
			1973:2–4	1974:3–1975:1
	1980s	1981:3–4	1980:1–1982:2	1981:4
		1986:3	1986:1	
	1990s	1992:4–1993:4	1989:2–1994:2	1994:1–4
			1998:1–4	
Finland	1960s			1965:3–4
	1970s	1976:1	1975:3–1977:4	1969:3–1970:2
		1978:4		
	1980s	1981:3–4	1983:2–1984:4	
		1984:4	1986:3	
		1987:4–1988:1		
	1990s	1993:3–1994:4		
France	1960s	1968:4–1969:3		
	1970s	1970:3	1970:1	
			1973:4–1974:4	
			1979:4	

Country[4]	Decade	Exchange Rate or Interest Rate[1]	Fiscal Policy[2]	Political Pressure[3]
			(Dates: Year.Quarter)	
	1980s	1981:3–4	1982:2	
	1990s	1992:4–1993:2	1992:2–1993:4	
Germany	1960s			
	1970s	1971:1–4	1973:3	
	1980s		1979:4–1982:2	1986:2–4
	1990s	1992:4–1993:2	1992:1–1993:2	1990:4
Italy	1960s			
	1970s	1971:4	1974:1–1975:1	1976:1–2
		1976:3–1977:4	1976:2–1977:2	
	1980s	1981:3–4	1980:1–1981:1	
			1984:1–1985:1	
			1986:1	
	1990s	1992:4	1998:1–4	1993:3
Japan	1960s	1961:2–1962:1		
		1968:2		
	1970s	1971:4–1972:1	1973:4–1975:2	
		1978:4		
	1980s	1981:3–4	1980:2–3	
		1986:3–4	1982:3	
			1985:3–1986:2	
	1990s		1991:2–1993:3	
Netherlands	1960s	1968:2		
	1970s		1978:4	
	1980s	1981:3–1982:1	1979:4–1980:3	1989:1
		1986:3–4	1981:3–4	
	1990s	1992:4		
New Zealand	1960s			
	1970s			
	1980s	1985:1–4	1985:1–1986:1	
		1987:2–3	1987:1–2	
	1990s			1990:2
				1994:3
				1995:3
Norway	1960s	1968:2	1969:3–1970:3	1961:4
	1970s	1973:3–1974:1	1973:2–1974:3	
	1980s	1981:3–1983:3	1977:3–1982:3	
		1984:4–1986:3	1985:4	
		1988:1	1989:4	
	1990s		1991:2–1993:4	
			1998:4	

(continued)

Table 5.2 *(continued)*

Country[4]	Decade	Exchange Rate or Interest Rate[1]	Fiscal Policy[2]	Political Pressure[3]
		(Dates: Year.Quarter)		
Portugal	1960s			
	1970s			
	1980s	1981:1–4	1983:4	1985:4
		1984:1–2	1985:1	1986:4–1987:4
		1985:2		
	1990s		1991:2–1994:2	
			1998:3–4	
Spain	1960s			
	1970s	1978:3–1979:1	1978:2–1983:4	
	1980s	1981:3	1985:2	
		1983:1–4	1987:1–3	
	1990s	1993:3	1993:1	
Sweden	1960s	1968:2–3	1969:4–1971:1	
	1970s	1973:4–1974:1	1974:3	1979:1
	1980s	1981:4–1982:1	1980:1–1982:3	
		1992:4–1994:1	1983:2	
			1985:2–3	
	1990s		1989:2–1994:1	1998:2–1999:2
Switzerland	1960s			
	1970s	1978:4–1979:1		
	1980s	1981:1–4	1989:1–1993:1	
	1990s			
United Kingdom	1960s	1968:2		
	1970s	1971:4–1972:1		1977:1
		1973:4–1974:1		
	1980s	1977:4–1978:1		1987:1
		1980:1		
		1981:3–4		
	1990s			1997:1–2
United States	1960s	1968:2		
	1970s	1971:2–4	1973:3–1974:4	
		1979:1		
	1980s	1981:3–1982:3	1979:4–1982:2	
		1986:2–1987:1		
	1990s			

[1] Full sample varies according to data availability. The table below gives sample length details. All data are quarterly. "Large" shocks are assumed to be consistent with a value for *ERP* > 1. See Equation 5.1.

Notes to Table 5.2 *(continued)*

Country	Sample	Country	Sample
Australia	1969:3–98:4	Japan	1961:1–99:4
Austria	1967:1–98:4	Netherlands	1961:1–98:4
Belgium	1961:1–98:4	New Zealand	1984:3–99:4
Canada	1961:1–98:4	Norway	1963:1–99:4
Denmark	1967:1–99:4	Portugal	1981:1–98:4
Finland	1975:3–98:4	Spain	1973:2–98:4
France	1961:1–98:4	Sweden	1963:1–99:4
Germany	1961:1–98:4	Switzerland	1975:4–99:4
Italy	1971:1–98:4	United Kingdom	1961:1–99:1
Ireland	1971:1–98:4	United States	1961:1–98:4

[2] Samples are comparable but not exactly the same as for series in note 1. "Large" shocks are assumed to be consistent with a value for *FP* > +.5. See Equation 5.2.
[3] See note 2. "Large" shocks are assumed to be consistent with a predicted probability for *PP* > .5, based on Equation 5.3.
[4] Additional details and data files may be found at http://www.wlu.ca/~wwwsbe/faculty/psiklos/centralbanks.htm.

bearing on the pressure to alter or abandon an exchange rate regime.[14] Though the index is meant to be most applicable to the European experience with fixed exchange rates there is no reason why the index cannot, in principle, signal pressure in any exchange rate environment. The index is a weighted average of an interest rate differential, the rate of change in the exchange rate and in foreign exchange reserves, and can be written in equation form as

$$ERP_t = \alpha_1(r_i - r_j) + \alpha_2 \Delta e_t + \alpha_3 \Delta FER_t \qquad (5.1)$$

where $r_i - r_j$ is the interest rate differential between country i and a benchmark country, usually Germany (or the United States), Δe is the rate of change in the nominal exchange rate, and ΔFER is the rate of change in foreign exchange reserves, again relative to some benchmark country.[15] The weights α are chosen to equalize the conditional variances of the three factors that vary widely.[16] Nevertheless, the chosen weights

[14] Fuller details about the construction of the various indicators are provided on the web site dedicated to this volume found at http://www.wlu.ca/~wwwsbe/faculty/psiklos/centralbanks.htm.
[15] Monetary aggregates are not specifically considered in large part for reasons already discussed in Chapter 4.
[16] A clear indication of the necessity of this transformation is apparent from an examination of the unconditional volatilities.

have been criticized (for example, Weber 1995) as not actually adding to our understanding of how the three factors contribute to creating speculative pressure on an exchange rate. In what follows we essentially standardize the sources of exchange market pressure in Equation 5.1 and find that the unweighted average is at least as informative as the weighting scheme suggested by ERW which are, in any event, less relevant for the selection of countries considered in this study. Figure 5.1 illustrates the *ERP* measure for Germany, Japan, and the United States.

While it is apparent that several "large" shocks raise the value of *ERP*, particularly in the early 1970s and then again in the mid to late 1980s, it is also the case that all three sources of speculative pressure are not equally important over time (plot not shown). Hence, while changes in foreign exchange reserves drive the ERP measure in the late 1960s and into the early 1970s, exchange rate movements tend to dominate the index throughout the late 1970s until roughly the mid 1980s. Interest rate differentials then become the dominant feature of the index in the 1990s. Nevertheless, while these are the main features of the data for all twenty countries considered there is only a modest contemporaneous correlation across "large" or outlier values of the unweighted measure of *ERP* for, say, the United States or Germany and most other countries.[17] Hence, periods of economic "stress" originating from the exchange rate regime are not necessarily transmitted immediately and do not tend to occur simultaneously, though, as noted earlier, there are some broad common features across the countries considered.[18]

Fiscal Pressure

Although it is common to link fiscal and monetary policies, there is comparatively little evidence that one affects the other in a significant fashion, other than at exceptional times when the treasury resorts to

---

[17] "Large" in this context is arbitrarily defined as values for *ERP* that exceed 1. One exception is a correlation of .55 between the United States and Japan, as well as sizeable correlations between Germany and Austria on the one hand, and the Netherlands on the other (.57 and .39, respectively).

[18] Additional analyses, admittedly of an exploratory kind, suggest that values of *ERP* across countries are not related to each other in the long run, at least in the statistical sense. Moreover, it would appear that the index responds mostly to own past shocks that tend to dissipate after approximately four to six quarters. There is, however, some evidence that shocks in the *ERP* index from the United States and Germany have a modest impact on the index of other countries and that these last for a period of approximately one to four quarters (results not shown).

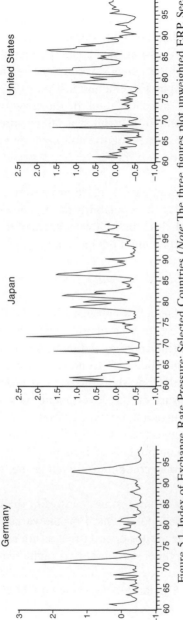

Figure 5.1 Index of Exchange Rate Pressure: Selected Countries (*Note*: The three figures plot unweighted ERP. See Equation 5.1. *Sources*: See text and http://www.wlu.ca/~wwwsbe/faculty/psiklos/centralbanks/htm.)

deficit financing on a large scale via the central bank. Nevertheless, it is conceivable that the impact of interest rates on the servicing of the public debt, as well as other indicators of pressures on the budget, such as recessions or the onset of a recession, may create pressures on central banks and lead to a change in the policy stance or the regime itself. There is evidence (see, for example, Estrella and Mishkin 1997) that the spread between domestic long and short rates, or the slope of the yield curve, predicts future recessions. In particular, a falling spread, say due to a rise in short-term interest rates relative to long-term yields is consistent with a tightening of monetary policy, and this would occur prior to a recession.

Unfortunately, as noted earlier, there are severe limitations on the available fiscal data and in the availability of recession dates at the quarterly frequency. Nevertheless, the following index of fiscal pressure (*FP*) was constructed, depending upon data availability.

$$FP_t = fiscal_t + recdur_t + \Delta spread_t \tag{5.2}$$

Fiscal is an estimate of the deficit (+)/surplus (−) to GDP ratio, *recdur* in an interaction variable capturing a quarter when the economy in question was in a recession (indicated by a dummy set to one in a recession and zero otherwise) multiplied by a trend to measure the length of the recession, and *spread* is the long-short interest rate differential. The basic idea is simply that pressure on the government budget is increased not only when there is a recession but pressure also increases with the length of the recession. The higher the value of *FP* the greater the pressure on fiscal policy, where all components of Equation 5.2 were standardized, and an unweighted average computed, as well as the individual components of the index.

There are a number of interesting features in the data. First, measures of the stance of fiscal policy based on the variable *fiscal* are fairly highly correlated among groups of countries, as are recession dates (not shown).[19] In particular, the *fiscal* variable is highly correlated between Germany and its major European partners, as is the correlation between the United States and Canada for the same variable.[20] Similarly, reces-

---

[19] The notes to Table 5.1 provide greater details.

[20] Correlations range between .5 and .9 between Germany and the Netherlands, Italy, Spain, and the United Kingdom.

sion indicators, for Australia and New Zealand indicators are also highly correlated with U.S. recessions.[21] The average duration of recessions does, however, differ somewhat across countries for which we have data (not shown).[22]

It is also instructive to examine the behavior of the yield curve across different groups of countries and across time. This is accomplished in Figure 5.2. Part a shows the strong common movements in the yield curve for Germany, Austria, and the Netherlands, most evident since their exchange rates became closely linked beginning in the 1980s. Hence, it is not surprising that there would be considerable common movement in their business cycles. Part b displays the yield curve for the G3 countries and it is apparent, to the extent that changes in the spread proxy business-cycle shocks, that there is a diversity of experiences between Germany, the United States, and Japan throughout most of the period examined. Indeed, the diversity of business cycle experiences is also a feature of a broader set of countries, as seen in Part c of the figure. There the U.S. spread is shown along with the unweighted average spread for the inflation targeting group of countries. Note, however, that while changes in the spread behave differently throughout the Bretton Woods period, and over much of the post-Bretton Wood era, there is a striking similarity in the spread across countries beginning in the mid 1990s.

The upshot then is that, as in the case of the index of exchange rate pressure, the index of fiscal pressure reflects the changing importance of the components of the index with recessions dominant in the late 1960s through to the late 1970s, the fiscal variable becoming relatively more important in the 1980s, while the yield curve plays an increasingly larger role throughout much of the 1990s. The index of fiscal pressure for the United States, for example, shown in Figure 5.3 is fairly typical of these changes but the principal source of crises from the fiscal side is a feature of the 1970s and 1980s (also see Table 5.2).

---

[21] Correlations range between .36 and .62 between Germany, France, Belgium, the Netherlands, Switzerland, and the United Kingdom. Correlations range between .53 and .58 between the United States, Canada, Australia, and New Zealand.

[22] Recession indicators for the United States are from the NBER (http://www.nber.org); Kim, Buckle, and Hall (1995) for New Zealand; Artis, Kontolemis, and Osborn (1997) for Canada, France, Germany, Italy, Japan, Switzerland, and the United Kingdom; and Reserve Bank of Australia for Australia. Also, see Siklos and Skoczylas (2002) who update the recession data.

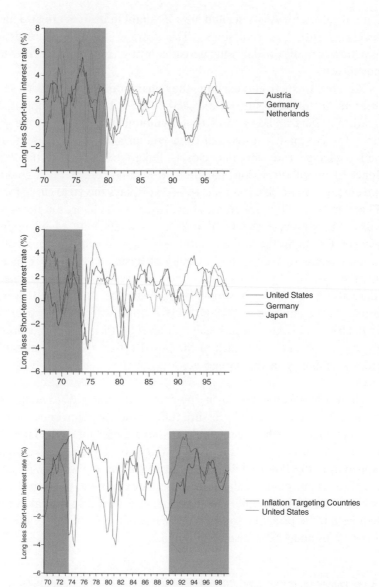

Figure 5.2 The Spread between Long and Short Interest Rates: Selected Comparisons (*Note*: See Chapter 1 for definition of long- and short-term interest rate for each country. Shaded areas in (a) post-Bretton Woods-pre ERM; (b) Bretton Woods; (c) Bretton Woods (until 1973) and inflation targeting (post-1990). For the purposes of Figure 5.3(c) inflation targeting countries include Australia, Canada, New Zealand, Sweden, and the United Kingdom. *Sources*: See text and http://www.wlu.ca/~wwwsbe/faculty/psiklos/centralbanks/htm.)

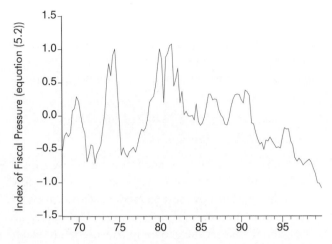

Figure 5.3 Index of Fiscal Pressure, United States, 1968–1999 (*Note*: See Equation 5.2. *Sources*: See text and http://www.wlu.ca/~wwwsbe/faculty/psiklos/centralbanks/htm.)

Political Pressure

The final catalyst for changes in monetary policy regimes is of the political variety. As noted earlier, Table 5.2 reveals relatively few instances of sharp political conflicts that can be directly, or indirectly, linked to monetary policy outcomes. Measuring political pressure is also made more difficult by the subtle manner in which political pressure influences the monetary policy regime in place. Nevertheless, one would expect that changes in inflation and unemployment, prolonged recessions, combined with a looming election, as well as the possibility of a partisan change in government would all contribute to political pressure that could spill over into the monetary policy arena.

It is assumed that political pressure (*PP*) is largely a feature of an approaching election and will be determined by the state of the economy, as measured by changes in unemployment and inflation in the months leading up to an election. In addition, it is also assumed that the prospect of a change in the party in power will also influence the degree of political pressure on monetary policy. While it is clear that such factors can contribute to influencing the stance of monetary policy, and possibly the monetary policy regime in place, any such indicator is only a probabilistic estimate of the likely forces of change that could influence monetary policy. As with the other indexes considered, the index of political pressure outlined below is, therefore, only suggestive of factors that can trigger policy changes and does not necessarily imply a causal interpretation of the relation between political pressure and the choice of a particular monetary policy regime.

Given the above discussion then the following expression is estimated:

$$PP_t = a_0 + a_1(L)\Delta\pi_t + a_2(L)\Delta U_t + a_3(L)EPRIOR_{t-1}$$
$$+ a_4(L)DRPT_t + a_5 recdur_t + \varepsilon_t \tag{5.3}$$

where all the variables have already been defined (see Chapter 4 and Equation 5.2). As noted earlier, the underlying model is somewhat ad hoc since it is not at all clear how best to model political pressure. Nevertheless, expression (Equation 5.3) does capture the widely accepted notion that the overall state of the economy, shortly before elections, as measured by changes in inflation, unemployment, whether the economy is in a recession, and the length of the recession, all contribute to increasing the likelihood that political authorities will apply political pressure of some kind on the central bank. The dependent variable is proxied by a binary variable, set to one during the quarter of the election and the two previous quarters, and so is estimated as a logit. Despite experimentation, Equation 5.3 produces reasonably satisfactory results with pseudo-R^2 ranging between 0.3 and 0.5.

Figure 5.4 illustrates the predicted values for the political pressure index for three countries, namely New Zealand, Germany, and the United States. Previously (see Chapters 2 and 3), the experience of these countries was highlighted.

It is interesting to note that political pressure, as measured here, begins to rise sharply in New Zealand, beginning in the mid 1980s, when reforms culminating in the adoption of inflation targets and an autonomous central bank were implemented. Political pressure rises again around the time of changes in the policy targets agreement and breeches in the inflation target. This result is not, however, driven by developments in inflation and unemployment alone as both show a tendency to fall, for the most part, during the sample considered. Rather the onset of elections, partisan changes in government (and a change in the electoral process) all contributed to the evolution of political pressure over time.

In Germany's case, political pressure appears to be a constant feature though it rarely exceeds the arbitrary threshold of .5 that might be considered "significant," except in the mid 1980s, that is, after a number of

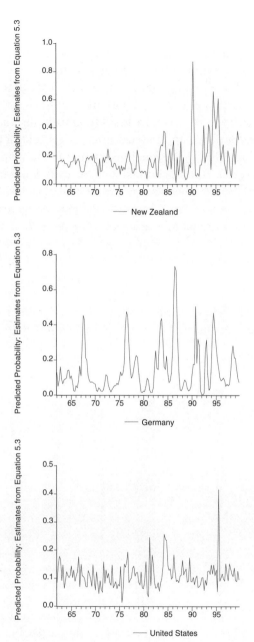

Figure 5.4 Index of Political Pressure: New Zealand, Germany, United States, 1962–1999 (*Note*: Predicted values from estimation of Equation 5.3. *Sources*: See text and http://www.wlu.ca/~wwwsbe/faculty/psiklos/centralbanks/htm.)

years of high inflation (by German standards). Turning to the U.S. evidence, we find little evidence of significant political pressure on the Fed since the 1960s. While perhaps inconsistent with the widespread belief, discussed earlier, that there exist political pressures on the U.S. Fed, the results are consistent with the finding that it is relatively difficult to find *statistical* evidence of such political pressures. By contrast, political pressure on the Bundesbank is easier to identify empirically though Germany's inflation performance and the autonomy of its central bank are not really in question. Clearly, the federal structure of German politics, and Germany's place in Europe, contrast with the experience of the U.S. Fed, at least since 1960. It may also be the case that, as has been said by many, while successive U.S. administrations may disagree with Fed policy at times they infrequently disagree with monetary policy outcomes.

AN ASSESSMENT

What are we to make of these disparate results? If we take Germany's inflationary experience as an example, Figure 5.5 illustrates that, as is

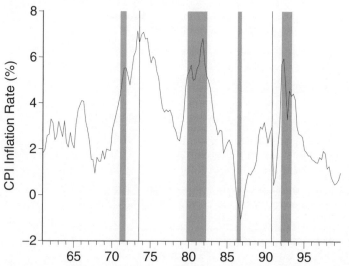

Figure 5.5 Germany's Inflation Rate and "Large" Economic Shocks, 1960–1999 (*Note*: Vertical lines and shaded areas based on data in Table 5.1. Inflation is rate of change in CPI. *Sources*: See text and http://www.wlu.ca/~wwwsbe/faculty/psiklos/centralbanks/htm.)

true of all the other countries in this study, it has experienced a succession of shocks over the past four decades. Hence, any policy regime that does not permit sufficient flexibility in accommodating numerous shocks from different sources, namely from exchange rates, fiscal and political considerations will be doomed to failure. Flexibility does not imply a loss of confidence or credibility, as the German example also illustrates. This is just another way of expressing, in perhaps more formal terms, the notion of limited discretion. It is this type of experience that may explain why a growing number of countries have adopted, implicitly, as in the German case, or explicitly, the policy of inflation targeting (see Chapter 7). The other contributing factor, documented in the preceding chapters, is the mounting, and often quantitative, evidence accumulated by central banks since World War II that has permitted them to assess the nature and source of the economic shocks they face and the appropriate remedies to tackle them.

SUMMARY

This chapter attempts to provide a reconciliation of the gap between the econometric and qualitative evidence concerning central bank behavior and performance. First, it appears that the gap between the two strands is narrowing as most countries in our study have found a greater degree of common purpose in defining what constitutes good monetary policy outcomes. Second, econometric evidence has difficulty capturing the occasional subtle nature and complex sources of institutional change that impact central banks. To illustrate, the chapter presents measures of exchange rate, fiscal, and political pressures on monetary policy. Broadly speaking, these have diminished in the 1990s, consistent with greater international agreement on what constitutes good monetary policy. However, the period between 1960 and 1990 is one of experimentation with different monetary policy strategies and differences across countries in the timing of "large" economic shocks. In general, the trend has been toward more flexibility (or discretion) in conducting monetary policy within a framework that constrains central banks sufficiently to deliver desirable economic outcomes but where the ultimate responsibility for policy outcomes is clearly defined. The mechanisms that are necessary to arrive at this outcome are addressed in the next chapter.

6 | Accountability, Disclosure, and Conflict Resolution

INTRODUCTION

The previous chapters have built the case for a view of central banks that recognizes the simultaneous role of institutional and economic factors on their performance in an historical context. In addition, the success of central bank policies will also be crucially dependent on how the central bank communicates its policies to the public. The importance of a greater public understanding of central bank policies is not new, as we have seen. However, the task of improving the quality and quantity of information disclosed in public has taken on greater urgency in recent years, in parallel with two other notable developments. They are: the clarification of the responsibilities of the monetary authority and the increase in accountability to governments and, by implication, to the public at large. It should be emphasized that accountability is not meant as an end run around the autonomy of the central bank. Instead, as we shall see, accountability cannot be entirely divorced from procedures to handle conflicts between the central bank and the government. As the Royal Commission of 1936 into the operations of the Bank of Canada fully recognized ". . . while the Bank should resist temporary gusts of public fancy, it must in the long-run show responsiveness to public opinion and be responsible to government" (Royal Commission 1936). Needless to say, finding the right balance of rights and responsibilities in this context is no easy matter.

Prior to the 1990s, there seems to have been little or no interest among academics or policy makers with the role of communication in the formation and validation of expectations formed by economic agents. Economic theory, especially following the widespread adoption of rational expectations, simply assumed that expectations were formed conditional on some information set and were, at least on average, correct. The marginal costs versus benefits calculus implicitly governed how much information was compiled and the notion that economic agents are forward looking was sufficient to essentially guarantee that individuals could not be fooled for long by policy makers who were thought to spring surprises on the public on a regular basis, regardless of the quality or quantity of information publicly available. Yet, these views cannot be defended once the monetary policy strategy in place is considered. As we shall see, the preference for quantified inflation control objectives is part and parcel of the developments outlined above. One advantage of explicit inflation targets is that, in principle, it should make it easier for the public to evaluate how well the central banks are performing (that is, reduce monitoring costs; see Walsh 1999).

Central banks can also improve their credibility and increase the trust placed in them according to how well and clearly they communicate their intentions, independently of the monetary policy strategy in place, and how they are prepared to react when fiscal and monetary authorities are in conflict over policy directions. While it is true that the role of communication may be seen as critical, regardless of the policy framework in place, inflation targeting has the distinct advantage of summarizing, using a fairly well-understood concept, the agreed upon *outcome* of monetary policy actions. By contrast, other policy frameworks, such as monetary or exchange rate targeting, are more easily misinterpreted by the public and manipulated by policy makers, thereby increasing the difficulty agents face in forming expectations. Moreover, economic theory gives pride of place to expectations of inflation. Even if, say, money growth or exchange rate behavior are key determinants of inflation, the links between them may be complex and interpretations of policy performance may be unduly influenced by econometric estimation rather than by purely economic considerations.

Hence, it is not surprising that discussions about how central banks communicate their policy actions are strongly linked with the adoption of inflation control objectives. By making it clear that inflation performance is the crucial measure of central bank performance it then becomes critical to explain what factors drive inflation, the limits of central bank actions in influencing its evolution over time, and how the statutory limitations placed on a central bank can also play a role in attaining the inflation control objectives.

Accordingly, the present chapter considers relatively new pressures faced by central banks whose aim is to clarify monetary policy objectives, and improve or solidify credibility. They are: accountability, disclosure,[1] governance, and conflict resolution procedures.

Existing work on quantifying the role of disclosure or transparency and accountability is limited. Briault, Haldane, and King (1996) report that more independent central banks are, on average, less accountable[2] whereas the two concepts might be expected to be positively related to each other. Eijffinger and de Haan (1996) argue that independence, if guaranteed via the conservative central banker model of Lohmann (1992; also see Chapter 4), need not lead to more accountability but instead is likely to enhance the prospect of central bank–government conflicts. de Haan, Amtenbrink, and Eijffinger (1999) revise the definition of accountability proposed by Briault et al. (1996) by adding characteristics relative to decisions about ultimate objectives of monetary policy and find that, thus defined, accountability and central bank independence are positively related in a sample of sixteen central banks (including the ECB) based on the most recent legislation governing their behavior. However, more independent central banks are also less transparent, contrary to what is believed to be desirable, as we shall see.

Existing work also tends to underemphasize the role of governance and conflict resolution procedures in assessing the implications of accountability and disclosure on policy formation. This chapter attempts to place each of these characteristics into the appropriate context and establish their significance in the conduct of monetary policy.

An important point made in this chapter is that attention devoted to central bank independence issues in academic and policy circles, while undoubtedly important, masks an increased emphasis on the role of communication in policy making. We begin with a brief explanation of the role, at least in theory, of the various dimensions along which central bank communication with the public takes place, and how these may be used to signal credibility. While it is clear that there are a variety of ways

---

[1] The literature typically refers to the concept of transparency. Transparency and disclosure have a similar meaning. However, rankings of central banks according to the transparency of their operations usually assume that the maximum release of inflation by the central bank is the most desirable outcome. The term disclosure also comes closest to being representative of the debate about how open a central bank should be with the public and markets. According to the Oxford English Dictionary disclosure is "The action of disclosing or opening up to view" while transparency has a less precise meaning, namely "the quality or condition of being transparent." Finally, in financial circles, the degree to which investors and regulators can gauge the operations of firms is measured by the degree of "disclosure" not transparency.

[2] A more precise definition of accountability will be provided later.

central banks can "talk," the remainder of the chapter focuses on some of the key ingredients only. Nevertheless, the indexes of accountability and disclosure introduced here include a broad set of characteristics, some of which play a role in the next chapter, where an outline of what constitutes a good "framework" for monetary policy is addressed in greater detail.

HOW MUCH TO TALK? CENTRAL BANK SIGNALING AND CREDIBILITY

Below, an approach is described that can help explain under what conditions it may be optimal for a central bank to signal more or less frequently. The approach relies on the notion that the central bank has some discretion and the manner in which discretion is practiced is multifaceted (and, therefore, potentially complex). Consider Figure 6.1 that measures the type of central bank on the vertical axis. Instead of viewing central

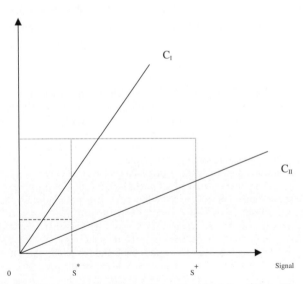

Figure 6.1 The Central Bank's Signal Extraction Problem (*Note*: The horizontal axis measures the signaling costs of monetary policy. The vertical axis measures credibility at attaining a particular monetary policy objective. There is some asymmetric information between the central bank and the public. Type I central bank has low credibility, type II has high credibility. S* is optimal for type II, S = 0 is optimal for type I, but equilibrium depend on how informative the signal is.)

banks as being "conservative" versus "accommodative,"[3] central banks are evaluated according to whether they are "credible" or not at achieving some stated objective.[4] The credibility of a central bank is affected by signaling costs.[5] I shall refer to these costs as the signaling costs of monetary policy. The problem for financial markets and the public is to evaluate the central bank's credibility according to the various signals emanating from the central banks. The chief purpose of the signals is to convey to the public whether the monetary policy process and stance are well understood by the bank. As the central bank's understanding of the underlying true state of the economy rises, and its ability to convey this information to the public, so does the credibility of the central bank.[6] I assume that the central bank knows what type it is while the financial market and the public assumes that signaling costs are negatively correlated with credibility. The latter is determined by some aggregation of four characteristics. They are, not in any order of importance: autonomy, disclosure, accountability, and past policy successes.[7] A low value for either of these characteristics translates into lower net returns in the form of credibility enhancement (that is, the difference between credibility and signaling costs).[8] Presumably, the payoffs are in the form of enhanced reputation. Figure 6.1 assumes there are two types of central banks: One has low credibility (type I), while another has relatively high

---

[3] These labels have been popular in the recent literature on central bank behavior but they strike me as having the same drawback as "partisan" labels used by economists and political scientists to describe central bank attitudes toward inflation versus unemployment changes. See Johnson and Siklos (1996) and Chapter 4.

[4] The precise form in which objectives are stated is, of course, important but this is a consideration that is ignored for the moment.

[5] The intellectual debt to Spence's original signaling model (1973) will be obvious. While it is quite likely that signaling costs might be a function of the type of signal, the resulting complication is ignored in what follows. An earlier outline of the model was discussed in Siklos (1999c).

[6] Earlier in this study (see Chapter 2), it was suggested that reputation is likened to a "stock." Alternatively, "credibility" may be thought of as a flow. Thus, in the context of a repeated "game" between the central bank and the public, the outcome of each game is measured in terms of credibility (with lower credibility reducing the reputational "stock" of the central bank). Also, see Cukierman (1986; 1996; 2000) and Posen (1998b).

[7] Autonomy and past policy successes have already been addressed in this study. The present chapter concentrates on the attributes of accountability and disclosure.

[8] For example, Fuhrer (1997) defines credibility as a condition that holds ". . . if businesses and consumers have come to believe that the bank will act systematically to attain a reasonably small set of ultimate objectives" (p. 26). His study raises the possibility that if there is more "noise" about which objective is currently being followed, due to the conflict between high- versus low-frequency data, this can serve to reduce credibility.

credibility (type II). If signaling costs are C_I then the optimal solution for central bank type I is not to signal at all (that is, $s = 0$). By contrast, if signaling costs for type II central bank are C_{II} then it is optimal to signal s^*. Clearly, there are an infinite number of signaling equilibria, that is, an infinite number of s^*. If signaling costs are primarily related to statutory factors, this result may partly explain why it is so difficult to extract meaningful information about central bank behavior based upon variables such as legal autonomy, whether the CEO of the central bank is "conservative" or not, or even based on the simple correlation between inflation performance and indicators of statutory autonomy. The reason is that it may be costly to determine the type of central bank based on statutory factors alone (that is, this signal is not sufficiently informative). An implication of this result then is that some central banks may require a higher s^* to signal their type thereby incurring greater signaling costs, as in the case where the optimal signal is, say, s^+ in Figure 6.1. Hence, some central banks with little reputation need to signal more frequently to be recognized as credible central banks, but it is not immediately clear that statutory reforms represent anything other than simply a necessary condition for such an outcome.[9] They are not, by themselves, sufficient to "buy" credibility.

It may be that a higher s is required because of existing deficiencies in the statutory relationship between the central bank and the government requiring more signaling, or the source of the difficulty may lie elsewhere, namely strong priors in the marketplace that the central bank is really type I (that is, low reputation) no matter how clearly or frequently the central bank signals that it is a type II central bank. In a sense, this requires the central bank to "overshoot" in terms of information provided to the marketplace or produce "excessive" information to remedy the failure of the signaling device. This is particularly true if more autonomy, disclosure, or accountability practices are not in place or the necessary stamp of approval requires outside bodies (for example, government or some commission recommending reform). Alternatively, the central bank may be hampered by too few policy successes. An obvious option is to search for other techniques that have the effect of reducing the effective signaling costs. How could this be accomplished? For

---

[9] Eijffinger, Hoeberichts, and Schaling (2000) reach the same conclusion but predict that openness will be associated with reduced flexibility. In the above setup this need not be the case because, with greater credibility and an enhanced reputation, the central bank also acquires some flexibility in implementing policies.

example, the more specific or clear the inflation target, and the consequences for the central bank's management of failure to meet the objective, the greater the incentive for the monetary authority to signal its type. Other devices might include the publication of inflation forecasts and the scenarios they are predicated upon, more speeches by central bank officials (noisy as these might be), the publication of an inflation report, or even the reporting of indices which effectively signal whether the central bank is attempting to focus on multiple objectives or not (for example, a monetary conditions index). Individually, or taken together, such devices have been viewed as increasing the likelihood that a central bank will behave more systematically or follow a "rule," that is, enhance the possibility that the public will look at the central bank and become convinced that it is a type II central bank. The implication of the above is that clear policy rules *increase* the likelihood and frequency of signals to financial markets and the public but at the risk that the central bank will be seen as shortsighted (also see Chapter 5).

The framework in Figure 6.1 can also be used to illustrate other possible outcomes. For example, suppose that if $s \geq s^*$ the central bank is of type II with a probability of 1, while there is a probability θ $(0 < \theta < 1)$ that a central bank is of type I if $s < s^*$, and a probability of $1 - \theta$ of being a type II central bank. The optimal amount of signaling is then 0 for both central banks. This could be viewed as the "free rider" case where signaling is not optimal so long as one of the nonsignaling central banks is type II or if an alternative technology exists which replaces the need for signaling (for example, as in fixing the exchange rate to a country whose central bank is type II with a high probability). Alternatively, a type II central bank may be secretive in nature and so it believes that the net credibility gains from signaling are lower than if it did not signal at all.

There is another interesting case to consider. Suppose that some identifiable characteristic or "technology" can be used to discriminate between central bank types but is unrelated to the type of central bank. In other words, the conditional probability of being a type I or a type II central bank is unaffected by the identifiable signal. Under these circumstances it is possible for the more credible central bank to be worse off than a central bank that chooses not to invest in the signaling device. Thus, for example, a country that targets inflation, whose governor is accountable to the government or the public, and whose operations are transparent, could still end up with less credibility (if s^* is high enough) than another central bank that did not resort to the additional signaling effort.[10] Hence, some central banks are more credible, not because of the signals, but because of the information structure of the market itself. An alternative interpretation of the above analysis is to suggest that it is possible that different policy rules can lead to observationally equivalent outcomes. The signaling technology fails to discriminate among central banks. It is perhaps for this reason that attempts to measure or understand how a central bank communicates with the public becomes an important issue. In other words, accountability and disclosure represent costly signals that may assist the public in deciding whether the central bank is credible or not and, in so doing, reduce the asymmetric information problems that lie at the core of the questions discussed here. Instead, the literature has tended to automatically assume that more of both is, regardless of content, better. Of course, assessing the "quality" of a signal is difficult but no less relevant to the issues under investigation. The analysis is also complicated by the nature of the event motivating the signal. For example, when the problem of identifying a central bank type arises because of the failure of governments to implement appropriate fiscal policies, the signals (or their cost) need not be the same as when the crisis stems not from the failure of some of the fundamentals of economic policy but from the behavior of the financial sector itself (as in the most recent Asian financial crisis). In this case, the signals that were previously appropriate need no longer convey the same information about the central bank's credibility.

THE MEANING OF ACCOUNTABILITY

This is not the first study to note that "inputs," such as central bank legislation, do not by themselves deliver the desired "output," namely "good" monetary policy outcomes. Briault, Haldane, and King (1996), Crow (1994), Posen (1993; 1995), Roll (1993), Siklos (1995), and several other authors, all deal with the potential impact on monetary policy actions of greater central bank accountability.[11]

Accountability is defined here in terms of the following criteria:

---

[10] This might also explain why the output and inflation gains of inflation targeting countries did not materialize as quickly as might have been expected.

[11] The papers given at the 1996 Jackson Hole conference, which brings together central bankers, policy makers, and academics, were, in the main, also devoted to the question of accountability. These are collected in Federal Reserve Bank of Kansas City (1996). Also, see Lindsay (1997).

1. The clarity and precision with which the objectives of monetary policy are stated and/or communicated;[12]
2. The degree and forms of communication of policy decisions and strategies to accomplish the stated objectives;
3. The extent to which the central bank is required to answer for past decisions, the form such responses must take, and the nature of the persons or bodies to whom the chief executive of the central bank is responsible.

How do the foregoing characteristics contribute to a clarification of what is meant by "good" monetary policy?

First, clarity and precision in outlining the objectives of monetary policy *simplifies* the outcome of monetary actions.[13] It becomes more difficult, therefore, to hide behind technical terms not widely understood or followed by the public. Nevertheless, clarity of objectives is not sufficient if the central bank is still able to portray its performance in the best possible light and is not sufficiently sensitive to alternative or critical views. The reason is that the public recognizes that even if a quantitative measure of inflation is the central bank's sole objective, a central bank is not entirely responsible for the outcome. Other domestic and international pressures can affect inflation in any given period. Moreover, a central bank cannot nor is it even expected to react to every economic shock. As noted previously, it faces the daunting task of distinguishing between temporary and permanent shocks in a world that does not permit their easy identification. As Milton Friedman (1962: p. 233) in reviewing how the U.S. Fed reported on its activities, put it long ago, central banks can be prey to an easy trap when communicating with the public (see Chapter 2).

Therefore, additional constraints are required to ensure objectivity in measuring central bank performance. One way of doing so, without unduly hampering the flexibility of a central bank, is by evaluating or

---

[12] Item 1 also appears in the definition put forward in Siklos (1995). Briault, Haldane, and King (1996) propose an index of accountability based on the sum of the following characteristics: parliamentary monitoring, minutes published, inflation or monetary report published, and the presence of an override clause. The contrast between their index and the one developed here will become apparent later.

[13] Winkler (2000) argues that the success of transparency in central banking depends on whether the public and the central bank are likely to share similar interpretations of the data. Hence, transparency and clarity need not be the same. Simplicity may go hand in hand with clarity if it is properly communicated and is consistent with the overall monetary policy strategy of the central bank. We return to this issue later.

requiring that the central bank communicate with the government and the public sufficiently regularly to allow both groups to independently form correct views about how well monetary policy is being conducted. This need not require that vast quantities of information be communicated. Rather, the value of communication is best measured via the quality of the information provided. Once again, the focus is on the "output" of the central bank and not simply inputs such as whether the central bank reports to the government, parliament, or the public but places the emphasis instead on the *content* of the reporting. For example, it may make a difference whether the central bank relies extensively on statistics or indicators constructed in-house as opposed to ones generated by other agencies or institutions. Additionally, it will also matter whether a central bank appears to be forward looking instead of providing only retrospective analyses which leaves open the possibility of an ex-post-facto justification of monetary policy outcomes. In this connection, of course, it is important to consider whether, as some have claimed (for example, Tarkka and Mayes 1999), this last requirement is greatly assisted via the publication of inflation forecasts.[14] However, as item 2 emphasizes, a central bank is more likely to be held accountable if the public knows the monetary policy strategy in place. After all, an inflation forecast is, once again, only one input into the central bank's decision-making process, and the assumptions and uncertainty around such forecasts must of necessity change over time. Finally, even if we put aside these questions, how are we to compare central bank forecasts with those of the private sector? The latter, of course, also publish forecasts but the details of the procedures and models used to generate such

---

[14] Unless stated, we do not emphasize the distinction between a "forecast" and a "projection." The latter are viewed as being conditional on a set of assumptions, such as an unchanged monetary policy. While such a distinction can be important it can also contribute to public confusion. As a member of the European Parliament pointed out, in response to a statement by the president of the European Central Bank who asked to clarify the usage of the term "projections": "I look forward to the notes that you will give to the Oxford English Dictionary on the difference in definition between projections and forecasts" (Committee on Economic and Monetary Affairs of the European Parliament 2000). A separate issue, to be addressed later in this chapter, is the location of responsibility for such forecasts. Central bankers have pointed out that projections or forecasts represent an input into the central bank decision-making body's decision on the appropriate policy stance. Consequently, evaluation of central bank performance cannot be made solely on the basis of such data nor can the central bank CEO be made "responsible" for such forecasts. Indeed, as will become clear later in this chapter, rather too much weight has been placed on this single piece of information that, after all, forms but one element of a well-developed communications strategy.

forecasts are not ordinarily made public for obvious reasons, as possibly only the forecasters' clients are privy to such information. Moreover, if the central bank achieves and maintains low inflation for some time it is conceivable that the private sector may find it more difficult to forecast inflation, especially if methods that forecast inflation based on historical extrapolations are used. The reason is that inflation may behave unpredictably inside a credible inflation target range.[15] In any event, even when a central bank attempts to overcome some of the problems referred to previously, the outcome may lead to further confusion rather than clarification about how the central bank sees the future.

In this connection, the procedures followed by the Bank of England are relevant for many of the issues concerning the difficulties of communicating monetary policy (Bowen 1995; Britton and Whittley 1996; Haldane 1996). Since 1993, it has published a quarterly *Inflation Report*. This document presents independent assessments of the past performance of monetary policy. (That is, central bank officials independently arrive at the conclusions before they are shown to or discussed by finance or treasury officials of the government.) The Bank of England also goes further by providing forecasts ("projections," as it calls them) up to two years ahead. However, rather than provide a confidence interval around such forecasts, it assigns a probability to actual inflation falling within a certain range.[16] It can then chart these forecasts and compare them with its own internally produced forecasts.

The appeal of this approach is that, given the different assumptions that go into producing various private sector forecasts, the range of projections gives an idea of the risks associated with different inflation outcomes. There are, however, some drawbacks. While the projections are informative about the range of possible inflation rates, their use relieves the bank from committing itself to a particular scenario. Indeed, since each projection band has a 10% probability of being correct, the band with a probability of being 90% correct can become quite wide. (For example, the May 2000 *Inflation Report* projected a 90% chance that actual inflation in 2002 would lie between approximately –0.80 and 3.8% – a wide range.) Moreover, unless the public is aware of the differences

---

[15] This outcome is consistent whether inflation is formally or informally (but credibly) targeted. See Siklos (1999b) and Akerlof, Dickens, and Perry (2000).

[16] Although, to the extent that a targeted inflation rate represents an upper limit with zero inflation as a lower limit, an implicit range of 0 to 2% is effectively assumed (see Åkerholm and Brunila 1995: p. 93).

in assumptions that lead to the various outcomes, it cannot make up its own mind about the most likely scenario.[17]

Sweden's Riksbank discusses a variety of scenarios for the key inputs into its projections for major price aggregates (for example, CPI inflation, core inflation) and presents a forecast for the "main" scenario, meaning the Riksbank's most likely views about the future course of the economy given constant future interest rates over a two-year horizon. While such an approach is certainly useful it reveals little about possible biases in future interest rates.[18]

By contrast, an understanding of a central bank's strategy for conducting monetary policy is more likely to give the public an overall assessment of the conditions under which the central bank will tighten or loosen future monetary policy. Even if this is accepted one must be clear about what constitutes an informative and useful communication of a monetary policy strategy. Recall that a strategy refers to a "plan for successful action . . ." (*Oxford English Dictionary*). However, not all attempts to communicate monetary policy intentions that do not involve the publication of inflation or other forecasts need be successful. The recent experience of the U.S. Federal Reserve is instructive in this connection. Historically, the Fed, like most other central banks, tended to raise or reduce interest rates following the appearance of economic evidence that required such action. However, since Alan Greenspan became chair of the Board of Governors in 1987, he has made it clear on several occasions that the Fed must act in advance of its expectations about the future course of the economy. "Because monetary policy works with a lag, we need to be forward looking, taking actions to forestall imbalances that may not be visible for months. There is no alternative to basing actions on forecasts, at least implicitly. It means that we often have to tighten or ease *before* the need for action is evident to the public at large, . . . This process is not easy to get right . . . and is often difficult to convey . . ." (Greenspan 1996). This has resulted in a series of "preemptive strikes" against expected upsurges of inflation, followed by a gradual reduction in the Fed funds rate, as fears of higher future inflation among the FOMC members subsided. The mechanism used to ensure that the

[17] Wallis (1999) points out that the Bank of England's "fan" charts assume that upside and downside inflation risks are the same that they need not be. The bank has since made some adjustments to the presentation of its forecast of risks.

[18] Goodhart (2000a) points out that such an approach, while seemingly sensible implies that projections will most likely differ from what a pure forecast would produce.

Fed provided more disclosure of monetary policy actions via the release of the "minutes of the FOMC meetings," as well as serving as a warning to the public and financial markets that the Fed would carry out policy based on its views of the future course of the U.S. economy. These minutes were intended to announce whether the Fed tilted toward interest rate increases or reductions. Unfortunately, soon after the practice began the Fed realized that its announcements could also confuse markets. In particular, market participants were unsure whether the Fed's "bias" in interest rate developments signaled an actual intention to change these rates or simply a probable change in rates.[19] Moreover, the horizon the Fed had in mind was also left unclear. Even Alan Greenspan noted that the Fed's directive in August 1999 ". . . was subject to differing interpretations."[20] Recognition of this problem has led to an attempt to ensure that the Fed's intentions are made clearer. Thus, for example, in the FOMC meeting of November 1999, the minutes stated ". . . all the members supported raising the Committee's target for the federal funds rate by 25 basis points at this meeting." The minutes then go on to state that ". . . any action might have to wait until the meeting in early February . . . [in the year 2000]" to contemplate further action. In January 2000 the Fed announced that, shortly after each FOMC meeting, a statement would be issued announcing its ". . . assessment of the risks in the foreseeable future to the attainment of its long-run goals of price stability and suitable economic growth."[21]

The bottom line is that a successful strategy involves being forward looking but without tying one's hand in advance in the event that some scenario, as is implicit in the case of the Fed's "bias" approach, does not accord with the facts as available to central bankers when they feel they must act. Note also that, as defined, the development of a monetary policy strategy permits governments and central banks to define their actions in relation to society's tolerance for inflation. This is another way of saying that the link between central bank autonomy and inflation performance can be severed. Consequently, it would appear that the Fed's approach of summarizing internal projections (as derived from the

---

[19] Thornton and Wheelock (2000; also see references therein) point out that while the inherent asymmetry in the FOMC statements were never defined it was intended as a consensus-building exercise. Moreover, the authors confirm that the FOMC typically did deliver on the signals.

[20] As quoted in R.W. Stevenson, "Fed Reconsiders Policy of Disclosing Tilt on Rates," *The New York Times*, October 8, 1999.

[21] Found at http://www.federalreserve.gov.

Greenbook), together with consensus projections from the private sector and the central government, as is done in its semiannual Monetary Policy Report to Congress, supplemented by an estimate of the uncertainty around its own internal forecast, offers a reasonable way of best communicating the strategy of monetary policy. It should also be added that the U.S. strategy offers one way of communicating disagreements within the FOMC about the best policy actions and the inherent risks such decisions entail.

The Bank of England is another recent addition to the list of central banks that make known the diversity of views within the policy-making body. Again, it is noteworthy that the diversity of views exists within a framework where the aim to maintain low and stable inflation rates is clearly enunciated. While it is certainly possible that an airing of views may increase uncertainty, it is more likely that such uncertainty is reduced because it is almost always the case that disagreements are finely balanced and that financial markets especially ought to be able to make their own assessments of the persuasiveness of each of the view expressed by committee members.[22] Note that, as defined, publication of minutes of central bank meetings can become harmful if the strategy of monetary policy is unclear. Otherwise, publication of minutes becomes useful as a means of confirming, ex post, that the chosen monetary strategy is not only suitable but is consistently being followed over time.[23] It is important to note that, in the examples considered previously, a committee serves as the crucial vehicle to deliver information to the public. We return, in the discussion that follows, to the role and significance of such committees in the conduct of monetary policy. Nevertheless, a few additional comments here are in order. First, while committees may be viewed as conducive to the garbling of information, via the strategic behavior of committee members, there are good theoretical reasons to suggest that they are a relatively more efficient structure than the single decision-maker alternative (Crawford and Sobel 1982; Li, Rosen, and Suen 2001). Nevertheless, complicating matters greatly is the fact that monetary policy committees must decide not only whether or not to change interest rates but also the size of the interest rate change. In this connection, it seems clear that vital importance ought to be attached to

---

[22] Siklos (2000b) provides some evidence supporting this contention using high-frequency (that is, daily) data.

[23] In this connection, the reluctance of the European Central Bank to release such minutes, becomes somewhat understandable. Also, see Lohmann (1999).

the clarity and persuasiveness of the evidence presented to the members of such committees. Accountability and disclosure can greatly assist in this cause as we shall see. Finally, committee structures enhance the possibility that a common set of goals can be developed for the conduct of monetary policy. This can be extremely useful as a means of enhancing the central bank's credibility when it must decide how quickly to respond to events that can call into question the primary objectives of monetary policy, as well as reinforcing the appropriateness of decisions concerning the nature of the response to economic shocks. In so doing, committees can also serve to counteract political pressure stemming from a disagreement with the political authorities over the current stance of monetary policy. Committee structures, especially when their *modus operandi* is explicit, suggest an efficient use of information in policy decisions, and that proper care is taken in the face of the inherent uncertainties that arise in attempting to deliver good monetary policy outcomes.

The lack of clarity in communicating the current thinking of the senior management of a central bank is illustrated by the recent experience of the newly formed European Central Bank. The practice of communicating the outcome of deliberations by the ECB's Governing Council immediately after meetings leaves no time for careful reflection of the disparate views especially when the publication of minutes is not permitted. Indeed, it is not at all uncommon for participants and interested observers of ECB policy to be confused by the public leanings of the ECB president and the occasionally contradictory statements of the members of the Governing Council. This despite the stated explanation for not releasing minutes of meetings meant to ostensibly protect the free flow of discussion within the Governing Council. Instead, the outcome creates more confusion and dissatisfaction with the communications policy of the ECB rather than undermining the work of the Council.[24]

In the ongoing debate about disclosure of central bank actions it is becoming abundantly clear that policy makers have, at times, confused the quantity of information provided with quality. Central bankers would be well advised to keep in mind Herbert Simon's admonition of long ago.

---

[24] The recent ECB publication (European Central Bank 2001) is silent on the pros and cons of different approaches to accountability and disclosure other than to essentially state that it makes the greatest efforts to be both open and accountable. Other critical views are in Eijffinger (2000) and also see Sims (2001).

"In a world where information is relatively scarce, and where problems for decision are few and simple, information is almost always a positive good. In a world where attention is a scarce resource, information may be a luxury, for it may turn attention from what is important to what is unimportant. We cannot afford to attend to information simply because it is there" (Simon 1978: p. 13). The result, as we shall see, is that while the ECB ranks high in accountability criteria it fails rather miserably in the disclosure ranking.

How a central bank communicates to the public has become a topic of considerable interest among economists.[25] Many of the developments surrounding this aspect of central bank performance have taken place during the 1990s and are related to the increased emphasis placed on the role of price stability and, in several cases, the mandate to achieve a certain inflation target. Accordingly, we return to this question in Chapter 7 where inflation control measures are discussed at greater length.

THE VALUE OF DISCLOSURE

It is useful to devote some space to deal with the nomenclature for it is easy to misrepresent the value of information disclosure by a central bank, also referred to as transparency. In what follows, notions of transparency focus on the role of information disclosure. Sanctions for failure to meet stipulated commitments are viewed as a separate, but crucial, characteristic of what constitutes "good" monetary policy. Disclosure or transparency is, of course, related to, but not the same as accountability.

"Transparency here plays the part of self-imposed commitment: by disclosing the basis of the policy decisions, the central bank enables the

---

[25] Indeed, Blinder, Goodhart, Hildebrand, Lipton, and Wyplosz (2001) consider many of the issues that have been discussed here. Their focus is on the U.S. Fed, the ECB, the Bank of Japan, the Bank of England, and the Reserve Bank of New Zealand. Their study does not rank those central banks, as such, according to the quality of their communications policies but it does make recommendations including a clearer policy objective for the Fed, a more transparent decision-making process for the ECB, a general redesign of the role and responsibilities of the Bank of Japan, and more clarity in the relationship between individual members of the Bank of England's Monetary Policy Committee and the decision of the group as a whole. It is interesting, and instructive, that the procedures used in implementing monetary policy in the United Kingdom and New Zealand have recently been the subject of comprehensive reviews. See Kohn (2001) and Svensson (2001).

general public to assess their adequacy and impose a sanction, if appropriate. At the same time, the central bank forfeits the option of pursuing a policy other than what it has announced" (Deutsche Bundesbank 2000a: p. 17).

The foregoing quote makes it clear that while transparency is a means toward attaining the objective of greater accountability, the latter is only achieved if, and only if, the information disclosed by the central bank does, in fact, enhance the public's understanding of how monetary policy decisions are made.

It is usually argued that transparency ought to be equated with making public a greater volume of information. This is undoubtedly correct, up to a point. However, beyond simply providing information, the ability to understand how monetary policy is made must of necessity be determined by the quality and clarity of the information provided. It is in large part for this reason that the term disclosure is used in preference over the expression transparency. The former better conveys the emphasis on the relative importance of assessing the content of what is being exposed by a central bank. Having made the point that there is more to transparency in central banking than the mere release of information, in what follows, transparency and disclosure will be used more or less interchangeably, unless otherwise indicated. Needless to say, there has been considerable interest in studying the role and functions of transparency. Buiter (1999), Geraats (2000), Issing (1999), Mayes and Razzak (1998), Remsperger and Worms (1999), and Winkler (2000) represent just a sampling of recent studies on the subject.

It is useful to begin by considering illustrations of some of the characteristics of central bank disclosure. In New Zealand, the governor of the Reserve Bank can, in principle, be dismissed if the RBNZ fails to meet the stated inflation targets. This arrangement is easily understood and monitored, so it is also transparent. Whether such a state of affairs is desirable ultimately depends on whether there are adequate mechanisms in place to act in the event of a breach in the target. Similarly, the RBNZ and the Bank of England, as have other central banks, made public details of the models used to generate forecasts used as inputs into monetary policy decisions. Such activities also increase the transparency of central bank operations. By contrast, central banks such as the U.S. Fed and the German Bundesbank are accountable to their governments and the public but enforcement is not transparent. Indeed, as the previous discussion makes clear, both central banks have either implicitly or explicitly advocated opacity in the implementation of monetary policy. In historical terms, this could be justified on the grounds that central banks knew too little about the structure of the economy to provide convincing information to the public.[26] It was, therefore, difficult to disclose considerable information when the ability to foresee how to respond to future economic shocks was limited. By the 1990s, however, this argument becomes less convincing.

As long as central banks did not have formal autonomy from government, disclosure was not an important issue. According to one view, political economy considerations would dictate that institutions such as central banks would shy away from taking responsibility for their actions.[27] A useful mechanism for doing so is to cloud the public's ability to understand or follow the monetary policy decision-making process. After all, central bankers have long been viewed as being motivated to be seen to do a good job. The issue then is whether this objective can best be accomplished via openness or vagueness in how their actions are carried out. Although the bureaucratic argument seems convincing at a superficial level it seems more likely, in light of the evidence presented in this study, that flaws in the institutional structure, rather than bureaucratic obfuscation, produced too little disclosure by central banks. Simply put, central banks needed to hide behind the statutes governing their activities. Statutes, and central bank–government relations in the 1950s and 1960s especially, effectively promulgated the views that central banks ought to stabilize economic activity, and implicitly assumed that they possessed the wherewithal to do so. Since, in fact, central banks were not equipped to carry out these responsibilities it comes perhaps as no surprise that they were seen as behaving in a bureaucratic fashion. Of course, the bureaucratic notion is silent about whether a central bank is in a position to obscure the facts. The evolutionary approach suggests that while this may have been the case decades ago it is no longer true.

Beyond this there is at least one other argument that contradicts bureaucratic notions of central bank behavior. Along with the growing tendency to provide more autonomy and accountability, it clearly became in the best interests of the central bank to become more open about how monetary policy is conducted and, perhaps equally important, to clarify the limitations of its actions and responsibilities. Interestingly, by providing more disclosure, a central bank is better able to communi-

---

[26] Alternatively, as was noted earlier in this study, this feature of central bank behavior would also be the result of the well-established caution of central bankers.

[27] The bureaucratic notion of central bank activities would suggest, in line with the earlier quote from Friedman, that central banks have an incentive to obscure the facts to their greatest possible advantage. In the literature on central banking this idea goes back at least to Acheson and Chant (1973).

cate the uncertainties in policy making and shift responsibility to others, notably governments, when its actions are believed to be outside its scope for action. As former Bank of Canada Governor John Crow once put it: "From my experience, a lot of the discussion on central bank accountability that takes place gives inadequate attention to this point – the need for a mandate for the central bank that is clear, and which it can achieve" (Crow 1994).

Consequently, accountability requires disclosure, but how much is necessary? Again, the overriding principle should be that disclosure ought to be sufficient to ensure that monetary policy actions are well understood and that the strategy of monetary policy is clear and consistent with the objectives of the central bank as set out in the statutes. It would appear difficult for a central bank without a stated price stability objective[28] to properly communicate its strategy if its decisions cannot be placed in the context of some overarching goal of monetary policy. Hence, disclosure and, by implication, accountability, lose a considerable amount of their meaning, and importance, if implemented without regard to defining a strategy for the conduct of monetary policy. In other words, disclosure and accountability require useful benchmarks against which the performance of the central bank can be evaluated. There is potentially a theoretical justification for this view. If, as in Faust and Svensson (1998), transparency means that the central bank's goals are directly observed but unconstrained then central banks may create both high and volatile inflation because their reputation, based on the economy's employment performance, cannot be related to its actions.[29] By contrast, introducing clear goals, and requiring disclosure of central bank actions, is socially optimal under these circumstances because the public can directly link economic observables (that is, inflation, employment) to central bank decisions.

THE IMPORTANCE OF CONFLICT RESOLUTION PROCEDURES AND GOVERNANCE

Accountability and disclosure, as defined here, refers to the operations of monetary policy and how central bank actions are communicated to

---

[28] Arguably, it need not be explicit, in the sense of some value, so long as there is a general consensus of what is meant by price stability. Of course, this is by no means a given.

[29] Transparency in the Faust and Svensson framework is not inconsistent with the concept of disclosure applied here since they are interested in the size and variability of "noise" (that is, deviations in policy from some anticipated pattern).

the public. By far the most common pressures on monetary policy are ones related to perceived excessive tightening or loosening of the stance of monetary policy. Moreover, in rare circumstances, conflicts can be more serious and lead to resignation and dismissal of the CEO of the central bank. While the face of central banking has changed, the potential for conflicts between the government and the central bank seems to be one of those immutable constants. These arise, in large part, because as Alan Greenspan, chair of the U.S. Fed once stated: "Despite waxing and waning over the decades, a deep-seated tension still exists over the government's role as an economic policy maker" (Greenspan 1996).

Fortunately, in industrial countries at least, these types of conflicts are comparatively rare not only because of the consequent damage to the reputation of the central bank but also the collateral damage to the government of the day.[30] The absence of formal autonomy or precise objectives of monetary policy thus combined in the past to reduce the likelihood that such conflicts would reach the public domain.

This view buttressed the attitude that central bankers should be seen but not heard. As a former deputy governor of the Bank of England put it:

> I've been convinced with all my years at the Bank that the influence we can exert behind closed doors, in private, not through newspaper head-lines, is well worth preserving, and that we probably have quite as much influence over what happens . . . as do other central banks who have got more ostensible independence.[31]

Central bankers (and economists) have also learned that influence over the ultimate direction of policy means little if it does not influence the public's expectations or contribute to reputation building. Indeed, it can fairly be said that it took most central banks over forty years following the end of World War II to turn their attention to how policy is communicated and begin sharing the views of one of the pioneers in this connection, namely the German Bundesbank. Karl Blessing, president of the Bundesbank and long-time central banker, shortly after passage of the landmark Bundesbank Law in 1957, put it in the following terms:

---

[30] Indeed, based on data in Cukierman, Webb, and Neyapti (1992) the turnover rate of central bankers in industrial countries is close to zero since the 1950s (also see Chapter 3).

[31] As quoted from Geddes (1987).

A central bank which never fights, which at times of economic tension never raises its voice, . . . that central bank will be viewed with mistrust.[32]

The previous quotes reflect to some extent the differences of views about the extent to which the public should be part of the overall strategy for the conduct of monetary policy. As Goodfriend (1986) remarks, the central banking mystique was, for years, viewed as consisting foremost of secrecy, with little concern for the public and its role in ensuring that monetary policy was successfully carried out. By the 1990s, however, openness was instead perceived as the essential ingredient of good conduct in monetary policy. "A central bank which is inscrutable gives the markets little or no way to ground perceptions in any underlying reality – thereby opening the door to expectational bubbles that can make the effects of its policies hard to predict. A more open central bank, by contrast, naturally conditions expectations by providing the markets with more information about its own view of the fundamental factors guiding monetary policy" (Blinder 1999: p. 72).

Greater emphasis on precise objectives, a clearer definition of the responsibility of monetary policy, and the consequent need for more disclosure, implies that influence and independence can no longer adequately be defended "behind closed doors." Consequently, the manner in which conflicts are resolved and the process by which central banks make decisions and convey these to the public become critical ingredients in building a successful institutional structure. Such arguments, as has been remarked earlier in this study, are not new. What is new is the recognition that goals and responsibilities are not easily divorced from the mechanisms needed to ensure that they are being carried out properly.

Governance and Central Bank Accountability

As expectations regarding the performance of central bankers have increased, in parallel with the growing autonomy and clarity in the objectives of monetary policy, conflicts are both more easily observed and their likelihood may be enhanced since, as pointed out earlier, precision in monetary policy objectives enhances the responsibilities for *both* the monetary authorities *and* governments. Clearly then, emphasis

---

[32] As quoted in Marsh (1992: pp. 256–7). Posen (2000) and Siklos and Bohl (2001) go into more detail about why the Bundesbank placed so much importance on communicating monetary policy views and decisions.

on how such conflicts are resolved is essential. In this connection history suggests two developments that have, in essence, converged. The first is the recognition that, as pointed out earlier, there needs to be consequences for the failure to meet clearly spelled-out objectives. The most extreme manifestation of this is the potential for dismissal in the event an inflation target is breached.[33] However, if the mechanism used to determine whether or not dismissal is warranted, as it is in New Zealand, is flawed then the threat in the event of conflict can become insignificant. In Chapter 3, the role of the directive in monetary policy was emphasized. The issuance of a directive is a symptom of government–central bank conflict. Here the focus is on how to resolve such disagreements and so issues relating to governance also become relevant.

New Zealand's experience underscores the significance of the problem alluded to above. In 1996, inflation exceeded the 2% ceiling of the inflation target band at the time – since revised upward to 3% following the 1997 elections – for the second time since 1990 (an earlier but brief episode took place in 1994). The then minister of finance asked the board of the RBNZ to determine whether the target breach could be "considered a matter which should call into question the Governor's performance or his continued employment" (RBNZ 1996b: p. 42). The board rejected the claim made against the governor, not on the basis of an independent assessment of the governor's performance but, in large part, on evidence provided by the staff working under the governor.

In light of this experience, together with a change of governing parties in 1999, the new government set out to review the conduct of monetary policy in New Zealand.[34] One of the important tasks of the Review was to examine the single decision-making model and to assess whether a more formal committee structure for decision making at the RBNZ ought to be introduced instead. Of particular interest is the submission of the

---

[33] The policy targets agreement (PTA), which forms the basis of the accountability of the governor of the RBNZ vis-à-vis the government, has evolved since it was first introduced in 1990. Indeed, strictly speaking, on occasion, certain breaches of the target will be permitted so long as measures are taken, and explained, to ensure that inflation reenters the target range. Moreover, the inflation rate the RBNZ is now held accountable for is defined in terms of core inflation and not the overall CPI inflation rate. As we shall see as follows, a major difficulty is the process used to decide how to deal with cases where the policy used to return inflation back into the target range is not acceptable to the government. After all, the PTA of 1999 also states "The Bank shall be fully accountable for its judgements and actions in implementing monetary policy."

[34] The submissions are posted on the Internet at http://www.monpolreview.govt.nz.

Directors of the Bank who were called upon to decide Governor Brash's fate in the episode just described. Their submission (Non-Executive Directors 2000) defends the status quo for essentially five reasons. Since the submission raises questions about the committee versus single individual models of central bank decision making their position is of general interest and are worth discussing at greater length.[35] They are:

1. The policy targets agreement (PTA) that outlines the inflation objectives agreed to between the treasurer and the governor provides a clear understanding of the objectives of monetary policy and places sufficient constraints on the decisions of the CEO and the central bank.
2. There is constant monitoring of the central bank from within and without. Additional monitoring via the committee arrangement is unnecessary.
3. The single decision-making model facilitates communication of policy actions with the government and the public. The governor cannot "hide" behind a committee.
4. Decision by committee risks a shift in emphasis from the reasons for a particular policy stance to the personalities of committee members.
5. Even if monetary policy decisions are made in a committee, the CEO is *primus inter pares* and to pretend otherwise sends the wrong signal to the public.

It should be pointed out at the outset that while there are no doubt *some* merits to the foregoing they utterly fail to convince as evidence in favor of the single decision-maker model.

First, any quantified inflation target does not preclude the possibility of government "override" or the possibility that a numerical objective is blurred by other considerations in the agreement between the government and the central bank.

Ironically, the directors (also see Mayes 2000) pointed out that the most recent policy targets agreement represented a weakening of the inflation objective. The reason is that, with the addition of an objective other than some indicator of changes in the cost of living alone, there is

---

[35] Svensson's (2001) report recommends in fact that the single decision-maker model be replaced by a committee structure. More generally, while proposing a few other more-or-less technical changes the report concludes that New Zealand's monetary policy is implemented rather well.

a danger that it can potentially interfere with the principal mandate of the central bank.[36] By contrast, a committee can act as a counterweight at attempts to influence an individual's position by bringing to light the weight of expert opinion on the desirability of any changes to central bank objectives.[37]

Moreover, in the case of other central banks, there can be doubts raised about the position of the CEO, if the central bank and the government interpret the numerical objective in terms of different price indexes,[38] or if there is uncertainty about the level of support for policies needed to return to a stated inflation objective in the event of a breach in the target. In either case, the weight of expert opinion places greater emphasis on governments to justify their actions and helps ensure the autonomy of the central bank.

The issues discussed above are not relevant to inflation targeting countries alone for a committee ensures that any policy is suitably vetted and discussed and provides an informed opinion based, presumably on a diversity of views.

The fact that monitoring by insiders and outsiders of central bank actions takes place at all times has no bearing on the choice of governing structures. The point is that a committee under most circumstances (see, however, the discussion that follows), ensures that no single opinion or ideology is decisive in policy decisions. Committees, by definition, improve accountability and, as we shall see, disclosure. Indeed, rather

---

[36] Indeed, clause 4(c) of the 1999 policy targets agreement (PTA) makes the following change to the 1997 PTA: "*In pursuing its price stability objective*, the Bank shall implement monetary policy in a sustainable, consistent and transparent manner *and shall seek to avoid unnecessary instability in output, interest rates and the exchange rate*" (amendments indicated in italics).

[37] To date there have been six PTAs since March 1990. Some (for example, Mayes 2000) expressed concern that frequent renegotiation of such agreements leads to an impression that governments (and the central bank) are attempting to induce fine tuning in monetary policy via the back door. In fairness to the process, the number of PTAs also reflect an attempt to produce a statement of central bank objectives that gets it "right" in the face of the myriad of shocks and other events it is unreasonable to expect a central bank to be able to deal with while maintaining inflation within the stated objectives. In addition, as has been pointed out already, regularly revisiting PTAs is a sign that ultimate responsibility for monetary policy outcomes rests with the government. In principle, regular revisions of such agreements can be helpful as long as the price stability objective and the central bank's autonomy are not fundamentally jeopardized.

[38] For example, in Canada, the inflation control objective is expressed in terms of the overall CPI. However, the Bank of Canada has made it clear that its responsibilities are limited to changes in core inflation that was redefined in 2001. Also, see Chapters 2 and 7, and http://www.bankofcanada.ca, Bank of Canada (1989a; 1991b).

than increase the focus on the personalities of board members, decision making by committee can enhance concentration on policy questions.[39] However, it must be emphasized that this outcome is likely to depend, as shall be argued, on whether diversity of views are aired in public.

Assuming the public does not believe that there is everywhere and always unanimity of opinion on the *future* course of inflation, and economic activity more generally, failure to air differences of opinion on such matters will instead produce an impression that the central bank's CEO is more of a consensus seeker than a decision maker. It seems curious that whereas financial markets, in particular, require a diversity of opinion to form expectations, we should expect that the decisions of a central bank must be an amalgam of an unknown variety expressed by a single individual. There is no surer way of creating a cult of personality than via the single decision-maker model.

Finally, the fact that a central bank CEO is first among equals is simply a measure to shift accountability of the institution in the direction of a particular individual. This does not solve the separate but central disclosure question which is enhanced via the means of communication to the public, regardless of how much authority the governor or the president of a central bank has.

The RBNZ's experience, therefore, highlights two important issues with general implications, one of which was discussed earlier in Chapter 2. First, the mere fact that responsibility for monetary policy rests entirely with the governor enhances the possibility that too much emphasis is placed on personalities as opposed to the policies of the central bank. In this connection, there has been growing recognition that, among the many consequences of more accountable and greater disclosure relating to policy decisions, is the need to communicate such policies in a more effective manner. As noted above, one obvious means of doing so is via the committee process. The committee approach gives credence to the view that monetary policy actions do not represent the views of a single individual. Moreover, as it is in the nature of committees to deliberate, the result is that the public is provided with some additional reassurance that different viewpoints are entertained and debated. But it is just as important to consider the legal basis of such committees and their

---

[39] Siklos (2000b) presents evidence suggesting that this is the case for the United Kingdom Monetary Policy Committee. In the case of the European Central Bank (ECB) failure to reveal the diversity of opinions within the Governing Council has instead increased focus on the president rather than the ECB's policies. See Dornbusch, Favero, and Giavazzi (1998); Goodfriend (1999); Gros (1999).

structure. Thus, for example, the structure of the Federal Open Market Committee of the U.S. Federal Reserve reflects the regional structure of the U.S. central bank. The FOMC consists of twelve members with considerable regional representation, a reflection of its historical origins. However, with the end of the Great Depression, decision making came to be centralized at the FOMC and, despite its regional structure, became the kind of deliberative body that fulfilled the committee functions highlighted above.

The Monetary Policy Committee (MPC) of the Bank of England, consists of the governor and eight other members, a majority of whom are appointed by the chancellor of the exchequer. The MPC is responsible for formulating monetary policy.[40] However, unlike the FOMC, the Bank of England's MPC includes outside experts, and the minutes of its meetings, as well as the degree of dissent, are both made public soon after the meeting takes place. While the amount of information disclosed about the decision making at the Bank of England is, arguably, far greater than that of central banks elsewhere in the industrial world, problems and tensions do remain. Decisions focus on the current round of interest rate decisions, not the intermediate term, despite the publication of an inflation report that takes a longer run view of monetary policy. This is, no doubt, partially a product of the role played by forecasts discussed earlier.[41] Thus, for example, while committee dissent is public it is unclear how individual MPC member's thinking relates to the Bank of England's published scenarios.[42] In other words, the "mapping" from the model projection and forecasts to the opinion of individual MPC members in relation to the central tendency around the "best collective judgment" of the group remains opaque.[43] It is clear that any solution to

---

[40] See Bank of England Act of 1998: ch. 11, sec. 13,
http://www.legislation.hmso.gov.uk/acts1998/8011-b.htm#13.
[41] Indeed, this is a point emphasized by Kohn (2001).
[42] The response, so far, by the Bank of England (also see Bank of England 2001) is a work in progress. However, in 2001, the minutes of the MPC began to be published separately, and a separate "annex," summarizing the data presented by the staff, was also incorporated. See Monetary Policy Committee (2001).
[43] Two other difficulties were highlighted by a Select Committee of the House of Lords (Select Committee on Monetary Affairs 2001). First, the process of voting for, or against, interest rate changes is sequential so that some votes are cast in the knowledge of other voters' positions. Second, there were questions raised about the frequency of MPC meetings. Frequent meetings can contribute to the interest rate smoothing phenomenon discussed in Chapter 4. On the other hand, frequent meetings can raise the chances of tunnel vision or myopia in monetary policy also addressed previously. In this connection, see Huizinga and Eijffinger (1998).

the problem requires either that more information be provided, without necessarily improving the quality of that information, or that the responsibilities of the governor and members of the MPC vis-à-vis the forecasts, be clarified or be more narrowly defined. Nevertheless, beyond these considerations are two others of crucial importance in delivering good monetary policy. First, since complexity and uncertainty permeate the implementation of monetary policy, retrospective examinations of past forecasts and performance would clearly enhance accountability and contribute to disclosure of central bank actions. Second, divorcing to some extent the forecasts and projections from the process of taking decisions about the appropriate stance of monetary policy, reduces the likelihood that the central bank is accused of myopia or tunnel vision. The latter are dangers that central banks are increasingly exposed to, as noted earlier, when transparency is enhanced without regard to the limits of accountability or to the underlying strategy of monetary policy.

In contrast to the above examples of formal committee structures, the Governing Council of the Bank of Canada is a creation of the Bank of Canada, whose members are senior central bank officials appointed by the governor. The committee has no legal standing, at least in terms of existing legislation.

How important is legal standing for such decision-making bodies? In terms of notions of disclosure and accountability discussed earlier, endowing the committee rather than the central bank's CEO with responsibility in formulating monetary policy would appear to be important. On the other hand, since senior, and presumably highly competent, officials are members of such a committee legal standing is perhaps less important so long as the public comes to accept that monetary policy decisions are not made solely by a single individual. Nevertheless, one of the difficulties with ad hoc committees is that public communication and responsibility for monetary policy decisions still rests, and must be officially communicated, by the CEO and not the committee.

Beyond responsibility for monetary policy actions is the question of conflict resolution. As the New Zealand experience dictates it is hardly credible to leave open the possibility of dismissal in the event of poor performance if an objective evaluation of the governor's performance is not possible under existing arrangements. However, not having any process whatsoever in place for the resolution of conflicts is just as unacceptable as a flawed arrangement for, in the event of a serious disagreement over policy, there can be no escape without damaging the central bank's reputation in the public's mind (and possibly the government's competence).

Of course, conflicts may eventually be resolved via the appointments process. In a setting where decisions are made at the level of a committee, the impact of appointments may be limited unless the entire committee can be dismissed at once or all committee members' terms expire at the same time, both rather unlikely events. Hence, monetary policy conducted by committee eases the problem of how to deal with conflicts when no formal conflict resolution procedures are in place.[44]

MEASURING CENTRAL BANK ACCOUNTABILITY AND DISCLOSURE

Having argued that the movement toward greater accountability and transparency in central banking is directly related to the increased clarity and precision of monetary policy objectives, how far are central banks from some ideal set of characteristics required to ensure that accountability and openness mirror the actual responsibilities of the central banks? Are some central banks actually more accountable or transparent than they need to be given their mandate? Is there a connection, keeping in mind that what is meant is correlation *not* causation, between economic performance, accountability, and disclosure? Answering these questions requires that we translate the discussion of the previous sections into measurable characteristics. Tables 6.1 and 6.2 list the characteristics thought to best represent the twin concepts of accountability and disclosure. A total of twenty-three characteristics are listed as comprising the elements of accountability and disclosure. At the outset, it needs to be emphasized that it is not always straightforward to neatly distinguish between the two concepts. For example, enhancing the clarity of the objective of monetary policy is obviously a sign of enhanced transparency but as it is intended to make it easier for the public and government to assess central bank performance, it seems preferable to add this feature to the list of measures that reflect improvements in accountability. Similar objections can no doubt also be raised about some of the other items under each classification. Nevertheless, every item reflects

---

[44] Since it is impractical in any piece of legislation to anticipate all contingencies that might lead a government to call into question a CEO's performance, the committee approach solves a complex problem. Even if a few contingencies are agreed to (for example, inflation relative to some target) these have to be precisely defined and it is unlikely than any government or central bank will want to tie its hands to that extent. The New Zealand example described earlier is a case in point. For a discussion of Sweden's experience, see Berg and Lundberg (2000).

Table 6.1. Characteristics of Accountability

Characteristics	Australia	Austria[1]	Belgium[1]	Canada	Denmark[1]	Finland[1]	France[2]	Germany[1]	Ireland[1]	Italy[1]	Japan
1. Clarity of objective (de jure)	No	Yes	No	No	No	Yes	Yes	Yes	No	No	No
2. Quantification of objective (de facto)	Yes	No	No	Yes	No	Yes	No	No	No	Yes	No
3. Publication of an economic outlook						√			√	√	√
i. in the form of explicit forecasts	√	√	√								
ii. forecasts with assessment of risks				√				√			
iii. general statement only		√			√						
4. Publication of statement of accountability and ultimate responsibility for monetary policy	Yes	No	No	Yes	No	Yes	No	No	No	No	Yes
5. Conflict resolution procedures (du jure)			None		None						
i. definition of conflict	Yes	Yes		Yes		No	No	Yes	No	Yes	Yes
ii. procedures to resolve conflict	Yes	Yes		Yes		Yes	Yes	Yes	Yes	Yes	Yes
iii. clear outcomes in the case of failure to resolve conflict	Yes	Yes		Yes		Yes	Yes	Yes	Yes	Yes	Yes
6. Reporting mechanisms and procedures (dealing with policy)											
a. to minister	√		√	√	√		√				√
b. to legislature			√			√		√	√	√	√
c. other (for example, board)	√	√									√

7. Decision-making structure (de jure)											
a. by committee (size)	√(9)	√(13)	√(7)	√	√(5)	√(5)	√(9)	√(17)	√	√	√(9)
b. CEO only	No	No	No	No	No	No	No	Yes	No	No	No
8. Gives explicit advice to government	Yes	Yes	No	Yes	Yes	No	Yes	Yes	No	No	Yes
9. Clear and detailed explanation of appointment procedures	Yes	No	Yes	Yes	Yes	Yes	Yes	Yes	Yes	No	Yes
10. Regular appearances before Parliament (de jure/de facto)	Yes	No	Yes	Yes	Yes	Yes	Yes	Yes	Yes	No	Yes
11. Is the central bank subject to possible interference in the conduct of monetary policy? (de jure)	Yes	No	Yes	Yes	No	No	Yes	Yes	Yes	Yes	Yes
12. Who sets the objectives of monetary policy?											
a. none/govt.	√										
b. management			√	√	√	√	√		√	√	
c. set by statute		√						√			
d. joint CB/govt.											√

249

Table 6.1 (*continued*)

Characteristics	Netherlands[1]	New Zealand	Norway	Portugal[1]	Spain[2]	Sweden[2]	Switzerland	United Kingdom	United States	ECB[3]
1. Clarity of objective (de jure)	Yes	Yes	No[5]	No	Yes	Yes	Yes	Yes	No	No
2. Quantification of objective (de facto)	No	Yes	No[5]	No	Yes	Yes	No[4]	Yes	No	Yes
3. Publication of an economic outlook					None					
i. in the form of explicit forecasts	√		√	√			√[4]			
ii. forecasts with assessment of risks		√			√	√		√	√	
iii. general statement only										√
4. Publication of statement of accountability and ultimate responsibility for monetary policy	No	No	Yes	Yes	No	Yes	No	No	No	No
5. Conflict resolution procedures (du jure)							None	None	None	
i. definition of conflict	Yes	Yes	No	No	No	No				No
ii. procedures to resolve conflict	Yes	Yes	Yes	Yes	Yes	Yes				Yes
iii. clear outcomes in the case of failure to resolve conflict	Yes	Yes	Yes	Yes	Yes	Yes				Yes
6. Reporting mechanisms and procedures (dealing with policy)										
a. to minister		√		√	√	√				
b. to legislature					√	√	√	√	√	
c. other (for example, board)	√		√							√

	√(5+)	√	√(7)	√(6)	√(8)	√(6)	√(3+)	√(9)	√(12)	√(6)
7. Decision-making structure (de jure)										
a. by committee		√								
b. CEO only										
8. Gives explicit advice to government	No	Yes	No	No	No	No	No	No	Yes	No
9. Clear and detailed explanation of appointment procedures	Yes	Yes	Yes	Yes	Yes	Yes	Yes	Yes	Yes	Yes
10. Regular appearances before Parliament (de jure/de facto)	No	Yes	Yes	Yes	Yes	No	No	Yes	Yes	Yes
11. Is the central bank subject to possible interference in the conduct of monetary policy? (de jure)	Yes	Yes	Yes	Yes	Yes	No	No	Yes	Yes	Yes
12. Who sets the objectives of monetary policy?										
a. none/govt.		√	√							
b. management				√	√	√		√	√	
c. set by statute										
d. joint CB/govt.	√						√			√

Information based on statutes since the mid 1980s or early 1990s. See http://www.wlu.ca/~wwwsbe/faculty/psiklos/centralbanks.htm for additional details and Table 6.2 for full set of notes for both Tables 6.1 and 6.2.

251

Table 6.2. Characteristics of Disclosure

Characteristics	Australia	Austria	Belgium	Canada	Denmark	Finland	France	Germany	Ireland	Italy	Japan
1. Publication of minutes of central bank meetings	No	No	No	Yes	No	Yes	No	No	No	No	Yes
2. Key assumptions in generating outlook	Yes	No	No	Yes	No	No	No	Yes	Yes	No	No
3. Publication of committee voting record	No	No	No	No	No	No	No	No	No	No	Yes
4. Regular information published about how monetary policy decisions are made and their justification	Yes	No	No	Yes	No	Yes	No	Yes	Yes	Yes	Yes
5. Operational instrument of monetary policy											
i. single	cash rate			ON			DR				ON
ii. multiple		OMO/ER	OMO/ER		OMO/ER	OMO/ER		OMO/ER	OMO/ER	OMO/ER	

252

	C1	C2	C3	C4	C5	C6	C7	C8	C9	C10	C11
6. Instrument independence?	Yes	No	No	Yes	Yes	No	No	Yes	Yes	Yes	Yes
7. Are monetary policy and operational objectives the same?	Yes	Yes	No	No	No	Yes	Yes	Yes	Yes*	Yes	Yes
8. Special recognition of the role of financial system stability (de jure)	Yes	No	No	Yes	Yes	Yes	Yes	No	No	No	Yes**
9. Economic modeling procedures:											
i. publicly available						✓			✓		
ii. described or discussed but complete details not provided		✓		✓				✓		✓	
iii. no information provided	✓		✓		✓		✓				✓
10. Forms of communication (public or private)											
i. statements or reports on inflation/monetary policy	✓	✓		✓	✓	✓	✓	✓	✓	✓	✓
ii. reports, bulletin on activities	✓	✓	✓	✓	✓	✓	✓	✓	✓	✓	✓
iii. regular speeches	✓			✓		✓		✓		✓	✓
iv. economic research	✓	✓	✓	✓		✓	✓	✓	✓	✓	✓
v. annual report/retrospective analysis	✓	✓		✓	✓	✓		✓	✓	✓	✓
11. Publication of a monetary policy strategy and/or limits of monetary policy	Yes	No	No	Yes	No	No	No	Yes	Yes	No	Yes

Table 6.2 (*continued*)

Characteristics	Netherlands[1]	New Zealand	Norway	Portugal[1]	Spain[2]	Sweden[2]	Switzerland	United Kingdom	United States	ECB
1. Publication of minutes of central bank meetings	No	No	No	No	No	Yes	No	Yes	Yes	No
2. Key assumptions in generating outlook	Yes	Yes	Yes	Yes	Yes	Yes	Yes	Yes	Yes	No
3. Publication of committee voting record	No	No	No	No	No	Yes	No	Yes	Yes	No
4. Regular information published about how monetary policy decisions are made and their justification	Yes	Yes	Yes	Yes	Yes	Yes	Yes	Yes	Yes	Yes
5. Operational instrument of monetary policy i. single ii. multiple	Repo rate	Cash rate	OMO/ER	OMO/ER	OMO/ER	Repo rate	Repo rate	Repo rate	FFR	ON
6. Instrument independence?	Yes	Yes	Yes	Yes	Yes	Yes	Yes	Yes	Yes	Yes
7. Are monetary policy and operational objectives the same?	Yes	Yes*	Yes	Yes	Yes	Yes	Yes	Yes	No	No
8. Special recognition of the role of financial system stability (de jure)	No	Yes	No	No	No	No	No	No	Yes	No
9. Economic modeling procedures: i. publicly available	√	√	√	√	√	√		√		

	1	2	3	4	5	6	7	8
ii. described or discussed but complete detail not provided					√		√	
iii. no information provided								
10. Forms of communication (public or private)								
i. statements or reports on inflation/monetary policy	√		√	√	√	√	√	√
ii. reports, bulletin on activities	√	√	√	√	√	√	√	√
iii. regular speeches	√	√	√	√	√	√	√	√
iv. economic research	√		√	√	√	√	√	√
v. annual report or retrospective analysis	√		√	√	√	√	√	√
11. Publication of a monetary policy strategy and/or the limits of monetary policy	Yes	Yes	No	No	Yes	Yes	Yes	Yes

(*Notes to Tables 6.1 and 6.2*)

[1] Pre-ECB provisions. Also applied to characteristics discussed in Table 6.2.

[2] Influenced by ECB provisions but introduced sufficiently prior to EMU in years to be considered separately. Also applies to characteristics in Table 6.2.

[3] ECB = European Central Bank.

[4] Beginning in 2000 the Swiss National Bank had an explicit inflation goal together with an explicit forecast beginning in 1999.

[5] A royal decree, dated March 29, 2001 pursuant to a change in the Norges Bank Act establishes an inflation target of 2.5% per year in the consumer price index (excluding taxes, duties, interest rate changes, and "extraordinary temporary disturbances"), the amendments to the Act further clarify the tasks of the central bank to be "oriented toward low and stable inflation." Additional information is available at http://www.norges-bank.no/english/nb/legislation/monetarypolicyregulation.htm.

* Signifies negative connotation of the term.

** The Bank of Japan Law refers to the need to guarantee an "orderly financial system" but does not define the term precisely.

OMO/ER = Open market operations/exchange rate; ON = overnight rate; DR = discount rate; FFR = federal funds rate.

Sources: National central banks or their web sites; Amtenbrink (1999); Aufricht (1967); Bini Smaghi and Gros (2000); Capie, Goodhart, Fischer, and Schnadt (1994); Dawe (1992); de Haan, Amtenbrink, and Eijffinger (1999); de Kock (1974); Deutsche Bundesbank (2000a); Freeman and Ammer (1995); International Monetary Fund (2000); Kisch and Elkin (1932); Pringle and Courtis (1999); and Treasury (1999).

the discussion so far about how the evolution of statutory features of central bank–government relations, the enhanced role of communication of monetary policy decisions to the public, and the evolutionary learning process over the decades about how monetary policy affects the economy, were the guiding principles in the choice of characteristics highlighted.

The next obvious question is how to aggregate each of the individual characteristics of accountability and disclosure into a usable index form. Since it is unclear, a priori, whether one characteristic is more important than another, each was coded in such a way that every element has roughly equal weight in the index.[45]

Indexes of Accountability and Disclosure

Tables 6.3 and 6.4 present the index values and analysis of the results. Figure 6.2 shows a plot of the relationship between the two indexes as well as the link between central bank independence and the disclosure index. The top scatter plot in Figure 6.2 suggests, as did the earlier discussion, that central bank autonomy and disclosure are positively related. The correlation is, however, far from perfect. The bottom scatter plot suggests, as expected, that accountability and disclosure go hand in hand as the two indexes are also positively related. As is clear from Table 6.3 no central bank is able to claim "perfect" accountability or "full" disclosure. However, the Reserve Bank of New Zealand is first in accountability while the Bank of England comes out on top in the disclosure ranking.

Table 6.4(a) examines the possibility that the various aggregations of characteristics of central bank behavior leading to the construction of indexes or measures of accountability, disclosure, stability, and supervision are sufficiently similar that, together, they do not add much to our understanding of what drives central bank autonomy or, for that matter, inflation. The table explores the principal components of five factors that

---

[45] Details of the construction of the index are in the appendix to the chapter at http://www.wlu.ca/~wwwsbe/faculty/psiklos/centralbanks.htm. Each characteristic is coded as a 0 or a 1, except for attributes 5 (conflict resolution procedures) and 12 (setting of monetary policy objectives). In the case of the disclosure index, all characteristics are coded 0–1 and are equally weighted, except for attribute 10 (forms of communication). The latter can take a maximum value of 1.5 if all five forms of communication are present.

Table 6.3. Indexes of Accountability and Disclosure

Country	Accountability (max. = 1)		Disclosure (max. = 1)	
	Index	Rank	Index	Rank
Australia	.73	4	.56	11
Austria	.56	13	.23	18
Belgium	.29	21	.04	20
Canada	.50	17	.83	4
Denmark	.35	20	.22	19
Finland	.63	9	.39	17
France	.58	12	.22	19
Germany	.74	3	.70	7
Ireland	.41	18	.41	15
Italy	.41	18	.43	14
Japan	.79	2	.74	6
Netherlands	.65	8	.65	8
New Zealand	.83	1	.83	4
Norway	.56	13	.52	12
Portugal	.62	10	.41	15
Spain	.72	5	.61	10
Sweden	.62	10	.87	3
Switzerland	.56	13	.65	8
United Kingdom	.69	7	.91	1
United States	.56	13	.87	2
ECB	.71	6	.52	12

Based on the characteristics listed in Tables 6.1 and 6.2. Also see http://www.wlu.ca/~wwwsbe/faculty/psiklos/centralbanks.htm for additional details about the construction of the index, as well as the commentary in the text.

can explain central bank autonomy or inflation.[46] Leaving aside some of the technical details of the statistical approach, Table 6.4(a) reveals that factors 1 and 2 are, in descending order, the two most important attributes of the five considered.[47] In other words, the analysis suggests that,

---

[46] Principal components analysis is widely used as a device to ascertain whether a multi-collinearity problem exists when several characteristics are believed to contribute or represent the variable of interest. In other words, it is conceivable that some of the indicators developed in this study, including ones examined in Table 6.4(a), measure essentially the same aspect of central bank behavior. That is, instead of having to regress inflation (or central bank independence) on all the various indicators generated in this study, we need only concern ourselves with a few since the remaining attributes are essentially linear combinations of the characteristics that significantly enter the relationship of interest. Nevertheless, it ought to be emphasized that principal components analysis is not without its problems. See, for example, Maddala (1977: pp. 193–4).

[47] See Joliffe (1986) who describes the selection of the factors that are empirically relevant for subsequent analysis. Recall, however, that each factor is a linear combination

Table 6.4. Principal Components and Determinants of Central Bank Independence or Inflation during the 1990s

(A) Principal Components

Indicator Variables[1]	Correlations		Correlations	
	Factor 1	**Factor 2**	**Factor 1**	**Factor 2**
Accountability	.56	−.07	.57	.36
Disclosure	.60	−.11	.60	.27
CBI	.46	.34	N/A	N/A
Stability	.17	.70	−.16	.71
Supervision	.29	−.61	.50	−.32
Inflation	N/A	N/A	.21	−.44

(B) Regressions

Independent Variables	Dependent Variables			
	Inflation	**t-statistic**	**CBI**	**t-statistic**
Constant	2.72	11.57	0.44	12.81
Factor 1	0.04	0.24	0.03	1.37
Factor 2	−0.18	−0.95	0.05	1.80
$\bar{R}^2$	0.05			.14
F	0.48 (.63)		2.56 (.10)	

Accountability and disclosure are the index values described in this chapter (also see Table 6.3). CBI is the index of central bank independence described in Chapters 2 and 3. Stability and supervision are the dummy variables described in Chapter 2. Inflation is average CPI inflation during the decade of the 1990s. $\bar{R}^2$ is the adjusted coefficient of determination and F is the F-test statistic for the joint significance of all the independent variables in the regression (significance levels in parenthesis).

of the variables considered, only two "latent" variables account for a significant variation in either average inflation or central bank independence. It seems likely that accountability and disclosure represent the principal components of inflation and central bank independence in the 1990s.[48] Most notably, greater disclosure is positively associated with inflation and central bank independence.

Similarly, the explicit assignment of a financial stability objective is a positive characteristic of both inflation and central bank independence

of the explanatory variables of interest that maximizes the variation in these same variables. Each factor is, by construction, uncorrelated (or orthogonal) to other factors.

[48] As Joliffe (1986: pp. 50–1) points out, identification of the principal components with the characteristics under investigation owes something to the imagination or ingenuity of the investigator. Nevertheless, the procedures for "identification" outlined in Joliffe (1986, especially chs. 4 and 6) were followed.

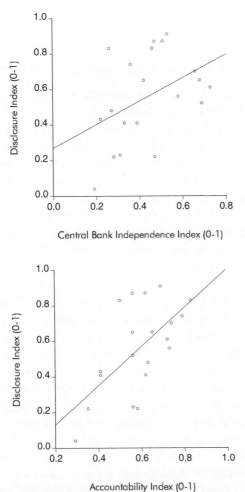

Figure 6.2 Accountability, Disclosure, and Central Bank Independence (*Sources*: Chapter 2 and Table 6.3.)

while joint banking supervision and central banking duties represent a negative feature of central bank independence.

Table 6.4(b), however, shows that while none of the factors significantly explain average inflation in the 1990s there is at least a significant factor explaining central bank independence in the last decade. Indeed, a statutory requirement to ensure the maintenance of financial stability, and greater transparency, are both consistent with a higher statutory level of central bank autonomy when the factors are unraveled to reveal the characteristics that are significant (not shown).[49]

Inflation Forecasts and Central Bank Communication Redux

Although the beneficial effects of transparency may be easily detected in high-frequency data, central banks no doubt also keenly hope that improvements in the manner in which policies are communicated impact private sector expectations of inflation, the primary goal of monetary policy. In the remainder of this chapter then we ask how some of the key elements in the movement to enhance accountability and disclosure may be reflected in private sector inflation forecasts.

Using monthly data, I first investigate whether the release of inflation reports influences private sector forecasts of inflation and whether there are any noticeable differences between countries that formally target inflation versus other major central banks with historically strong inflation records.

Two sets of regressions were estimated in a panel setting. The first asks whether private sector inflation forecasts are influenced by the previous forecast as well as by the publication of an inflation report in the context of an inflation target. For comparison, a second regression examines the persistence properties of inflation via the estimation of an AR(1) model of inflation (also see Chapter 2). Two panels are considered: a group of twelve countries, six of which do not formally target inflation but are considered to have exemplary inflation records. They are: the United States, Germany, Switzerland, Austria, the Netherlands, and Japan. The remaining countries formally target inflation and the same models are reestimated for this separate group of countries. They are: Australia, Canada, Sweden, New Zealand, Spain, and the United Kingdom.

The results in Table 6.5 reveal that inflation reports, largely in place among the inflation targeting group of countries by the mid 1990s, significantly reduced inflation forecasts since 1995. In contrast, the adoption of inflation targeting, a feature in place since the early 1990s in most

---

[49] It is conceivable that some of the attributes in both the disclosure and accountability indexes are more important than others. Additional principal components analysis along these lines indicate that, for example, forms of communication, whether decision making at the central bank is the responsibility of a committee, and whether setting monetary policy goals is a joint government–central bank responsibility, are perhaps relatively more important attributes of central bank statutory structure.

Table 6.5. Pooled Cross-Section Time Series Estimates: Monthly Data, 1988–1999

| Independent Variables | All Countries | | | | | Inflation Targeting Countries | | | |
| | Inflation Forecast (π_t^f) | | | Realized Inflation (π_t) | | Inflation Forecast (π_t^f) | | Realized Inflation (π_t) | |
Samples	88–99	90–99	95–99	85–99	90–99	90–99	95–99	85–99	90–99
π_{t-1}^f	.09 (.02)⊥	.08 (.02)⊥	.06 (.03)@	–	–	.15 (.04)⊥	.20 (.05)⊥	–	–
π_{t-1}	–	–	–	.41 (.02)⊥	.32 (.02)⊥	–	–	.59 (.03)⊥	.69 (.07)⊥
Inflation Report	–	-.02 (.02)	-.05 (.02)@	–	–	-.05 (.03)*	-.05 (.02)⊥	-.01 (.02)	-.01 (.02)
IT dummy	–	-.02 (.01)⊥	-.01 (.01)	–	–	–	–	–	–
Log Likelihood	-26.90	10.59	171.08	-531.08	-286.35	-159.57	22.56	38.57	152.60
SSR	129.40	122.56	37.20	279.08	186.71	98.56	26.98	87.30	17.33
Number of Observations	1393	1364	780	2194	1560	740	420	856	420

@ signifies statistically significant at the 5% level (* at the 10% level; ⊥ at the 1% level).

Data are monthly. SSR = Sum of squared residuals.

Inflation Reports is a dummy variable set to 1 in the month the report is released, and is 0 otherwise.

All estimates are obtained with GLS (using cross-section weights) and standard errors are heteroskedasticity corrected. The panels are unbalanced as data availability is not the same for all countries. See http://www.wlu.ca/~wwwsbe/faculty/psiklos/centralbanks.htm for details.

The twelve countries in the sample are: Australia, Canada, Sweden, the United States, Germany, Switzerland, New Zealand, Spain, the United Kingdom, Austria, Netherlands, Japan, and Finland.

The inflation targeting countries are: Australia, Canada, Sweden, New Zealand, Spain, the United Kingdom, and Finland.

Table 6.6. The Determinants of Inflation Forecast Errors, 1994–1999

	Dependent Variable: Forecast Errors Samples		
Independent variables	1994–99	1995–99	1995–99
GDP growth (–2)	.03 (.03)	.02 (.04)	.02 (.04)
Interest rate (–1)	.13 (.03)+	.10 (.04)⊥	.11 (.04)⊥
Inflation forecast	–.88 (.05)+	–.86 (.05)⊥	–.86 (.05)⊥
Inflation target	–	–.02 (.01)*	–
Inflation report	–	–	–.01 (.03)
$\bar{R}^2$	.37	.37	.36
F-statistic	225.29	123.07	121.45

See Table 6.5 for estimation details. Data are monthly. Heteroskedasticity corrected standard errors are in parentheses. Panel consists of 13 countries (cross sections) for a total of 708 observations (588 when the sample is 1995–99).

of the countries sampled, also has a negative impact on forecasts of inflation. While it is difficult to assign the relative contribution of inflation targets, an indication of increased accountability, as opposed to the publication of an inflation report, a proxy for more information disclosure, panel estimates for the group of inflation targeting countries suggest that transparency played a significant role. Finally, the results reveal that while inflation persistence fell in all thirteen countries during the sample considered, as measured by the coefficient on lagged inflation, the impact was relatively larger for the inflation targeting countries. The results confirm, in a panel setting, similar results obtained for individual inflation targeting countries (Siklos 1999b). Both increased accountability and disclosure can explain these results. In particular, the drop in persistence can be interpreted as the outcome of attempts by central banks to be more forward looking, that is, effectively target a forecast for inflation, rather than being backward looking as was perhaps previously the case.

A further test of the impact of changes in central bank policies on inflation may be obtained by asking two related questions. First, are private sector forecasts efficient and unbiased? Second, has the adoption of inflation targets, and the publication of inflation reports, had any impact on forecast efficiency and unbiasedness? Table 6.6 provides some suggestive answers. The basic form of the regressions can be summarized as follows:

$$\pi_t - E[\pi_t | I_{t-1}] = \alpha + \beta(L)X_{t-1} + (\delta - 1)E[\pi_t | I_{t-1}] + v_t \qquad (6.1)$$

where π_t is the CPI inflation rate, $E[\pi_t | I_{t-1}]$ is the inflation forecast conditional on information at time $t - 1$, X_{t-1} is a vector of observables describing economic activity of time $t - 1$, and $\beta(L)$ is a distributed lag function. X_{t-1} is assumed to be composed of two variables, namely output growth and the interest rate. The left-hand side is, therefore, the forecast error and expression Equation 6.1 seeks to determine whether the error could have been affected by omitted economic fundamentals that, with hindsight, ought to have been relevant in the forecast or is, to some extent, influenced by the forecast which immediately preceded it.

If inflation targeting increases accountability, transparency, or both, these can serve to reduce forecast errors. Indeed, the results in Table 6.6 reveal this to be the case. It is also noteworthy that the result fails to hold prior to 1995 (not shown). This result is consistent with the view that inflation targeting reduces forecast errors beyond their possible impact on credibility since, by 1995, inflation targets had been in place for a few years and were largely unchanged following transitional targets sometimes referred to as inflation reduction targets (see Siklos 1999b for the details). Note, however, that the publication of inflation reports does not impact forecast errors. There are two possible explanations for this result. First, any impact from these kinds of statements may be quickly dissipated and need not, therefore, show up at the monthly frequency (see, for example, Joyce and Read (1999) for the United Kingdom and Levin, McManus, and Watt (1999) for Canada). Alternatively, inflation reports may, over time, have proven not to contain a "surprise" element, thereby contributing to the stability of short-term inflation expectations.

Indeed, in the Canadian case alone, an impulse response function measuring the impact of the release of the Bank of Canada's Monetary Policy Report on inflation forecast errors shows no "statistically" significant impact over ten months.[50] Nevertheless, a positive result is that inflation forecasts add significantly to the regression's explanatory power though the null hypothesis that $\alpha = 0$ in Equation 6.1 is rejected. However, the hypotheses that $\alpha = 1$ and $\beta(L) = 0$ in Equation 6.1 are easily rejected. Therefore, inflation forecasts are neither efficient nor unbiased.[51]

---

[50] The impulse response function is akin to the familiar multiplier concept in economics. It is used to statistically evaluate how economic shocks affect, in this case, forecast errors over time. For additional details see, for example, Enders (1995).

[51] A couple of technical features about the panel estimates in Tables 6.5 and 6.6 should be mentioned. First, all variables are in first differences thus eliminating the constant term in the regressions. The appropriateness of this transformation was also confirmed via testing, as noted in the text. This is due to Nickell's (1981) result that estimators in levels are biased and the bias is especially serious when the time dimension is small. Second, an F-test easily rejects the fixed effects in favor of the results shown in the tables.

SUMMARY

Successful economic outcomes, at least to the extent that a central bank is responsible for them, requires a "contract" between the monetary authorities and the state but not necessarily of the variety that some academic economists have been advocating, namely a contract between the CEO and the government. Instead, accountability, disclosure, conflict resolution procedures, in addition to adequate governance structures, represent key inputs into the creation of conditions conducive to delivering good monetary policy outcomes. The locus of good institutional design ought to rest with institutional structure.

This chapter defines, develops, and analyzes indexes of central bank accountability and disclosure and asks how well these help us understand central bank behavior and institutional structure. They, hopefully, also assist us in understanding how far away central banks are from some ideal combination of the factors that ultimately explain "good" monetary policy outcomes. The chapter also explores how these measures can shed new light on central bank performance in conjunction with the choice of monetary policies. Finally, some attention was devoted to the role of enhanced accountability and disclosure in influencing private sector inflation forecasts. Unlike changes in statutory requirements, changes in inflation forecasts stemming from central bank activities represent concrete indicators of the effects of greater accountability and disclosure.

The indexes of accountability and disclosure are positively related to each other, and were also found to be informative about central bank independence indicators in the 1990s. Moreover, key elements of accountability and disclosure, namely the adoption of inflation targets, and the release of inflation or monetary policy reports, have had a noticeable impact on inflation, private sector forecasts of inflation, and their persistence levels. Accordingly, the study continues with a deeper exploration of the significance of the adoption of inflation targets.

7 | Inflation Targets versus Other Inflation Control Measures: Two Sides of the Same Coin?

INTRODUCTION

This study has documented and traced the evolution of central bank policies and institutions since World War II. Evolution describes well the process by which monetary policy has changed over time and the forces that reshaped the institutional relationship between central banks and government on the one hand, and the public on the other. In essence the current state of affairs recognizes the role of inflation as the fulcrum of monetary policy more explicitly than has heretofore been possible or even desirable. The reason has to do with a search for a coherent policy framework in which monetary policy could operate. Through experimentation policy makers have concluded that, to date, the most coherent policy framework is to focus on some inflation objective.

Indeed, as this is written, it is becoming increasingly commonplace for central banks to adopt some kind of inflation objective. Whether as a guideline, or via more formal mechanisms, inflation targeting certainly strikes some as taking on a kind of flavor-of-the-month role among the existing menu of monetary policy frameworks. While it is difficult to find instances of central banks that did not have some kind of inflation control objective in mind throughout their history, the performance of inflation since the end of World War II lends credence to the view that good intentions alone in the realm of inflation are not enough. Either the hands of central bankers need somehow to be tied or the institutional relationship between the state and the central bank was flawed because, more often than not, central banks have not been able to deliver low and stable inflation rates for long stretches of time. This chapter first considers how economic theory has led to the formulation of models or approaches where the policy framework is central to the determination of inflation outcomes. Next, an attempt is made to link the broad evolution of macroeconomic policies to the theoretical developments sketched in the previous section. The evolution of policy frameworks led to the neglect, for a time, of one critical aspect in institutional design. The provision of autonomy to central banks can only represent one part of the possible solution to the inflation control puzzle. The "authorities" need to provide more disclosure about their operations. However, as noted in the previous chapter, the mere gesture of openness is, by itself, not enough unless the relations with the political authorities who, after all, appoint and interact with central bankers are properly structured or sufficiently clear.

The desirability of openness and greater disclosure also suggests that the instruments of monetary policy considered in existing models omit an important element, in particular how the central bank communicates with political authorities, financial markets, and the public. As discussed as follows, the form in which communication proceeds is also relevant. A distinction is made between what used to be referred to as moral suasion, namely the attempt to either persuade the authorities, the public, or both, to change their behavior voluntarily, as opposed to devices that inform markets in more concrete or decisive ways about their outlook for the economy or policy. The distinction is important not only because of considerations surrounding the openness, disclosure, and accountability criteria previously discussed but also because of the conflict central banks face today between low frequency outcomes (for example, an inflation objective) and high frequency outcomes (for example, volatility in financial markets).

The chapter concludes by exploring some of the practical issues surrounding inflation targeting.[1]

---

[1] There is also the, as yet, untried policy of nominal income targeting. Some have argued (for example, McCallum 1997b) that a target for nominal GDP growth might have the advantage of being in a sense "fairer" because it would be easier for everyone in the population to follow and incorporate the effect of changes in the prices of all goods and services. However, implementing such a nominal anchor requires assumptions about changes in the velocity of circulation. This is viewed as either unpredictable or a function of institutional factors (for example, see Bordo and Jonung 1987; Bordo, Jonung, and Siklos 1997; and Siklos 1993). Moreover, a nominal income target still leaves open how much real income growth is implicit in the objective, another quantity that appears to be difficult to measure. In part for these reasons, the policy has never been adopted by any central bank. Consequently, in the absence of any experience with such a policy, we do not consider it any further.

THE END OF PERSONALITIES AND THE EMERGENCE OF A FRAMEWORK FOR MONETARY POLICY

As discussed in Chapter 2, Milton Friedman (1962; also see Friedman and Schwartz 1963) long ago suggested that the personalities who head central banks significantly dictate the course of actual policies taken. Anecdotal evidence, particularly for the United States, Canada, and the United Kingdom, to name but three countries, appears to support this view (for example, see Siklos 1999a; and Timberlake 1993: ch. 20).[2] Friedman (1962) ascribes this outcome to the manner in which the Fed has always conducted monetary policy, namely a desire to "avoid accountability and its efforts to maintain a favorable public image" (Friedman and Schwartz 1993). This outcome can be traced to flaws in the institutional design of the Fed. However, the record of U.S. inflation, relative to that of virtually every industrial country, has been a good one. Indeed, the relatively high inflation of the 1970s is the historical exception (for example, see DeLong 1997; 2000). Taylor (1999) also notes the importance of "ideology" concerning inflation by arguing that changes in views about the consequences of inflation had measurable impact in policy makers' attitudes toward inflation. Sargent (1999), in contrast, argues that while the Lucas critique helped convince policy makers that policy evaluation via econometric modeling was futile, adaptive type estimation approaches would have led to an earlier conquest of inflation. Therefore econometric policy evaluation can be vindicated. Nevertheless, whether the record of inflation alone is sufficient to maximize society's social welfare is a separate question. We have already seen, in Chapter 4, that there is a great deal of consensus among economists about the contents of the objective function of a central bank, namely the inclusion of both price developments as well as developments in the real side of the economy. What is unclear, of course, are the relative weights placed on each objective, and how these might change over time. Openness and accountability then become important attributes because they represent mechanisms through which the public and the political authorities can

---

[2] The early history of central banking, that is, prior to World War II, were formative years during which central banks were for the most part concerned with establishing their authority vis-à-vis the treasury. Also see, for example, Fratianni and von Hagen 1992; Meltzer 2001; Sylla 1988; Wicker 1993; and references therein. For the British case prior to World War II see the description in Moggridge (1992: pp. 270–4) and Keynes' role in the process, as well as Sayers (1976). Also, see Bordo and Schwartz (1997).

evaluate performance relative to their respective objectives. It has long been argued that, unless such institutional mechanisms are in place, a bureaucracy will not pursue the same objectives as society (Acheson and Chant 1973). It is in such a setting that, for example, a central bank will be perceived as favoring one group over another. Indeed, a somewhat different set of bureaucratic notions of central bank behavior, in the form of opposition to inflation in the financial sector, led Posen (1993; 1995) to suggest that laws are not enough and, consequently, that legal remedies that give central banks autonomy from the political authorities will be insufficient to deliver desirable inflation outcomes. All this means is that the debate over the independence of central banks should be placed in the political and financial environment in which they operate. Hence, personalities become less important than the institutional environment. To be sure, personalities matter, but the lessons from history are that personalities matter most during defining moments in history, such as when there is some kind of economic or financial crisis. The reason, as discussed in Chapter 2, is that effective monetary policy is about dealing with unexpected events. Presumably then, the greater the "shock" the more likely it is that the decisions of the central bank CEO will matter most. Personalities may also matter because there is no single recipe for a successful monetary policy. If such a formula existed there would be no need for a central bank or to worry about which type of monetary policy is most effective.

Therefore, institutional design and reform, and the choice of monetary policy frameworks, are not independent of each other. If we ignore the institutional and financial environments for the moment, then, as we have seen in Chapter 4, the central bank's loss function leads to the result that, given rational expectations, there is a bias in favor of inflation for the simple reason that the monetary authorities can react more quickly to such shocks than either wage or price setters. Avoiding the time inconsistency problem is easy, in principle, since all that is required is some rule that sets the desired inflation rate at some level. At its most basic level an inflation target can be interpreted as such a rule. Notice that advocates of rules also believe that the benefits of activist stabilization policies are smaller than the costs, in part because of the long and variable lags in monetary policy combined with the view that the impact of monetary policy on output is relatively small and, at best, temporary, whereas the impact on inflation is relatively larger. Consequently, the net costs of actively resorting to monetary policy actions are too great.

For many years the debate about the role of monetary policy was framed around the question of rules versus discretion. However, casual evidence and the results discussed in Chapter 4 suggest that actual policy choices are neither of the pure discretion or ruleslike behavior outlined in theory. Moreover, there are no obvious avenues through which personalities, partisan politics, or bureaucratic behavior, can influence inflation performance in the current setup.

As a first step one can simply declare, backed by legislation, that the central bank is an autonomous institution that is free of instructions from the finance ministry. However, not even the most independent of central banks can be entirely free from political influence since the institution remains a creature of the state. At best, political influence is limited and, if the institutional relationship between the state and the central bank is clearly defined and credible, then the outcome can be superior to either a simple rule or to discretion. As we have seen, the requisite conditions are unlikely to be met in reality so it is quite likely that central bank independence is not enough. Indeed, it is telling that de jure independence is a phenomenon that appeared to gather momentum after a consensus had been reached to reduce inflation, and not as a direct vehicle through which lower inflation per se was attained. In countries with historically good inflation performance, statutory independence was vaguely assured, or not explicitly mentioned at all.

Since merely declaring central banks independent is not enough, an alternative is to appoint a central banker who ostensibly places a relatively greater weight on inflation performance than either the government, the public, or both.[3] To prevent the time inconsistency problem from manifesting itself in a different manner, it is clear, in principle, that the central banker cannot easily be dismissed from the post of CEO once appointed. This gives rise to the notion of the "conservative" central banker due to Rogoff (1985). Lohmann (1992) extends the idea to account for the possibility that the conservative central banker may wish to be reappointed. In this case even the conservative central banker can

---

[3] It is not always clear where the public stands in models where the central bank interacts with the rest of society. Surveys of the kind conducted by Shiller (1997) contend that the public does care about inflation and yet suffers from money illusion. It is quite conceivable that the importance the public places on inflation control is not as great as that of the central banker but is higher than that of the government. Although the full implications of these complications have not been fully worked out, some of the relevant considerations emerge when discussing the role of partisan politics, as shown in Chapter 4.

accommodate some shocks that might lead the government to block reappointment. Clearly, this is a third avenue through which the cult of personality notion of central banking can be explained. From a practical perspective, however, this "solution" to the inflation bias problem presents a number of difficulties. First, of course, is the matter of establishing whether the central banker in question is, in fact, more conservative than policy makers in government. Is the evaluation to be done solely prior to the appointment of the central banker? Does the conservative central banker have to prove himself, or herself, as it were, by implementing a policy that demonstrates a relatively lower inflation bias? Does it matter whether the central banker is appointed from within the central bank or from outside? One can very well imagine an ex ante conservative central banker, appointed externally who, once in office, becomes less conservative, either because the data or deliberations within the bank convince the CEO to alter course, or because the institution succeeds in influencing the head of the central bank to adopt the preexisting level of conservatism at the central bank. If, as in Sargent (1999), a form of adaptive reasoning rules central bank behavior, prior beliefs within the institution are likely to be a key determinant of policy actions, regardless of the appointment of a more-or-less conservative central banker. Presumably, there exist signals that can assist in establishing the inflation fighting credentials of the central banker, whether he or she is appointed from within.

Next, the appointment of a conservative central banker who eventually wishes to be reappointed need not, as in Lohmann (1992), be necessarily accommodating of large shocks that might otherwise damage the chances of reelection of the current government, especially if governance questions are appropriately dealt with. Moreover, failure to reappoint could be costly to the government, or result in modification of future appointment procedures that prove unacceptable to some future government, thereby resulting in a deferral of the original problem. Finally, dismissal or failure to reappoint may not be so critical after all if the replacement is also considered to be conservative by markets or the public at large. These difficulties, combined with the recognition that even the most autonomous of central banks ultimately remain accountable either to the elected representatives or the public, need not imply, as assumed for example in Alesina and Summers (1993), that one can equate the degree of central bank independence with inflation performance. Moreover, under the typical set up for the loss function described in Chapter 4, the reduced inflation bias displayed by the conservative central banker translates into relatively greater output variability. The reason, to exaggerate a bit to make the point, is that conservative central bankers care more about inflation than output, and are consequently unmoved by departures in overall economic activity from the target or its natural rate.

Despite some peripheral role for the central bank as an institution, its role remains in the background and is secondary to the personality at the head of the central bank. So far, however, and other than for the role of governance within the central bank, the choice of appointments has been ignored. Yet it is the government in power that is crucial in the appointment of the central bank's CEO and, as the results in Chapter 4 indicate, partisan and/or electoral considerations must play a role in the appointment process.

This aspect of the problem has been recognized by, among others, Waller (1989), and Alesina and Gatti (1995). The situation is most easily understood by assuming that there are two parties vying for power who are distinguished by their preference for output stabilization. In addition, there is uncertainty about the election outcome and, therefore, the type of monetary policy to be implemented following the election. Central bank independence, in the form of a conservative central banker, can reduce political business influences thereby increasing the importance attached to central bank independence. Moreover, as discussed in Waller and Walsh (1996), the longer the term of office the less likely a central bank will be politically motivated. The irony is that while the theory is plausible, it is precisely in countries where the central bank has delivered relatively low inflation rates (for example, the United States) that political business cycle activity is most pronounced. Yet, countries where partisan cycles cannot by definition be detected (for example, Switzerland and Japan), but where the central banks are considered to be autonomous, have produced inflation and economic records comparable to that of other countries with apparently politically motivated business cycles. Hence, despite the explicit addition of political factors into the reaction function framework, there remain difficulties with both the anecdotal and empirical evidence supportive of partisan or political business cycles.

Ultimately, the difficulty in distinguishing the role of personalities versus policies arises because these same personalities must operate within some kind of institutional or policy environment. However, if we define a policy framework, following the Oxford English Dictionary's definition as a *structure composed of parts framed together*, then the task of distinguishing between personalities and policies becomes somewhat easier. The following section argues that the policy of inflation targeting completely satisfies the requirement of the definition, with exchange rate regimes based monetary policies coming behind and, finally, with monetary targeting regimes a distant third. It is precisely for this reason that inflation targeting versus other measures to control inflation do not represent two sides of the same coin.

EXCHANGE RATE REGIMES, MONEY, INFLATION, AND TARGETING: WHICH ONE IS A COHERENT POLICY FRAMEWORK?

The post-World War II era has seen three major policy regimes in place with a direct bearing on central bank behavior and performance. They are: various types of exchange rate regimes which, for the time being we combine under one umbrella; monetary targeting regimes where some money supply measure is formally or informally targeted; and, finally, inflation targeting regimes where some indicator of the cost of living is explicitly targeted.

Good monetary policy requires that the objectives of the central bank be properly spelled out, that the statutes delineate the responsibilities of the monetary and political authorities, and that adequate instruments must be available to accomplish the stated objectives. Fulfilling these conditions precisely requires that a policy framework be in place. The natural question is then to ask whether any of the three regimes of the post-World War II era satisfy the necessary criteria. It is to this question that we now turn.

Exchange Rate Regimes

The classification of exchange rate regimes might appear straightforward at first glance yet this is not necessarily the case. Theory tends to focus on the two extremes of fixed versus floating since, under the former, there is total loss of independent monetary policy action while, under the latter regime, there is complete maneuverability in the realm of monetary policy. In practice, however, few countries have either rigidly fixed their exchange rates or allowed them to float freely without intervention. Table 7.1 shows a version of the International Monetary Fund's de jure classification scheme for the countries considered in this study

Table 7.1. Exchange Rate Arrangements, 1980–1999: The IMF's Classification Scheme and Some Modifications

Country	1980	1981	1982	1983	1984	1985	1986	1987	1988	1989	1990	1991	1992	1993	1994	1995	1996	1997	1998	1999
United States	F	F	F	F	F	F	F	F	F	F	F	F	F	F	F	F	F	F	F	F
Canada	F	F	F	F	F	F	F	F	F	F	F	F	F	F	F	F	F	F	F	F
Australia	F	F	F	MA	MA	MA	F	F	F	F	F	F	F	F	F	F	F	F	F	F
Japan	F	F	F	F	F	F	F	F	F	F	F	F	F	F	F	F	F	F	F	F
New Zealand*	F	F	F	MA	MA	MA	F	F	F	F	F	F	F	F	F	F	F	F	F[1]	F
Austria	PC	PC	PC	PC	PC	PC	PC	PC	PC	PC	PC[2]	PC[2]	PC[2]	PC[2]	PC[2]	PC[2]	PC[2]	PC[2]	LC[2]	F
Belgium	LC	LC	LC	LC	LC	LC	LC	LC	LC	LC	LC[2]	LC[2]	LC[2]	LC[3]	LC[2]	LC	LC	LC[2]	LC[2]	F
Denmark*	LC	LC	LC	LC	LC	LC	LC	LC	LC	LC	LC[4]	LC[1]	LC[1]	LC[1]	LC[1]	LC[1]	LC[1]	LC[1]	LC[1]	F
Finland*	PC	PC	PC	PC	PC	PC	PC	PC	PC	PC	PC	PC[1]	LC[1]	LC[1]	LC[3]	F[1]	F[1]	F[1]	F[1]	F
France*	LC	LC	LC	LC	LC	LC	LC	LC	LC	LC	LC[4]	LC[4]	LC[4]	LC[1]	LC[1]	LC[3]	LC[4]	LC[2]	LC[2]	F
Germany*	LC	LC	LC	LC	LC	LC	LC	LC	LC	LC	LC[6]	LC[6]	LC[6]	LC[6]	LC[6]	LC[6]	LC[6]	LC[6]	LC[6]	F
Ireland*	LC	LC	LC	LC	LC	LC	LC	LC	LC	LC	LC[1]	LC[1]	LC[1]	LC[1]	LC[1]	LC[5]	LC[1]	LC[1]	LC[1]	F
Italy*	LC	LC	LC	LC	LC	LC	LC	LC	LC	LC	LC[5]	LC[6]	LC[6]	LC[4]	F	LC[5]	LC[5]	LC[4]	LC[4]	F
Netherlands	LC	LC	LC	LC	LC	LC	LC	LC	LC	LC	LC[2]	LC[4]	LC[4]	LC[4]	LC[4]	F	LC[1]	LC[2]	LC[2]	F
Norway*	PC	PC	PC	PC	PC	PC	PC	PC	PC	PC	PC	PC	PC	LC[4]	F[1]	F[1]	MA[1]	MA[1]	MA[1]	MA
Portugal*	IA	IA	IA	IA	IA	IA	IA	IA	IA	IA	IA[1]	MA[1]	LC[1]	LC[1]	LC[1]	LC[1]	LC[1]	LC[1]	LC[1]	F
Spain*	F	F	F	MA	MA	MA	MA	MA	MA	F	LC[5]	LC[5]	LC[5]	LC[5]	LC[5]	LC[5]	LC[4]	LC[4]	LC[1]	F
Sweden*	PC	PC	PC	PC	PC	PC	PC	PC	PC	PC	PC[5]	PC[4]	PC[1]	PC[1]	F	F	F	LC[3]	LC[5]	LC
Switzerland	F	F	F	F	F	F	F	F	F	F	F	F	F	F	F	F	F	F	F	F
United Kingdom*	F	F	F	F	F	F	F	F	F	F	LC[5]	LC[5]	LC[5]	F	LC[1]	F	F	F	F	F

F = Float
LC = Limited flexibility in a cooperative arrangement
IA = Exchange rates adjusted according to "indicators" which may vary by country
MA = Managed float
PC = Pegged currency whose value may change through time
The classifications are based on the de jure classification of the International Monetary Fund found in *Exchange Arrangements and Exchange Restrictions and International Financial Statistics*. Levy-Yeyati and Stuzenegger (1999) obtain a different classification based on measures of exchange rate volatility, the volatility of

international reserves, and the volatility of exchange rate changes. Where their classification differs from the IMFs – they consider the 1990–98 sample – these are noted as follows:
1. Fixed exchange rate regime
2. Inconclusive
3. Dirty float
4. Dirty float, crawling peg
5. Floating exchange rate
* signifies that a difference exists between the de jure and de facto classifications

273

since 1980.[4] The table shows that at least five different types of de jure exchange rate regimes have been in place over the past two decades. Indeed, other classifications are possible and these, as well as the ones in Table 7.1, have been used by some to investigate overall economic performance across countries with decidedly mixed results (for example, Cukierman, Rodriguez, and Webb 1995; Frieden, Gros, and Jones 1998; Ghosh, Gulde, Ostry, and Wolf 1995; Siklos 1997b). Levy-Yeyati and Struzenegger (1999) raise a point that is a familiar one to those who study central banks, namely that there is a potential difference between de jure and de facto exchange rate arrangements. They argue that a proper classification of exchange rate regimes also requires capturing how policy makers react to exchange rate volatility and not just to how their levels are set or are permitted to evolve over time. As a result, for fifteen of the twenty countries listed in Table 7.1, differences between actual and legal exchange rate regime definitions are significant over much of the sample considered by these authors. Nevertheless, the delineation of exchange rate regimes is clouded by the fact that some exchange rate arrangements after the end of Bretton Woods permitted limited flexibility vis-à-vis their major trading or economic partners (for example, the European ERM) while remaining flexible vis-à-vis other major currencies (for example, the U.S. dollar). Moreover, the period under study is also influenced by some major economic shocks that are difficult to neatly distinguish from the ending of Bretton Woods. These are: the oil price shocks in 1973–4 and again in 1979–80 and the German economic and monetary union in 1990.

A far simpler classification, used in Chapter 4, is one based on the dating of the end of the Bretton Woods system of pegged exchange rates in with limited flexibility.[5] This delineation provides a useful way for our purposes to understand the role of exchange rate regimes in explaining economic performance than either version of the classifications considered in Table 7.1.

---

[4] For reasons that should be apparent by now, going back in time prior to the 1980s is not likely to be terribly informative about exchange rate arrangements owing largely to the existence of the Bretton Woods system of pegged exchange rates. Many authors are continuing to wrestle with the difficulty of defining de facto exchange rate regimes. The original, and widely used source from the International Monetary Fund (see notes to Table 7.1) is currently being revised. Also see, in this connection, Fischer (2001).

[5] Bordo (1993) provides a comprehensive review of the Bretton Woods era for a select group of industrial countries. Also, see Flood, Bhandari, and Horne (1989); Isard (1996); Obstfeld (1995); and Obstfeld and Rogoff (1995).

There now remains the question of why an exchange rate regime does not fulfill all of the criteria for a policy framework as understood in this study. The choice of exchange rate regimes is foremost under the control of the political authorities. As a result, in a world of fixed exchange rates, responsibility for inflation performance shifts to the country the currency is being pegged to. In a floating world there is the possibility, if not the strong likelihood, of intervention. In some countries (for example, Canada), intervention has been aimed at reducing exchange rate volatility but the case is not clear in many other industrial countries.[6] Intervention is often shrouded in secrecy, or is nontransparent, with the result that there is a clouding of central bank objectives.[7] Moreover, since legal authority over foreign exchange reserves ultimately rests with the government, the delineation of responsibilities with consequences for monetary policy performance is less clear. Also, if exchange rate levels or their volatility could be equilibrated or stabilized via the use of foreign exchange reserves alone then, arguably, the choice of exchange rate regimes might not influence the degree of instrument independence available to a central bank. However, many central banks, either formally or informally, can use interest rate changes to try to accomplish exchange rate objectives. In principle then, the choice of exchange rate regimes can compromise instrument independence even under a floating exchange rate regime. Of course, as noted previously, there is loss of instrument independence under any form of exchange rate pegging.

In all of the foregoing scenarios flexibility in the exchange rate, while perhaps complete, nevertheless requires the adoption of some monetary policy strategy. The reason, of course, is that even a managed floating regime requires a nominal anchor. Therefore, the choice is fundamentally not one between fixed, or a variant of floating, but rather between an exchange rate peg and another nominal anchor, namely monetary targets, inflation, or nominal income targeting.

---

[6] Berg and Jonung (1999) discuss Sweden's experiment with price level targeting during the 1930s. In the United States, there have been many attempts to reform the Federal Reserve Act to mandate some form of inflation control. In the 1920s, congressional bills that would have mandated price stability failed, as did several bills introduced in the 105th Congress (1997). Also see Chapters 1 and 2.

[7] The empirical literature has marshaled considerable evidence that intervention is not successful at permanently influencing equilibrium exchange rate levels. The matter is less clear concerning the impact of intervention on volatility and uncertainty in exchange rate movements. See, inter alia, Edison (1993); Garber and Svensson (1995); and Murray, Zelmer, and McManus (1997).

Finally, while the monetary authorities continue to be responsible for interest rates and inflation, there is clearly the potential for conflict between the two institutions. The early years of Europe's Exchange Rate Mechanism, its effective collapse in 1992, and the choice of exchange rates at the time of German Economic and Monetary Union, are but two vivid examples that illustrate the point. The problem is partly exacerbated under a pegged type of exchange rate regime, or a floating regime with a strong expectation of intervention. Precisely because such conflicts are likely, the focus can shift toward the personalities in government and at the central bank. As a result, the structure of monetary policy is poorly framed so that policies that target the exchange rate in one fashion or another cannot fulfill the criteria required of a coherent policy framework.

Money Growth Targets[8]

Monetary targeting saw the light of day shortly after the breakup of Bretton Woods in several industrialized countries as they searched for a new anchor for monetary policy. The Bundesbank has, from the outset, been at the forefront of the policy of money growth targeting and has continued to defend the practice as best exemplified by the choice of policy practices followed by the newly created European Central Bank.[9] Bernanke and Mishkin (1992) have exhaustively reviewed the record of official money growth targets in six major economies (the United States, the United Kingdom, Canada, Germany, Switzerland, and Japan), Rich (1997) has reviewed the Swiss experience, and von Hagen (1995; 1999a; 1999b) has separately analyzed the German episodes. Accordingly, the discussion below focuses on why monetary targeting fails the criteria required of a coherent policy framework.

It is almost always the case that a money growth target is specified in terms of an aggregate that is both imprecisely measured and is, over time, heavily influenced by financial innovations. Indeed, it is considera-

---

[8] For an alternative view that, arguably, relies on circumstances specific to a particular country, namely Austria, see Hochreiter (1995), and Hochreiter and Winckler (1995).

[9] The ECB, reflecting differing views among member countries about how monetary policy should be conducted in practice, has developed a monetary policy based on the "two pillars" concept. The first pillar is based on a "prominent" role for money growth target for eurowide M3. The second pillar involves an assessment of monetary conditions based on "other economic and financial indicators" such as the exchange rate. The strategy has been referred to as "confusing" by its critics. See, for example, Svensson (1999a).

tions such as these that led, first, to a proliferation worldwide in the variety of definitions for "the" money supply, and later the choice of an interest rate as the proxy for the instrument of monetary policy such as in the empirical work presented in Chapter 4. Moreover, unless velocity is a will-o'-the-wisp, as Friedman and Schwartz (1982) put it, it will be unclear to markets and the public about how money supply growth translates into inflation. The latter point suggests that, in a monetary targeting environment, the objectives of monetary policy will be unclear. A possible caveat to this conclusion arises in those instances where the central bank is explicitly mandated to maintain price stability. Under such circumstances one could then argue that money targets serve to signal or inform the public how price stability might be achieved, and the location of potential risks for failure to reach the stipulated targets. However, with the possible exception of the Bundesbank (and perhaps the Swiss National Bank), which has also supplemented its money growth targets with information about changes in velocity, as well as a target for inflation, no other central bank considered in this study approaches the requirements outlined above.[10]

Monetary targeting does appear to fulfill, for the most part, the remaining two criteria required of a policy framework. Hence, a policy of monetary targeting does not appear to influence the relationship between the monetary and political authorities though, as in the U.S. and German cases especially, the failure to meet the targets can be grounds for applying political pressure to alter the existing monetary policy stance or to weaken the position of the central bank vis-à-vis elected officials. Also, the policy of targeting growth in a particular monetary aggregate should not limit the instruments at the disposal of the central bank. This is especially true since targets are generally expressed in terms of an aggregate over which the central bank does not have full control, namely a measure that is often broader than just the monetary base. It is conceivable that monetary targeting can be implemented under any exchange rate regime. In a fixed exchange rate regime sterilization will dictate how successfully the central bank can attain a particular target. Serious reservations expressed in the literature about the ability of central banks to adequately sterilize foreign currency flows, together with their apparent high cost, can destroy the connection between the money growth target and price stability.

---

[10] Even though the Swiss National Bank has adopted an inflation target it is reluctant to refer to itself as an inflation targeting country (see Rich 2000).

Under a floating regime the success of money growth targets depends on the stability of the relationship between the targeted aggregate and inflation, unless the central has considerable reputation, and the noise implicit in the money growth signal will not seriously impair the authorities' reputation.

With the possible exception of Germany, Switzerland, and the United States, the era of monetary targeting is too brief in most countries to permit an effective formal statistical analysis of its performance. Indeed, the brief interlude during which monetary targets were in place would seem to represent indirect evidence of the dissatisfaction among central banks with its performance as a nominal anchor. Even the Bundesbank, which nominally has targeted money growth for over two decades, is now thought of as having effectively targeted inflation. Money targets provided sufficient flexibility for the Bundesbank to gradually achieve its objectives without any loss of credibility (for example, Deutsche Bundesbank 1999).[11] Moreover, as pointed out previously, central banks appear to view money growth targets as secondary to whatever the underlying principal objective of monetary policy ought to be, namely the stability of prices in one form or another. The base drift phenomenon, combined with the sometimes exceedingly wide bands for money growth targets, renders an objective evaluation more difficult still. Finally, monetary targeting may be viewed as a "backward looking" policy, that is, it usually adds precious little information about future economic prospects in the form of some forecast, say, of future inflation.

Inflation Targeting

Arguably, the most significant shift in the apparently never-ending search for the Holy Grail of monetary policy took place during the 1980s. The poor performance of key economic aggregates beginning in the late 1970s made it clear that monetary policy in the industrial world was not sufficiently well anchored to deliver low and stable inflation together with adequate economic performance. At the same time, however, fiscal policy became exceedingly lax by peacetime historical standards. Whether by accident or by design, central bankers succeeded in per-

---

[11] Theoretical models of the kind developed by Cukierman and Meltzer (1986a; 1986b) also interpret money targets as a noisy signal rather than an ultimate target. This view persists in the extensions to the original Cukierman-Meltzer framework by Garfinkel and Oh (1995) and Eijffinger et al. (2000).

suading the public at least that monetary policy was largely responsible for inflation and interest rate developments, but it was less clear whether the relationship between the treasuries and the central banks would permit sufficient coordination to allow the two institutions to seek common goals. In particular, it became increasingly clear that some central banks had the requisite instruments to attain some desirable policy objectives, while others did not. In some countries, this realization came from the political institutions, as in New Zealand, where room to maneuver either fiscally, or in the realm of monetary policy, no longer appeared to exist. Elsewhere, as in Canada, the stimulus came from the central bank as it sought a mechanism first to persuade, then to ensure, that price stability be placed at the forefront as an objective of monetary policy. Ultimately, in several countries, the loss of monetary and fiscal discipline in the 1980s led several countries to consider an alternative, but not fundamentally new, form of monetary policy, referred to as inflation targeting.

Table 7.2 outlines some of the key attributes of an inflation targeting regime, and the question of interest here is whether such a policy constitutes a coherent policy framework as defined earlier.[12] In principle, an inflation target, since it is specified in terms of a general cost of living measure the public and markets understand reasonably well, quantifies in an objective fashion the measurement of central bank performance. But this is not necessarily the same as saying that the responsibilities for monetary policy performance, as between the treasury and the central bank, have been clarified. Indeed, as shown in Table 7.2, the legislation governing the central banks that have formally adopted an inflation targeting regime, has been largely unchanged in many countries where the policy has been adopted.[13] Moreover, with the possible exception of New

---

[12] Readers will not be surprised that some of the attributes listed in Table 7.2 also appear in earlier discussions of autonomy (Chapter 2), accountability, and disclosure (Chapter 6). Also see Chapter 6 in terms of corporate governance issues. Switzerland joined the list of inflation targeting countries in 2000 (see, however, Rich 2000) while Iceland (not part of the sample) adopted a target in March 2001.

[13] To be more precise, we have seen (for example, as in Chapter 2) that New Zealand introduced inflation targets at the same time as new legislation was introduced (actually shortly thereafter in the form of a policy targets agreement, see Table 7.4). Canada and Australia did not revise their legislation upon the introduction of formal targets. Spain also changed its legislation at about the same time as it announced inflation targets while legislation formally enshrining the price stability was passed after targets were introduced in the United Kingdom. Finally, Sweden made some legislative changes prior to, as well as following, the announcement of inflation targets. Also, see Debelle (1997) and Haldane (1995a).

Table 7.2. Varieties of Inflation Targets

Country/ Index Targeted	Inflation Objective Defined	Calculation Period	Contingencies for Breaches of the Inflation Target	Consequences for Failure to Meet the Target	Targeting Horizon	Adoption Date (dd/mm/yy)
Australia/CPI	Average of 2% to 3%	Over the cycle	Mortgage interest Government-controlled prices	None	None	01/01/93
Canada/CPI[2]	2% to 4% by end of 1992 1.5% to 3.5% by mid 1994 (original) (revised) 1% to 3% Dec. 1993 to Feb 2001[3] (revised) 1% to 3% to Dec. 2006[11]	Annual	Energy prices Indirect taxes Food and energy prices (selected)[10]	None	Yes	26/02/91
Finland/CPI[9]	2% from 1995	Annual	Housing capital costs Indirect taxes Government subsidies	None	No	02/02/93
New Zealand/ CPI[5]	3% to 5% (Dec. 1990) 2.5% to 4.5% (Dec. 1991) 1.5% to 3.5% (1992:Q1–Q4) 0% to 2% (1993:Q1–Q4) 0% to 3% (1994:Q1–1997:Q1) 0% to 3% (1997:Q4–)[6]	Annual	Commodity prices Government-controlled prices Interest, credit charges	Yes	Yes	02/03/90
Spain/CPI[9]	3.5% to 4% (1996:Q1) 3% to 3.25% (1997:Q1) 3% upper limit for 1997 2.5% to 2.75% upper limit for late 1997 2% (1998)[7]	Annual	Mortgage interest	None	Yes	01/01/95
Sweden/CPI	2% 1% to 3% since 1995	Annual	Nominally none but conditional on indirect taxes, subsidies	None	No	15/01/93
United Kingdom/RPI	1% to 4% until June 1997 elections 2.5% since June 1997[12]	Annual	Mortgage interest	None	No	8/10/92

Country/Index Targeted	Separate Inflation Report?	Who Sets Target?	Publishes Inflation Forecast?	Was Central Bank Legislation Changed? When	Instrument Independence? (dominant)
Australia/CPI	No	Government	No	No	Yes (interest rate)
Canada/CPI[2]	Yes	Joint	No	No	Yes (interest rate)
Finland/CPI[9]	No[4]	Central bank	No	Yes (after)	Limited (interest rate)
New Zealand/CPI[5]	Yes	Joint	Yes	Yes (before)	Limited to yes (interest rate)
Spain/CPI[9]	Yes	Central bank	No	Yes (after)	Limited (interest rate)
Sweden/CPI	Yes	Central bank	Yes	No	Limited (interest rate)
United Kingdom/RPI	Yes[8]	Government	Yes	Yes (after)	Yes (interest rate)

[1] The governor is, however, "available" to report on the conduct of monetary policy twice a year to the House of Representatives Standing Committee on Financial Institutions and Public Administration.

[2] Although the target is formally specified in terms of overall CPI, the bank focuses on the CPI excluding food, energy, and the effect of indirect taxes. The target represents an agreement between the minister of finance and the governor of the Bank of Canada.

[3] Renewed in February 1998.

[4] Finland reports quarterly on the inflation outlook in its *Monthly Bulletin*.

[5] Since December 1997, the CPI excluding credit services is targeted. Before that date, overall CPI was targeted.

[6] The term of the new PTA coincides with the current term of the governor, which expires August 31, 2003. The PTAs were agreed to in December but are dated as beginning the following quarter for compatibility with subsequent empirical work.

[7] The Law of Autonomy was put in place in June 1994 and, although the inflation target was announced in December 1994, it was formally adopted only as of January 1, 1995. Between 1995 and 1997 the aim was to reduce inflation to the 2% range. In 1998, the aim is to keep the annual inflation rate "close to 2 percent" during the year.

[8] Only since June 12, 1997.

[9] Superceded by admission to the European Monetary Union.

[10] A new measure of "core" inflation was introduced in 2001. See http://www.bankofcanada.ca/en/press/background.pdf.

[11] Renewed in a press release dated May 18, 2001. See http://www.bankofcanada.ca/en/press/pr01-g.htm.

[12] The Bank of England Act (June 1, 1998) requires that the chancellor of the exchequer specify, at least once in a twelve-month period, what price stability is taken to be.

Sources: Siklos (1997a; 1997b); http://www.rbnz.govt.nz/bulletin/contents.htm; Bank of England Quarterly Bulletin (May 1998); http://www.bof.fi; http://www.bde.es, http://www.rba.gov.au; and Almeida and Goodhart (1998).

Zealand, there appear to be no formal consequences for failing to achieve the target other than loss of reputation, of course, an issue to which we return below.[14]

If there is then a potential flaw with inflation targets as a framework for policy such a conclusion requires that the evaluation of central bank performance be based almost entirely on de jure considerations. While this is an important aspect, as discussed in earlier chapters, every central bank with an inflation target has also taken additional steps that permit inflation targeting, at least in the public's mind, to effectively clearly delineate the responsibilities, if not the consequences for failure, to achieve the targets. Because these are potentially important considerations, we examine these additional steps separately below.

Finally, we turn to the question whether the central bank has adequate instruments to achieve the stated objective. Table 7.2 indicates the degree of instrument independence for the inflation targeting central banks. Freed from a quantitative objective for the exchange rate or money growth, central banks generally have freedom over *how* to attain the specified inflation objective. As discussed in Chapter 6, an interest rate is generally the preferred instrument chosen by the central bank but it is not the only one available. However, most of these central banks have disavowed any formal exchange rate objectives or even systematic intervention in foreign exchange markets.[15] Nevertheless, this development raises an important difficulty for central banks, because by increasing the focus of the public and markets on interest rate developments, while avoiding excessive reactions to development in the economy (see Chapter 3), there is the danger of increasing the *perception* that their actions are, in effect, consistent with a loss of instrument independence. How these perceptions can be countered is the next topic to be considered.

DISCLOSURE VERSUS FLEXIBILITY REDUX

As noted above, the policy of inflation targeting comes closest to meeting the definition of a coherent policy framework. However, in large part due to the manner in which governments and central banks came to the conclusion that the adoption of inflation targets was both viable and nec-

[14] Also see Chapter 6 in terms of governance issues.
[15] There is a trade-off because, as noted earlier (in Chapter 6), more disclosure presumably means less scope for secrecy in central bank actions.

essary, combined perhaps with political aspects involving changes in the legislation governing central banks, the delineation of the responsibility for the outcome of monetary policy, and the potential for conflicts under an inflation targeting regime, have not been fully resolved in current statutes. While many who study central banks will bemoan this problem it should be clear from this study, as well as the literature dealing with central banks more generally, that de jure classifications offer an incomplete assessment of what central banks actually do.

In particular, since inflation outcomes are the product of various shocks, some of which the central banks cannot or ought not respond to, it is vital that the public be made to understand the limitations of the instruments employed by the monetary authorities to attain a particular objective. Precisely because of these limitations, an inflation targeting policy needs to be flexible to accommodate not only the suspension of the targets themselves, but, rather, that allowances be made notably for large unanticipated shocks, especially ones originating from abroad, or ones arising from the short-term implications of financial crises. Moreover, this can only be accomplished if the public, markets, and governments, are clearly informed about the assumptions under which monetary policy is conducted. A device used to address this trade-off is the publication of a separate inflation report or monetary policy statement but it is as much, if not more, the content of such publications that matter rather than their mere existence. Such a situation may be thought of as adding a dose of pragmatism to inflation targeting.[16]

THE APPEAL OF "COMMUNICATION" AS AN INSTRUMENT OF MONETARY POLICY

In the era when the instruments available to central banks were limited by regulation, tradition, or caution, many resorted to the practice of

---

[16] The term is used instead of the one suggested by Svensson (1997a) who distinguishes between strict and flexible variants of inflation targeting. The former refers to a policy that effectively places differences between actual and targeted inflation rates alone in the central bank's loss function. By contrast, flexible inflation targeting permits other determinants, including the output gap, exchange rates, etc. (also see Svensson 2001). The distinction is not explicitly relied upon in the present study for a couple of reasons. First, it is doubtful that any central bank, let alone an inflation targeting one, can be interpreted as an "inflation nutter," the term used to describe such a central bank. Second, flexible inflation targeting, as defined above, would mean that central banks might argue that they are effectively all alike, whether they explicitly target inflation or not. Clearly, this is not the case, as we have seen.

"moral suasion," namely the attempt by a central bank to persuade certain groups (for example, banks) to act in a manner they would not otherwise choose voluntarily. Typically, however, this form of communication was not made via public means but rather by exhorting key financial institutions to restrain the growth of credit when central bank instruments could not do so in an effective fashion. Reliance on moral suasion ebbed as central banks gained influence over money markets through a growing variety of instruments at its disposal. Nevertheless, as central banks in the 1970s and 1980s ceased, at least in several industrial countries, to be viewed solely in terms of the lender of last resort function traditionally associated with central banking,[17] there was a return to an emphasis on how monetary policy could be communicated. Therefore, instead of moral suasion, the public communication function became increasingly important. Nowhere is this more evident perhaps than in the case of the German Bundesbank.

An important feature of monetary policy in Germany lies in public (and private) communications by senior Bundesbank officials with the general public (and government officials). As Bundesbank President Tietmeyer (1998a: p. 5) wrote:

> [T]he Bundesbank's role as a guardian of monetary stability must of necessity extend beyond its decision-making powers in the field of monetary policy. It has to draw attention – at as early a stage as possible – to potential risks to stability in other areas and parallel behavioral patterns in the economy or in society.

Later he goes on to add:

> [The Bundesbank] has placed itself under the obligation to explain and justify its policy as well as its assessment of developments that are relevant to monetary policy. Its target group is the general public, which it addresses through the speeches of the members of its governing bodies. (Ibid: p. 5)

To be sure, the instrument of monetary policy implied by the foregoing discussion, namely central bank communication as a signal, is a subtle one. Moreover, such an approach can only represent a noisy indicator of the Bundesbank's competence. Communication with the public is also, of course, a means through which the Bundesbank can maintain favorable public opinion of its policies, deemed to be a key ingredient of

---

[17] Another factor may have been the spread of financial innovations that may have impacted the effectiveness of short-run monetary policies.

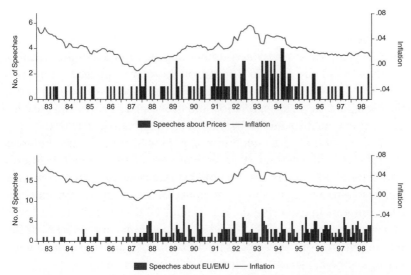

Figure 7.1 German Inflation and Speeches Given by the Bundesbank President, 1983–1998 (*Source*: Siklos and Bohl (2001) and BIS (various issues).)

its success (for example, Neumann 1999). This form of communication may or may not be "cheap talk" (for example, see Stein 1989), but such an instrument is not intended to compromise its stated objective. Rather, the goal of communication is quite the opposite. In terms of Garfinkel and Oh's (1995) framework then, the Bundesbank "speaks" precisely to minimize the "ambiguity" of its policies. Unlike the Bundesbank, however, communication will be less ambiguous[18] in the context of an inflation target precisely because such a policy is more likely to force a central bank over time to match deeds with words. Hence, an explicit inflation target and effective communication must go hand in hand as part of an overall policy framework.

Figure 7.1 illustrates how one form of communication, namely speeches given by the president of the Bundesbank by topic, might be used to supplement interest rate policy.[19] The plot shows that the number

---

[18] Ambiguity is, of course, partly a function of the track record of a central bank over time. As noted earlier in this study, central banks that earn the public's trust about their competence suffer from fewer credibility problems, and are less likely to require an explicit inflation target to reduce the noise level in their communication with the public.

[19] The data are from Siklos and Bohl (2001) who provide the details of the series construction. The correlations range from .35 to .50 depending upon the chosen sample.

of speeches dealing with inflation delivered by the president of the Bundesbank since the early 1980s is positively correlated with inflation developments.[20] By contrast, speeches dealing with the European Union or European Monetary Union do not appear to be related to inflation as revealed in the bottom portion of the figure. Instead, there is in appearance a level jump in the number of speeches toward the end of the 1980s, that is, once negotiation and eventual agreement was reached on what eventually came to be known as the Maastricht Treaty.

The upshot is that understanding how central banks influence markets and expectations requires more than just a model of interest rate behavior. The reason is that interest rate changes represent just one form of communicating monetary policy decisions. Although there has been progress in exploring the use of nontraditional data sets, in particular in the analysis of U.S. and German monetary policies, future research should turn more of its attention to further assessing and quantifying the more qualitative forms of central bank behavior.[21]

The principal obstacle, of course, for progress lies with the communications policy of a central bank. As indicated previously one could proxy the impact of such signals via the number of speeches by senior central bankers. The Bank for International Settlements has, for years, collected "important speeches and articles by senior central bankers."[22]

---

[20] Siklos and Bohl (2001) mix count models and traditional estimation techniques such as the ones used throughout this study to show how speeches, in particular ones dealing with inflation and economic policy more generally, can be used to explain the Bundesbank's monetary policy since the early 1980s.

[21] Siklos (1999c) collects data on "important" speeches collected by the Bank for International Settlements for a cross-section of countries. Larger central banks (for example, Germany, the United States) have relatively more of their speeches recorded than smaller central banks while central banks with inflation targets also have had more recognition of their speeches in recent years. Unfortunately, however, there are difficulties with this type of data set that prevent them from being used extensively in empirical work at the present time. Speeches are not, of course, the only way a central bank communicates with markets or the public. See, for example, Guthrie and Wright (1998) and Kuttner and Posen (1999).

[22] The information is supplied to the Bank for International Settlements by member central banks. The title of "senior central banker" refers to the president, governor, deputy-governor, or chief economist of the central bank. However, in the case of the United States and Germany, speeches by some members of the Board of Governors of the Federal Reserve System and the Board of the Bundesbank are also recorded. It is unclear whether the definition of an "important speech" has remained unchanged since 1980. In addition, central bank reporting requirements at individual central banks can differ, and may have changed through time, which may affect the number of speeches given. The data do not represent the sum of all speeches given by each country's central banker. Since Siklos and Bohl (2001) compile *all* the speeches by Bundesbank senior officials, we can at least ascertain the correlation between the two series. Interestingly,

As noted already, central banks in the 1990s communicate in a variety of ways and it is by no means obvious that speeches represent the best signal of monetary policy next to interest rate changes or other forms of communication. Nevertheless, it is interesting to consider the possible connection between these two instruments of monetary policy. Accordingly, Table 7.3 considers all twenty countries in this study and asks whether, conditional on some of the determinants of interest rates and the number of speeches given, the extent to which the two instruments substitute or complement each other. Again, as with all such empirical exercises, there are a number of technical issues that cannot be discussed here but potentially have a bearing on the results.[23]

Part A of the table gives the correlation between changes in the number of speeches and in interest rates. The former may be used as a signaling device to influence inflationary expectations instead of an interest rate change. Recall that central banks smooth interest rates and their communication policies can assist in that cause. The first column of the table shows the unconditional country-by-country correlation coefficient while the second column is the conditional correlation based on estimates from the following model estimated in a cross-section setting

$$\Delta Y_{it} = \Delta Y'_{it-1}\beta + \Delta X'_{it}\gamma + \Delta\varepsilon_{it} \tag{7.1}$$

where Y is a vector consisting of the short-term interest rate for each country and the number of speeches while X is a vector of exogenous variables. For the purposes of the present empirical analysis X_{it} is simply a dummy variable that identifies inflation targeting countries.[24]

---

speeches classified by the Bundesbank as dealing with either inflation or economic policy more generally were found to have a .30 correlation with the BIS data in the 1989–98 period. A similar exercise for New Zealand for a much shorter sample (second half of 1999) yields a correlation coefficient of .63. The New Zealand data were taken from the RBNZ's submission to the New Zealand Monetary Policy Review.

[23] For example, as will be seen, the estimated relationship has a lagged dependent variable. In a panel this can create biased estimates, unless the time dimension of the cross-section is large – it is twenty years in the present case. Consequently, Anderson and Hsiao (1982) propose instrumental variable estimation.

[24] As the objective of the empirical analysis is exploratory in nature, the intention was to keep the estimated relationship as simple as possible. The identification of inflation targeting countries seemed an obvious control in a sample covering only the decade of the 1980s and 1990s. The reader will also note that Equation 7.1 is written in the form of a panel vector autoregression. This is used to take advantage of the potential endogeneity between speeches and interest rate changes. See Holz-Eakin, Newey, and Rosen (1988) and Judson and Owen (1996) for additional details. Given the sample and data limitations, the estimated panel VAR is of order 1. For a general analysis of panel econometrics see, for example, Hayashi (2000: ch. 5) and Hsiao (1986).

Table 7.3. Communication and Interest Rates as Signals of Monetary Policy: An Exploratory Analysis, 1980–1999*

(A) Conditional and Unconditional Correlations[1]

Country	Unconditional	Conditional
Australia	−.01	−.01
Austria	.05	.03
Belgium	.10	.07
Canada	.12	.09
Denmark	.18	.18
Finland	.02	.02
France	.07	.07
Germany	−.01	−.01
Ireland	−.15	−.16
Italy	.03	.01
Japan	−.01	−.06
Netherlands	.03	.04
New Zealand	−.03	−.05
Norway	−.07	−.07
Portugal	−.11	−.12
Spain	.30	.30
Sweden	.12	.12
Switzerland	.01	.01
United Kingdom	−.01	−.02
United States	−.13	−.16

(B) Panel Estimates of the Determinants of Changes in the Number of Speeches[2]

Dependent Variable: Number of Speeches

Independent Variables	Coefficient (t-value)
Constant	−0.01 (0.02)
Lagged interest rates	0.08 (0.04)[@]
Lagged speeches	−0.04 (0.01)*
Inflation targeting dummy	−.02 (.06)
F-statistic (sig. level)	3.43 (.02)

* Data are monthly. Interest rates are short term as defined in Chapter 2. Data on the number of speeches are from the BIS. Additional information may be found at http://www.wlu.ca/~wwwsbe/faculty/psiklos/centralbanks.htm.

[1] The unconditional correlations are the sample correlations between changes in the number of speeches and changes in interest rates. The conditional correlations are the correlations between the residuals in Equation 7.1 by individual country.

[2] All variables are in first differences, as recommended. See, for example, Judson and Owen (1996). The interest rate variable is instrumented via the actual inflation rate also lagged. Both the interest rate and the speeches variable are lagged two periods. Other combinations were examined without any impact on the conclusions. The inflation targeting dummy is set to 1 for Australia, Canada, Finland, New Zealand, Spain, Sweden, and the United Kingdom, and is zero otherwise.

Both conditional and unconditional correlations are low and insignificant which would appear to indicate, overall, that speeches do not serve the role as substitutes for changes in interest rates. However, as revealed by the cross-section estimates in Part B of the table, speeches can serve to complement interest rate changes, as indicated by the positive and statistically significant coefficient on lagged interest rate changes.[25] Estimation evaluates the impact of interest rate changes on speeches, and not vice-versa. As pointed out above, and supported by the results in Table 7.4A, one can easily reject any effect from speeches to interest rate changes but not vice-versa.[26]

For reasons already stated these results are instructive at best, and the data omit the richness and variety with which central banks, particularly in the 1990s, communicate to the public their thinking about the conduct of monetary policy. It is too early, therefore, to draw any strong conclusions from the empirical analysis.

It should be clear that communication, while a vital ingredient in the inflation targeting framework, still leaves open an important aspect of what constitutes a policy framework, namely an indication of how the central bank sees the future.

The Importance of Forecasts

As noted earlier, a crucial drawback with exchange rate and monetary targeting based policies is that they limit the scope and maneuverbility of central bank actions in the face of unexpected shocks.

In contrast, an inflation targeting policy permits the central bank to be more forward looking. But how does a central bank communicate "forward lookingness" to a public without jeopardizing pragmatic inflation targeting? As shown in Table 7.2 central banks in inflation targeting

---

[25] Again, the bias issue (see notes 2 and 3) requires that we instrument the lagged dependent variable. This is accomplished via the inflation rate and changes in the number of speeches lagged two periods. The results were not sensitive either to the exclusion of Spain as belonging to the inflation targeting group of countries nor to estimation for data from the 1990s only. Note also that the estimates assume a common intercept. A separate test (not shown) strongly rejected the fixed effects model.

[26] An additional difficulty with the estimates is that they are dependent on a count of the number of speeches. Count model estimation in this context (for example, see Cameron and Trivedi 1998; Siklos and Bohl 2001; and Winkelmann 2000) would be more appropriate. Estimates of the impact of speeches appear to be consistent in this framework for the individual countries in the sample (results not shown), however, with the results presented in Table 7.4 B.

Table 7.4. Monetary Policy and Inflation Reports: An International Comparison

Country	Title	Authorship	First Issue/ Annual Frequency	Thrust of Discussion	Policy-making Uncertainties?	Specific Content of Report		
						Inflation Outlook or Projection?	Explanation of Policy Decision?	Policy Board Deliberations Made Public?
Australia	Semi-annual statement on monetary policy	RBA[1]	May 1997/ 2 per year	Broad macroeconomic developments (international, domestic, etc.)	No[2]	No	No	No
Canada	Monetary policy report	Governing council	May 1995/ 2 per year (+2 interim updates)	Inflation developments, aggregate demand/ supply, etc.	Yes	Yes[3]	Yes[4]	No[4]
Finland	Monetary policy and economic outlook[4]	None specified	March 1999/ 2 per year[5]	Inflation developments, euro area	No	Yes	No	No
Germany	Monthly report	None specified	1989/4 (with interquarter updates)[6]	General economic developments	Yes	Yes[7]	Yes[7]	No
Japan	Monthly report of recent economic and financial developments	Policy board	Winter 1997/12[8]	General economic developments (all sectors)	Yes	Yes[9]	Yes	No

New Zealand	Monetary policy statement	Governor	April 1990/4 (+4 interim updates)	General discussion of macroeconomic conditions	Yes	Yes	Yes	No[10]
Norway	Inflation report	Executive board	Sept. 1996/ 4 per year	Developments in inflation, exchange rate and "cyclical" developments	Yes	Yes	No	No
Sweden	Inflation report	Governor/ governing board	Oct. 1993/ 4 per year	Inflation developments, interest rate effects	Yes	Yes	Yes	No
Switzerland	Bulletin trimestriel[11]	Report from SNB for the directorate[12]	1983/ 4 per year	General economic developments	No	Yes	Yes	No
United Kingdom	Inflation report	Monetary policy committee	Feb. 1993/ 4 per year	Macroeconomic conditions	Yes	Yes[13]	Yes	Yes
United States	Humphrey-Hawkins report (1978–2000); Monetary policy report (2000–)	Board of governors	Feb. 1979/ 2 per year	General economic developments incl. prices	Yes	Yes	Yes	Yes
ECB	Monthly bulletin	Executive board	Jan. 1999/ 12 per year[14]	Euro area developments	Yes	Yes[15]	Yes[16]	No

Table 7.4 (*continued*)

Country	Formal Inflation Target?	Report Mandated?	Advance Meeting Dates Announced?	Focus Boxes on Current Issues?	Approx. Length (pages)
Australia	Yes	Yes	Yes	Yes	≈50 pgs
Canada	Yes	No	Yes (2001)	Yes	<50 pgs
Finland	Yes	No	Yes	No	≈10 pgs
Germany	No	No	No	No	<50 pgs
Japan	No	Yes	Yes	No	<100 pgs
New Zealand	Yes	Yes	Yes	Yes	<50 pgs
Norway	No	No	Yes	Yes	<50 pgs
Sweden	Yes	Yes	Yes	Yes	<100 pgs
Switzerland	Yes[17]	No	No	No	≈100 pgs[18]
United Kingdom	Yes	Yes	Yes	Yes	≈100 pgs
United States	No	Yes (until 2000)	Yes	No	<50 pgs
ECB	Yes[19]	Yes	Yes	No	<50 pgs

[1] Based on statutes the report is from the governor.

[2] An outlook is provided as well as information based on private sector forecasts.

[3] An outlook is provided as well as information based on private sector expectations.

[4] Prior to December 2000, only when overnight target band changed. Extracts from minutes released with a short lag.

[5] Originally part of the Bank of Finland Bulletin. Date refers to separate availability of the document.

[6] In addition there are monthly updates under a different title.

[7] Periodically, the Bundesbank announced an "unavoidable" inflation rate. Decisions explained retrospectively, especially via the annual report.

[8] Monthly Report supplemented by a publication known as *The Bank's View.*

[9] Beginning in December 2000, *Outlook and Risk Assessment of the Economy and Prices.*

[10] Governor is alone responsible for monetary policy decisions.

[11] In French and German with an English summary.

[12] The report is addressed to the Directorate of the SNB (Swiss National Bank).

[13] Risks of future inflation rather than a point target.

[14] The ECB began formal responsibility for monetary policy in January 1999.

[15] Beginning December 2000.

[16] An announcement is followed immediately by a press conference held by the president of the ECB.

[17] Beginning in 2000.

[18] Increased from approximately fifty pages following the granting of statutory autonomy in July 1997.

[19] Inflation target is, however, part of an overall monetary policy strategy that includes exchange rates and targets for money growth in the euro arena (see *A Strategy-Oriented Monetary Policy Strategy for the ESCB*).

292

countries are split between ones that publish an explicit inflation forecast and others that do not (also see Chapter 6). All, however, discuss with varying degrees of precision the "outlook" in the medium term for inflation, in particular, and economic activity more generally.

Theoretical work (for example, Bernanke and Woodford 1997; Woodford 1999b) has suggested that central banks should target an inflation forecast. However, inflation forecast targeting could be destabilizing for essentially two reasons. First, if the target is credible in the first place, the inflation forecast is not likely to provide much useful information. Indeed, there is the potential for a negative externality since the incentive to produce private sector forecasts will disappear. Second, inflation forecast targeting leads to increased volatility in inflation even if, on average, the target is met. This is approximately true whether the forecast being targeted is some consensus forecast or the central bank's own inflation forecast.

Moreover, the theoretical predictions presume a considerably greater amount of openness and disclosure in central bank operations than is in fact the case. Also, it is doubtful that private sector forecasts, especially of the consensus variety, would be the aim of inflation targets without knowledge of the structure or the information set used to generate the forecasts in the first place. Additionally, as pointed out earlier, agents are not only interested in one moment in the distribution of inflation or inflation forecasts. Monetary policy operates in an inherently uncertain world and point forecasts are of limited usefulness. Finally, even if we put aside all of the foregoing objectives, there remains the question of whether central banks would eventually be held accountable for their forecasts only or inflation performance more generally. Also, would the central bank's loss function now be determined by a forecast error relative to forecasts or relative to actual inflation? This position also presumes that there are measurable economic consequences from missing inflation forecasts, and there is no economic theory that can help us interpret the implications of such a policy. The upshot is that inflation forecast targeting strays away from a pragmatic inflation targeting policy, and would also violate one of the criteria of a coherent policy framework. Nevertheless, this is not the same as saying that the publication of an inflation forecast is unnecessary. Quite the contrary. Since all such useful forecasts are conditional, their availability simply reflects an important element of disclosure in central bank operations discussed earlier in this study.

Finally, recall (see Chapters 2 and 4) that there is an important distinction to be made between a forecast and a projection. Yet, even if the public is made to understand the differences between these two concepts, one might well ask how informative such forecasts are once the inflation target is unchanged and is being met for a considerable amount of time? After all, this might be the best indication of all that long-run success in targeting inflation has been attained.

As seen from Table 7.2, most inflation targeting countries instituted inflation *reduction* targets in the early phase of the strategy. Subsequently, these became inflation *control* targets. Earlier (see Chapters 2 and 6), the relatively high persistence in inflation forecasts was noted. It is, therefore, conceivable that, in such an environment, changes in inflation will not be terribly informative if they consistently remain within the target range. It is precisely under these circumstances that communication of monetary policy conditions becomes still more important. First, by transmitting to the public the *risks* of failing to meet the target under certain scenarios precisely via well articulated projections. Second, by emphasizing the importance of constantly aiming for the midpoint of any target range, and the symmetry of central bank responses to inflation rates that drift above or below the range.[27] Finally, by underlining the fact that even small deviations in actual inflation from the center of the target can, over time, lead to significant permanent losses in purchasing power.[28]

COMMUNICATING MONETARY POLICY

Indeed, a reflection of the pragmatic approach is evident in the proliferation of inflation and monetary policy reports in both inflation targeting and noninflation targeting countries. Moreover, since the European Central Bank represents ten of twenty central banks considered in this study, this type of communication has now essentially been adopted by virtually all central banks in the industrial world. Table 7.4 summarizes some of the key features of this and other forms of communication now undertaken by central banks.

The table provides key summary information regarding the authorship and content of the reports, and the degree to which deliberations within the central bank are made public. Broadly speaking, the "typical"

---

[27] The Bank of England, for example, is explicit about treating departures from the midpoint of the target in a symmetric fashion. Other inflation targeting countries (for example, Canada) were, initially at least, less explicit in this connection.

[28] The Bank of Canada, for example, introduced an "inflation calculator" that makes it easy for anyone to evaluate such losses. See
http://www.bankofcanada.ca/eu/inflation_calc.htm.

report is fairly short, published roughly quarterly, and deals with broad macroeconomic developments, not simply with inflation performance. Few central banks release details of deliberations within the committees responsible for making monetary policy decisions. In contrast, the vast majority of decisions are explained and differences of views within the central bank may be publicly disclosed in that manner. With the exception of Germany, Switzerland, and the United States, reporting on monetary policy is primarily a phenomenon of the 1990s.[29] In addition, in several countries (for example, Canada and New Zealand), the frequency with which monetary or inflation reports are published has increased over time. By 2001 the vast majority of countries considered in this study provide some kind of explicit forecast of inflation and of other key macroeconomic aggregates. Even the holdout countries (for example, Canada, Australia, and Germany (prior to EMU)) provide considerable detail about the inflation outlook.

Most of these reports are less than fifty pages, although four central banks publish such reports that come in at just under one hundred pages. While it is, of course, impossible to estimate the "optimal" length for reporting monetary policy there is surely a loss of clarity with an increase in length (though, in other instances, financial markets might appreciate more frequent reports). It is also instructive to note that such reporting is mandated in only half of the countries considered, while, at the time of writing, almost all the countries have decided to notify markets in advance of scheduled meeting dates for the policy-making body of the central bank.

Finally, the vast majority of countries do not use such reporting mechanisms to discuss inflation developments alone. Only four of the central banks can be said to focus the discussion solely on inflation. Even these central banks are careful to point out that its sources are varied, and require a broad view of economic developments.

PRACTICAL ISSUES WITH INFLATION TARGETS: THE CRUCIAL ROLE OF THE INSTITUTIONAL FRAMEWORK

Supporters and critics of inflation targeting point out that the policy raises some practical problems. As these are well known (for example,

---

[29] That is not to say that information concerning monetary policy was not available at the other central banks listed in the table. Instead, the reporting that was publicly available was not directly aimed at communicating central bank strategy in achieving a particular inflation objective.

see Bernanke, Laubach, Mishkin, and Posen 1999; Haldane 1997; Mishkin 2000; and Siklos 1997a; 1999b) they are only briefly reviewed here.

Table 7.1 reveals that policy makers must decide on whether the target is to be a range of inflation rates or a point target. Moreover, a decision must be taken on whether the midpoint of the range is a target as well, and whether the central bank ought to be indifferent between inflation rates above or below the target. In general, experience with inflation targets has shown that central banks constantly aim for the middle of the target range, where defined, and so they do not treat inflation rates above or below the target in an asymmetric fashion. However, inflation targeting does not eliminate the long and variable lags of monetary policy. Hence, it seems reasonable to treat the target as a goal that cannot *always* be *certain* of being attained. The width of the target range is an open question since a wide band has greater chances of meeting some accountability criterion but is unlikely to be transparent precisely because the target range might become uninformative. Similarly, too narrow a band might be taken as a sign of a strong desire for central bank accountability but, due to the variety and size of economic shocks that are inevitable, would require a considerable amount of disclosure that could have a negative impact on the public's perception of central bank performance. Consequently, a target that is considerably narrower than the historical experience, but is wide enough to prevent the central bank from having to "talk" too frequently, would appear to be adequate. The specification of the targets, as outlined in Table 7.1, together with the historical experience with inflation reviewed throughout this study, suggests that policy makers had the foregoing considerations in mind. The point is to specify a target such that breaches are an exception and permit the disclosure mechanisms of the central bank to be adequate enough to prevent a permanent change in inflationary expectations.

The foregoing discussion also raises the question of the problem of escape clauses, and the choice of the indicator of inflation to target, that is, what shocks are admissible as being beyond the control of the central bank and the terms in which these should be evaluated. As first discussed in Chapter 2, there is a tension between targets specified in terms of some indicator of core inflation versus others set in relation to a headline or overall inflation rate. Considerations of disclosure and accountability outlined in Chapter 6 suggest that a target should be understood in terms of a broad measure of consumer prices but that monetary policy should primarily be geared toward an underlying inflation rate. This appears to be sensible not only to prevent perverse forms of monetary policy discussed earlier[30] but because it highlights the need for the central bank to be flexible, and reinforces the important role of the communication of monetary policy decisions. Finally, despite the myriad of ways to measure changes in the purchasing power of money, and the inherent biases in all such measures, the general level of consumer prices remains the most widely understood benchmark in policy discussions.

In Chapter 6 the problem of "tunnel vision" in the conduct of monetary policy was also raised and, in this connection, policy makers need to define the horizon over which the target is to be met. Tradition suggests that inflation on an annual basis is the metric of choice across most central banks (see Table 7.1). Inflation calculated on a monthly or quarterly basis clearly displays considerably more volatility than annual or inflation rates measured over longer horizons (see Chapter 2). Longer horizons, while reducing the chances that the central bank will react too quickly to some perceived shock also raises the possibility of greater political influence over monetary policy as the length of the horizon approaches that of the political cycle. However, this also serves to increase accountability on both the central bank and the government. After all, this study has emphasized the importance of joint responsibility over monetary policy decisions. Maintaining the annual horizon but requiring a preelection briefing by the central bank over the electoral horizon, as is currently the practice in New Zealand, is a suitable compromise.

Finally, there are the relatively less commonly addressed questions of volatility and interdependence. The public is not likely to favor an inflation target unless it also promises less volatile inflation rates.[31] Moreover, even if an inflation targeting regime operates in an environment where

---

[30] For example, in the event of an adverse aggregate supply shock which raises inflation, it is clearly inappropriate to raise interest rates.

[31] In this connection, mention should be made about the possibility of price level targeting as opposed to inflation targeting. With possible exception of Sweden in the 1930s (Berg and Jonung 1999; Jonung 1979), price level targeting has not been adopted in the post-war era nor is it viewed by central banks as a practical possibility in part because of fears of deflation. Under a price level target, a rise in the price level must at some point be followed by a fall in the price level to meet the target. It is generally assumed that price level targets are point targets but if the price level target is a range it can merely be thought of as just a stricter form of inflation targeting. However, theoretical models suggest that price level targeting reduces inflation volatility (Svensson 1997b) but not necessarily uncertainty (for example, Fischer 1994). An alternative, of course, is to permit some drift in the price level target but then we are back to a fixed inflation target.

exchange rates are permitted to float freely without intervention, central banks must contend with external shocks as well. The importance of these is likely to be a function of the proximity of principal trading partners and the economy's openness.[32] How the target band is defined, and the circumstances under which volatility and international links in inflation lead to breaches in the inflation target, are measures that are designed to deal with these questions.

The bottom line, as the foregoing discussion implies, is that the practical difficulties with inflation targets underline the crucial importance attached to the institutional framework in which they operate. Without these, inflation targeting alone need not necessarily be a more coherent framework than others considered in this study.

SUMMARY

Economists are interested in the comparative advantage of inflation targeting as a framework for monetary policy. To understand this development requires a historical detour to ask how monetary policy objectives have evolved over time and what were the main catalysts for change. The chapter provides an explanation for the emergence of each form of policy making in terms of the accountability, disclosure, and conflict resolution issues highlighted earlier in this study. An argument is then made that the growth of international capital markets, and their enhanced linkages, have contributed to this outcome. Moreover, after a lull of sorts, "moral suasion" as a policy tool has apparently made a comeback in a different modern form. This highlights the role of communication as a separate instrument of monetary policy. Siklos (1999c) and Siklos and Bohl (2001) show how the "words" of central bankers, namely speeches, can potentially represent a separate but important instrument of monetary policy. It is necessary to construct a variable able to capture the signaling content of central bank communication, how these interact and influence the setting of more conventional instruments of monetary policy (for example, interest rates). One possibility explored in this chapter is to use the number of speeches given by senior central bank officials as an instrument to supplement the traditional resort to interest

---

[32] Romer (1993) associates greater openness with lower inflation. Recognition of external shocks in the reaction function, and in the description and analysis of the inflationary experience of the countries considered in this study, is the means through which openness is recognized here.

rate changes as the main indicator of monetary policy actions. Finally, the chapter concludes that inflation targeting fulfills the requirements of a coherent monetary policy "framework," while other strategies adopted in earlier decades of the post-World War II era did not.

8 | The Changing Face of Central Banking: Epilogue

INTRODUCTION

Monetary policy is the most flexible economic policy tool of government, and possibly its most potent one as well. Nevertheless, as World War II ended, the experience of the 1920s and 1930s revealed a deep mistrust of monetary policy, and perhaps to a greater extent, of central bankers. Governments yearned for some form of stability, after decades of large fluctuations in the price level and in other major macroeconomic aggregates. Policy coordination failed and there was a strong undercurrent of desire for countries to find their own destiny, as it were, in economic terms. While fiscal policy would dominate the scene as the principal tool of policy, three concurrent forces lead to a shift back to the view that the central bank must occupy a central place in the implementation of economic policy. First, exchange rate stability is an illusion and must of necessity come in conflict with domestic objectives that diverge across countries. Second, the growth of trade and of capital mobility leads to international imbalances that are exacerbated by artificial attempts to maintain exchange rate regimes ill suited to such an environment. Third, fiscal policy is slow to act and is increasingly an inept instrument for attaining particular economic objectives. This is especially true in a world of high-frequency data. The impression is sometimes given that what has changed, in the 1990s especially, is the greater recognition of the importance of price stability. Nothing could be further from the truth. Economists and policy makers long ago felt that monetary policy was about delivering low and stable inflation rates. "It may be assumed . . . that the whole of the economic world is agreed upon the desirability of securing some degree of stability in the general level of prices . . ." (Bellerby 1924: p. 177). Indeed, the era of extremely volatile prices that marked the

300

period of the 1920s and 1930s led many to advocate policies that would ". . . aim merely at lessening price fluctuations within a particular business cycle, checking somewhat the upward movement and thereby lessening the subsequent decline" (Sprague 1921: p. 24). The reason for such views are simple: ". . . we know this: Periods of serious price disturbances are period of industrial and financial disturbance and social unrest. Practically never one without the other. And periods of price stability are periods of industrial and social equilibrium and sanity" (Snyder 1935).

What has changed is the recognition that price stability can be achieved in a framework that provides flexibility in policy making without jeopardizing credibility or reputation. Moreover, the last fifty years has provided an opportunity for learning by central bankers and policy makers. As such, economic history has indeed taught us something that has been put to good use.

Hence, any understanding of economic performance more generally, and of inflation performance in particular, must come to grips with what central banks have done over the past half century or so of economic history. The study began by emphasizing the role of central banks as institutions, for it is easy to fall prey to the notion that institutions matter little in a world where the conduct of monetary policy, especially nowadays, appears to follow rules-like behavior. The rest of the study examined the tension between attempts at oversimplifying what central banks are supposed to do with what they are designed to do. Needless to say, the analysis reveals the largely evolutionary nature of central banking institutions and policies, and hence the complexities one must face in attempting to summarize the economic history of central banking over the past half century. The concluding chapter retraces the main steps in the journey and broadly assesses what has been learned along the way.

DE JURE OR DE FACTO AUTONOMY: DOES IT MATTER?

First and foremost, central banks are institutions that operate within government and not apart from it. Hence, any attempt at legislating autonomy can never entirely eliminate all potential sources of tension between the political and monetary authorities. There are plenty of examples of central banks that do not appear to possess what, in retrospect, is the desired level of autonomy and yet are able to deliver consistently good economic performance. One reason, as we saw in Chapter 2, is that inflation performance, for example, is not likely to be entirely independent of political structures that set out the "rules of the game" for central banks. Divisive forms of government may be more apt to create conditions that favor more inflation, regardless of the degree of statutory autonomy enjoyed by the central bank.

Moreover, the narrow statutory view of central banking leaves open the question of the ingredients that are crucial to delivering good monetary policy, for any given political structure. Indeed, as shown in Chapter 2, three features of the legal relationship between the government and the central bank stand out. They are: the nature and limits of the responsibilities of the head of the central bank vis-à-vis the treasury, or the government more generally, the clarity of objectives, and the manner in which conflicts are resolved.

The economics literature has shown considerable interest in the question of how best to design a "contract" for a central banker; it is becoming clearer that such a view shifts too much responsibility onto too few individuals. Delivering good monetary policy, gaining credibility, and gaining a strong reputation require competence and due diligence toward differences of opinion among a small group entrusted with the task of implementing monetary policy. Therefore, the focus ought to be on policy-making boards of central banks since, whether de facto or de jure, this is how monetary policy is effectively carried out, and has been for decades. The role of bodies is evident throughout the study but especially in Chapters 5 through 7 for they help define the concept of a *framework* for monetary policy.

Clarity of objectives becomes crucial, not only because it assists in making public the extent of the responsibilities of central banks and governments for certain economic outcomes, but also because it emphasizes the importance of accountability and disclosure of information by the central bank, the subject of Chapter 6.

Conflict resolution is one issue that the existing literature has largely ignored or downplayed. Yet, the question is a crucial one for it not only helps decide how effective statutory factors are in central bank–government relations, but such events are at the core of the notion that the central bank is defined by the personality that heads the institution. Chapter 3 uses a mix of statistical evidence and case studies to show that personalities tend to define the central banking institution infrequently but at times of crises. Moreover, the severity of the conflict can often be traced to the imprecision or even absence of clear conflict resolution procedures.

So, what can we conclude about de jure versus de facto measures of independence? First, the former form of independence tends to be lagging indicators of the true state of the autonomy of central banks. Second, overall statutory autonomy is probably less important than some of the key elements in the legal position of central banks. Third, the 1990s appear to have ushered in a new era of sorts in that de facto and de jure indicators of central bank autonomy appear to be closer than ever. Previous decades saw occasionally large divergences between the two forms of independence.

WHITHER CENTRAL BANK PERSONALITIES?

Central bankers appear to be constantly in the news these days. The ease and speed with which financial transactions are processed has led to calls for more vigilance on the part of central bankers. No doubt a decade of more-or-less solid growth in the 1990s, in many parts of the industrial world, together with fiscal policies that were in retrenchment, elevated the role of some central bankers at least, to the level of "maestro."[1] The high regard that some central bankers are held in recalls the hypothesis put forward by Milton Friedman in 1962. He argued in part for rules in monetary policy as a way of counterbalancing the excessive influence of the personalities in charge of monetary affairs. Using a mix of econometric and historical cases, this study finds that, while there is some merit to Friedman's views, the data actually support a restatement of the original hypothesis: Personalities at the helm of a central bank dominate the monetary policy landscape only at defining moments in the history of the central bank. These typically occur at times of crises and are exacerbated when the objectives of the central bank are opaque, governance structures do not permit defusing a conflict or crisis, or the statutes of the central bank do not outline procedures to resolve serious differences of opinion. Indeed, Chapter 3 devoted considerable space to what, next to clarity of objectives, is perhaps the most important aspect of the relationship between the central bank and government, namely an understanding of the concept of joint central bank–government responsibility in monetary policy, and the power of governments to ultimately override central bank decisions via a directive.

The personalities aspect of central banking also emerges in a modern setting because clarity of objectives does not preclude the necessity to

---

[1] Alan Greenspan, chair of the U.S. Board of Governors of the Federal Reserve System, was referred to as such by Michael G. Oxley, chair of the House of Representatives Committee on Financial Services. See http://www.house.gov/financial services/022801ox.htm.

react to shocks that may not immediately threaten the objectives of the central bank but has implications for the stability of the financial system. This forces a much greater emphasis on the role of communications by central bank officials with the public but there is the danger that the central bank can become myopic or develop a form of "tunnel vision." Once again, however, the dividing line between a state where personalities dominate versus one where the conduct of monetary policy comes to the fore is a fine one. As argued in Chapters 3, 6, and 7, the side of the fence one ends up on depends on the type of monetary policy framework in place. Some strategies, such as money growth targeting are simply ill suited to preventing personalities from dominating monetary policy. In contrast, inflation targeting is a strategy that does permit a focus on the policies.

QUALITATIVE VERSUS QUANTITATIVE FORMS OF ANALYSIS OF CENTRAL BANK PERFORMANCE

The 1960s ushered in an era of quantitative assessments of central bank behavior. Central banks were viewed as maximizing agents that responded to developments in inflation and in the real economy. This approach was soon abandoned for two reasons. First, the resulting "reaction functions" were unstable, presaging an instability that would be uncovered later and alleged to afflict many fundamental economic relationships that dominated macroeconomic thinking at the time (for example, the Phillips curve). Second, economists found that the estimated reaction functions mixed the preferences of the central bank and those of government. Since central banks were not thought to be independent at the time, the estimated coefficients really did not tell us what central banks did. Political scientists, however, evinced less concern for separating the preferences of the central bank from those of government officials since the monetary authority was simply an agency of government and, presumably, shared similar preferences.

Over two decades later, two developments produced a reincarnation of the reaction function approach in economics. First, as an independent central bank, a central bank would be expected to respond to both inflation and output developments that were "excessive" in relation to some benchmark. In several countries, most notably the United States and Germany, the objectives were implicit. In a growing number of countries, however, the benchmarks were explicit, at least insofar as inflation is concerned. In any event, once calibrated, the new reaction function was seen as reflecting the preferences of the central bank. Political influences were ignored, again the product of central bank autonomy in the setting of interest rates. Many economists, and political economists, however, never abandoned the view that electoral and/or partisan features influence monetary policy. Moreover, the notion that central banks are optimizing institutions that respond to certain economic shocks presumes that they are somewhat forward looking institutions. This requires at least a view of the structure of the economy and a process by which central banks use the interest rate instrument to anticipate, and perhaps, opportunistically influence expectations. "Because monetary policy works with a lag, we need to be forward looking, taking actions to forestall imbalances that may not be visible for months. There is no alternative to basing actions on forecasts, at least implicitly. It means that we often have to tighten or ease before the need for action is evident to the public at large, . . . this process is not easy to get right . . . and it is often difficult to convey . . ." (Greenspan 1996).

After reviewing the technical, and practical, difficulties in replicating the decision-making process at a central bank, Chapter 4 proposes an evolutionary statistical model. The model recognizes changes in the information set available to central banks over the decades, but also constrains that information set to include as far as possible no more data than the monetary authority could have had at its disposal when interest rate decisions were made. In addition, the model recognizes the institutional, and political pressures on monetary policy and, as such, attempts to bridge an important gap in the existing literature, namely the gulf that exists between qualitative and quantitative forms of evidence about central bank performance. Finally, the approach is extended to a cross-section format in order to ascertain the degree to which the "one size fits all" philosophy can be said to apply to central banks in the industrial world, as a group.

Estimates reveal that central banks for the most part do react to positive inflation shocks and unemployment shocks by, respectively, raising and lowering interest rates. In addition, there is plenty of evidence that central banks are not immune to political, institutional, or international pressures. Moreover, while there is some persistence in interest rate changes it is not as large as the existing literature suggests because most reaction functions ignore the variety of influences on monetary policy.

Other evidence was marshaled to show not only that fiscal policy appears to directly influence the setting of interest rates by central banks but also that interest rate volatility may indeed play a role in the monetary authority's loss function. Cross-country reaction function estimates clearly show the important function of institutional characteristics in explaining central bank behavior, as well as the significant role played by exchange rate and inflation targeting regimes. There is also some evidence that central banks in certain groups of countries, such as the countries forming the European Monetary Union, react somewhat differently than the rest to the various sources of influences on monetary policy behavior. While the statement that "one size fits all" may not, strictly speaking, be an accurate description of reaction function estimates presented here there are clearly a number of important common features in how central banks change interest rates that seem to be adequately captured by the panel approach. The panel estimates also highlight a role for central bank–government relations that cannot be so readily evaluated at the level of individual country estimates, the typical vehicle used to examine central bank performance in the relevant literature.

As explained in Chapter 5, the qualitative and quantitative evidence suggests that central banks not only have, for the most part, behaved differently, but that the institutional and political pressures on monetary policy have evolved over time. There is, however, one important sense in which the two distinct approaches to the study of central banks can be reconciled. The worldwide emphasis on finding the right mix of rules and discretion in the conduct of monetary policy has produced a narrowing of the gap of sorts between the qualitative and econometric assessments of central bank behavior. The evidence also suggests that central banks in the industrial world behave more like each other beginning in the 1990s. Earlier decades, in contrast, reveal significant differences in institutional structures, responses to economic shocks, and, as a result, in inflation performance.

TOWARD THE HOLY GRAIL IN MONETARY POLICY?

As noted in the introduction, inflation has always been the fulcrum of monetary policy. What is substantially different by the mid to late 1980s is the realization that the central bank ought to be made accountable, preferably explicitly so, for a particular level or range of inflation objectives, with government responsible for establishing the overall goals of the central bank. In addition, mechanisms must be put in place to ensure that the objectives are clearly explained to the public. The latter requires adequate disclosure of policy decisions and the means by which they were reached. Chapters 6 develops, therefore, indexes of accountability and disclosure and sets out to determine whether robust relationships exist between the proposed indicators and measures of central bank performance. It is found that accountability and disclosure are reliably and positively related to each other. Moreover, a reasonably strong link exists between measures of central bank autonomy and accountability and disclosure. Finally, various modern devices used by most central banks to communicate the implementation of monetary policy are examined for their impact, for example, on measures of inflationary expectations. The link between forms of communication and expectations is found to be significant but especially so when the framework of monetary policy is one of inflation targeting. Successful communication of policy proposals and monetary policy decisions requires emphasis on the quality of information, not its quantity, for, as Simon (1978) asserts, there is a danger that too much information will divert our attention away sufficiently to create scope for major new policy errors. "Some of the practical consequences of attention scarcity have already been noticed ... where ... 'management information systems' flooded executives with trivial data and, until they learned to ignore them, distracted their attention from more important matters" (Simon 1978: p. 13). Note that the emphasis here is on the distinction between quality and quantity. As argued throughout this study, the substantial increase in the availability of information that enables private markets to better understand what central bankers are *planning* to do does not reduce the effectiveness of monetary but instead has led to substantial improvements in the delivery of monetary policy.[2]

Consequently, Chapter 7 asks which among the various policy regimes implemented in the last half century, satisfies the definition of a framework, where this is taken to mean a *structure composed of parts framed together*. Contrasting exchange-rate–based monetary regimes, policies based on monetary targets, and inflation-control–based regimes, it is found that only inflation targeting policies fulfill all of the requirements of a policy framework. The reason is that an inflation target, properly designed, clearly assigns the location for the ultimate responsibility of monetary policy to government, with short-term objectives assigned to the central bank. Moreover, the clarity of responsibilities puts the onus on the central bank to explain the outcomes of its actions as well as

---

[2] A recent, and elegant, discussion of this last point is also found in Woodford (2001).

provide information about its outlook for the future. Inflation targeting forces into the open the forward-looking nature of monetary policy decision previously hidden from the public by a secretive central bank.

It is always premature to declare that policy makers have found the Holy Grail in the current design of monetary policy (for example, see Posen 1998a). Nevertheless, it should be noted that the inflation targeting regime will soon surpass in longevity all the other monetary policy regimes implemented over the last half century or so of economic history. As more central banks become enamored by inflation targeting, it is useful to recall that the success enjoyed by this regime is partly dictated by currently fashionable theories of inflation, and the benefits of disclosure and accountability. As Keynes himself admonished almost eight decades ago, "A new theory can never win its way in the field of practical affairs unless it is illuminated by vivid facts and supported by events" (Keynes 1924). To be sure, the facts supporting the "case" have been building for over a decade in some countries but it is as yet unclear whether there have been sufficiently "vivid" events to reach a verdict. Nevertheless, the events of 1997–8 and 2001 do seem to augur well for the destiny of the inflation targeting regime. Yet, the European Central Bank remains an important, and stubborn, exception to these developments insisting, as it does (see ECB 2001: p. 48), that the "best" policy must rest with the "twin pillars" that give a prominent role for money growth and a range of other economic indicators. Time will tell whether one type of monetary regime will come to surpass another in popularity and longevity for history also shows that, once the hard fought battles over the choice of a policy regime are won, there is a tendency to pursue it even after the facts dictate that another strategy may well be preferable.

We may very well conclude that the changing face of central banking, born out of the turbulence of the first half of the last century, nurtured by evolution and revolution in policy making, will define the history of central banking in the second half of the twentieth century.

Bibliography

Abrams, R.K., R. Froyen, and R.N. Waud (1980), "Monetary Policy Reaction Functions, Consistent Expectations, and the Burns Era," *Journal of Money, Credit and Banking*, 12 (1): 30–42, February.

Acheson, K., and J.F. Chant (1973), "Bureaucratic Theory and the Choice of Central Bank Goals: The Case of the Bank of Canada," *Journal of Money, Credit and Banking*, 5: 637–55.

Åkerholm, J., and A. Brunila (1995), "Inflation Targeting: The Finnish Experience," in L. Liederman and L.E.O. Svensson (Eds.), *Inflation Targets* (London: CEPR), pp. 90–106.

Akerlof, G.A., W.T. Dickens, and G.L. Perry (2000), "Near-Rational Wage and Price Setting and the Long-Run Phillips Curve," *Brookings Papers on Economic Activity*, 1: 1–44.

Alesina, A. (1989), "Politics and Business Cycles in Industrial Democracies," *Economic Policy*, 8: 57–98.

(1988), "Macroeconomics and Politics," in S. Fischer (Ed.), *Macroeconomics Annual 1988* (Cambridge, MA: MIT Press), pp. 13–62.

Alesina, A., and S. Ardagna (1998), "Fiscal Adjustments: Why They Can Be Expansionary," *Economic Policy*, 27 (October): 487–517.

Alesina, A., G.D. Cohen, and N. Roubini (1997), *Political Cycles and Macroeconomy* (Cambridge, MA: MIT Press).

(1992), "Macroeconomic Policy and Elections in OECD Democracies," in A. Cukierman, Z. Hercowitz, and L. Leiderman (Eds.), *Political Economy, Growth and Business Cycles* (Cambridge, MA: MIT Press), pp. 227–62.

Alesina, A., and R. Gatti (1995), "Independent Central Banks: Low Inflation at No Cost?," *American Economic Review*, 85 (2): 196–200, May.

Alesina, A., and R. Perotti (1996), "Budget Deficits and Budget Institutions," NBER Working Paper 5556.

Alesina, A., and H. Rosenthal (1995), *Partisan Politics, Divided Government, and the Economy* (Cambridge: Cambridge University Press).

Alesina, A., and N. Roubini (1992), "Political Cycles: Evidence from OECD Countries," *Review of Economic Studies*, 59 (October): 663–88.

Alesina, A., and J. Sachs (1988), "Political Parties and the Business Cycle in the United States, 1948–84," *Journal of Money, Credit and Banking*, 20: 63–82.

309

Alesina, A., and L. Summers (1993), "Central Bank Independence and Macro-economic Performance: Some Comparative Evidence," *Journal of Money, Credit and Banking*, 25 (May): 151–62.

Almeida, A., and C.A.E. Goodhart (1998), "Does the Adoption of Inflation Targets Affect Central Bank Behaviour?," *Banca Nazionale del Lavoro Quarterly Review*, 51, Supplement (March): 19–107.

Amano, R., and S. van Norden (1993), "A Forecasting Equation for the Canada-US Dollar Exchange Rate," in *The Exchange Rate and the Economy*, Proceedings of a Conference Held at the Bank of Canada, June 22–23, 1992 (Ottawa: Bank of Canada), pp. 207–65.

Amtenbrink, F. (1999), *The Democratic Accountability of Central Banks: A Comparative Study of the European Central Bank* (Portland, OR: Hart Publishers).

Anderson, T.W., and C. Hsiao (1982), " Formulation and Estimation of Dynamic Models Using Panel Data," *Journal of Econometrics*, 18: 47–82.

Arellano, M., and S. Bond (1991), "Some Tests of Specification for Panel Data: Monte Carlo Evidence and an Application to Employment Equations," *The Review of Economic Studies*, 58 (2): 277–97, April.

Artis, M., G. Kontolemis, and D.R. Osborn (1997), "Business Cycles for G7 and European Countries," *Journal of Business*, 70 (April): 249–80.

Aufricht, H. (1967), *Central Banking Legislation*, Vols. 1 and 2 (Washington, DC: International Monetary Fund).

Bach, G.L. (1949), "The Federal Reserve and Monetary Policy Formation," *American Economic Review*, 39: 1173–91.

Bai, J., and P. Perron (1998), "Estimating and Testing Linear Models with Multiple Structural Changes," *Econometrica*, 66 (January): 47–78.

Ball, L. (1999), "Policy Rules for Open Economies," in J.B. Taylor (Ed.), *Monetary Policy Rules* (Chicago: University of Chicago Press).

   (1994), "What Determines the Sacrifice Ratio?," in N. Gregory Mankiw (Ed.), *Monetary Policy* (Chicago: University of Chicago Press), pp. 155–82.

Ball, L., and N.G. Mankiw (1994), "Asymmetric Price Adjustment and Economic Flucatuations," *Economic Journal*, 104 (March): 247–61.

Baltensperger, E. (1999), "Monetary Policy Under Conditions of Increasing Integration (1979–96)," in *Fifty Years of the Deutsche Mark* (Oxford: Oxford University Press), pp. 439–523.

Banaian, K., R. Burdekin, and T. Willett (1998), "Reconsidering The Principal Components Of Central Bank Independence: The More the Merrier?," *Public Choice*, 97 (October): 1–12.

Banaian, K., R.C.K. Burdekin, and T.D. Willett (1995), "On the Political Economy of Central Bank Independence," in K.D. Hoover and S.M. Sheffrin (Eds.), *Monetarism and the Methodology of Economics: Essays in Honor of Thomas Mayer* (London: Edward Elgar), pp. 178–97.

Banaian, K., L.O. Laney, and T.D. Willett (1986), "Central Bank Independence: An International Comparison," in E.F. Toma and M. Toma (Eds.), *Central Bankers, Bureaucratic Incentives, and Monetary Policy*, Financial and Monetary Policy Studies series, Vol. 13 (Boston: Kluwer Academic Publishers), pp. 199–217. Previously published in 1983.

Bank of Canada (1991a), "Targets for Reducing Inflation: Further Operational and Measurement Considerations," *Bank of Canada Review*, September: 3–23.

(1991b), "Background Note on the Targets," *Bank of Canada Review*, March.

(1995), *Monetary Policy Report*, May.

Bank of England (2001), "Bank of England Response to the Kohn Report," *Bank of England Quarterly Bulletin*, 41 (Spring): 50–4.

(2001), *Inflation Report*, February.

Bank of International Settlements (various issues), *BIS Review*.

Bank for International Settlements (2000), *Annual Report*.

Barber, T. (2001), "ECB Watch: Rate Cut Reasoning Not To Everyone's Taste," *Financial Times*, May 15.

Barro, R.J. (1990), "The Ricardian Approach to Budget Deficits," *Macroeconomic Policy* (Cambridge, MA and London: Harvard University Press), pp. 213–35.

Barro, R., and D. Gordon (1983), "Rules, Discretion and Reputations in a Model of Monetary Policy," *Journal of Monetary Economics*, 12: 101–22.

Batchelor, R. (1998), "How Useful are the Forecasts of Intergovernmental Agencies? The IMF and OECD versus the Consensus," Working Paper, City University Business School, London, July.

Behrens, E.B. (1932), "A Practical Monetary Policy for the Ottawa Conference" (London: St. Clements Press) PRO T 175/70.

Bellerby, J.R. (1924), "The Monetary Policy of the Future," *The Economic Journal*, 34 (June): 177–87.

Bennett, R.B. (1932), "Statements made before the Committee on Monetary and Financial Questions," 1932 Imperial Economic Conference, Ottawa, Canada, PRO T208/167 "British Monetary Policy: A Collection of Various Public Statements, Feb. 1932 to Feb. 1939," p. 41.

Berg, C., and L. Jonung (1999), "Pioneering Price Level Targeting: The Swedish Experience 1931–37," *Journal of Monetary Economics*, 43 (June): 525–51.

Berg, C., and H. Lundberg (2000), "Conducting Monetary Policy with a Collegial Board: The New Swedish Legislation One Year On," Working Paper, Sverige Riksbank, March.

Berger, H. (1997), "The Bundesbank's Path to Independence: Evidence from the 1950s," *Public Choice*, 93: 427–53.

Berger, H., and F. Schneider (2000), "The Bundesbank's Reactions to Policy Conflicts," in J. De Haan (Ed.), *Fifty Years if the Bundesbank: Lessons for the ECB* (London: Routledge), pp. 43–66.

(1997), "Does the Bundesbank Give Way in Conflicts with the West German Government?," Working Paper 9716, University of Linz.

Berman, S., and K.R. McNamara (1999), "Bank Democracy: Why Central Banks Need Public Oversight," *Foreign Affairs*, 78 (March/April): 2–8.

Bernanke, B., and A.S. Blinder (1992), "The Federal Funds Rate and the Channels of Monetary Transmission," *American Economic Review*, 82 (September): 901–21.

Bernanke, B.S., and J. Boivin (2000), "Monetary Policy in a Data-Rich Environment," prepared for the Conference on Monetary Policy Under Incomplete Information, Gerzensee, Switzerland, October, *Journal of Monetary Economics* (forthcoming).

Bernanke, B., and M. Gertler (1999), "Monetary Policy and Asset Price Volatility," *Economic Review*, Federal Reserve Bank of Kansas City (Fourth Quarter): 17–51.

Bernanke, B.S., T. Laubach, F.S. Mishkin, and A.S. Posen (1999), *Inflation Targeting: Lessons from the International Experience* (Princeton, NJ: Princeton University Press).

Bernanke, B., and I. Mihov (1998), "Measuring Monetary Policy," *Quarterly Journal of Economics*, 113 (August): 869–902.

(1996), "What Does the Bundesbank Target?," *European Economic Review*, 41 (June): 1025–53.

Bernanke, B., and F.S. Mishkin (1992), "Central Bank Behavior and the Strategy of Monetary Policy: Observations from Six Industrialized Countries," in O.J. Blanchard and S. Fischer (Eds.), *Macroeconomics Annual 1992* (Cambridge, MA: MIT Press), pp. 183–227.

Bernanke, B., and M. Woodford (1997), "Inflation Forecasts and Monetary Policy," *Journal of Money, Credit and Banking*, 29, part 2 (November): 653–84.

Bernard, H., and S. Gerlach (1996), "Does the Term Structure Predict Recessions: The International Evidence," BIS Working Paper No. 3 (September).

Bini Smaghi, L., and D. Gros (2000), *Open Issues in European Central Banking* (New York: St. Martin's Press; London: Macmillan Press; in association with Centre for European Policy Studies), pp. ix, 209.

Blinder, A.S. (1999), *Central Banking in Theory and Practice* (Cambridge, MA: MIT Press).

(1998a), "Survey Evidence on Central Bank Credibility," Working Paper, Princeton University.

(1998b), "Is Government too Political?," *Foreign Affairs*, 76 (6): 115–26.

Blinder, A., C. Goodhart, P. Hildebrand, D. Lipton, and C. Wyplosz (2001), *How do Central Bankers Talk?*, Report prepared for presentation at the Third Geneva Conference to the World Economy, May, CEPR and International Center for Monetary and Banking Studies.

Boivin, J. (1999), "The Fed's Conduct of Monetary Policy: Has it Changed and Does it Matter?," Working Paper, Columbia University, October.

Bollard, A., and D. Mayes (1993), "Lessons for Europe from New Zealand's Liberalisation Experience," *National Institute Economic Review*, 143 (February): 81–97.

Bonin, B. (2000), *La Politique Monitaire* [Monetary Policy], unpublished manuscript.

Bonser-Neal, C., and T.R. Morley (1997), "Does the Yield Spread Predict Real Economic Activity? A Multicountry Analysis," *Economic Review* (Federal Reserve Bank of Kansas City), 82 (3): 37–53.

Bopp, K.R. (1944), "Central Banking at the Crossroads," *American Economic Review*, 34, 260–77.

Bordo, M.D. (1993), "The Bretton Woods International Monetary System: A Historical Overview," in M.D. Bordo and B. Eichengreen (Eds.), *A Retrospective on the Bretton Woods System* (Chicago: University of Chicago Press), pp. 3–98.

Bordo, M., and L. Jonung (1987), *The Long-Run Behavior of the Velocity of Circulation: The International Evidence* (Cambridge: Cambridge University Press).

Bordo, M., L. Jonung, and P.L. Siklos (1997), "Institutional Change and the Velocity of Money: A Century of Evidence," *Economic Inquiry*, 35 (October): 710–24.

Bordo, M.D., and A. Redish (1990), "Credible Commitment and Exchange Rate Stability: Canada's Interwar Experience," *Canadian Journal of Economics*, 23 (May): 357–80.

(1987), "Why Did the Bank of Canada Emerge in 1935?," *Journal of Economic History*, 47 (June): 405–17.

Bordo, M.D., and A.J. Schwartz (1997), "Monetary Policy Regimes and Economic Performance: The Historical Record," NBER Working Paper 6201, September.

Bowen, A. (1995), "Inflation Targetry in the United Kingdom," in A.G. Haldane (Ed.), *Targeting Inflation* (London: Bank of England), pp. 59–74.

Brainard, W. (1967), "Uncertainty and the Effectiveness of Policy," *American Economic Review*, 57 (May): 411–25.

Briault, C.B., A.G. Haldane, and M.A. King (1996), "Independence and Accountability," Bank of England Working Paper 49, April.

Britton, E., and J. Whittley (1996), "Asymmetry, Risks, and the Probability Distribution of Inflation," mimeo, Bank of England.

Brumm, H.J. (2000), "Inflation and Central Bank Independence: Conventional Wisdom Redux," *Journal of Money, Credit and Banking*, 32 (November, part 1): 807–19.

Brunner, A.D. (2000), "On the Derivation of Monetary Policy Shocks: Should We Throw the VAR Out with Bath Water?," *Journal of Money, Credit and Banking*, 32 (May): 254–79.

Bruno, M., and W. Easterly (1998), "Inflation Crises and Long-Run Growth," *Journal of Monetary Economics*, 41 (February): 3–26.

Buiter, W. (1999), "Alice in Euroland," *Journal of Common Market Studies*, 37 (June): 181–209.

Burdekin, R.C.K., and P.L. Siklos (1999), "Exchange Rate Regimes and Shifts in Inflation Persistence: Does Nothing Else Matter?," *Journal of Money, Credit and Banking*, 31 (May): 235–47.

(1998), "Central Bank Behaviour, the Exchange Rate Regime, and the Persistence of Inflation in Historical Perspective," in T.J.O. Dick (Ed.), *Business Cycles Since 1820: New Perspectives from Historical Data* (London: Edward Elgar), pp. 232–58.

Burdekin, R.C.K., and T.D. Willett (1991), "Central Bank Reform: The Federal Reserve in International Perspective," *Public Budgeting and Financial Management*, 3: 619–50.

Burdekin, R.C.K., and M.E. Wohar (1990), "Deficit Monetisation, Output and Inflation in the United States, 1923–1982," *Journal of Economic Studies*, 17 (6): 50–63.

Cairns, J.P., and H.H. Binhammer (1965), *Canadian Banking and Monetary Policy* (Toronto: McGraw-Hill).

Calvo, G.A. (1978), "On the Time Consistency of Optimal Policy in a Monetary Economy," *Econometrica*, 46 (6): 1411–28, November.

Cameron, C.A., and P.K. Trivedi (1998), *Regression Analysis of Count Data*, Econometric Society Monograph No. 30 (Cambridge: Cambridge University Press).

Capie, F., S. Fischer, C.A.E. Goodhart, and N. Schnadt (1994), *The Future of Central Banking* (Cambridge: Cambridge University Press).

Cargill, T.F. (1989), "Central Bank Independence and Regulatory Responsibilities: The Bank of Japan and the Federal Reserve," Salomon Brothers Center for the Study of Financial Institutions Monograph Series on Finance and Economics, No: 1989–2.

Cargill, T.F., M.M. Hutchison, and T. Ito (2000), *Financial Policy and Central Banking in Japan* (Cambridge, MA: MIT Press).

Cassel, G. (1932), "The Destruction of the World's Monetary System," address to the Conservative Party Finance Committee at the House of Commons, May; Public Records Office [PRO] T 175/70.

Cecchetti, S.G. (2000), "The Cult of Alan Greenspan: Why the Fed Needs a Policy Framework," Occasional Essays on Current Policy Issues No. 2, December.

(1999), "The Uncertainty of Making Monetary Policy: Do the New FOMC Statements Clarify Anything?," Occasional Essays on Current Policy Issues, No. 1, December.

Cecchetti, S.G., H. Genberg, J. Lipsky, and S. Wadhwani (2000), *Asset Prices and Central Bank Policy*, Geneva Report on the World Economy No. 2 (London: Center for Economic Policy Research). Available at http://www.cepr.org.

Central Banking (2001), *Key Events in Central Banking, 1609–1999* (London: Central Banking Publications).

Chandler, L.V. (1971), *American Monetary Policy 1928–1941* (New York: Harper and Row).

(1958), *Benjamin Strong: Central Banker* (Washington, DC: The Brookings Institution).

Chinn, M., and M.P. Dooley (1997), "Monetary Policy in Japan, Germany, and the United States: Does One Size Fit All?," NBER Working Paper 6092, July.

Chong, Y.Y., and D.F. Hendry (1986), "Econometric Evaluation of Linear Macro-Economic Models," *The Review of Economic Studies*, 53 (4): 671–90, August.

Christian, J.W. (1968), "A Further Analysis of the Objectives of American Monetary Policy," *Journal of Finance*, 23 (3): 465–77.

Ciampi, C. (1983), *Caucus and Practices in Central Banking* (Naples: Isveimer).

Clarida, R., J. Gali, and M. Gertler (1999), "The Science of Monetary Policy: A New Keynesian Perspective," *Journal of Economic Literature*, 37 (December): 1661–707.

(1998), "Monetary Policy Rules in Practice: Some International Evidence," *European Economic Review*, 42 (June): 1033–67.

Clarida, R., and M. Gertler (1997), "How the Bundesbank Conducts Monetary Policy," in C. Romer and D. Romer (Eds.), *Reducing Inflation* (Chicago: Chicago University Press), pp. 363–406.

Claus, J., P. Conway, and A. Scott (2000), "The Output Gap: Measurement, Comparisons and Assessment," Reserve Bank of New Zealand Research Paper No. 44, June.

Clemen, Robert T. (1989), "Combining Forecasts: A Review and Annotated Bibliography," *International Journal of Forecasting*, 5 (4): 559–83.

Cogley, T., and J. Nason (1995), "The Effects of the Hodrick-Prescott Filter on Trend and Difference Stationary Time Series: Implications for Business Cycle Research," *Journal of Economic Dynamics and Control*, 19 (Jan–Feb): 253–78.

Cohen, D. (2001), "Défense de la banque centrale européenne [Defending the European Central Bank]," *Le Monde*, May 5.

Collins, S., and P.L. Siklos (2001), "Optimal Reaction Functions, Taylor Rules, and Inflation Targets: How Strict Are the Dollar Bloc Countries?," unpublished, Wilfrid Laurier University.

Committee on Economic and Monetary Affairs of the European Parliament (2000), "Hearings with the President of the European Central Bank," November 23, 2000.

Committee to Review the Functioning of Financial Institutions (1980), "Appendices" (London: Her Majesty's Stationary Office).

Compass Inc. (1999), *Bank of Canada General Public Survey*, October. Summary available at http://www.bankofcanada.ca/en/poll-results.htm.

Crawford, V.P., and J. Sobel (1982), "Strategic Information Transmission," *Econometrica*, 50 (6): 1431–51.

Croushore, D., and C.L. Evans (2000), "Data Revisions and the Identification of Monetary Policy Shocks," Working Paper 2000–26, Federal Reserve Bank of Chicago, September.

Croushore, Dean (1996), "Inflation Forecasts: How Good are They?," *Federal Reserve Bank of Philadelphia Business Review*, (May/June): 15–26. Available at http://www.phil.frb.org/econ/br/brmj96dc.html.

Crow, J. (1994), "Central Banks: Independence, Mandates and Accountability," manuscript, Bank of Canada, May.

Crow, J.W. (1988), "The Work of Canadian Monetary Policy," manuscript, *Bank of Canada Review*, February.

Cukierman, A. (2000), "Accountability, Credibility, Transparency and Stabilization Policy in the Eurosystem," in Charles Wyplosz (Ed.), *The EMU and its Impact on Europe and the World*.

(1996), Economics of Central Banking (Tel Aviv: The Sackler Institute for Economic Studies, Tel Aviv University).

(1992), *Central Bank Strategy, Credibility, and Independence* (Cambridge: MIT Press).

(1986), "Central Bank Behavior and Credibility: Some Recent Theoretical Developments," *Review of the Federal Reserve Bank of St. Louis*, 68: 5–17.

Cukierman, A.S., P. Kalaitzidakis, L.H. Summers, and S.B. Webb (1993), "Central Bank Independence, Growth, Investment and Real Rates," in A.H. Meltzer and C.I. Plosser (Eds.), *Carnegie-Rochester Conference Series on Public Policy*, Vol. 39, December (Amsterdam: Elsevier), pp. 95–140.

Cukierman, A., and A.H. Meltzer (1986a), "A Theory of Ambiguity, Credibility and Inflation Under Discretion and Asymmetric Information," *Econometrica*, 54 (September): 1099–128.

(1986b), "The Credibility of Monetary Announcements," in M.J.M Neuman (Ed.), *Monetary Policy and Uncertainty* (Baden-Baden: Nomos Verlagsgesellschaft), pp. 39–67.

Cukierman, A., P. Rodriquez, and S.B. Webb (1998), "Central Bank Autonomy and Exchange Rate Regimes – Their Effects on Monetary Accommodation and Activism," in S. Eijffinger and H. Hunzinga (Eds.), *Positive Political Economy: Theory and Evidence* (Cambridge: Cambridge University Press), pp. 78–110.

Cukierman, A., and S.B. Webb (1997), "Political Influence on the Central Bank – International Evidence," in S.W. Eijffinger (Ed.), *Independent Central Banks and Economic Performance* (Cheltenham, UK: Edward Elgar), pp. 567–93.

(1995), "Political Influences on the Central Bank: International Evidence," *The World Bank Economic Review*, 9 (September): 397–42.

Cukierman, A., S.B. Webb, and B. Neyapti (1992), "The Measurement of Central Bank Independence and Its Effects on Policy Outcomes," *World Bank Economic Review*, 6, 353–98.

Dalziel, P. (1998), "New Zealand's Experience with an Independent Central Bank Since 1989," in P. Arestis and M.C. Sawyer (Eds.), *The Political Economy of Central Banking* (Cheltenham, UK: Edward Elgar), pp. 199–216.

Dawe, S. (1992), "Reserve Bank Act of 1989," in *Monetary Policy and the New Zealand Financial System*, Third Edition, pp. 31–40.

Deacon, P.S. (1960), "Have They Really Got a Case Against the Bank of Canada?," *Financial Post*, December 24.

Deane, M., and R. Pringle (1995), *The Central Banks* (New York: Viking).

Debelle, G. (1997), "Inflation Targeting in Practice," IMF Working Paper 97/35, March.

(1996), "The Ends of Three Small Inflations: Australia, New Zealand and Canada," *Canadian Public Policy*, 22 (1): 56–78.

Debelle, G., and S. Fischer (1994), "How Independent Should a Central Bank Be?," in J.C. Fisher (Ed.), *Goals, Guidelines and Constraints Facing Monetary Policy* (Boston: Federal Reserve Bank of Boston).

DeGrauwe, P. (1992), *The Economics of Monetary Integration*, Second Revised Edition (Oxford: Oxford University Press).

de Haan, J., (Ed.) (2000), *The History of the Bundesbank* (London and New York: Routledge).

de Haan, J., F. Amtenbrink, and S.C.W. Eijffinger (1999), "Accountability of Central Banks: Aspects and Quantification," *Banca Nazionale del Lavoro Quarterly Review*, 52 (June): 169–93.

DeKock, M.H. (1974), *Central Banking*, Fourth Edition (London: Crosby Lockwood Staples).

DeLong, B. (1997), "America's Only Peacetime Inflation: The 1970s," in C.D. Romer and D.H. Romer (Eds.), *Reducing Inflation: Motivation and Strategy* (Chicago and London: University of Chicago Press), pp. 247–76.

DeLong, J.B. (2000), "America's Experience with Low Inflation," *Journal of Money, Credit and Banking*, 32 (November, part 2): 979–93.

Deutsche Bundesbank (2000a), "Monetary Policy Transparency," *Monthly Report*, 52 (March): 15–30.

(2000b), "Core Inflation Rates as a Tool of Price Analysis," *Monthly Report*, 52 (April): 45–58.

(2000c), "The Deutsche Bundesbank's Involvement in Banking Supervision," *Monthly Report*, 52 (September): 31–44.

(1999), *Fifty Years of the Deutsche Mark* (Oxford: Oxford University Press).

(1998a), *Opinion of the Central Bank Council Concerning Convergence in the European Union in View of Stage Three of Economic and Monetary Union*, Frankfurt, March 26.

(1998b), *50 Jahre Deutsche Mark: Monetäre Statistiken*, 1948–1997 (CD-ROM).

(1995), *The Monetary Policy of the Bundesbank* (Frankfurt a. Main: Deutsche Bundesbank), October.

Di Noia, C., and G. Di Giorgio (1999), "Should Banking Supervision and Monetary Policy Tasks be Given to Different Agencies?," *International Finance*, 2 (November): 361–78.

Dornbusch, R., C.A. Favero, and F. Giavazzi (1998), "The Immediate Challenges for the European Central Bank," *Economic Policy: A European Forum*, No. 26, April.

Drazen, A. (2000a), "The Political Business Cycle After 25 Years," Working Paper, University of Maryland and University of Jerusalem, May, forthcoming in *Macroeconomics Annual 2001* (Cambridge, MA: MIT Press).

(2000b), *Political Economy In Macroeconomics*, (Princeton, NJ: Princeton University Press).

Drazen, A., and P. Masson (1994), "Credibility of Policies Versus Credibility of Policy Makers," *Quarterly Journal of Economics* (August): 735–54.

Dupasquier, C., A. Guay, and P. St-Amant (1999), "A Survey of Alternative Methodologies for Estimating Potential Output and the Output Gap," *Journal of Macroeconomics*, 21 (3): 577–95, Summer.

Edison, H. (1993), "The Effectiveness of Central Bank Intervention: A Survey of the Post-1992 Literature," *Special Papers in International Economics*, No. 18. Princeton, NJ: Princeton University Press.

Edison, H., and J. Marquez (1998), "U.S. Monetary Policy and Econometric Modelling: Tales from the FOMC Transcripts 1984–1991," *Economic Modelling*, 15 (July): 411–28.

Eichengreen, B. (1995), "The Endogeneity of Exchange Rate Regimes," in J. Reis (Ed.), *International Monetary Arrangements in Historical Perspective* (London: Macmillan), pp. 3–33.

(1992a), *Golden Fetters* (Oxford: Oxford University Press).

(1992b), "Designing a Central Bank for Europe: A Cautionary Tale from the Early Years of the Federal Reserve," in M.B. Canzonin, V. Grilli, and P.R. Mason (Eds.), *Establishing a Central Bank: Issues in Europe and Lessons from the US* (Cambridge: Cambridge University Press), pp. 13–40.

Eichengreen, B., A.K. Rose, and C. Wyplosz (1996a), "Contagious Currency Crises," *Scandinavian Journal of Economics*, 98 (December): 463–84.

Eichengreen, B., A. Rose, and C. Wyplosz (1996b), "Speculative Attacks on Pegged Exchange Rates: An Empirical Exploration with Special Reference to the European Monetary System," in H.B. Canzoneri, W.J. Ethier, V. Grilli (Eds.), *The New Transatlantic Economy* (Cambridge: Cambridge University Press), pp. 191–288.

Eichengreen, B., and J. von Hagen (1997), "Fiscal Policy and Monetary Union: Is There a Tradeoff Between Federalism and Budgetary Restrictions?," in B. Eichengreen (Ed.), *European Monetary Unification: Theory, Practice and Analysis* (Cambridge and London: MIT Press), pp. 235–45.

Eichengreen, B., and C. Wyplosz (1998), "The Stability Pact: More than a Minor Nuisance?," *Economic Policy*, 26 (April): 65–104.

Eijffinger, S.C.W. (2000), "How Can the European Central Bank Imporve the Transparency of Monetary Policy in Europe," Briefing Paper on the Conduct of Monetary and an Evaluation of the Economic Situation in Europe – 3rd Quarter 2000 for the European Parliament, available at http://www.europarl.eu.int/comparl/econ/pdf/emu/speeches/20000912/eijfinger/default_en.pdf.

Eijffinger, S., and J. de Haan (1996), "The Political Economy of Central Bank Independence," *Princeton Special Papers in International Economics*, No. 19 (May).

Eijffinger, S.W., M. Hoebrichts, and E. Schalling (2000), "Why Money Talks and Wealth Whispers: Monetary Uncertainty and Mystique," *Journal of Money, Credit and Banking*, 32 (May): 218–35.

(1998), "A Theory of Central Bank Accountability," Center for Economic Research, Tilburg University, September.

Eijffinger, S., E. Schalling, and W. Verhagen (1999), "A Theory of Interest Rate Stepping: Inflation-Targeting in a Dynamic Menu Cost Model," CEPR Discussion Paper 2168, June.

Elgie, R., and H. Thompson (1998), *The Politics of Central Banks* (New York: Routledge).

Enders, W. (1995), *Applied Econometric Time Series* (New York: John Wiley and Sons).

Enders, W., and P.L. Siklos (2001), "Cointegration and Threshold Adjustment," *Journal of Business and Economic Statistics*, 19 (April): 166–77.

Engle, R.F., Takatoshi Ito, and Weng-Ling Lin (1995), "Meteor Showers or Heat Waves? Heteroskedastic Intra-Daily Volatility in the Foreign Exchange Market," *Econometrica*, 58 (3): 525–42.

Estrella, A., and F.S. Mishkin (1998), "Predicting U.S. Recessions: Financial Variables as Leading Indicators," *Review of Economics and Statistics*, 80 (1): 45–61, February.

(1997), "The Predictive Power of the Term Structure of Interest Rates in Europe and the United States: Implications for the European Central Bank," *European Economic Review*, 41 (7): 1375–1401, July.

European Central Bank (2001), *The Monetary Policy of the ECB* (Frankfurt/ Main: European Central Bank).

(1998), "A Stability-Oriented Monetary Policy Strategy for the ECSB." Available at http://www.ecb.int/press/pr981013_1.htm.

Evans, C.L., and K.N. Kuttner (1998), "Can VARs Describe Monetary Policy?," Federal Reserve Bank of New York, April.

Farrell, J., and M. Rubin (1996), "Cheap Talk," *Journal of Economic Perspectives*, 10 (Summer): 103–18.

Faust, J., and J. Irons (1999), "Money, Politics and the Post-War Business Cycle," *Journal of Monetary Economics*, 43 (February): 61–89.

Faust, J., and L.E.O. Svensson (1998), "Transparency and Credibility: Monetary Policy with Unobservable Goals," NBER Working Paper 6452, March.

Favero, C.A., and R. Rovelli (2000), "Modelling and Identifying Central Banks' Preferences," Working Paper, Bocconi and Bologna, June.

Federal Reserve Bank of Kansas City (1996), *Achieving Price Stability*, A Symposium sponsored by the Federal Reserve Bank of Kansas City, 29–31 August. Available at http://www.kc.frb.org/Publicat/sympos/1996/Sym96prg.htm.

Feldstein, M., and J.H. Stock (1996), "Measuring Money Growth When Financial Markets Are Changing," *Journal of Monetary Economics*, 37 (1): 3–27, February.

Fischer, S. (2001), "Exchange Rate Regimes: Is the Bipolar View Correct?," Distinguished Lecture on Economics in Government, American Economics Association and Society of Government Economists, New Orleans January 6. Available at http://www.imf.orgexternal/np/speeches/2001/010601a.htm.

(2000), "Opening Remarks," IMF Institute's High-Level Seminar on Implementing Inflation Targets, IMF, Washington DC. Available at http://www.imf.org/external/np/speeches/2000/032000.htm.

(1998), "The IMF and the Asian Crisis," March 20. Available at http://www.imf.org/external/np/speeches/1998/032098.htm.

(1996), "Why Are Central Banks Pursuing Long-Run Price Stability," in *Achieving Price Stability*, A Symposium Sponsored by the Federal Reserve Bank of Kansas City (Kansas City: Federal Reserve Bank of Kansas City), pp. 7–34.

(1995), "The Unending Search for Monetary Salvation," *NBER Macroeconomics Annual 1995* (Cambridge, MA: MIT Press), pp. 275–86.

(1994), "Modern Central Banking," in F. Capie, C. Goodhart, S. Fischer, and N. Schnadt (Eds.), *The Future of Central Banking* (Cambridge: Cambridge University Press), pp. 262–308.

(1990), "Rules Versus Discretion in Monetary Policy," in B.M. Friedman and F. Hahn (Eds.), *Handbook of Monetary Economics*, Vol. II, (Amsterdam: Elsevier), pp. 1156–84.

Flood, R.S., J.S. Bhandari, and J.P. Horne (1989), "Evolution of Exchange Rate Regimes," *IMF Staff Papers*, 36 (December): 810–35.

Flood, R.P., and P. Isard (1989), "Monetary Policy Strategies," *IMF Staff Papers*, 36 (September): 612–32.

Forder, J. (2000), "Central Bank Independence and Credibility: Is There a Shred of Evidence?," *International Finance*, 3 (1): 167–85.

(1998), "Central Bank Independence-Conceptual Clarifications and Interim Assessment," *Oxford Economic Papers*, 50: 307–34.

Fortin, P. (1996), "The Great Canadian Slump," *Canadian Journal of Economics*, 29 (November): 761–87.

(1990), "Do We Measure Inflation Correctly?," in R.G. Lipsey (Eds.), *Zero Inflation: The Goal of Price Stability* (Toronto: C.D. Howe Institute), pp. 109–30.

Fratianni, M., and F. Spinelli (2001), "Fiscal Dominance and Money Growth in Italy: The Long Record," *Exploration in Economic History*, 38: 252–72.

Fratianni, M., J. von Hagen, and C.J. Waller (1997), "Central Banking as a Political Principal-Agent Problem," *Economic Inquiry*, 35 (April): 378–93.

Fratianni, M., and J. von Hagen (1992), *The European Monetary System and European Monetary Union* (Boulder, CO: The Westview Press).

Freedman, C. (1999), "Monetary Policy Making and Uncertainty," in *Monetary Policy-Making Under Uncertainty*, Conference organized jointly by the European Central Bank and the Centre for Financial Studies of the University of Frankfurt, pp. 38–47.

(1995), "The Role of Monetary Conditions and the Monetary Conditions Index in Canada," *Bank of Canada Review* (Autumn), 53–9.

Freeman, J.R., Williams, J.T., and Lin Tse-Min (1989), "Vector Autoregression and the Study of Politics," *American Journal of Political Science*, 33 (November): 842–77.

Freeman, R.T., and J.L. Ammer (1995), "Targeting Inflation in the 1990s: Recent Challenges," *Journal of Economics and Business*, 47 (May): 165–92.

Frey, B.S., and F. Schneider (1981), "Central Bank Behavior: A Positive Empirical Analysis," *Journal of Monetary Economics*, 7: 291–315.

Frieden, J., D. Gros, and E. Jones (Eds.), (1998), *The New Political Economy of EMU* (Lonham, MD and Oxford: Rowman and Littlefield).

Friedman, B.M. (2000a), "The Role of Interest Rates in Federal Reserve Policy Making," NBER Working Paper 8047, December.

(2000b), "Monetary Policy," in N.J. Smelser and P.B. Bates (Eds.), *International Encyclopedia of the Social and Behavioral Sciences* (Amsterdam: Elsevier).

(1999), "The Future of Monetary Policy: The Central Bank as an Army with Only a Signal Corps?," *International Finance*, 2 (3): 321–38, November.

(1992), *Money Mischief* (New York: Harcourt, Brace, and Jovanovich).

(1977), "Inflation and Unemployment: Nobel Lecture," *Journal of Political Economy*, 85 (June 1977): 451–72.

(1962), "Should There Be an Independent Monetary Authority?," in L.B. Yeager (Ed.), *In Search of a Monetary Constitution* (Cambridge, MA: Harvard University Press).

Friedman, M., and A.J. Schwartz (1993), "A Tale of Fed Transcripts," *Wall Street Journal*, December 20, 1993, p. A12.

——— (1982), *Monetary Trends in the United States and the United Kingdom* (Chicago: University of Chicago Press for the NBER).

——— (1963), *A Monetary History of the United States, 1870–1960* (Princeton, NJ: Princeton University Press).

Frowen, S.F., and R. Pringle (Eds.) (1998), *Inside the Bundesbank* (London: Macmillan).

Fuhrer, J.C. (1997), "The (Un)Importance of Forward-Looking Behavior in Price Specifications," *Journal of Money, Credit and Banking*, 29 (3): 338–50. August.

Fuhrer, J.C., and G. Moore (1992), "Monetary Policy Rules and the Indicator Properties of Asset Prices," *Journal of Monetary Economics*, 29 (April): 303–36.

Garber, P.M., and L.E.O. Svensson (1995), "The Operation and Collapse of Fixed Exchange Rate Regimes," in G. Grossman and K. Rogoff (Eds.), *Handbook of International Economics*, Vol. III (Amsterdam: Elsevier), pp. 1865–911.

Garfinkel, M., and S. Oh (1995), "When and How Much to Talk: Credibility and Flexibility in Monetary Policy with Private Information," *Journal of Monetary Economics*, 35 (April): 341–57.

Gavin, W.T., and R.J. Mandal (2001), "Forecasting Inflation: Do Private Forecasts Match Those of Policymaking," *Federal Reserve Bank of St. Louis Review*, 83 (May/June): 21–36.

Geddes, P. (1987), *Inside the Bank of England* (London: Boxtree).

General Accounting Office (1996), "Mexico's Financial Crisis," Report to the Chairman, Committee on Banking and Financial Services, House of Representatives (February).

Geraats, P.M. (2000), "Why Adopt Transparency? The Publication of Central Bank Forecasts," Working Paper, University of California, Berkeley, July.

Ghosh, A., A.M. Gulde, J. Ostry, and H.F. Wolf (1995), "Does the Nominal Exchange Rate Regime Matter?," IMF Working Paper 95/121.

Giavazzi, F., and M. Pagano (1988), "The Advantage of Tying One's Hand: EMS Discipline and Central Bank Credibility," *European Economic Review*, June, 1055–82.

Giblin, L.F. (1951), *The Growth of a Central Bank: The Development of the Commonwealth Bank of Australia, 1924–1945* (Melbourne: Melbourne University Press).

Giovannini, A. (1993), "Bretton Woods and Its Precursors: Rules Versus Discretion in the History of International Monetary Regimes," in M.D. Bordo and B. Eichengreen (Eds.), *A Retrospective on the Bretton Woods System* (Chicago: University of Chicago Press), pp. 109–47.

Goodfriend, M. (1999), "The Role of a Regional Bank in a System of Central Banks," *Carnegie-Rochester Conference Series on Public Policy*, 51: 51–71, December.

——— (1986), "Monetary Mystique: Secrecy and Central Banking," *Journal of Monetary Economics*, 17 (January): 63–92.

(1991), "Interest Rates and the Conduct of Monetary Policy," *Carnegie-Rochester Conference Series on Public Policy*, 34: 7–30.

Goodhart, C.A.E. (2000a), "Monetary Transmission and the Formulation of the Policy Decision on Interest Rates," unpublished, Bank of England.

(2000b), "Can Central Banking Survive the IT Revolution?," *International Finance*, 3 (July): 189–209.

(1999), "Central Bankers and Uncertainty," *Bank of England Quarterly Bulletin*, 39 (February): 102–14.

(1995), "Price Stability and Financial Fragility," in C.A.E. Goodhart (Ed.), *The Central Bank and the Financial System* (Cambridge: MIT Press), pp. 263–302.

(1988), *The Evolution of Central Banks* (Cambridge, MA: MIT Press).

Goodhart, C.A.E., and B. Hofmann (2000a), "Do Asset Prices Help Predict Consumer Price Inflation?," *Manchester School*, 68 (Supplement): 122–40.

(2000b), "Deflation, Credit and Asset Prices," Unpublished (Financial Markets Group: London School of Economics).

(2000c), "Financial Variables and the Conduct of Monetary Policy," Svenges Riksbank Working Paper No. 112.

Goodhart, C.A.E., and D. Schoenmaker (1995), "Institutional Separation between Supervisory and Monetary Agencies," *The Central Bank and the Financial System* (Cambridge, MA: MIT Press), pp. 333–413.

Goodman, J.B. (1991), *Central Bank – Government Relations in Major OECD Countries*, Study prepared for the Joint Economic Committee of the U.S. Congress (Washington, DC: U.S. Government Printing Office, 1991).

Gordon, H.S. (1961), "The Bank of Canada in a System of Responsible Government," *Canadian Journal of Economics and Political Science*, (February): 1–22.

Gorvin, I. (Gen. Ed.), (1989), *Elections Since 1945: A Worldwide Reference Compendium* (Harlow, Essex: Longman Inc.).

Granger, C.W.J. (1999), "Comments on the Evaluation of Econometric Models and of Forecasts," Working Paper, University of California, San Diego, January.

Granger, C.W.J., Z. Ding, and S. Spear (1997), "Stylized Facts on Temporal and Distributional Properties of Daily Data from Speculative Markets," University of California, San Diego, April.

Gregory, T.E. (1955), *The Present Position of Central Banks* (London: Athlone Press).

Greenspan, A. (1996), "The Challenge of Central Banking in a Democratic Society," Speech given at the Annual Dinner and Francis Boyer Lecture of the American Enterprise Institute for Public Policy Research, Washington, DC, December 5. Available at http://www.federalreserve.gov/boardocs/speeches/1996/19961205.htm.

Greider, W. (1987), *Secrets of the Temple: How the Federal Reserve Runs the Country* (New York: Simon and Schuster).

Grier, K.B., and M.J. Perry (1998), "On Inflation and Inflation Uncertainty in the G7 Countries," *Journal of International Money and Finance*, 17: 671–89.

Gros, D. (1999), "Briefing Paper on 'Improvement of the Democratic Account-ability Process'." Available at
http://www.europarl.eu.int/dg2/ECON/EMU/EN/defulat.htm.

Guthrie, G., and J. Wright (1998), "Open Mouth Operations," *Journal of Monetary Economics*, 46 (October): 489–576.

Grilli, V., D. Masciandaro, and G. Tabellini (1991), "Political and Monetary Institutions and Public Financial Policies in the Industrial Countries," *Economic Policy*, 13: 342–92.

Hadri, K., B. Lochwood, and J. Maloney (1998), "Does Central Bank Independence Smooth the Political Business Cycle in Inflation? Some OECD Evidence," *The Manchester School*, 66 (September): 377–95.

Haldane, A.G. (1997), "Some Issues in Inflation Targeting," Bank of England Working Paper.

——— (1996), "Some Thoughts on Inflation Targeting," Presented at the 1996 Konstanz Seminar on Monetary Theory and Policy, Konstanz, Germany.

——— (1995a), "Inflation Targets," *Bank of England Quarterly Bulletin*, (August): 250–59.

——— (1995b) (Ed.), *Targeting Inflation* (London: Bank of England).

Hamilton, J.D. (1994), *Time Series Analysis* (Princeton, NJ: Princeton University Press).

Hanright, D. (1960), "Economists Claim Bank of Canada Coloured Report," *Halifax Mail Star*, 6 June.

Harris, S.E. (1933), *Twenty Years of Federal Reserve Policy*, Vol. 3: *The Monetary Crisis* (Cambridge, MA.: Harvard University Press).

Harvey, A.C. (1993), "Modeling Nonlinearity over the Business Cycle: Comment," in J.H. Stock and M. Watson (Eds.), Business Cycles, Indicators, and Forecasting. NBER Studies in Business Cycles, Vol. 28 (Chicago and London: University of Chicago Press), p. 326.

——— (1989), *Forecasting, Structural Time Series Models and the Kalman Filter* (Cambridge, New York, and Melbourne: Cambridge University Press), pp. xvi, 554.

Haubrich, J.G., and A.M. Dombrosky (1996), "Predicting Real Growth Using the Yield Curve," *Economic Review*, Federal Reserve Bank of Cleveland 32 (Quarter 1).

Havrilesky, T. (1995a), *The Pressures on American Monetary Policy*, Second Edition (Boston: Kluwer Academic Publishers).

——— (1995b), "Restructuring the Fed," *Journal of Economics and Business*, 47: 95–111.

——— (1995c), "Central Bank Autonomy, Central Bank Accountability and Inflation Performance," Duke University, July.

——— (1993), *The Pressures on American Monetary Policy* (Boston: Kluwer Academic Publishers).

——— (1991), "The Frequency of Monetary Policy Signalling from the Administration to the Federal Reserve," *Journal of Money, Credit and Banking*, (August, part I): 422–30.

——— (1990), "The Influence of the Federal Advisory Council on Monetary Policy," *Journal of Money, Credit and Banking*, 22: 37–50.

(1967), "A Test of Monetary Policy Actions," *Journal of Political Economy*, June, 399–404.

Hawtrey, R.G. (1970), *The Art of Central Banking* (New York: Kelly).

Hayashi, F. (2000), *Econometrics* (Princeton, NJ: Princeton University Press).

Heisenberg, D. (1999), *The Mark of the Bundesbank: Germany's Role in European Monetary Cooperation* (Boulder, CO: Lynne Reiner).

Hendry, D.F. (1995), *Dynamic Econometrics* (New York and Oxford: Oxford University Press).

Hermalin B.E., and M.S. Weisbach (2000), "Boards of Directors as an Endogenously Determined Institution: A Survey of the Economic Literature," Working Paper, University of California Berkeley, June.

(1998), "Endogenously Chosen Boards of Directors and their Monitoring of the CEO," *American Economic Review*, 88 (March): 96–118.

Hess, G.D., and R.D. Porter (1993), "Comparing Interest-Rate Spreads and Money Growth as Predictors of Output Growth: Granger Causality in the Sense Granger Intended," *Journal of Economics and Business*, 45 (3–4): 247–68.

Hetzel, R.L. (2000), "The Taylor Rule: Is It a Useful Guide to Understanding Monetary Policy?," *Federal Reserve Bank of Richmond Economic Quarterly*, 86 (Spring): 1–33.

(1998), "Arthur Burns and Inflation," *Federal Reserve Bank of Richmond Economic Quarterly*, 84 (Winter): 21–44.

Hochreiter, E. (1995), "Necessary Conditions for a Successful Pursuit of Hard Currency Strategy," mimeo, Austrian National Bank.

Hochreiter, E., and G. Winckler (1995), "The Advantage of Tying Austria's Hand: The Success of the Austrian Hard Currency Policy," *European Journal of Political Economy*, 11 (March): 83–111.

Hodgetts, B. (1992), "Chronology of Monetary Policy Structural Changes Since 1960," in *Monetary Policy and the New Zealand Financial System*, Third Edition (Wellington: Reserve Bank of New Zealand), pp. 232–53.

Hodrick, R.J., and E.C. Prescott (1997), "Postwar US Business Cycles: An Empirical Investigation," *Journal of Money, Credit and Banking*, 29 (February): 1–16.

Hoffmeyer, E. (1994), *Thirty Years in Central Banking*, Occasional Paper 48, (Washington, DC: Group of Thirty).

Holtfrerich, C.L. (1988), "Relations Between Monetary Authorities and Governmental Institutions: The Case of Germany from the 19th Century to the Present," in G. Tomiolo (Ed.), *Central Banks' Independence in Historical Perspective* (Berlin: Walter de Gruyter), pp. 105–59.

Holtz-Eakin, D., W. Newey, and H. Rosen (1988), "Estimating Vector Autoregressions with Panel Data," *Econometrica*, 56 (6): 1371–95.

Hooker, M. (1999), "Oil and the Macroeconomy Revisited," Board of Governors of the Federal Reserve System, Finance and Economics Discussion Paper Series: 99/43, p. 13. August.

Howitt, P. (2001), "Learning About Monetary Theory and Policy," in the reissue of S. Gordon (Ed.), *The Economists versus the Bank of Canada* (Montreal: McGill-Queen's University Press, forthcoming).

(1993), "Canada," in M.V. Fratianni and D. Salvatore (Eds.), *Monetary Policy in Developed Economies*, Vol. 3, Handbook of Comparative Economic Policies (Westport, CT: Greenwood Press), pp. 459–508.

Hsiao, C. (1986), *Analysis Of Panel Data*, Econometric Society Monographs, No. 11 (Cambridge: Cambridge University Press).

Huizinga, H., and S. Eijffinger (1998), "Should Central Bank Councils Convene Often?," Working Paper, Humboldt and Tilburg University, November.

Hyman, S. (1976), *Marriner S. Eccles, Private Entrepreneur and Public Servant* (Stranford, CA: Stanford University Graduate School of Business).

International Financial Statistics (Washington, DC: International Monetary Fund, CD-ROM).

International Monetary Fund (2000), "Supporting Document to the Codes of Good Practices on Transparency in Monetary and Financial Policies," Part 2 – Good Transparency Practices for Monetary Policy by Central Banks, July. Available at http://www.imf.org.

Isard, P. (1996), *Exchange Rate Economics* (Cambridge: Cambridge University Press).

Issing, O. (1999), "The Eurosystem: Transparent and Accountable or 'Willeni in Euroland'," *Journal of Common Market Studies*, 37 (September): 503–19.

(1993), *Central Bank Independence and Monetary Stability* (London: Institute of Economic Affairs).

Jenkins, R. (2001), *Churchill: A Biography* (London: Macmillan).

John, K., and L.W. Senbir (1998), "Corporate Governance and Board Effectiveness," *Journal Banking and Finance*, 22: 371–403.

Johnson, D. (1999), "The Effect of Inflation Targeting on the Behavior of Expected Inflation: Evidence from an 11 Country Panel," Working Paper, Wilfrid Laurier University, July.

(1998), "The Credibility of Monetary Policy: International Evidence Based on Surveys of Expected Inflation," in *Price Stability, Inflation Targets, and Monetary Policy*, Proceedings of a conference held by the Bank of Canada, March 1997, pp. 361–95.

(1997), "Expected Inflation in Canada 1988–1995: An Evaluation of Bank of Canada Credibility and the Effect of Inflation Targets," *Canadian Public Policy-Analyse de Politiques*, 23 (3): 233–58, September.

(1994), "Ricardian Equivalence: Assessing the Evidence for Canada," in W.R. Robson and W.M. Scarth (Eds.), *Deficit Reduction: What Pain, What Gain?* (Toronto: C.D. Howe), pp. 81–118.

(1990), "The Zero Inflation Target: Do Wilson and John Crow Agree?," *Canadian Public Policy*, 14 (September): 308–25.

Johnson, D., and P.L. Siklos (1996), "Political and Economic Determinants of Interest Rate Behavior: Are Central Banks Different?," *Economic Inquiry*, (October): 708–29.

(1994), "Political Effects on Central Bank Behavior: Some International Evidence," in P.L. Siklos (Ed.), *Varieties of Monetary Reforms: Lessons and Experiences on the Road to Monetary Union* (Boston: Kluwer Academic Publishers), pp. 133–62.

Johnson, M., and R.E. Keleher (1996), *Monetary Policy, A Market Price Approach* (Westport, CT: Quorum Books).

Joint Economic Committee (1999), "Establishing Federal Reserve Inflation Goals," April. Available at http://www.house.gov/jec/fed/fed/goals.htm.

——— (1991), *Central Bank-Government Relations in Major OECD Countries* (Washington, DC: U.S. Government Printing Office), August.

Joliffe, I.T. (1986), *Principal Component Analysis* (New York: Springer-Verlag).

Jonung, L. (1979), "Knut Wicksel's Norm of Price Stabilisation and Swedish Monetary Policy in the 1930s," *Journal of Monetary Economics*, 5: 459–96.

Joyce, M., and V. Read (1999), "The Impact of Inflation News on Financial Markets," *Bank of England Quarterly Bulletin*, 39 (February): 48–59.

Judd, P.J., and G. Rudebusch (1998), "Taylor's Rule and The Fed: 1970–1997," Federal Reserve Bank of San Francisco, *Economic Review*, 2 (3): 3–16.

Judson, R.A., and A. Owen (1996), "Estimating Dynamic Panel Data Models: A Practical Guide for Macroeconomists," Board of Governors of the Federal Reserve.

Kennedy, E. (1991), *The Bundesbank: Germany's Central Bank in the International Monetary System* (London: Pinter for the Royal Institute of International Affairs).

Kettl, D.F. (1986), *Leadership at the Fed* (New Haven and London: Yale University Press).

Keynes, J.M. (1924), "The Policy of the Bank of England," *The Nation and the Athenaeum*, July 19, PRO T176/5 "Monetary Policy."

——— (1923), *A Tract on Monetary Reform* (London: Macmillan).

Khoury, S.S. (1990), "The Federal Reserve Reaction Function: A Specification Search," in T. Mayer (Ed.), *The Political Economy of American Monetary Policy* (Cambridge: Cambridge University Press), pp. 27–49.

Kim, C-J., and C.R. Nelson (1999), *State-Space Models With Regime Switching: Classical and Gibbs-Sampling Approaches With Applications* (Cambridge and London: MIT Press), pp. x, 297.

Kim, K., R.A. Buckle, and V. Hall (1995), "Dating New Zealand Business Cycles," *New Zealand Economic Papers*, 29: 142–71.

Kisch, Sir C.H., and W.A. Elkin (1932), *Central Banks* (London: Macmillan).

Kohn, D.L. (2001), "The Kohn Report on MPC Procedures," *Bank of England Quarterly Bulletin* (Spring): 35–49.

Kozicki, S. (1999), "How Useful are Taylor Rules for Monetary Policy?," *Economic Review*, Federal Reserve Bank of Kansas City (2): 5–33.

Krugman, P. (1996), "Stable Prices and Fast Growth: Just Say No," *The Economist*, August 31–September 6, 1996, pp. 19–22.

Kuttner, K.N., and A.S. Posen (1999), "Does Talk Matter After All? Inflation Targeting and Central Bank Behavior," Federal Reserve Bank of New York, Staff Report #88, October.

Kydland, F.E., and E.C. Prescott (1977), "Rules Rather Than Discretion: The Inconsistency of Optimal Plans," *Journal of Political Economy*, 85 (3): 473–91, June.

Laidler, D.E.W. (1991), *How Shall We Govern the Governor? A Critique of the Governance of the Bank of Canada* (Toronto: C.D. Howe Institute).

Laidler, D., and S. Aba (2000), "It's Time to Ignore Core Inflation," C.D. Howe Institute Backgrounder, November. Available at http://www.cdhowe.org.

Laidler, D.E.W., and W. Robson (1993), *The Great Canadian Disinflation* (Toronto: C.D. Howe Institute).

Laidler, D.E.W., and M. Parkin (1975), "Inflation: A Survey," *Economic Journal*, 85 (December): 741–809.

Laubach, T., and A. Posen (1997), "Some Comparative Evidence on the Effectiveness of Inflation Targeting," Federal Reserve Bank of New York Research Paper 9714, April.

Leiderman, L., and L.E.O. Svensson (Eds.), (1995), *Inflation Targets* (London: CEPR).

Leitemo, K. (1999), "Inflation Targeting Strategies in Small Open Economies," Norges Bank.

Levin, A., D. McManus, and D. Watt (1999), "The Information Content of Canadian Dollar Futures Options," in *Information in Financial Asset Prices*, Proceedings of a Conference held by the Bank of Canada, May 1998 (Ottawa: Bank of Canada), pp. 229–88.

Levin, A., V. Wieland, and J.C. Williams (1998), "Robustness of Simple Monetary Policy Rules under Model Uncertainty," National Bureau of Economic Research Working Paper 6570, May.

Levy-Yeyati, E.X., and F. Sturzenegger (1999), "Classifying Exchange Rate Regimes: Deeds vs. Words," Working Paper, Universidad Torcuato Di Tella, December.

Li, H., S. Rosen, and W. Suen (2001), "Conflicts and Common Interests in Committees," *American Economic Review*, 91 (December): 1478–97.

Lijphart, A. (1999), *Patterns of Democracy* (New Haven and London: Yale University Press).

(1997), "Reflections: Dimensions of Democracy," *European Journal of Political Science Research*, 31: 195–204.

Lindsay, L. (1997), "Central Banking in a Democracy: Balancing Independence and Accountability," presentation at the North American Economic and Finance Association, New Orleans, LA, January.

Linklater, J. (1992), *Inside the Bank: The Role of the Reserve Bank of Australia in the Economic, Banking, and Financial Systems* (St. Leonards, NSW, Australia: Allen & Unwin).

Lohmann, S. (2000), "Sollbruchstelle: Deep Uncertainty and the Design of Monetary Institutions," *International Finance*, 3 (November): 391–412.

(1999), "The Dark Side of European Monetary Union," in E. Meade (Ed.), *The European Central Bank: How Decentralized? How Accountable? Lessons from the Bundesbank and the Federal Reserve System* (Washington, DC: American Institute for German Studies), pp. 15–37.

(1998), "Federalism and Central Bank Independence: The Politics of German Monetary Policy, 1957–92," *World Politics*, 50 (April): 401–46.

(1994), "Designing a Central Bank in a Federal System: The Deutsche Bundesbank, 1957–92," in P.L. Siklos (Ed.), *Variety of Monetary Reforms:*

Lessons and Experiences on the Road to Monetary Union (Boston: Kluwer Academic Publishers), pp. 247–78.

(1992), "Optimal Commitment in Monetary Policy: Credibility Versus Flexibility," *American Economic Review*, 82: 273–86.

Longworth, D., and C. Freedman (1995), "The Role of the Staff Economic Projection in Conducting Canadian Monetary Policy," in A. Haldane (Ed.), *Targeting Inflation* (London: Bank of England), pp. 10–112.

Lucas, R.F. (1989), "The Bank of Canada and Zero Inflation: A New Cross of Gold?," *Canadian Public Policy*, 15 (March): 84–93.

Lucas, R.E, Jr. (1976), "Econometric Policy Evaluation: A Critique," *Journal of Monetary Economics*, 1 (2): 19–46.

Maddala, G.S. (1977), *Econometrics*, (New York: McGraw-Hill).

Mahadeva, J., and G. Sterne (2000), *Monetary Policy Frameworks in a Global Context* (London: Routledge).

Maier, P., and J. de Haan (2000), "How Independent is the Bundesbank Really? A Survey," in J. de Haan (Ed.), *The History of the Bundesbank: Lessons for the European Central Bank* (London and New York: Routledge), pp. 6–42.

Makridakis, S., S.C. Wheelwright, and R. Hyndman (1993), *Forecasting: Methods and Applications*, Third Edition (New York: John Wiley and Sons).

Mangano, G. (1998), "Measuring Central Bank Independence: A Tale of Subjectivity and of its Consequences," *Oxford Economic Papers,* 50: 468–92.

Manley Report (1992), *The Mandate and Governance of the Bank of Canada*, First Report of the Sub-Committee on the Bank of Canada (February).

Mansel, S.J. (1973), *Managing the Dollar* (New York: W.W. Norton and Co.).

Marsh, D. (1992), *The Bundesbank: The Bank That Rules Europe* (London: Heinemann).

Marshall, M. (1999), *The Bank* (London: Random House Business Books).

Masciandaro, D. (1993a), "Monetary Policy, Banking Supervision and Inflation: Do We Need a Multitask Agency?," Manuscript, Paolo Baffi Centre for Monetary and Financial Economics.

(1993b), "Policymaking Hazards, Monetary Policy and Central Bank Design," Manuscript, Paolo Baffi Centre for Monetary and Financial Economics.

Masson, P. (1995), "Gaining and Losing ERM Credibility: The Case of the United Kingdom," *Economic Journal*, 105 (May): 571–82.

Mátyás, L. (Ed.) (1999), *Generalized Method Of Moments Estimation* (Cambridge: Cambridge University Press).

Mayer, M. (2001), *The Fed* (New York: Free Press).

Mayes, D.G. (2000), "The Operation of Monetary Policy in New Zealand," Submission to the Independent Review of the Operation of Monetary Policy. Available at http://www.rbnz.govt.nz.

Mayes, D., and B. Chapple (1995), "The Costs and Benefits of Disinflation: A Critique of the Sacrifice Ratio," *Reserve Bank Bulletin*, 58 (March): 9–21.

Mayes, D.G., and W. Razzak (1998), "Transparency and Accountability: Empirical Models and Policy Making at the Reserve Bank of New Zealand," *Economic Modelling*, 15: 377–94.

McCallum, B.T. (1998), "Robustness Properties of a Rule for Monetary Policy," *Carnegie-Rochester Conference Series on Public Policy*, 29 (Autumn): 213–14.

(2000a), "The Present and Future of Monetary Policy Rules," *International Finance*, 3 (April): 273–86.

(2000b), "Alternative Policy Rules: A Comparison with Historical Settings for the United States, the United Kingdom and Japan," *Economic Quarterly*, Federal Reserve Bank of Richmond, 86 (Winter): 49–79.

(1999), "Recent Developments in the Analysis of Monetary Policy Rules," Federal Reserve Bank of St. Louis Review, 81 (6): 3–11, November.

(1997a), "Inflation Targeting in Canada, New Zealand, Sweden, The United Kingdom, and in General," in I. Kuroda (Ed.), *Towards More Effective Monetary Policy* (New York: St. Martin's Press), pp. 211–41.

(1997b), "Crucial Issues Concerning Central Bank Independence," *Journal of Monetary Economics*, 39 (June): 99–112.

(1996), "Commentary: How Should Central Banks Reduce Inflation? – Conceptual Issues," in *Achieving Price Stability*, A Symposium Sponsored by the Federal Reserve Bank of Kansas City, Jackson Hole, Wyoming, August 29–31, pp. 105–14.

(1995), "Two Fallacies Concerning Central Bank Independence," *American Economic Review Papers and Proceedings*, 85 (May): 207–11.

(1990), "Inflation: Theory and Evidence," in B.M. Friedman and F. Hahn (Eds.), *Handbook of Monetary Economics*, Vol. II (Amsterdam: Elsevier), pp. 964–1012.

(1989), *Monetary Economics* (New York: Macmillan).

(1988), "Robustness Properties of a Rule for Monetary Policy," *Carnegie-Rochester Conference Series on Public Policy*, 29 (Autumn): 213–14.

McCallum, B.T., and E. Nelson (1999), "Performance of Operational Policy Rules in an Estimated Semi-Classical Structural Model," in J.B. Taylor (Ed.), *Monetary Policy Rules* (Chicago: University of Chicago Press), pp. 15–45.

Melitz, J. (1988), "Monetary Discipline, Germany, and the European Monetary System: A Synthesis," in F. Giavazzi, S. Micossi, and M. Miller (Eds.), *The European Monetary System* (Cambridge: Cambridge University Press), pp. 51–79.

Meltzer, A.H. (2001), *A History of the Federal Reserve* (Chicago: University of Chicago Press), forthcoming.

Memoranda concerning the Federal Reserve Board taken from the Diaries of Charles S. Hamlin (1984), (Washington, DC: Library of Congress).

Mieno, Y. (1994), "The Development of Central Banking: Discussion," in *Future of Central Banking: The Tercentenary Symposium of the Bank of England* (Cambridge: Cambridge University Press), pp. 250–52.

Miller, A.C. (1921), "Federal Reserve Policy," *American Economic Review*, 11 (June): 177–206.

Miller, G.P. (1996), "Decision-Making at the Bank of Japan," *Law and Policy in International Business*, 28 (Fall): 1–47.

Mishkin, F.S. (2000), "Issues in Inflation Targeting," Working Paper, Columbia University.

(1995), "Symposium on the Monetary Transmission Mechanism," *Journal of Economic Perspectives*, 9 (Fall): 3–10.

Mitchell, B.R. (1993), *International Historical Statistics: The Americas, 1750–1988*, Second Edition (New York: Stockton Press).

(1992), *International Historical Statistics, Europe, 1750–1988* (Basingstoke, Hants, England: Macmillan).

Moggridge, D.E. (1992), *Maynard Keynes: An Economist's Biography* (London and New York: Routledge).

Monetary Policy Committee (2001), "Minutes and Press Notices," Bank of England, February.

Moynihan, M. (1975), *Currency and Central Banking in Ireland, 1922–1960* (Dublin: Gill and Macmillan).

Muirhead, B. (1999), *Against the Odds: The Public Life and Times of Louis Rasminsky* (Toronto: University of Toronto Press).

Murchison, S.C., and P.L. Siklos (1999), "A Suggestion for a Simple Cross-Country Empirical Proxy for Trend Unemployment," *Applied Economics Letters*, 6 (7): 447–51, July.

Murray, J. (2000), "Why Canada Needs a Flexible Exchange Rate," *North American Journal of Economics and Finance*, 11 (August): 41–60.

Murray, J., M. Zelmer, and D. McManus (1997), "The Effectiveness of Official Intervention and the Volatility of the Canadian Dollar," in *Exchange Rates and Monetary Policy*, Proceedings of a conference held at the Bank of Canada, October 1996 (Ottawa: Bank of Canada), pp. 311–60.

Neufeld, E. (1958), *Bank of Canada Operations and Policy* (Toronto: University of Toronto Press).

Neumann, M.J.M. (1999), "Monetary Stability: Threat and Proven Response," in Deutsche Bundesbank (Eds.), *Fifty Years of the Deutsche Mark* (Oxford: Oxford University Press), pp. 269–306.

Nickell, S.J. (1981), "Biases in Dynamic Models with Fixed Effects," *Econometrica*, 49 (6): 1417–26, November.

Non-Executive Directors of the Reserve Bank of New Zealand (2000), "Submission to the Independent Review of Monetary Policy." Available at http://www.rbnz.govt.nz.

Nordhaus, W. (1975), "The Political Business Cycle," *Review of Economic Studies*, April: 169–90.

Obstfeld, M. (1995), "International Currency Experience: New Lessons and Lessons Relearned," *Brookings Papers on Economic Activity*, 1, 119–96.

Obstfeld, M., and K. Rogoff (1995), "The Mirage of Fixed Exchange Rates," *Journal of Economic Perspectives*, 9 (Fall): 73–96.

OECD (1995), *Budgeting for Results: Perspectives on Public Expenditures Management* (Paris: OECD).

Orphanides, A. (2000), "Activist Stabilization Policy and Inflation: The Taylor Rule in the 1970s," Board of Governors of the Federal Reserve System, February.

(1998), "Monetary Policy Rules Based on Real-Time Data," Board of Governors of the Federal Reserve System Finance and Economics Discussion Paper 1998–03.

Orphanides, A., R.D. Porter, D. Reifschneider, R. Tetlow, and F. Finan (1999), "Errors in the Measurement of the Output Gap and the Design of Monetary Policy," Finance and Economics Discussion Paper 45, Board of Governors of the Federal Reserve System, August.

Orphanides, A., D.H. Small, V. Wieland, and D.W. Wilcox (1996), "A Quantitative Exploration of the Opportunistic Approach to Disinflation," Board of Governers of the Federal Reserve System, May.

Orphanides, A., and S. van Norden (1999), "The Reliability of Output Gap Estimates in Real Time," Board of Governors of the Federal Reserve System, August.

Parkin, M. (2000), "What Have We Learned About Price Stability?," Working Paper, University of Western Ontario, June.

——— (1986), "Domestic Monetary Institutions and Deficits," in J.M. Buchanan, C.K. Rowley, and R.D. Tollison (Eds.), *Deficits* (London: Basil Blackwell), pp. 310–37.

Persson, T., and G. Tabellini (1997), "Political Economics and Macroeconomic Policy," NBER Working Paper 6329, December.

——— (Eds.) (1994), *Monetary and Fiscal Policy* (Cambridge, MA: MIT Press).

——— (1993), "Designing Institutions for Monetary Stability," *Carnegie-Rocheseter Conference Series on Public Policy*, Vol. 39.

——— (1990), "Macroeconomic Policy, Credibility and Politics," *Fundamentals of Pure and Applied Economics*, Vol. 38, Macroeconomic Theory Section (Chur, Switzerland: Harwood Academic).

Pesaran, M.H., Y. Shin, and R. Smith (1997), "Pooled Estimation of Long-Run Relationships in Dynamic Heterogeneous Panels," University of Cambridge, Department of Applied Economics Working Paper Amalgamated Series: 97/21, pp. 18. August.

Posen, A. (1998a), "Do Better Institutions Make Better Policy?," *International Finance*, 1 (October): 173–205.

——— (1998b), "Central Bank Independence and Disinflationary Credibility: A Missing Link?," *Oxford Economic Papers*, 50 (July): 335–59.

——— (1995), "Declarations are Not Enough: Financial Sector Sources of Central Bank Independence," in B.S. Bernanke and J.J. Rotemberg (Eds.), *Macroeconomics Annual 1995* (Cambridge, MA: MIT Press), pp. 253–74.

——— (1993), "Why Central Bank Independence Does Not Cause Low Inflation: There is No Institutional Fix for Politics," in F.R. O'Brien (Ed.), *Finance and the International Economy* (Oxford: Oxford University Press), pp. 40–65.

Posen, A.S. (2000), "Lessons from the Bundesbank on the Occasion of its Early Retirement," in L. Mahadeva and G. Sterne (Eds.), *Monetary Policy Frameworks in a Global Context* (London: Routledge), pp. 393–420.

Poterba, J.M. (1994), "Do Budget Rules Work?," in A.J. Duerbach (Ed.), *Fiscal Policy: Lessons from Economic Research* (Cambridge, MA: MIT Press), pp. 53–86.

Powell, J. (1999), *A History of the Canadian Dollar* (Ottawa: Bank of Canada).

Pringle, R. (1995), *The Morgan Stanley Central Bank Directory* (London: Central Banking Publications).

Pringle, R., and N. Courtis (1999), *Objectives, Governance and Profits of Central Banks* (London: Central Banking Publications).

Public Records Office [PRO] (1933), "US Monetary Policy," T172/2081.

Pusey, M.J. (1974), *Eugene Meyer* (New York: Knopf).

Quigley, N. (1992), "Monetary Policy and the New Zealand Financial System: An Historical Perspective," in *Monetary Policy and the New Zealand Financial System*, Third Edition (Wellington: Reserve Bank of New Zealand), pp. 205–231.

Radcliffe Committee (1959), Committee on the Working of the Monetary System: Report (London: Her Majesty's Stationary Office).

Rasminsky, L. (1966), "Role of the Central Banker Today," Per Jacobsson Memorial Lecture (Washington, DC: Per Jacobsson Foundation).

Reeves, T. (2001), *President Nixon: Alone in the White House* (New York: Simon and Schuster).

Remsperger, H., and A. Worms (1999), "Transparency in Monetary Policy," CFS Working Paper 1999/16, January.

Report of the Royal Commission on Banking and Finance (1964), Ottawa: Queen's Printers.

Reserve Bank of New Zealand (1996a), *Briefing on the Reserve Bank of New Zealand* (Wellington, New Zealand) October.

(1996b), "Letter from Sir Peter Elworthy to the Minister of Finance, 19 April 1996," in *Monetary Policy Statement*, June.

(1996c), *Briefing on the Reserve Bank of New Zealand* (Wellington: New Zealand) October.

(1996d), "Summary Indicators of Monetary Conditions," *Reserve Bank Bulletin*, 59 (September): 223–28.

(1993), *Post-Election Briefing Paper* (Wellington: New Zealand), November.

Reuber, G.L. (1964), "The Objectives of Canadian Monetary Policy, 1949–61: Empirical Trade-Offs and the Reaction Function of the Authorities," *Journal of Political Economy*, 52 (April): 109–32.

Rich, G. (2000), "Money Policy Without Central Bank Money: A Swiss Perspective," *International Finance*, 3 (November): 439–70.

(1997), "Monetary Targets as a Policy Rule: Lessons from the Swiss Experience," *Journal of Monetary Economics*, 39: 113–41.

Richter, R. (1999), "Germany Monetary Policy as Reflected in the Academic Debate," in Deutsche Bundesbank (Eds.), *Fifty Years of the Deutsche Mark* (Oxford: Oxford University Press), pp. 525–71.

Roberts, P. (2000), "Benjamin Strong, The Federal Reserve, and the Limits of Interwar American Nationalism," *Economic Quarterly*, Federal Reserve Bank of Richard, 86 (Spring): 61–98.

Rogoff, K. (1985), "The Optimal Degree of Commitment to an Intermediate Monetary Target," *The Quarterly Journal of Economics*, 100 (4): 1169–89, November.

Rogoff, K.F. (1987), "Reputational Constraints in Monetary Policy," in K. Brunner and A.H. Meltzer (Eds.), *Carnegie-Rochester Conference Series on Public Policy*, Vol. 26 (Amsterdam: Elsevier), pp. 141–81.

Roll, E. (1993), *Independent and Accountable: A New Mandate for the Bank of England* (London: CEPR).

Romer, C.D., and D.H. Romer (2000), "Federal Reserve Private Information and the Behavior of Interest Rates," *American Economic Review*, 90 (June): 429–57.

—— (1996), "Institutions for Monetary Stability," in C.D. Romer and D.H. Romer (Eds.), *Reducing Inflation: Motivation and Strategy* (Chicago and London: University of Chicago Press), pp. 307–29.

Romer, D. (1996), *Advanced Macroeconomics* (New York: McGraw-Hill).

Romer, D.H. (1993), "Openness and Inflation: Theory and Evidence," *Quarterly Journal of Economics*, 108 (November), 869–903.

Royal Commission into Bank of Canada Operations (1936), Report, Ottawa, Ontario.

Royal Commission on Banking and Currency (1933), Ottawa, Ontario.

Rudebusch, G.D. (2001), "Is the Fed Too Timid? Monetary Policy in an Uncertain World," *Review of Economics and Statistics*, 83 (May): 203–17.

—— (1998), "Do Measures of Monetary Policy in a VAR Make Sense?," *International Economic Review*, 39 (November): 907–47.

Rudebusch, G.D., and L.E.O. Svensson (1999), "Eurosystem Monetary Targeting: Lessons from the U.S. Date," NBER Working Paper 7179, June.

Rymes, T.K. (1994), "On the Coyne-Rasminsky Directive and Responsibility for Monetary Policy in Canada," in P.L. Siklos (Ed.), *Varieties of Monetary Reforms: Lessons and Experiences on the Road to Monetary Union* (Dordecht: Kluwer Academic Publishers), pp. 351–66.

Sack, B. (1998), "Does the Fed Act Gradually? A VAR Analysis," *Journal of Monetary Economics*, 46 (August): 229–56.

Sack, B., and V. Wieland (2000), "Interest Rate Smoothing and Optimal Monetary Policy: A Review of Recent Empirical Literature," *Journal of Economics and Business*, 52 (Jan–Apr): 205–28.

Sargent, T.J. (1999), *The Conquest of American Inflation* (Princeton, NJ: Princeton University Press).

Sarno, L., and M.P. Taylor (2001), "Official Intervention in the Foreign Exchange Market: Is it Effective and, if so, How Does it Work?," *Journal of Economic Literature*, 39 (September): 839–68.

Sayers, R.S. (1976), *The Bank of England, 1891–1944* (Cambridge: Cambridge University Press).

Schuster F. (1906), "The Bank of England and the State," Lecture delivered November 14, 1905 (Manchester: Manchester University Press).

Schwartz, A.J. (2000), "The Rise and Fall of Foreign Exchange Market Intervention as a Policy Tool," *Journal of Financial Services Research*, 18 (2–3): 319–39, December.

Select Committee on Monetary Policy, Committee of the Bank of England (2001), "Report," London, House of Lords, February 13.

Shapiro, M.D., and D.W. Wilcox (1996), "Mismeasurement of the Consumer Price Index: An Evaluation," NBER *Macroeconomics Annual 1996* (Cambridge, MA: MIT Press), pp. 93–142.

Shiller, R.J. (1997), "Why Do People Dislike Inflation?," in C.D. Romer and D.H. Romer (Eds), *Reducing Inflation: Motivation and Strategy* (Chicago and London: University of Chicago Press), pp. 13–65.

Shleifer, A., and R. Vishny (1997), "A Survey of Corporate Governance," *Journal of Finance*, 52, 737–83.

Sibert, A. (1999), "Monetary Policy Committees: Individual and Collective Reputations," Working Paper, Birbeck College, November.

Sicilia, D.B., and J.L. Cruikshank (2000), *The Greenspan Effect* (New York: McGraw-Hill).

Siklos, P.L. (2002a), "The Coyne Affair Revisited: Disagreement over Monetary Policy in Canada, 1957–1961," Working Paper.

(2002b), "How Cautious are Central Banks? International Evidence," Working Paper, Wilfrid Laurier University.

(2001), "Central Bank Behavior, the Institutional Framework, and Policy Regimes: Inflation vs. Non-Inflation Targeting Countries," Working Paper, Wilfrid Laurier University.

(2000a), "Inflation and Hyperinflation," in *The Oxford Encyclopedia of Economic History* (Oxford: Oxford University Press), forthcoming.

(2000b), "Accountability, Transparency, and Perceptions About Monetary Policy in Canada," Working Paper, Wilfrid Laurier University.

(2000c), "Is the MCI a Useful Signal of Monetary Conditions? An Empirical Investigation," *International Finance*, 3 (November): 413–37.

(2000d), "Inflation Targets and the Yield Curve: New Zealand and Australia vs. the US," *International Journal of Economics and Finance*, 5 (February): 15–32.

(1999a), "Inflation Target Design, Changing Inflation Performance and Persistence in Industrial Countries," *Review of the Federal Reserve Bank of St. Louis*, 81 (March/April): 47–58.

(1999b), "US and Canadian Central Banking: The Triumph of Personalities Over Politics?," in C.L. Holtferich, G. Toniolo, and J. Reis (Eds.), *The Emergence of Modern Central Banking from 1918 to the Present* (Aldershot: Ashgate), pp. 231–78.

(1999c), "Pitfalls and Opportunities for Central Banks in A World of High Frequency Data," *Information in Financial Asset Prices* (Ottawa: Bank of Canada), pp. 331–69.

(1997a), "Charting a Future for the Bank of Canada: Inflation Targets and the Balance Between Autonomy and Accountability," in D.E.W. Laidler (Ed.), *Where We Go From Here: Inflation Targets in Canada's Monetary Policy* (Toronto: C.D. Howe Institute), pp. 101–84.

(1997b), "The Connection Between Exchange Rate Regimes and Credibility: An International Perspective," in *Exchange Rates and Monetary Policy* (Ottawa: Bank of Canada), pp. 73–121.

(1995), "Establishing Central Bank Independence: Recent Experiences in Developing Countries," *Journal of International Trade and Economic Development*, 4 (November): 351–84.

(1993), "Income Velocity and Institutional Change: Some New Time Series Evidence," *Journal of Money, Credit and Banking*, 25 (August): 377–92.

(1988), "The Deficit-Interest Rate Link: Empirical Evidence for Canada," *Applied Economics*, 20 (December): 1563–78.

Siklos, P.L., and A. Barton (2001), "Monetary Aggregates as Indicators of Economic Activity in Canada: Empirical Evidence," *Canadian Journal of Economics*, 34 (February): 1–20.

Siklos, P.L., and M.T. Bohl (2001), "Do Words Speak Louder than Actions? The Conduct of Monetary Policy at the Bundesbank," Working Paper, Wilfrid Laurier Univeristy.

Siklos, P.L., and L. Skoczylas (2002), "Volatility Clustering in Real Interest Rates: International Evidence," *Journal of Macroeconomics* (Spring).

Simon, H.A. (1978), "Richard T. Ely Lecture: Rationality as Process and as Product of Thought," *American Economic Review*, 68 (May): 1–16.

Simons, H.C. (1936), "Rules Versus Authorities in Monetary Policy," *Journal of Political Economy*, 44 (February): 1–30.

Sims, C.A. (1998), Comment on Glenn Rudebusch's "Do Measures of Monetary Policy in a VAR Make Sense?," *International Economic Review*, 39 (November): 933–41.

Sims, G.T. (2001), "ECB's Rate-Cut Scorecard Comes with an Asterisk," *Wall Street Journal Europe*, November 8, p. 1.

Smets, F. (1997), "Financial Asset Prices and Monetary Policy: Theory and Evidence," BIS Working Paper 47, September, Basle, Switzerland.

Snyder, C. (1935), "The Problem of Monetary and Economic Stability," *Quarterly Journal of Economics*, (February): 173–205.

Spence, M. (1973), "Job Market Signalling," *Quarterly Journal of Economics*, 87 (August): 355–74.

Sprague, O.M.W. (1921), "The Discount Policy of the Federal Reserve Banks," *American Economic Review*, 11 (March): 16–29.

Sproul, A. (1947), "Monetary Management and Credit Control," *American Economics Review*, 37.

Staiger, D., J.H. Stock, and M.W. Watson (1997a), "The NAIRU, Unemployment and Monetary Policy," *Journal of Economic Perspectives*, 11 (Summer): 33–50.

(1997b), "How Precise are Estimates of the Natural Rate of Unemployment," in C.D. Romer and D.H. Romer (Eds.), *Reducing Inflation: Motivation and Strategy* (Chicago: University of Chicago Press), pp. 195–242.

Stein, J.C. (1989), "Cheap Talk and the Fed: A Theory of Imprecise Policy Announcements," *American Economic Review*, 79 (March): 32–42.

Stiglitz, J.E. (1997), "Up the NAIRU without a Paddle," *The Economist* (8 March).

Stock, J.H., and M.W. Watson (2001), "Forecasting Output and Inflation: The Role of Asset Prices," Working Paper, Harvard University.

Svensson, L.E.O. (2001), *Independent Review of the Operation of Monetary Policy in New Zealand: Report to the Minister of Finance*, February. Available at http://www.monpolreview.govt.nz.

(2000), "Open Economy Inflation Targeting," *Journal of International Economics*, 50 (February): 155–83.

(1999a), "Monetary Policy Issues for the Eurosystem," *Carnegie-Rochester Conference Series on Public Policy*, Vol. 51 (Amsterdam, North-Holland: Elsevier), pp. 79–136.

(1999b), "Price Stability as a Target for Monetary Policy: Defining and Maintaining Price Stability," NBER Working Paper 7276, August.

(1997a), "Inflation Targeting in an Open Economy: Strict or Flexible Inflation Targeting?," Reserve Bank of New Zealand Discussion Paper G97/8, November.

(1997b), "Optional Inflation Targets, 'Conservative' Central Banks, and Linear Inflation Targets," *American Economic Review*, 87 (March): 98–114.

(1995), "The Swedish Experience of an Inflation Target," in L. Leiderman and L.E.O. Svensson (Eds.), *Inflation Targets* (London: Centre for Economic Policy Research; distributed in North America by the Brookings Institution, Washington, DC), pp. 69–89.

Sylla, R. (1988), "The Autonomy of Monetary Authorities: The Con of the US Federal Reserve System," in G. Toniolo (Ed.), *Central Banks' Independence in Historical Perspective* (Berlin and New York: Walter de Gruyter), pp. 17–38.

Symposium (1997), "The Natural Rate of Unemployment," *Journal of Economic Perspectives*, 11 (Winter): 3–108.

Tarkka, J., and D.G. Mayes (1999), "The Value of Publishing Official Central Bank Forecast," Bank of Finland Discussion Paper 22/99, December.

Taylor, J.B. (2000), "Using Monetary Policy Rules in Emerging Market Economies," Unpublished, Stanford University, December.

(1999), "A Historical Analysis of Monetary Policy Rules," in J.B. Taylor (Ed.), *Monetary Policy Rules* (Chicago and London: University of Chicago Press), pp. 319–41.

(1998a), "The Robustness and Efficiency of Monetary Policy Rules as Guidelines for Interest Rate Setting by the European Central Bank," *Journal of Monetary Economics*, 43 (June): 655–79.

(1998b), "Monetary Policy and the Long Boom," *Review of the Federal Reserve Bank of St. Louis*, 80 (November/December): 3–12.

(1996), "How Should Monetary Policy Respond to Shocks While Maintaining Long-Run Price Stability? Conceptual Issues," in *Achieving Price Stability*, A Symposium Sponsored by the Federal Reserve Bank of Kansas City (Jackson Hole, Wyoming), pp. 181–95.

(1993), "Discretion versus Policy Rules in Practice 4," *Carnegie-Rochester Conference on Public Policy*, 45 (December): 195–214.

Tetlow, R., and P. von zur Muehlen (1999), "Simplicity Versus Optimality: The Choice of Monetary Policy Rules when Agents Must Learn," Finance and Economics Discussion Paper 10, Board of Governors of the Federal Reserve System, January.

Thiessen, G. (2000a), "Can A Bank Change? The Evolution of Monetary Policy at the Bank of Canada, 1935–2000," Lecture to the Faculty of Social Science, University of Western Ontario, October. Available at http://www.bankofcanada.ca/en/speeches/sp00-6.htm.

(2000b), "Accountability and Transparency in Canada's Monetary Policy," *Bank of Canada Review*, (Spring): 19–22.

Thornton, D.L., and D.C. Wheelock (2000), "A History of the Asymmetric Policy Directive," *Federal Reserve Bank of St. Louis Review*, 82 (5): 1–16, Sept.–Oct.

Tietmeyer, H. (1998a), "The Bundesbank: Committed to Stability," in S.F. Frowen and R. Pringle (Eds.), *Inside the Bundesbank* (London: Macmillan), pp. 1–10.

(1998b), "Reflection on the German Treaty Negotiations of 1990," in S.F. Frowen and R. Pringle (Eds.), *Inside the Bundesbank* (London: Macmillan), pp. 68–109.

Timberlake, R. (1993), *Monetary Policy in the United States* (Chicago and London: University of Chicago Press).

Toniolo, G. (Ed.) (1988), *Central Banks' Independence In Historical Perspective* (Berlin and New York: de Gruyter).

Treasury, H.M. (1999), *The Monetary Policy Framework* Available at http://www.hm-treasury.gov.uk.

Vaubel, R. (1997), "The Bureaucratic and Partisan Behavior of Independent Central Banks: German and International Evidence," *European Journal of Political Economy*, 13: 201–24.

Volcker, P. (1994), "The Human Factor and the Fed," in D.C. Colander and D. Deane (Eds.), *The Art of Monetary Policy* (Armonk, NY: M.E. Sharpe), pp. 21–32.

Volcker, P.A. (1990), "The Triumph of Central Banking," Per Jacobsson Lecture, International Monetary Fund.

Volcker, P.A., and T. Gyohten (1992), *Changing Fortunes: The World's Money and the Threat to American Leadership* (New York: Times Books).

von Furstenberg, G.M., and M.K. Ulan (1998), *Learning From The World's Best Central Bankers: Principles And Policies For Subduing Inflation* (Boston, Dordrecht, and London: Kluwer Academic Publishers).

von Hayek, F.A. (1931), *Prices and Production* (London: Routledge).

von Hagen, J. (1999a), "Money Growth Targeting by the Bundesbank," *Journal of Monetary Economics*, 43, 681–701.

(1999b), "A New Approach to Monetary Policy (1971–78)," in Deutsche Bundesbank (Eds.), *Fifty Years of the Deutsche Mark* (Oxford: Oxford University Press), pp. 403–38.

(1995), "Inflation and Monetary Targeting in Germany," in L. Leiderman and L.E.O. Svenson (Eds.), *Inflation Targets* (London: Center for Economic Policy Research), pp. 107–21.

von Hagen, J., and R. Suppal (1994), "Central Bank Constitutions for Federal Monetary Unions," *European Economic Review*, 38 (April): 774–82.

Wahlig, B. (1998), "Relations Between the Bundesbank and the Federal Government," in S.F. Frowen and R. Pringle (Eds.), *Inside the Bundesbank* (London: Macmillan), pp. 45–55.

Waller, C.J. (2000), "Policy Boards and Policy Smoothing," *Quarterly Journal of Economics*, 115 (February): 305–39.

(1992), "The Choice of a Conservative Central Banker in a Multisector Economy," *American Economic Review*, 82 (September): 1006–12.

(1992), "A Bargaining Model of Partisan Appointments to the Central Bank," *Journal of Monetary Economics*, 29 (3): 411–28, June.

(1989), "Monetary Policy Games and Central Bank Politics," *Journal of Money, Credit and Banking*, 21 (4): 422–31, November.

Waller, C.J., and C.E. Walsh (1996a), "Central-Bank Independence, Economic Behavior, and Optimal Term Lengths," *American Economic Review*, 86 (5): pp. 1139–53, December.

(1996b), "Central-Bank Independence, Economic Behavior, and Optimal Term Lengths," *American Economic Review*, 86 (5): 1139–53, December.

Wallis, K. (1999), "Asymmetric Density Forecasts of Inflation and the Bank of England's Chart," *National Institute Economic Review*, (January): 106–12.

Walsh, C.E. (2001), "The Output Gap and Optimal Monetary Policy," Working Paper, University of California, Santa Cruz, March.

(2000a), "Monetary Policy Design: Institutional Developments from a Contractual Perspective," *International Finance*, 3 (November): 375–90.

(2000b), "Accountability, Transparency, and Inflation Targeting," University of California, Santa Cruz, June.

(1999), "Announcements, Inflation Targeting and Central Bank Incentives," *Economica*, 66 (May): 255–69.

(1997), "Inflation and Central Bank Independence: Is Japan Really an Outlier?," *Bank of Japan Monetary and Economic Studies*, 15 (May): 89–117.

(1995a), "Optimal Contracts for Central Bankers," *American Economic Review*, 85 (March): 150–67.

(1995b), "Recent Central-Bank Reforms and the Role of Price Stability on the Sole Objective of Monetary Policy," *NBER Macroeconomics Annual 1995* (Cambridge, MA: MIT Press), pp. 237–52.

Walsh, G.O. (1981), *Federal Reserve Act of 1913: with Amendments and Laws Relating to Banking* (Washington, DC: U.S. Government Printing Office).

Watts, G.S. (1993), *The Bank of Canada: Origins and Early History*, T.K. Rymes (Ed.) (Ottawa: Carleton University Press).

Weber, A. (1995), "Exchange Market Mayhem: The Antecedents and Aftermath of Speculative Attacks: Discussion," *Economic Policy*, 21 (October): 300–07.

Wells, W.C. (1994), *An Economist in An Uncertain World: Arthur F. Burns and the Federal Reserve, 1970–78* (New York: Columbia University Press).

Wheelock, D.C. (1991), *The Strategy and Consistency of Federal Reserve Monetary Policy, 1924–1933* (Cambridge: Cambridge University Press).

Whittlesey, C.R. (1970), "Central Bank Leaders and Central Bank Credibility," in David P. Eastburn (Ed.), *Men, Money and Policy: Essays in Honor of Karl R. Bopp* (Philadelphia, PA: Federal Reserve Bank of Philadelphia).

Wicker, E. (1993), "The U.S. Central Banking Experience: A Theoretical Perspective," in M.V. Fratianni and D. Salvatore (Eds.), *Monetary Policy in Developed Economies*, Vol. 3, *Handbook of Comparative Economic Policy* (Westport, CT: Greenwood Press), pp. 195–243.

(1966), *Federal Reserve Monetary Policy, 1917–33* (New York: Random House).

Wieland, V. (2000a), "Monetary Policy, Parameter Uncertainty and Optimal Learning," *Journal of Monetary Economics*, 46 (August): 199–228.

(2000b), "Learning by Doing and the Value of Optimal Experimentation," *Journal of Economic Dynamics and Control*, 24 (April): 501–34.

Williamson, J.E. (2000), "The New Institutional Economies: Taking Stock, Looking Ahead," *Journal of Economic Literature*, 38 (September): 595–613.

Willis, H.P. (1923), *The Federal Reserve System: Legislation, Organization and Operations* (New York: The Ronal Press Co.).

Winkelman, R. (2000), *Econometric Analysis of Count Data*, Third Edition (Heidelberg and New York: Springer).

Winkler, B. (2000), "What Kind of Transparency? On the Need for Clarity in Monetary Policy-Making," Working Paper 26, European Central Bank, Frankfurt.

Wood, E. (1939), *English Theories of Central Banking Control* (Cambridge, MA: Harvard University Press).

Woodford, M. (2000), "Pitfalls of Forward-Looking Monetary Policy," *American Economic Review Papers and Proceedings*, 90 (May): 100–04.

——— (2001), "Monetary Policy in the Information Economy," NBER Working Paper 8674, December.

——— (1999a), "Revolution and Evolution to Twentieth-Century Macroeconomics," Working Paper, Princeton University, June.

——— (1999b), "Optimal Monetary Policy Inertia," *Manchester School*, 67 (Supplement): 1–35.

Woolley, J.R. (1995), "Nixon, Burns, 1972, and Independence in Practice," Unpublished, University of California, Santa Barbara, May.

Woolley, J.T. (1984), *Monetary Politics: The Federal Reserve and the Politics of Monetary Policy* (Cambridge: Cambridge University Press).

——— (1983), "Political Factors in Monetary Policy," in D.R. Hodgman (Ed.), *The Political Economy of Monetary Policy* (Boston: Federal Reserve Bank of Boston), pp. 177–203.

Wueschner, S.A. (1999), *Charting Twentieth-Century Monetary Policy: Herbert Hoover And Benjamin Strong, 1917–1927*, Contributions in Economics and Economic History, No. 210 (Westport, CT and London: Greenwood Press).

Young, C. (1961), "Coyne Unmasks Mystery Advisor," *Ottawa Citizen*, July 11.

Zelmer, M. (1996), "Strategies versus Tactics for Monetary Policy Operations," in *Money Markets and Central Bank Operations*, Proceedings of a Conference held by the Bank of Canada (Ottawa: Bank of Canada), pp. 211–59.

Index